Minerva Rules Your Future

Other Books by Barrie Dolnick

How to Write a Love Letter (2001)

Simple Spells for Hearth and Home (1999)

Simple Spells for Success (1996)

Simple Spells for Love (1995)

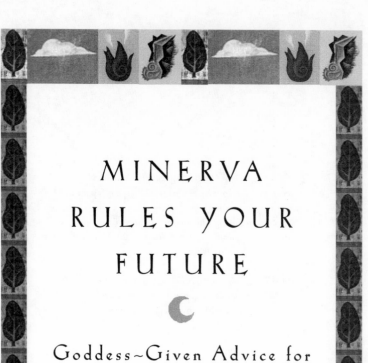

MINERVA
RULES YOUR
FUTURE

Goddess~Given Advice for

Smart Moves at Work

BARRIE DOLNICK

Harmony Books 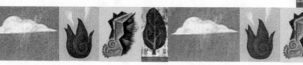 New York

Published by Harmony Books, New York, New York.
Member of the Crown Publishing Group,
a division of Random House, Inc.
www.randomhouse.com

HARMONY BOOKS is a registered trademark and the
Harmony Books colophon is a trademark of
Random House, Inc.
Printed in the United States of America

Design by Donna Sinisgalli

Library of Congress Cataloging-in-Publication Data
Dolnick, Barrie.
Minerva rules your future : goddess-given advice for smart
moves at work / by Barrie Dolnick.— 1st ed.
(hardcover)
1. Vocational interests. 2. Vocational guidance. 3. Career
development. 4. Career changes. I. Title.
HF5381.5 .D65 2003
650.13—dc21
2002014717

ISBN 0-609-60428-7

10 9 8 7 6 5 4 3 2 1

First Edition

For Randy

Acknowledgments

I extend my gratitude to my family for their constant support and belief in my work—Gero; Elisabeth; my sisters Randy, Amy, and Carol, my home away from home; Halo and Friedel.

I thank my agent, Emma Sweeney, for the wonderful guidance and intelligence she contributes to my work, and I thank Shaye Areheart, my special friend and editor, whose magical soul guides so many meaningful messages into the world.

I am continually grateful to the many outstanding, sharp, intuitive women who grace my life with their presence: Cheryl Callan, Julia Condon, Sheila Davidson, Jennie Emil, Marilyn Levey, Liz Nickles, Mary Lou Quinlan, Ann Ross, Betsy Schecter, Ann Skalski, Susan Strong . . .

And special thanks to CCRC Horoscope Program for valuable help with Moon Sign Tables.

Contents

Preface

Trapped. Bored. Stilted. Angry. Disconnected.

These are the words most often used by my clients about their jobs (or lack of). Sound familiar?

Nancy, a thirty-six-year-old media sales rep, hates her job and her field but can't imagine any way to get out and still pay her bills. She puts in fifty-hour weeks and endures a strenuous commute for the precious few hours she has on weekends, when she can do something she really likes.

Gloria, a forty-six-year-old editor at a major publishing house, just doesn't feel the passion for her career that she used to, but insists there are few alternatives that would guarantee her the income level she worked so hard to achieve.

Todd, a forty-eight-year-old money manager, feels trapped by his six-figure salary. He wants to go back to school and get a degree in psychology, but his wife and three kids are expensive dependents. How can he walk away from their security?

Rick, a sixty-eight-year-old public affairs executive forced into retirement, is stunned by the enormous amount of free time he faces and claims he no longer has a sense of his own identity. He wants meaningful work but worries about ageism and lack of opportunity in his field.

We are all vulnerable to these inhibitions—the circumstances of dependents and current responsibilities, fear of losing financial security, fear of failure, feeling you're too old or it's too late to start over. Some of us are even being criticized for trying to make a change happen. There are mountains of reasons why we don't "go for the brass ring" in our careers or follow our true desires and creative impulses. You can add your own reasons to these. But these mountains are easy to scale when you get to know Minerva.

Maybe your feelings are not so dramatic or you're not desperate to find new career paths. Maybe you just want to do something you really love instead of making do because of the security it provides. You don't have to be in a negative mindset or an unhappy state to work with Minerva, you just need to be a willing adventurer in the story of your life.

I've worked with Minerva myself, and I doubt I'll ever stop, because I find it so interesting to constantly reinvent and morph into new forms of creativity. I left a thirteen-year career in advertising to pursue a career in writing, which led to opening my own business, which led to speaking on my business expertise and being assigned the title of "expert" in my field.

Minerva's way is not a formulaic approach to reaching a goal. It's more like a blossoming of your talents, strengths, and vision, and watching the world respond with opportunities as you open yourself to them. It's honing power and creativity to demand and receive what brings you satisfaction and prosperity.

Still, many of us are conditioned to resist pursuing our real creative goals:

"You can't make any money doing that."
"Who's going to hire me to do that?"
"No one gets paid for loving their job."
"My family will never understand this."

There are lots more. These are long-standing, time-tested career cop-outs that keep you from being the person who "has it all." You can live and breathe these barriers to self-actualization, but when you see others going for their dreams, you're going to get cranky.

A lot of people thought I was crazy to give up a successful career in advertising for a chance (not even a firm promise) to write and publish a book. At the time, I hadn't sold anything, but I felt it was the right time to go. In six months I did land a book contract, but not without burning through my savings, and generating many improbable ideas for making money. I did start to think that I should get another advertising job, but just when I hit that point, Minerva took over.

There is a great deal of faith involved in working with Minerva. It's the greatest bungee jump you'll ever take—the greatest thrill you'll ever seek. She'll lead you through a profound journey, exploring your deepest sense of truth, facing fear, and learning about your strength. It requires spiritual stamina and courage—qualities we have at any age, at any stage of physical health.

You may be asking yourself: Why on earth should I do this? I propose several answers. One or two may hit home to you.

1. Life is too short not to maximize enjoyment and satisfaction at all times—not just on weekends.
2. You spend too much time at work not to make it something you like to do.
3. Midlife and late-life crises can be avoided when you feel that you are accomplishing what you've set out to do and have a real sense of purpose.
4. Physical and mental illness can be averted when you increase your satisfaction with life. Spiritual, emotional, and creative components are essential to good health.

You're ready to go with Minerva when you know you want to make a change. This book will provide you with the way to go about it. This book will guide you to a great adventure that will lead you along the road to your best destiny.

It is really a thrill to watch your efforts pay off. Working with Minerva, you won't be a victim of fate. She takes you into a realm where your own experiences, desires, wishes, skills, gifts, and even weaknesses have a chance to surface—you'll open up to a powerful new, energetic you—and then find the right career shift as a result.

No longer will you feel so unheard, helpless, or frustrated about where you are in your life, because you won't feel so out of control. You'll have influence, power, and real substance. Minerva will help you find it, see it, use it, and relish it in that bright new light you bring to your world.

ONE

INTRODUCTION TO MINERVA

Welcome to the realm of Minerva. You're about to step into a new dimension, one where you can find ultimate satisfaction in your life and work. If you think this isn't for real, you're half right. Minerva's world integrates your reality with your possible future, where you use a little magic from the gods to get what you want. Minerva greets you, eager with the anticipation of making your life what you want it to be.

If you're not familiar with Minerva, she'll excuse you. She knows that her presence has been rather low-key since the fall of the Roman Empire, but her powers are no less potent. Minerva is a goddess celebrated in many ancient cultures, from Greece, where her name was Athena, to Ireland, where she was called Brigid. Minerva is her name from the Etruscan civilization, the people who preceded the Romans and modern-day Italians.

Minerva's powers were widely respected. She held a place

among the "big three" gods—sitting beside Jupiter (Zeus), king of the gods, and his wife, Juno (Hera). Minerva is the goddess of handicrafts, the professions, the arts, and strategic warfare. Her likeness is still found in ruins around Pompeii, Rome, and throughout Europe and Britain.

You won't have to erect a shrine to Minerva in order to enlist her help (although I'm sure she'd be flattered); in fact, you don't need to recognize her as a "goddess" in the old-fashioned, seriously pagan way. For purposes of this book, Minerva is your cosmic guide, your help in the heavens in getting what you want. You won't find her very intrusive, but you'll soon rely on her constant support.

> ☾ "Soon, I wearied and called out to men and the gods for help . . . I pleaded, desperate . . .
>
> As I stretched out my arms to heaven, I felt them change and darken, sprouting pennate projections—feathers? Indeed! And my arms and hands were turning to wings. My feet on the sand no longer slipped but now flew along lightly, on top of the ground, and then up in to the air, soaring, floating, wheeling. . . . Thus, I became Minerva's companion."
>
> —OVID, *METAMORPHOSES*

MINERVA AND THE ANCIENT ART OF SHAPE-SHIFTING

Shape-shifting is a term borrowed from ancient cultures that essentially means "magical powers to change form, power, and purpose." Shape-shifting, in its historic sense, was the ability to take on different physical forms in order to enact a deed or purpose that would be otherwise impossible. For instance, in myth, a mortal could be transformed into an animal or plant, usually at the whim of the gods; in other legends, a magician or shaman would shape-shift into a deer in order to pass undetected onto someone else's land, or a bird, to get an aerial view of the landscape. Medicine men and healers today employ more energetic, nonliteral shape-shifting through meditation, to access the powers of healing or vision associated with animals.

Career shape-shifting is not so mysterious; it is a method of deriving buried creativity, power, and opportunity that will allow you to pursue your real ambitions. Career shape-shifting is both practical and actionable—through somewhat unconventional (but safe and nontoxic) means.

Successful career shape-shifters are all around us. They're the people who go back to school, who quit their jobs to start their own businesses or change careers, who even "drop out" of mainstream business life to pursue their heart's desires. Career shape-shifters have courage to pursue their happiness and fulfillment, and have somehow found a way to break the ties that bind them to only limited satisfaction. Minerva knows the way, and with her as your companion, you can shape-shift, too.

WHAT TO EXPECT FROM MINERVA

Minerva Rules Your Future will take you through a process of creative rejuvenation, as well as career exploration, that is unlike any method you've heard about to help you shape-shift into a new career persona. While you may think these exercises are strange, I assure you they work.

Minerva uses some ancient tricks and methods to put the push behind career changes and advances. To go with Minerva, though, you have to have an open mind. If you're accustomed to rational procedures, you may find that Minerva's way doesn't make sense. She doesn't care about phones, faxes, résumés, and meetings the way you would. She actually helps the psychic and mental energy around your goal become healthy, actionable, and magnetic.

Each step with Minerva complements any real-world actions you'll be taking on your career-shifting journey. For instance, when you know that you want to make a change, she'll help you consider your options. Like vocational testing for career aptitude, Minerva will offer you her insight into your gifts—through your stars.

When you're ready to put some energy out there—like making phone calls, sending résumés, making new contacts—Minerva will polish up your power to give you the best chance of gaining what you want. Her nontraditional exercises create considerable results in your psychic energy. You and your efforts can appear smarter, sharper, faster, or just plain better than others. And this won't be smoke and mirrors, either; you can actually be better than others when you get your psychic energy aligned with your real-world affairs.

Minerva is also extremely understanding and helpful when the inevitable disappointments are encountered. Not even Minerva can make it happen for you right away; you're bound to encounter obstacles, including your own fears, when you forge this new path. Particularly when it comes to career changes, "rerouting" is common. This occurs when your original goal becomes the wrong answer and you decide to change your mind . . . again.

My client Edie is a good example of this. She was working with some of these exercises in her effort to change professions, from lab technician to a profession more involved with helping people. Her first solution was to obtain an advanced degree—an M.B.A.—to add to her undergraduate degree in biochemistry. This, she thought, would enable her to become a sales representative for a drug company and hence work more with people. Yet Edie didn't really like her M.B.A. classes. She found her energy going down every time she left work to go to night school. She became more tired as her schedule became more demanding. She also heard from fellow scientists that the drug companies were only interested in hiring graduates with a Ph.D. in biochemistry, a far cry from undergraduate work. It seemed to Edie that every time she turned around the universe was trying to tell her that her goal wasn't right. Eventually we talked and I suggested a clearing—Minerva's way of allowing things to settle out and letting go of the negativity. Maybe the universe was only telling her to slow down, or maybe there really was a suggestion that she look into a different field for fulfillment. After the clearing, Edie realized that she wasn't being honest with herself. She went the M.B.A. route only because she thought it made the most sense. In fact, she just didn't want to learn about business; she found herself yearning for something more human.

Edie decided to take a break from the stress of night school, but her anxiety level seemed to increase. Seeking help to reduce her headaches, sleeplessness, and nervousness, she looked into herbal remedies. Edie said it was like a light suddenly turned on: Her glance into natural medicine opened her eyes to a new career path. While this was a far cry from biochemistry and drug sales, she found her energy went up at the thought of taking classes on this subject. Edie eventually found her way out of traditional biological sciences and today is a successful practitioner of natural healing and nutrition—a very nice shape-shift.

You, too, may be a candidate for rerouting, and if you are, Minerva will help you through it and you'll be that much closer to your goal.

Frankly, there are a lot of obstacles to encounter when you decide to change careers. I don't know if it's always the case, but I haven't seen anyone yet who has been able to make a smooth, swift shift without some dips here and there.

Let's go to the end of the process, though, when you've come to the point where you can say "Okay, I did it." This is sweet victory because it's been earned through your heart's efforts. What now? Does Minerva bail out?

Smart career-shifters never lose touch with Minerva, often just by relaying anecdotes to others about how they got where they are. Minerva doesn't demand that you honor her for her help, but she does make one request: You should share your magic by remembering it and, in some way, become a mentor to others. Minerva likes to see the positive vibes being passed around, so when you're done, when you've accomplished your goal, tell someone how you did it and encourage them to do the same.

LIVING UP TO MINERVA
RULES YOUR FUTURE

Before you begin to transform your life and work, you'll need to consider a few peculiarities of this process.

Do You Believe in Magic?

First and foremost, you must believe in magic. I'm not asking you to join a coven, perform weird rites, or pull rabbits from hats. You must, however, take stock in what magic really is: the indefinable, irreducible acts of harmony, synchronicity, and miracle that happen to all of us one time or another. Magic happens when you don't expect it, dictate it, or pull at it. Magic happens in what I would call a graceful moment—when some divine force can intervene in a tiny space of possibility and effect change. Magic is most often found when something mundane becomes amazing or something "coincidental" answers your prayers. Magic can be found in personal ways, like meeting your spouse, or it can happen in more worldly circumstances, like finding that an old friend is now running the company you want to work for. There are infinite ways magic can happen, but you need to believe in it to experience it.

Do You Know How to Ask for Help?

Once you accept that magic isn't so silly or elusive, you're ready for the next step: asking for it. You may not have realized that magic doesn't have to be so random; you can actually attract more of it consciously into your life. You just have to know where to go. God can make magic, but many of us don't want to burden the divine being with what we think of as worldly or nonspiritual matters. Minerva can be the liaison, as it were, between you and heavenly intervention. Minerva doesn't work outside of God's world; she's actually one of its angels. That's why so many people believed in her and worshiped her for so long: She can make things happen.

Can You Let It Happen?

This leads me to my next requirement: relinquishing control—and this is a tough one, especially when you're trying to change something that seems so practical, like getting into a new profession or changing the focus of your work. These goals sound very reasonable—learn about what you want to do, explore it, generate opportunities, et cetera—and there is nothing wrong with going about things matter-of-factly and rationally. It only makes sense. But when you seek Minerva, each step you take will carry with it something more than you alone could do. You'll have some spiritual energy on your team, too. This makes each part of the process less predictable and much more difficult to control. After all, you're not the only one working on it.

Control issues are pretty tough to overcome. I don't believe any of us ever really relinquish control while we're going through this process—we secretly hold out, as if we know what will happen. It's human nature. But usually, in this process, your desire to control will create a crisis before your results are achieved. I've seen it happen many times; surrender prior to victory, giving up just in time to win. Control over the outcome is often unconscious—you think you're very hands-off until something you haven't counted on happens and, *oops!*, you feel out of control.

My client Linda had been working on her career change for a long time. She was a public relations executive and wanted to work in a more socially conscious environment. Her investigations into cause-related institutions depressed her—the salary structure was much lower than her current job and there were few positions available in general. After almost a year, Linda heard about a great position at a wealthy foundation that sponsored sporting events to raise money for health-related issues. With her public relations background she was perfect for the job, and contacted the executive director right away. She had reason to expect to be called for an interview. Not hearing from them, Linda called to follow up and was told the position had been filled. That did it. Linda threw her hands to the heavens in despair.

I saw Linda not long after this happened and it didn't take long to see her fear—of failure, of being stuck in her current job forever, of not being "heard" by the universe. She couldn't comprehend why such an "obvious" opportunity didn't work out. As for my counsel, I simply reinforced that there was something more suitable coming. I held the faith for her, while she claimed she'd given up.

Only a few weeks later Linda was in a meeting with one of her clients who announced that his company was setting up a new corporate philanthropy division and was in the midst of recruiting for it. Privately, Linda communicated to her client her interest in the new division. He set her up with the right people and it wasn't hard to convince them that she was right for the job. Linda got what she wanted after all.

Magic is easy. Control is hard.

WHAT'S THE PURPOSE OF YOUR CHANGE?

Lots of people want to make changes to their working lives. They'd like less pressure and stress, more money and satisfaction. Those are perfectly reasonable goals, but they aren't necessarily grounds for advancement or for making a career change.

The desire for change—at least the kind of change Minerva can create—must come from a kind of primal urge, an energy or pulse, that's undeniable. It's like a calling, but it doesn't have to be grounded in spiritual or teaching work. You can have a calling to be a stockbroker, a lawyer, a building contractor. Your calling is the desire to do work you love, whatever that may be. Working with Minerva takes you to places deep within yourself to create your best path, and at the same time you'll be reigniting old passions and wishes. It's not just about being better at your job; it's about finding the right work and being alive at work in the most positive way possible.

If you've picked up this book to get a better salary, put it down. Minerva doesn't deal with dollars; prosperity is what happens when you fulfill your desire for change. If you want to venture into possibilities that can better satisfy your creative potential, keep going. Only you know the integrity of your purpose.

ARE YOU READY?

Check how many of these statements accurately describe you or your behavior.

_____ 1. When I'm at work, I spend a lot of my time making plans for my leisure time.

_____ 2. I buy lottery tickets and make lists of things I would do with the money.

_____ 3. When someone says something positive about my work, I don't feel anything, good or bad.

_____ 4. I calculate my net worth and how long I could live without a job if I cash out.

_____ 5. Every morning seems like a bad Monday morning.

_____ 6. Even when something goes very wrong at work, I don't care.

_____ 7. When I am asked to set goals for myself, I can't think of any.

_____ 8. I own and wear a "Thank God It's Friday" T-shirt.

_____ 9. I avoid farewell parties because I'm jealous of those leaving.

_____10. I look at the faces of happy people on the street and wonder what they do for a living.

Analysis

If you've checked more than half of these questions, you're really ready for *Minerva Rules Your Future.*

If you've checked under half as true for you, you're on your way to career burnout—Minerva can help you avoid more dramatic symptoms.

If you are unfamiliar with the dissatisfactions described above, you're lucky. You can still be Minerva's companion, seeking new opportunities and avenues for your creativity, but you won't be in as much of a hurry.

EXERCISE: WHAT YOU DON'T WANT TO DO

If you've touched some nerves in your career discontent, assess your current situation for what you really don't like. Not the people, not the hours, but the actual tasks or responsibilities that make you yawn or groan. Even though we haven't begun to identify what you want to do next, you probably know what it is you want to avoid.

- My client Gary can't stand to think about one more quarterly sales report.
- Natasha claims one more inventory audit will put her in an asylum.
- I used to roll my eyes and crash with fatigue when preparing marketing reviews for my former advertising job.
- Sherry says she just can't stand working with people anymore and wants to do freelance work from a home office.

Now is the time to list the things about your current job

that don't work for you. For instance, if you hate working with numbers, say so. If you don't want to work in the public or private sector, say that. Make a list of what you hope to leave behind. You can change your mind later, and people often do, but for now, list what it is that makes this job or career the wrong one for you. You'll be referring back to it later.

A WORD TO SURVIVORS OF LAYOFFS, DOWNSIZING, OR FIRINGS

Our workforce is constantly transforming and shifting as technology advances, market needs change, and resources dwindle. If you have experienced layoffs, downsizing, or have been let go for the wrong reasons, you are the perfect companion for Minerva.

Minerva's process can rid you of any residue from the bad experience as well as open you up to power and skills you didn't use before. Minerva's methods work best when you have "nothing to lose." If you're between jobs, you can really put her power to use.

If the experience that led to your unemployment was particularly tough, you will need to work through the negativity of that past job. Pay special attention to chapter two, "Groundwork: Personal Archaeology," where you will be unearthing wounds and grudges that might prevent you from moving on. As someone in need of a new job, you are in the unique position to create your next career, and you certainly don't want to taint it with the past.

THE INTEGRITY
OF SHAPE=SHIFTING WORK

There is a little matter of psychic kickback that Minerva would like to warn you about before you begin. This process demands a certain kind of integrity that you don't often have to muster. Since you're going to be shifting your work, your career persona, and most likely your source of prosperity, you do need to face up to something: you.

You can't lie or fake it when you work with Minerva. There's no point. Sure, you can cheat on a diet and still be able to lose weight, but cheat on your work with Minerva and you won't get the full benefit of your efforts.

This integrity is especially important now, at the beginning. You will soon be cleaning out some pretty powerful psychic storage space, and that can make you feel things you may not want to feel. If you feel like quitting before you've even started, you're already facing up to some internal pressure to just stay put.

The most powerful force—both positive and negative—that you will encounter on this journey with Minerva is going to be you. There are certain steps you're going to take that may cause you to want to turn back, and it's here that you need the most staying power. Make a commitment to yourself right now that you're going to see this through. Once you start on this road, it is actually harder to turn back.

A WORD TO THE
CONSERVATIVE COMPANION

There is no doubt that some companions are going to wince at some of the exercises. Even if you're not a hard-nosed, straight-line kind of person, you might feel silly lighting a candle, sitting in the dark, listening to a tape of your voice. There are plenty of opportunities to feel uncomfortable if you're not accustomed to more creative methods of unleashing power.

You can't help what you feel. I've had plenty of experience in this area myself. When I was just learning about metaphysics and inner power, I took classes given by a gifted metaphysician in New York. She commenced her class with a group chant. I couldn't help but think back to first grade, but instead of standing up in a classroom and reciting the pledge of allegiance, we were grown-ups (many in business attire) sitting on pillows on the floor, holding hands and chanting with our eyes closed. Naturally, my first time I peeked through my eyelashes to watch how seriously everyone was acting; they were serious. Yet I couldn't summon the courage to let go in a free chant (which can sound much like howling at the moon). There was always some really loud chanter reaching new heights of vocal disparity that would make me want to giggle instead of join in. I took that class for four or five years, and by the end I was the howler.

This isn't a case of "if you can't beat 'em, join 'em." Rather, after finally allowing my own silly judgments, nervousness, and adolescent sneering to fade, I realized that it felt damned good to let out a little chanting, and it often made very harmonious melody. I also realized that it changed me from an uptight, by-the-book businessperson to a more easygoing, open, playful woman. This energy shift was important to my overall career shape-shift, for if I couldn't relax enough to participate in a simple chant, I certainly wouldn't have been open to becoming an author.

Humor, though, is important. I don't doubt that there will be times Minerva's antics will cause chuckles, eye rolls, and the occasional giggles. That happens and it's not a bad thing. I still laugh thinking about that first class, where I sat so stiffly on the floor in my short red suit, trying to keep the skirt from being too revealing while trying to hold hands and take that chant seriously. It's still funny.

I caution you now, though, that if you are too conservative and timid about performing some of Minerva's exercises, you won't get as much out of it. You don't have to behave like a priest and wear sacred robes, but do try to respect the process even if you don't understand it.

To help you out, there are some alternative exercises that may not seem as "out there" or risky to you. If you just can't or don't want to do one exercise, see if there's an alternative that feels better. You're best off doing something rather than nothing, and the alternatives, though less potent, can be productive.

With Minerva, I've made an attempt to demystify as much as possible while still maintaining the integrity of this very creative and magical journey. If you don't feel that "someone out there is watching out for you" yet, you will soon.

SO HOW LONG IS
THIS GOING TO TAKE?

I anticipate that you will ask this question sooner or later, so you may as well know now: I don't know. Typically, a career shift takes longer than you think before it happens, and seems to have happened all at once in retrospect. Your efforts will take on the speed of light when you feel you're gaining ground, and time will drag its feet when you don't feel so productive. That's the key: Time is malleable.

Trying to predict how long it will take you to find yourself happily working away in a productive, new capacity is like asking How high is up? Your own potential dictates how your shape will shift and how many stages it actually takes—and some people never really stop shifting by choice. As you set upon Minerva's way, you'll notice that each piece brings you new awareness, a new accomplishment, and new learning. Each step builds on the last, and each exercise opens you to another facet of your potential. You are piecing together an extraordinary jigsaw puzzle of your own talents, gifts, desires, and energy, all while venturing out into a new landscape and seeking new adventures. This is quite a busy process, even when you don't feel like you're really "moving."

For a few, Minerva's energy rockets them into something new right away, leaving them to catch up to their potential while already in a new career; trust me, this isn't easy. For most of us, though, Minerva allows us to get ready before we get to the new career that is a much easier transition. It can feel slow at times, no doubt, but the creativity and force you are access-ing through Minerva needs to flow in its own way, in its own magical time.

Take your time, enjoy the path as it unfolds, and know that your upcoming experience is possibly the most unique and awe-inspiring project you will ever attempt.

TWO

GROUNDWORK:
PERSONAL ARCHAEOLOGY

To get right down to work with Minerva, you have to open up to your own potential and passions. This is crucial to your ultimate success, but it can be difficult. Minerva will take you on your own archaeological dig—into your own past—to uncover long-forgotten, put-aside passions, values, and desires.

THE IMPORTANCE OF THE DIG

The reason Minerva takes you into your dark and dusty past is to clear your creative ground of the shards and shrapnel of a broken creative spirit—you can't plant seeds for a new career if your creative ground is littered with apprehension, judgments, self-esteem issues, and buried regrets. Ever since you were in your mother's womb you probably heard things about yourself, some of it inaccurate or critical. This stuff sticks to you and gets buried in your subconscious.

What if you heard your mother say, when she was nine months pregnant with you, "This kid is really lazy. He hardly moves at all." Or "I can tell this baby is going to be a real fighter—he kicks all the time and never lets me rest." And what if you remembered it? Maybe some of it colored your decisions in life. And don't forget later, when you're in school, all of those evaluations, grades, ratings from both teachers and peers.

I'm the perfect example. I have an older sister who was always in the class one year ahead of mine. For those of you with older siblings, you might be able to relate to this: I was struggling to find my place, my identity, in a world that knew her first. One day, when I was about ten years old, my teacher, who had my sister the previous year, handed me back a composition I wrote. Here's the conversation I remember (I am paraphrasing).

Teacher: You and your sister are very different.

Me: I guess so.

Teacher: She always wrote very well. I remember her stories.

Me (unsure of this message): Yeah, she writes good stories.

Teacher: Yes, but you're better at math and science than she was.

In retrospect, this seems like a pretty tame conversation. I'm sure the teacher only meant to acknowledge my sister and encourage me. So why did it haunt me? I had earned an A— on that composition, but I walked away from that brief encounter with this understanding:

1. My sister was a better writer than I was.
2. I should stick to math and science if I want to excel at something and distinguish myself from my sister.
3. Even though I got an A—, my work wasn't good.

It took me years to consider myself a good writer. I couldn't shift my career from advertising to author until I had faced that perception and changed it.

There are so many examples of these kinds of messages invading our minds, touching on insecurities, and eventually bruising our creative potential and self-esteem.

Chances are, you aren't going to dig up everything that ever damaged your sense of self or your creative potential—at least I hope not. You still need to access some of these judgments to help defuse their impact on your creative energy.

DIGGING UP TOXIC NOSTALGIA

By thinking back to your past you may come up with a culprit or two responsible for some of your apprehension to take a risk or follow your dream. You might also remember some judgments couched in "niceness" that hurt your self-esteem ("Sweetheart, you know you just don't have a head for business"). This is toxic nostalgia—a kind of memory that reinforces negative beliefs about your own potential. Toxic nostalgia taints your ability to move forward with your career shape-shift because it holds back a certain amount of energy

COMMON CULPRITS OF YOUR CREATIVE BRUISES

Older Siblings

Kate loved to work with hair but her brother told her that that was for sissies. She still wants to be a stylist but judges it as "not real work."

Teachers

Terry remembered his art teacher telling him he should stick to academics. He combined his love of form with his talent for math and became an architect who now longs to be a sculptor.

Parents

Tristan wants to give up his accounting practice and become a partner in a new technology firm. His mother's voice still keeps him from doing it ("Stick with what you know"). She was against risk in all forms.

Friends

Dorrie's best girlfriend in high school told her she wasn't cool enough to be in the drama club. Dorrie wants to work in a local theater group but doesn't feel she'd fit in.

Other Grown-Ups

Austin's aunt Sylvie spoke disparagingly about his uncle Otto, "the bum," who lost money in a real estate deal. Austin wants to work with real estate investments but is worried he'll "be a bum," too. ☾

and talent you might need. Even if your silly old aunt's assessment of your singing voice seems irrelevant ("Darling, you're no Julie Andrews"), it could hurt you. It might seem like a long shot, but a comment like that could reappear at any moment and cause you to keep your mouth shut just when it would be best to say your peace. Maybe that comment makes you afraid to open your mouth while interviewing with someone who reminds you of your aunt, maybe her words make you hate Julie Andrews, maybe her comment is just buried along with a bunch of other mean things she said. You don't have to anticipate or even understand just how her comment might have affected your creative potential; if you remember it and her words still sting, it's done some damage.

Exercise: Identifying Toxic Nostalgia

Tools: Family photos, memorabilia from your youth or schooling, things given to you in the past—awards, certificates, anything that can take you back to your upbringing.

Go through your memorabilia. *Make a list of everything you remember anyone ever telling you about your skills, abilities, talents (or lack thereof), intelligence, capabilities, strengths, and weaknesses.* Take your time, be thorough. Take breaks of a day or two while making your lists. You will be loosening up buried memories and they might trickle out slowly.

Here are some examples of what some of my clients found when they looked back.

Parents' Opinions

"You're not good at math."

"We always knew your brother would do very well, and
that you could, too, if you really tried."

"It's very hard to make it as a writer; why don't you go
to business school as a fallback?"

"You're very good at drawing, but it's so competitive,
why don't you try computer programming?"

"You don't have to love your job, you just have to
keep it."

"You should always have this to fall back on."

"You can't make any money doing that."

"You'll never find a husband/wife if you're so picky."

"Just take what you can get."

"Don't be so weird."

Scarring Social Circumstances from Friends

Voted most likely to end up in jail

Being picked last for teams

Not being in the "cool" crowd

Being in the "cool" crowd

Losing a debate

Dropping out

Even silence can be a powerful judgment.

That old saying "If you don't have something nice to say,
don't say anything at all" leaves us to interpret silence as a tacit
negative judgment. Your interpretation of someone's silence
can plant a seed of failure where there is no ground for it:

DELIA, THIRTY-EIGHT

I must say I was startled to learn that my mother had
bragged about the public speaking I used to do in high
school. I used to love to debate and I wanted to be a trial
lawyer—just to get up and argue in front of an audience was
thrilling and satisfying. My parents used to come to my
debates but never mentioned if they thought I was good. I
won several trophies but I was never encouraged to
compete beyond our high school's scope. I interpreted
their silence as disapproval—my brother was on the tennis
team and they seemed more into that. I never pursued it
further, and though I went to law school, I took a job as a
tax attorney. Now that my mother tells me that she and my
dad were just naive about debating (they'd have been scared
to do what I did) and didn't want to push me into going on
with it, I feel I really denied myself my true love and I'm
looking for ways to integrate my love of public speaking
into my career.

MINERVA'S NEUTRALIZING CLEANSER FOR TOXIC NOSTALGIA

Part One: Conscious Detox

Now that you've unearthed a bunch of unpleasantness, get rid
of it!

EXERCISE

TOOLS: Blank paper, crayons.

I. Sit on the floor in a room by yourself (really, sit on the floor) with your blank paper and crayons in front of you. Look at the list of judgments you've made from the last exercise. *Using the crayons, color those comments you wish to destroy* on the paper. You can write them out, but you don't have to simply color what those judgments make you feel. You can also write the name of the culprit or draw the person who put that idea into your head. Let your emotions go as you draw, scribble, or stab the paper. It's not unusual to feel angry or sad as you work it through. Use both sides of the paper and keep going until you feel spent. By the time you finish, your paper is likely to be covered with crayon and indistinguishable figures and words. This is not a work of art; it is a toxic archaeological find that should be neutralized.

2. When you feel finished with the coloring part of the exercise, take the paper over to the sink in your kitchen. Light the paper on fire—you're doing this in the sink so that you won't start a major fire. If you get nervous with the flames, just turn on the water in your sink. If possible, let the paper burn out.

3. Take the ashes or whatever is left of the work and throw it away *outside of your home.*

If you feel you need to do it again because there's more in you, repeat the process. If your paper doesn't burn well, you might want to do it again. Sometimes this is a sign of not wanting to let those negative perceptions go.

Alternate Exercise: Neutralizing Toxic Nostalgia for Skittish Companions

(This exercise isn't as powerful as the preceding one, but it may be more comfortable to some readers.)

TOOLS: Blank paper, pen or pencils.

Complete the exercise above using a pen or pencil. Then, instead of burning the paper, tear it up into little pieces and throw it away outside of your home or office.

Caution: Releasing psychic toxins can render temporary side effects of sadness, depression, or anger. Allow these feelings to surface and know that they are temporary. They surface as part of the release.

Part Two: Psychic Detox

Next, Minerva now takes you into a deeper dig where you won't need such rational skills as thinking and writing. Your toxic nostalgia—what you can consciously remember—has entered the cleansing process, but there are more deeply embedded fragments of negativity to be found. Your psychic energy has also been tainted by the many naysayers in your past. Since your psychic energy is linked to your creativity, it is very important to perform some releases and clearings here, too.

For beginners, Minerva's tactics may seem odd and without explanation. In order to dig into the psychic part of your energy, you will be using nonrational (*not* irrational) methods to loosen up the dirt. The exercises below use symbolic means to clean up your unconscious self. You will be working with elemental energies that are very powerful helpers once you know how to use them.

THE ELEMENTS

The elements that give you the tools to dig up and release negativity are literally the elements that make up daily life: fire, earth, air, and water. Since the elements make up what we call reality, you can use them to shift, change, and shape your present and your future—and the key to that is reshaping the past. Each element symbolizes a different part of you.

Fire

Fire is the element of your passion, courage, and force. Your fire element may easily have been dimmed or discouraged by events or people in your past. Your relationship to risk-taking, for instance, has to do with your fire element. Your ability to face and navigate conflict is also a fire-driven characteristic. Fire emits a lot of energy and heat—it's about what kind of "heat" you exude in the world.

You used fire in the previous exercise because of another property it holds: purification. Fire reduces things to barest ashes, and in doing so, whatever is burned becomes heat and light, then nothing. Your personal fire element can burn through impurities in your life; this part of your detox will do just that.

Earth

Earth is a physical element—about land, food, your physical body, and, important, wealth and riches. Earth is literally about the stuff in your life. For purposes of releasing, earth is the great recycler. What goes into the earth is broken down and reintegrated into useful, productive soil—even if it takes thousands of years to get there. In the case of psychic detox, earth can take on the stuff that weighs you down so you can feel your own light energy again.

Your personal earth element is about your relationship to being physical. Are you grounded, in your body, alive and vibrant, or are you disconnected, lackluster, gloomy? Your earth element connects you to health and prosperity, both of which are key to making your shape-shift happen.

Air

Air is the element of the intellectual and is associated with thinking, writing, evaluating, contracts, ideas, and concepts. It's important that your air element be clear, not cloudy, smoggy, or heavy, if you want to be smart and sharp. Air holds certain beliefs about yourself that may need to be released. Writing down your toxic nostalgia was an air-element release.

When your personal air element is toxic, you may hold beliefs about yourself or others that are negative, or you may have a mental block about being able to do something you want to do. That's where air needs to be cleared; in order to make the most of working with Minerva, you'll need to be able to rid yourself of blocks or belief patterns that keep you from attaining your goals. Air needs as much space as possible so the winds of change can blow gently upon you.

Water

Water is the last element and the one most often ignored in business and career advancement; it is the element of emotions. Water is the easiest element to use in releasings because it literally washes away and evaporates into thin air. The water element is often put aside in your work life because of silly comments like "don't take it personally" or "it's only business," which tell you not to feel what you're feeling. Sure, you can get angry or upset when you're working, but by not releasing it you allow it to build up a dam of discontent.

Your toxic water element holds grudges, regrets, and insecurities that could keep you from making your career change. Water is an element that needs to keep flowing, but when it's toxic, it can get stagnant or frozen. It's tough to release pent-up frustrations and disappointments all at once, so whenever you work with the element of water, do so slowly and gently. Particularly if you've been building up some negative emotions for a while, beware of doing anything abruptly. Tidal waves are tough to handle.

ELEMENTAL DETOX

The following exercises put you back in touch with the basic energy of each element and, in doing so, rid your psyche of toxins and impediments. Like sifting through dirt at an ancient site, you'll be sifting through each element, ridding it of bits and pieces of impurities and clearing the ground, yet again, for new growth.

Exercise: Fire Detox

Tools: A candle.

Light a small (birthday) candle and pass your finger quickly through the flame—it should not hurt if you are quick enough! As you do this say aloud: "I allow the fire to purify my creative energy so that the fire of my creative passions comes alive again."

When you feel as if you're done, blow out the candle and throw it away.

RELEASING YOUR PSYCHIC TOXINS

1. Use a full moon or waning moon for all releasing rituals.
2. Allow for privacy and time (you won't need more than thirty minutes and can do them in as little as five minutes).
3. Be sure you're ready to let go.

Caution: Releasing psychic toxins can render temporary side effects of sadness, depression, or anger. Allow these feelings to surface and know that they are temporary. ☾

Exercise: Earth Detox

TOOLS: Your garden or a pot of soil without a plant.

Dig your hands into the soil. Feel its soft, supportive essence. As you hold the soil or dig into it say aloud: "I release any toxins my body holds back into the earth for recycling and I join with the fertility of the land and support growth, prosperity, and abundance."

Wash your hands when you're finished. Toss the soil out to recycle those toxins.

Exercise: Air Detox

TOOLS: Go outside into fresh air.

Take in a deep breath and slowly release it. As you let your breath go, say *"aaahhhh,"* like the first part of the word *Amen.*

Repeat this three times but do not hurry your breathing—you should not hyperventilate. Say aloud: "With these 'ah' breaths I release the ideas or memories that block me from my true intelligence, inventiveness, and clarity."

Repeat one more "ah" breath.

Exercise: Water Detox

TOOLS: A bowl of salt water—use sea salt (or seawater) if possible.

Wash your hands in the bowl of salt water. Say aloud: "I cleanse the emotional toxins I have harbored over the years and gently release them into this salt water where they can heal. I reconnect with emotional spaciousness and inner creativity through this cleansing."

A FINAL POWER RELEASE

You've done a great deal of work thus far, and Minerva smiles upon your ability to set aside your desire to skip the exercises. You've loosened up and released a lot of toxic blockages and you're almost ready to get into some serious power-building. Just one more step and you're free to engage in magical magnetism.

First, however, I encourage you to release a few more bits and pieces that may impede your ultimate success: Clear your relationship to power. To be a skillful shape-shifter you need to know how to use and when to use your powers—not just your talents, charisma, or charm, but your real ability to influence yourself, others, and the world beyond you.

You may not even understand what I'm getting at because

THE MOON AND UNCONSCIOUS POWER

Since ancient times, the moon has been a symbol of the unconscious, what is mysterious, changing, unseen, and creative. Where the sun is rational, the moon is not. Where the sun illuminates, the moon reflects.

Moon Cycles

Farmers have long believed that the moon governs growth. Minerva's ancient worshipers understood that the moon's influence was real and important, yet subtle and unseen. Tides were highest on a full moon, but why? People acted in high spirits (hence the term *lunacy*) during the full moon, why? The full moon still creates its powerful pull today—ask any hospital emergency room doctor or nurse.

The full moon is the greatest point of lunar energy we can see (the unconscious emerging into the conscious) and therefore brings hidden things to light.

Once the moon finishes its peak energy, it wanes, eventually disappearing in the sky. Ancient farmers took this time to harvest crops, pull weeds, and get rid of pests, since the waning moon is the energy of diminishing rather than growing. Minerva's companion makes use of the waning energy to cut away obstacles.

The new moon, when the night sky is dark, is opposite of a full moon. Ancients stayed indoors rather than travel on a moonless night. The new moon evokes an internal energy, a time to be quiet, cautious, and still. The new moon is a good time to plant seeds; the next two weeks are

> the waxing moon, a time of growing light and energy. As Minerva's companion, you will use this time to go out in the world and plant the seeds for your future.
>
> For now, the moon will help you rid your psychic energy of deeply held beliefs or judgments that may be keeping you from pursuing the right career path. You will be using the waning moon for psychic detox. ☾

we have little chance to understand the principle of power in our culture. Here's a place to start.

Personal power is your ability to influence, change, or shape your environment.

Sure, this can mean taking a shovel in your hand and digging up a garden—that takes personal physical and motivational (fire) power. On a more subtle and much less conscious level, though, is the power to shift an atmosphere just by walking into a room—or, conversely, being able to walk into a room completely unnoticed. This personal power is fundamental to a great shape-shifter and helpful to anyone who wants to change careers. Personal power works on both a real, obvious, cause-effect level and on a purely psychic, nonphysical level.

Your relationship to your personal power is probably undefined. You most likely understand what I'm talking about, but you haven't noticed if and when you use your power.

The following exercises are designed to put you in touch with your personal power. Once again, Minerva uses the elements, hence four exercises.

Exercise: Fire Power Purifier

Tools: A candle.

Light the candle and place it on a table. Sit in front of the candle. Gaze at its flame. See how the flame shifts and reaches, bends and subtly transforms. Be with the flame, just watching it for a while.

Say aloud: "I own my power of fire, and allow my fire to reach, to warm, to bend with the atmosphere. My fire power is renewed."

Blow out the flame when you feel ready. Save the candle for more power-building to come.

Exercise: Earth Power Purifier

Tools: Money—both bills and coins, domestic or foreign, as much as you want.

Place the money before you on a table. Sit down in front of it. Pick up the coins and bills, studying them and turning them. See what they really are: metal and paper, printed images and symbols.

Say aloud: "I own my relationship to earth and prosperity. Abundance is infinite and real, earthly and rich. I release my fear around money and welcome it into my life as a symbol of the infinite riches the earth offers me."

Put the money away except for one coin, which you will save as a symbol of prosperity and use in future exercises.

Exercise: Air Power Purifier

Tools: A place you can scream loudly without feeling inhibited.

Stand in a place where you can be as loud as you want.

Think about how you want the world to hear what you have to say—all the ideas you have, and what you want to make happen.

Say aloud (when you feel ready, shout): "I have a voice and I claim it."

Afterward, inhale deeply and exhale with an "ah."

Exercise: Water Power Purifier

TOOLS: An ice cube and a bowl.

Place the ice cube in the bowl. Leave it on a windowsill or table by the window.

Say aloud: "As this ice melts so do my emotional blockages; I release that which keeps me from flowing freely with my emotions and intuition and claim my power of water."

Wait a day or two for the ice to melt and then evaporate entirely. Wash the bowl when it is all gone.

The Kickbacks of Power-Clearing

So far, I have never seen a release or clearing that didn't bear some sort of kickback in the form of temporary discomfort. Some people feel angry, others depressed, some get sick. Whatever you feel, it is temporary and very much a part of clearing.

My friend Julia was intent on clearing out obstacles in her personal power and did clearings with great enthusiasm. After every clearing, she either got a cold or a headache, which was her form of "kickback." My client Greg also did lots of elemental purifying during his initial efforts with Minerva, and he says that for every element he cleared, that issue would come up.

For instance, after Greg's Fire Power Purifier, he had a bout of procrastination and didn't do the next elemental purifier for three weeks—his motivation and energy level went down—the exact opposite of the intention of the clearing. When he did the Earth Power Purifier, he felt poor and had a self-proclaimed "money meltdown," and after the Air Power Purifier, he was afraid to speak up to a waiter when he was served the wrong food. Did that mean he didn't succeed? Actually, it meant his exercises were working. The blocks to his power were surfacing so that he could reckon with them. The water exercise really showed him how much he'd loosened, for when his mother, the voice of negativity in his life, telephoned and began a critical riff, he was actually able to tell her to stop or he'd hang up, which shocked them both. As a result of his newfound fire/courage, earth/security, and air/voice, he took an emotional risk and survived.

Your own experience is bound to be different since your relationship to power and each element is based on your personal history. Allow for what might come up after each exercise; don't plan to do them all at once.

THE COMPLETION OF PERSONAL ARCHAEOLOGY

Your digging is done. Your results are . . . obvious? Perhaps not yet. Your last exercise in Personal Archaeology is taking your act on the road. Get up and get out—and see how different the world is to you now.

☾ "I felt as though I could do anything. Even watching a construction crew putting a building up . . . I thought to myself, 'I could do that.' "

—FRED, THIRTY-THREE, ACCOUNTANT

☾ "I looked at those busy executives hurrying off to work and knew I would soon be one of them."

—TERRY, FORTY-FOUR, MOTHER

RETURNING TO THE WORKFORCE

☾ "I stopped envying those people sitting at cafés during the day while I sat chained to my desk. I know I can get out of this job whenever I want to."

—MARTIN, TWENTY-SIX, RECEPTIONIST

Pay attention to how you see the world and how you feel about yourself. If your dig worked well, you're carrying around a lot less resentment, fear, and limitation. You can see opportunity, hope, and a whole panorama of possibility. I hope you're feeling lighter and freer, for it's time to move on with Minerva.

THREE

MINERVA CHARTS YOUR ASSETS

Minerva belongs to a generation of humanity that used many different kinds of tools to understand life. While we don't always appreciate how insightful, progressive, and creative society was so long ago, there were certainly many ways they interpreted and used information. For instance, omens were constantly read and interpreted—and some still survive today: "Red sky at night, sailors delight. Red sky in morning, sailors take warning." In addition to omens, astrological influences—or the interpretation of planets as they move through the twelve constellations of the zodiac—were used much more commonly. Most households were versed in the stars, and astrology was a respected profession. Although astrology has enjoyed a comeback in popular culture, many people are unfamiliar with how interesting and accurate it can be.

I've worked with astrological information for over ten years, and never tire of the zodiac's archetypes and how accurate they are at predicting inborn predilections and gifts. For purposes of Minerva, however, you won't need to go into a full astrological frenzy. Instead, we'll be looking at only two main features of your personal astrological makeup, using them to identify some basic traits to help you with your career shift.

Minerva chooses to work with the sun and moon signs in order to define two separate dimensions of your personal energy. The sun sign is the easiest to pinpoint, since it is simply based on your birthday. The moon sign is slightly more specific, since the moon changes signs every two and a half days; the moon moves through the whole zodiac in about a month's time. To know your moon sign it is helpful if you know the time of your birth.

THE SUNNY SIDE OF YOU

In astrology, the sun is interpreted as a symbol of your conscious self. The sun stands for your basic nature, your natural life force energy. Your sun sign is most likely the one thing you know about yourself astrologically. Western astrology (very different from Chinese or Indian astrology) denotes twelve signs of the zodiac throughout the year. Each sign has many dimensions to its nature, and they aren't as simple as you may think.

Knowing more about your sun sign can help you understand some basic talents you might have ignored or forgotten, and also increase your awareness of the issues your character faces and what to do when you encounter them.

Ron, a physical therapist, liked to get to know his clients as he worked with them, asking them about their lives, their opinions, even their emotional relationships. He found those clients who didn't talk much tougher to work with, and he often referred them to other therapists just to avoid them; he felt there was no point in working with someone with whom he felt no connection.

Ron knew he didn't want to do physical therapy his whole life; he had gone into the field after being unable to make "medical school grades" in college. He thought working with people in a healing profession was a good compromise. After reading more about his sun sign, Gemini, he realized his need to communicate with people wasn't just a "nice to have" aspect of his work, it was very necessary. That explained his disinterest (and guilt) in not wanting to deal with clients who didn't talk. Since he liked helping people, he wanted to stay with healing work, but in areas where conversation and communication were more important. As a result, he looked into social work with the intention of working with group therapy.

Ron's appreciation for his talent for communicating opened up new horizons for his career change and also, in one way, narrowed the field. He was able to dismiss some ideas for new careers as inappropriate when he realized he wouldn't be using verbal communication as a tool.

Not everyone will find their sun sign so revealing or directly applicable to their career. Sarah, a Pisces, is now a hotel concierge after working with Minerva. Her sun sign is creative, loving, sometimes shy, and often very intuitive. Is this an obvious connection to her new career path? Although you wouldn't look at Pisces and immediately say "hospitality provider," her career choice does make sense in that she can use her sensitivity to relate to guests and her creativity to offer interesting suggestions.

Sun signs are an interesting place to start when you look at your astrological makeup. They will remind you a lot about yourself and light up areas of your nature you may have left unexplored.

MOON SIGNS

As we briefly explored in the previous chapter, the moon addresses a different part of your energy. Where the sun is your conscious self, the moon is your unconscious and subconscious, the part of you that exists beneath your obvious, rational energy.

As you know, the moon waxes and wanes, from full moon to new moon in the sky. Its power is felt physically, but if you pay closer attention, you'll realize that you feel it creatively and emotionally, too. The moon is associated with

- Instincts
- Habits
- Imagination
- Receptivity
- Emotions
- Sensitivity
- Intuition

Unlike the sun, which changes signs every month, the moon changes signs every two and a half days. Ron, the soon-to-be group therapist, is a Gemini with a Cancer moon, as opposed to Gina, another Gemini, who has a Libra moon. A

Cancer moon usually endows an individual with a caring, nurturing sensibility, which gives credence to Ron's desire to be in a healing profession. The moon in Libra, however, is different, and brings a different energy to Gina's career desires.

Gina, too, wanted to make a career change. She was working as a sales manager in a big department store where her communications skills were constantly in use—with buyers, corporate staff, and the many customers she constantly came in contact with. It seemed as if Gina was in a job well-suited to a Gemini, but she was getting very tired of it. Why? Because many of her tasks on the job had to do with conflict. She had a mountain of customer service issues (most of them unhappy), an erratic sales staff in which there was always someone complaining, and tough internal politics that made her feel unappreciated. Certainly, a Gemini would be able to handle all of that communication, but Gina's Libra moon was simply overtaxed. The moon in Libra brings an emotional desire for calm, peace, and harmony. Emotionally, Gina's job was far too conflict-ridden to be healthy for her.

When Gina learned this about her moon sign, she understood why she was having such a hard time. She also learned that both Gemini and Libra are good at thinking, writing, evaluating, and dealing with people. Eventually, Gina opted out of her retail career altogether. She joined a small promotions company that provided her with a chance to exercise her writing skills, creativity, and love of variety. Since the company was small, she could form close relationships with coworkers and feel part of a team instead of acting as referee.

The moon brings another, more subtle dimension of your energy and yields another layer of talent, motivation, and creativity.

Sun	Moon
Individuality	Personality
Character	Emotion
Power	Instinct
Authority	Creativity
Rational	Intuitive

THE DIFFERENCE OF THE SUN AND MOON IN SIGNS

While the twelve zodiac signs remain the same, how the sun and moon act in each one varies. The sun in a sign is your conscious motivation—much more familiar—while the moon's influence can be more like an emotional craving or subtle pull. It's important to know both signs so that you can bring them into use and be more deeply satisfied with your work.

THE SIGNS AND THEIR ARCHETYPES

Astrological signs also define certain qualities that affect your ability to create and move into change. Each sign is ruled by an element (fire, earth, air, or water) and has an energetic nature to it—cardinal, fixed, or mutable. These facets are less well known but afford valuable insight into your strengths.

Elements

You're already familiar with the elements from the previous chapter, but it is worth reviewing them, this time with the signs of the zodiac in mind.

FIRE SIGNS: ARIES, LEO, AND SAGITTARIUS

Fire is a fearless energy, one that takes risks and follows its will and desire. Fire is also known to be tactless, brash, and willful. Each fire sign has its own spin on these qualities.

In my experience, fire signs put out a lot of energy (like the flame), which is great for getting work done. Where fire signs can fall short, though, is in subtleties. While fire signs are so busy burning up fuel, they don't always take in the details and signals around them. Fire signs need to be reminded to pay attention to others once in a while.

EARTH SIGNS: TAURUS, VIRGO, AND CAPRICORN

We all need our earth signs these days; these people offer common sense, practicality, patience, and fortitude. The Calvinist work ethic must have earth sign roots, for earth signs are all about prosperity. Earth signs are great at keeping people and businesses running; they don't often make trouble and can even be very healing and nurturing energies.

Earth signs take in a lot of energy; they can be highly intuitive in a very subtle way—not "suddenly psychic" but more grounded and soft about what is right. Earth signs are sometimes risk-averse (this can inhibit Minerva), but most often just study their options carefully before pursuing a goal.

AIR SIGNS: GEMINI, LIBRA, AND AQUARIUS

Air signs live the world of words, thoughts, ideas, concepts, and communications. Weighing words or forming policy, it's all an airy domain. Air signs are usually good at brainstorming sessions but can be arrogant, nervous, and sharp.

Air signs are usually good at assessing situations when they pay attention, but they can't always be counted on to listen. Sometimes air signs are so busy thinking or pondering that they miss something rather obvious. Air signs need to be grounded.

WATER SIGNS: CANCER, SCORPIO, AND PISCES

Since water is the emotional element, these signs tend to have deep emotions, intuition, and imagination. Water signs can be sensitive, which is great for creativity but challenging to taking risk or facing conflict. Since water takes on three forms—liquid, gas, and solid—those who are water signs can also be complex.

Most water signs are smart in nonverbal ways. They are patient and careful; they are also good at detail. On a bad day, water signs can lose touch with the world. Water signs need to stay in tune with their work's purpose.

Energetic Nature

There are three energetic modalities in the zodiac. This is the way the energy of the sign works—cardinal, fixed, or mutable.

CARDINAL SIGNS: ARIES, CANCER, LIBRA, AND CAPRICORN

A cardinal sign is like an arrow sailing through the air, going toward its target and nowhere else. Cardinal signs set about their tasks with purpose, direction, and determination. They don't look around to see what others are doing; they just get it done. A cardinal sign is very effective when that kind of "get it done" energy is appropriate, but if there are complications, moderations, or new findings that merit consideration, it's hard to set the arrow on a different path.

The challenge to those in the cardinal sign is to remember to reevaluate their position now and then. Care should be taken by those who try to control a cardinal sign—they aren't very agreeable. And if cardinal energy is in your stars, be aware that your peripheral vision may need some work.

FIXED SIGNS: TAURUS, LEO, SCORPIO, AND AQUARIUS

The fixed sign is just that: fixed, stable, committed, rooted, and sure. Fixed signs can be described as tenacious, committed, and patient, because they just don't change unless they absolutely have to. Fixed signs are great at what they've set their hearts on doing; they don't give up. If you find that you have a fixed sun or moon, you can be sure you're going to see Minerva through.

Changing course is the biggest problem for a fixed energy, because change is very, very difficult. Fixed signs are not flexible, malleable, or even a little bending. Loyalty to their cause is both an asset and, at times, a liability. Fixed signs need to be aware of the tendency to talk about change but not actually participate in it.

MUTABLE SIGNS: GEMINI, VIRGO, SAGITTARIUS,
AND PISCES

Change isn't the problem for mutable signs; rather, it's sticking to the path they've chosen. Mutable signs are very good at shifting, turning, or just zigzagging along to get to where they want to go. Mutable signs can think, act, and feel more than one thing at a time, making for very perceptive, creative energies.

Working with or having a relationship with a mutable sign can be both invigorating and exasperating, as they need to be guided back "to the point" now and then. Given their propensity to morph, mutable signs need to learn how to commit, stay with the program, and keep their eyes on their goal.

Your sun and moon signs are evaluated here simply to guide you to what you may not know about yourself.

HOW TO KNOW WHAT SIGN YOU ARE

Sun Sign

All you need to know is the day you were born to know what sign your sun is in. Here are the dates.

Aries	March 21–April 19
Taurus	April 20–May 20
Gemini	May 21–June 20
Cancer	June 21–July 22

Leo	July 23–August 22
Virgo	August 23–September 22
Libra	September 23–October 22
Scorpio	October 23–November 21
Sagittarius	November 22–December 21
Capricorn	December 22–January 19
Aquarius	January 20–February 18
Pisces	February 19–March 20

If your birthday falls on the first or last day of the sign, you may be on the cusp. The sun doesn't change to the next sign exactly at midnight, so there is a chance, if you were born on, say, October 23, that the sun might still have been in Libra and not yet in Scorpio. It's best in this case to read both signs, Libra and Scorpio, to see which describes you best.

Moon Sign

Find your birthday on the charts at the back of the book (pages 161–226). This chart lists each day the moon changed signs and at what time—in Eastern Standard Time. To adjust the time to your time zone, do as follows:

1. For Daylight Savings Time, subtract one hour.
2. For Central Time, subtract one hour.
3. For Mountain Time, subtract two hours.
4. For Pacific Time, subtract three hours.

The times listed use the twenty-four-hour clock. This means that after twelve noon, the hours are listed as follows:

13 = 1 P.M.

14 = 2 P.M.

15 = 3 P.M.

16 = 4 P.M.

17 = 5 P.M.

18 = 6 P.M.

19 = 7 P.M.

20 = 8 P.M.

21 = 9 P.M.

22 = 10 P.M.

23 = 11 P.M.

24 = 12 P.M.

The only dates listed are the days the moon changed signs. If you don't see your birthday listed, your moon fell in the sign above. For instance, if you were born on January 25, 1940, your birthday would not be listed but your moon would be in Leo because the moon went into Leo on January 24, 1940, and didn't move into another sign until January 26, 1940.

If your birthday is mentioned, the moon went into a new sign that day. If you know the time of your birth, you can look to see if the moon changed signs before or after you were born. If you don't know the time of your birth, simply read each sign—the one before the date of your birth and the sign the moon entered that day—and decide which one best describes you.

For instance, if you were born on June 29, 1964, at 9:00 P.M. Pacific Time, you would see that the moon entered Pisces at 16:56 Eastern Time. If you were born in Pacific Time, subtract three hours from here.

$$16:56 - 3 = 13:56 \text{ (or 1:56 P.M.)}$$

This means that the moon went into Pisces at almost 2:00 P.M. If you were born at 6:00 A.M., you know that the moon was still in Aquarius at that time so your moon would be Aquarius.

If you don't know the time of your birth, you would read both Aquarius and Pisces to see how you relate to each—they are very different signs and it will be easy to ascertain which describes you better.

THE SIGNS

ARIES

Element: Fire	*Energy: Cardinal*
Creed: I am.	
Ruling planet: Mars	

Positive Qualities

Courageous Enterprising Forgiving
Generous Good willpower Independent
Industrious Mentally energetic Pioneering

Challenging Qualities

Foolhardy Headstrong Impatient
Impulsive Insubordinate Quick-tempered
Selfish Tactless Willful

Notes

☾ Most people with Aries energy hate having a boss.

☾ Headaches are common maladies for stressed-out Aries.

Aries Sun (March 21–April 19)

Those born in Aries need to create an existence that provides refreshing challenges and territories that can be explored and conquered. Constant setback is preferable to monotony—and surprise is better than predictability. Work needs to allow the freedom of movement, time, and goals. Aries is an arrow; it travels with speed and purpose, hopefully to hit its target. Even if the arrow misses, it flies off again. Your exuberance for life is exalted in new challenges.

Aries people are tireless workers, usually optimistic and reliable. The danger herein is the will to get the job done: They can push toward a goal while stepping on others to get there— and not even notice. One of an Aries's spiritual tasks is to learn that not everyone is a competitor or opponent; partnership and cooperation need to be learned wherever you go.

Aries Moon

The person with an Aries moon needs to feel accomplishment in his work. Boredom is bad, lack of recognition is worse. They have strong imaginative faculties—a good mind and daring sense of inventiveness. They may tire of working for others and find a way to be their own boss. They lack diplomacy when they feel strongly but excel at motivating others around a heartfelt project.

The Aries moon is often so forceful in its gush of feelings that its exuberance can put more reserved types off. They should not try to squash that impulse to react—it always comes out one way or another. Instead, they need to watch out for signs that others are uncomfortable with their strength. They can always use humor to ease their way. An Aries moon feels its way through change and easily discards emotional setbacks to get on with the task at hand.

Aries and Career Shifts

An Aries sun or moon will look upon a career shift with gusto. It's a great challenge and an interesting crusade where there may be dragons to slay, mountains to scale, and riches to be won. If there is one sign that does well with the idea of Minerva, it's Aries. Mars, the ruling planet, shares Minerva's domain of strategic warfare. This makes most Aries natural career shape-shifters.

Aries is challenged when the career shape-shift is prolonged or delayed, for Aries lacks patience. Aries is also disgruntled when others are slow to understand their cause or too shy or reluctant to help out. Those of you who have Aries sun or moon need to constantly monitor your willfulness, pushiness, or aggression so that you don't become your own worst enemy.

TAURUS

Element: Earth	*Energy: Fixed*
Creed: I have.	
Ruling planet: Venus	

Positive Qualities
Cautious Committed Composed
Magnetic Mellow Persevering
Self-reliant Sympathetic Trustworthy

Challenging Qualities
Conceited Covetous Exacting
Grudge-holding Lazy Narrow
Possessive Stubborn Timid

Notes

- Taureans are known to manage money well (but they can be cheap, too).
- Taurus rules the neck, so stress often settles in the upper shoulder and neck area.

Taurus Sun (April 20–May 20)

The nature of the Taurus sun energy is to create or work with tangible, physical reality, even if Taureans don't actually hold on to it. Luxury goods, money, beautiful things, real estate— earthly assets come into view with Taurus energy. Work that produces measurable results or reaction from the outside world is satisfying. Work that requires caution, measure, or patience is also rewarding.

Taureans may feel frustrated if their careers demand a lot of verbal activity, since actions and deeds speak louder than mere words. They may also feel physically ill if they are around negative people or places, since their bodies are so sensitive to physical energy. Taureans are natural healers for this reason, too, since they innately understand what is healthy and productive versus challenging and toxic.

Taurus Moon

An environment that provides support or positive feedback is preferable. Work where loyalty counts, goals are measurable, and people respect each other. The instincts of those with a Taurus moon are good when it comes to art, money, land, precious metals, and fashion. Their mood and self-worth can sour, however, if they are surrounded by cheapness, ugliness, or discomfort.

Always listen to that fine Taurean intuition; it is right, especially when taking risks. Taureans do not allow themselves to be pushed into doing something they don't want to do; they will regret it. To a Taurus, change is serious business and requires real research and commitment. Taurus moons work through change with serious intent to feel the right solution.

Taurus and Career Shifts

If you've got either sun or moon in Taurus, you'll want to pay close attention to your security issues. You don't have to take the aggressive fast track to get to that new career unless you have some strong fire energy to help you. You need to go at your own pace, comfortably approach your goal and even test it out a bit before you commit. You are not made for quick change (remember the stubborn thing) and you can't be told what to do.

Taurus is cautious, which often guarantees success. You won't recklessly jump to something that doesn't work out; instead, you will take the time to feel it through and appreciate the impact on every part of your life. Money and prosperity issues will most definitely come up in your shift, so don't be surprised and use some of the clearing exercises you've learned to ease you through the fears. Venus is your ruler and she really likes to keep you in the comfort and style you deserve.

GEMINI

Element: Air	*Energy: Mutable*
Creed: I think.	
Ruling planet: Mercury	

Positive Qualities
Ambitious Eloquent Flexible
Inquiring Intelligent Quick
Resourceful Responsive Tolerant

Challenging Qualities
Curious Distractible Impulsive
Inconsistent Irritable Rash
Restless Verbose Wasteful

Notes

- Geminis are known to love gossip, fun, and making lots of connections.
- Gemini is a sign prone to nervous exhaustion—and as ruler of the lungs is also prone to bronchitis.

Gemini Sun May 21–June 20

Satisfaction for Geminis is multilayered. They need variety in everyday life, subjects that grip their intellectual interest, some degree of movement, and connection to others. Working quietly in solitude is not an ideal condition unless they are writing to someone or (like me) a book or article. Communication in all of its many forms are fitting for Gemini talent.

Geminis also need to satisfy their need for variety and to be able to comment on what is seen, heard, or created. The most challenging situation for a Gemini is to keep his or her mouth shut. Denying the Gemini a way to be heard, be it through art, music, the written word, actions, or speaking, is tantamount to killing a life force. To seek, to know, to tell is the Gemini's primary nature.

Gemini Moon

High-speed intellectual energy is common to the moon in Gemini, as are anxiety and nervousness. An environment that appreciates thinking and provides a variety of creative outlets is ideal. Stability, predictability, or frequent evaluations are desirable to keep the Gemini energy grounded, interested, and feeling "heard."

Gemini moons are challenged to feel emotions rather than

think them. This is hard for such a verbal sign. There is often a tendency to rationalize feelings or to talk their way out of what they feel if they just don't want to deal with it. Intuition is very sharp for those Geminis who can tone down the thinking energy. Gemini moons benefit from work that allows them to think, create, and relax in cycles.

Geminis and Career Shifts

Mercury-ruled Gemini is shifty and changeable, good for being interested in a career shift but in constant need of grounding throughout the process. Symbolically, Gemini is the twins, two sides to one whole—and this is often seen in the way a Gemini does two things at once and sometimes even carries on two professions at once. Being a Gemini, I know how that is. I am also intimately familiar with how hard it is to stick with a program. Geminis are easily distracted.

If you have a Gemini sun or moon you need to keep your attention on your goal. You are bound to get bored when things don't happen fast enough, and you may even change your mind several hundred times when you begin your shift. That's all very natural to you, but you must remember to find ways to keep going, be patient, and follow through. Otherwise you could start this over and over again and never see the last chapter.

CANCER

Element: Water	*Energy: Cardinal*

Creed: I feel.

Ruling planet: The Moon

Positive Qualities
Adaptable Conscientious Devoted
Domestic Economical Intuitive
Patient Sociable Sympathetic

Challenging Qualities
Lazy Moody Proud
Resentful Sentimental Suspicious
Timid Untruthful Vain

Notes
- ☾ Cancer rules the stomach and holds the stress—ulcers, aches, and acid.
- ☾ Cancers are hard on the outside, soft on the inside.

Cancer Sun (June 21–July 22)

With subtle leadership qualities, those with a Cancer sun sign know how to make others feel comfortable and heard. It is important that they find a work environment that is stable and secure. While they enjoy rational and methodical approaches, their own creative nature and ability to investigate beyond the surface should be recognized. They are stimulated by the people around them both positively and negatively, and take their loyalty and character seriously.

Cancers are usually reluctant to venture out alone as entrepreneurs and are cautious as investors. This is not to say they can't work alone or take risks, but they appreciate calculation and consideration before they sail into uncharted waters. They work well as a balance to other people who need tempering, moderation, or smoothing out.

Cancer Moon

Recognition and appreciation for their work is important, as are compatible coworkers and reasonable rules for promotion. Their intuitive and creative senses need some outlet as do their moods. Strict emotional boundaries are fine as long as they fit their mode of behavior. Rash acts, outbursts, and grandstanding displays of emotion from others can be very uncomfortable for them, but under stress, they, too, are prone to act from emotion and not from reason.

Cancer moon is a great nurturer and well-suited as a mentor, leader, or supporter. Taking care of people who are sincere and willing is easy. Serving those who seem less deserving is hard. There is a dignified, judgmental nature to the Cancer moon that can seem standoffish and unapproachable.

Since the moon is the ruling planet of the sign, the moon in Cancer is very powerful.

Cancers and Career Shifts

The claws of the Cancer crab hold on to something or someone dear harder than any other sign of the zodiac. Sun or moon in Cancer, you must be ready to leave behind what has been good or well-loved when you career shape-shift. It's hard, to be sure, but it's necessary. Cancers need to work on emotionally disengaging from the old career to get into making the new one. Even if you hate-hate-hate your job, you still probably have friends there and they will be hard to leave.

Cancers do set about things with purpose, being a cardinal sign, and are therefore successful. Crabs walk sideways—they sidle—and so will you—into finding the right work. As long as you keep your heart open and your emotions flowing (do clearings with water frequently), you won't have too much reluctance to achieve your goal.

LEO

Element: Fire	*Energy: Fixed*
Creed: I will.	
Ruling planet: The Sun	

Positive Qualities
Chivalrous Hopeful Impressive
Industrious Inspiring Kind
Loyal Passionate Sincere

Challenging Qualities
Arrogant Condescending Dominating
Fussy Gullible Hotheaded
Impetuous Pompous Vain

Notes

- ☾ Leos like to be treated as visiting dignitaries and awarded respect if not admiration.
- ☾ Leo rules the heart, which can make them loving as well as out of reach.

Leo Sun (July 23–August 22)

With the sun as ruling planet, Leos are endowed with an inner light and are usually optimistic and without fear. Leos have a tendency to wait until they fully understand a situation before they take over with their opinion. As a fixed sign, Leos are likely to listen to others for information but make decisions based on their own will. Leos are often well-liked because of their energy and can rise easily in the ranks of any profession; the hard part is the start, when they haven't earned esteem or respect.

Leos are fueled by creative inspiration, amusement, liveliness, and life itself. Professions that allow a Leo to be happy, creative, and respected are best. Leos can be entrepreneurs or lead a small team in a big company, as long as they can shine. The fiery nature of the Leo sun is not the most perceptive; they might miss some subtle signal while they generate their work energy.

Leo Moon

Leo moons are bright emotional energies that glow and bask in admiration and playfulness. A Leo moon is loyal and optimistic and it takes a great deal to bring them down. There is a certain daring, "look at me" quality to a Leo moon that brings a thirst for entertaining or coming before the public in some way. "Shy" is not a word often linked to a Leo moon.

The emotional buoyancy of Leo moons is probably much admired, and their ability to work through difficulties with dignity is also valued. Leo moons are often so bright that they miss deeper, less direct communication or subtleties. They might spend so much time putting out energy that they don't have time to take it in. For this reason, Leo moons can be surprised by unpleasant situations or problems after everyone else is in the know.

Leos and Career Shifts

Sun or moon in Leo is a glowing, fixed light. Leo energy is great for conquering (the lion, and king of the zodiac), but like most leaders, Leos don't like to do the "grunt work." Their pride might get in the way when it comes to asking for favors or doing things they feel are too amateurish or beneath them. While they are naturally endowed with personal power, they don't want to put people off, either.

Leos are great optimists, which helps in Minerva's process. They are likely to be patient as their future unfolds and undaunted by challenges or obstacles. The natural flow of well-being and radiance that exudes from them will inspire others and keep them on the track to success.

VIRGO

Element: Earth	*Energy: Mutable*

Creed: I analyze.

Ruling planet: Mercury

Positive Qualities
Active Discreet Efficient
Industrious Intuitive Methodical
Prudent Serious Thoughtful

Challenging Qualities
Anxious Apprehensive Calculating
Cold Critical Discontented
Inconsistent Indecisive Irritable

Notes
- Virgo is a natural caretaker who all too often puts others first.
- Virgo rules the lower digestive tract, and stress creates problems in that area.

Virgo Sun (August 23–September 22)

Virgos were put on this planet to sort the rest of us out. Virgos have a unique talent at untangling, perfecting, and smoothing out whatever needs to get done. They are really gifted in knowing "who, what, where, when, and why" all at once. Virgos are, for instance, healers, communicators, and diagnosticians, and they use these talents in everyday life, not just in work. Virgos need variety and problems to sort out and a place to effect the change they want.

Virgos are often very sharp and can pick up on subtleties in their environment. They often know just what is wrong and how to fix it, and, being so good at problem-solving, they often fix things that aren't their responsibility. They can be guilty of putting others before themselves, which leaves them exhausted and depleted and not just a little irritable. They have an amazing ability and simply need to learn where they want to put their energy—and then rest.

Virgo Moon

Those with the moon in Virgo are highly intuitive. They take so much information from the environment, that it isn't always easy to process it. This makes them nervous, anxious, or highstrung for no apparent reason. Those with the moon in Virgo are also prone to worry, since they notice so many things to worry about. When not overtaxed, they are finely tuned perceivers, ready and willing to use vast amounts of knowledge to solve problems.

Those with the moon in Virgo are excellent critics, always looking for ways to perfect what exists now. Their dark side is self-criticism ("I could have done it better"), which is not helpful at all. Discerning tastes, high standards, and clarity need to be addressed in any work they do. They can't work for sloppy, mediocre anything—it's bad for their health.

Virgos and Career Shifts

For career-shifting, Virgo suns and moons have mutability and perceptiveness that contribute a great deal to their ability to react appropriately when opportunity comes up. They will respond well to Minerva, allowing their process to unfold with interest. It is important, however, for them to support themselves with positive thoughts and to be aware of the self-critic that lives within them. Especially when they are worried, stressed, or in a state of anticipation, their default mind-set is to wonder what they could have done differently or where they might have gone wrong. Their intuition, capability, and natural propensity to find answers will lead them to the right place—don't think too hard.

LIBRA

Element: Air	*Energy: Cardinal*
Creed: I balance.	
Ruling planet: Venus	

Positive Qualities
Affectionate Cheerful Forgiving
Impartial Intelligent Persuasive
Purposeful Sympathetic Tactful

Challenging Qualities
Aloof Careless Choosy
Demanding Extreme Gullible
Indecisive Pedantic Vain

Notes

c Libras are best in problem-solving situations where personal relationships are not at stake.

c The lumbar region (lower back) is Libra-ruled and is therefore subject to trouble when under stress.

Libra Sun (September 23–October 22)

Those with the sun in Libra love beauty, peace, harmony, and ideals. Where beauty and good feelings are strong, Libras thrive. When conflict or negativity are constant, they are most challenged. They are intelligent, endowed with scholarly curiosity and the ability to grasp complicated situations quickly (Libras make great judges and lawyers). Answers come to them without too much effort, both rationally and intuitively. They have a natural generosity and an ability to soothe others—diplomacy and peace-keeping are strong skills.

Libra energy can get bogged down when conflict is continual and problems can't be solved. This is also the case when things are always peaceful—they won't make trouble for the sake of it, but without challenges or new pursuits, Libras can be too self-interested and indolent. The balance Libras strive for is also internal, but too much peace won't be satisfying either.

Libra Moon

Those with the moon in Libra strive not only for balance in life but in partnerships, too. Both in marriage and business, a Libra moon likes to keep company with someone else. The desire for partnership is innate and finding the right person brings a sense of completion. Problems with partnerships are also common, since working out conflict and keeping the peace is part of their purpose.

They also have a great sense of fun—not slapstick but witty, word humor—and are excellent party guests. They don't seek the spotlight but they do well in it, and their appreciation of the arts—music, art, dancing, singing—gives them pleasure. Clothes, adornments—anything that brings beauty into the world—is easy and enjoyable for them.

Libra and Career Shifts

Looking for a new career while you're working is a naturally unbalanced state; this can be hard on you if your sun or moon is in Libra. While you are an excellent problem-solver and good at directing your energy toward a purpose or goal, Minerva's method and the process of investigation may make you feel disloyal or dishonest while you are supposed to be committed elsewhere. It's natural to feel uncomfortable at times.

Your cardinal energy and swift intellectual power will contribute to your success. Be firm about pleasing yourself and your goals first, since your propensity for diplomacy can lead you to compromise your own ideals. Allow yourself to use your intuition, not your strong ability to reason, when you are making decisions. Your sixth sense is your strongest sense of all.

SCORPIO

Element: Water	*Energy: Fixed*
Creed: I create.	
Ruling planet: Pluto	

Positive Qualities
Ambitious Creative Eloquent
Energetic Fearless Honorable
Loyal Patient Thoughtful

Challenging Qualities
Cold Dark Destructive
Dogmatic Miserly Sarcastic
Secretive Severe Suspicious

Notes
c Scorpios have an intense, innate power that sometimes unnerves others.
c Scorpio rules the pelvic region.

Scorpio Sun (October 23–November 21)

Scorpios are strong, intent, and creative—a great combination of strengths. They have all the energy it takes to make something happen, yet, in contrast, they can destroy as easily as they build. Their intensity is apparent in their sincerity and steadfastness, but can turn darkly into suspicion and animosity; people rarely want to make trouble with a Scorpio, for the price of tangling with this force can be steep.

This intensity and innate power endows Scorpios with innocence, which is necessary for invention and pragmatism, and helps in achieving a goal. Being vulnerable, though, feels very threatening and can make them withdraw from the fray, often to their disadvantage. The famous Scorpio attack comes from their most endangered state. They are arguably the most creative sign of the zodiac; if you are a Scorpio, do not be afraid of your own power.

Scorpio Moon

Loyal, committed, deep, and private, those with a Scorpio moon need respect to function. There are no bounds to their ability to sense; they are deeply intuitive beings. Again, vulnerability is not easy. As a result, they like to control their environment and achieve some sense of security from the relationships that surround them. They can't abide criticism or deception from those they trust, so their friendships and associations must stand the test of time. They aren't likely to be impulsive about liking someone else, and their words can sound very sharp and judgmental when they're being self-protective.

The fixed nature of those with a Scorpio moon is great for commitment but is reluctant to "see the writing on the wall." What is obvious to others can come as a surprise when they just don't want to believe it. Their will can be overpowering and argumentative, even when the struggle is internal.

Scorpio and Career Shifts

Your fixed nature challenges the idea of shifting at all, even if you really want to make a change. This is common to all fixed signs but even more so to sun or moon in Scorpio, since your intensity can displace your objectivity. You have a singular ability to create the change you want, and as a strongly intuitive individual, you have a great rapport with Minerva and her ways. However, when it comes back to earth and making your change real, you're the only one who can take the steps toward your goal, and you might talk yourself out of it ("What if I stumble?" "What if I don't make it?") since failure is like public humiliation—the worst thing a Scorpio can face.

Scorpio is a survivor, though, and, like the phoenix rising out of ashes, you can make a new, better existence from your last one. Direct some of your intensity in the direction of allowing, embrace the unknown as your friend and not your enemy, and you will find an easier path to your next career.

SAGITTARIUS

Element: Fire	*Energy: Mutable*
Creed: I seek.	
Ruling planet: Jupiter	

Positive Qualities
Adventurous Charitable Energetic
Fearless Generous Honest
Logical Prophetic Sincere

Challenging Qualities
Aggressive Blunt Boastful
Changeable Defiant Overconfident
Rash Speculative Uncompromising

Note
- Sagittarius rules the sacrum and sciatic nerve, innervating the hips and thighs.
- Sagittarians are said to be "frank to a fault."

Sagittarius Sun (November 22–December 21)

High spirits and can-do energy are typical of adventurous Sagittarians. Anything that presents new terrain is interesting, both physical thrills and new knowledge. They can try almost anything for a first time, and master it if they feel like it. They are all about expanding horizons and finding answers—then moving on and doing it all over again. Rather than use their knowledge for themselves, they are bound to want to share what they know with others. Their advice is usually good, but they often don't follow it themselves.

Although Sagittarians can be fickle, they don't give up easily and will persevere even when others don't. As a risk-taker and gambler of sorts, they often have good results. Sagittarius is symbolized by the archer, shooting into the distance to seek—new lands, new cultures, new ideas. Whatever they find compelling and motivating is surely attractive and probably fruitful.

Sagittarius Moon

Mutability and fire combine in Sagittarius to form an impulsive, passionate emotional nature that loves the thrill of the chase. Their motive for work and creativity is sincere and they will enjoy challenge and risk, but when their pursuit loses its luster, they have to learn about willpower. Sagittarius has a strong humane streak that makes causes, justice, and issues of culture compelling. Their generosity and ardent commitment are apparent.

Seeking and sharing knowledge brings satisfaction. They tend to have strong philosophical beliefs. Those who cross them may come up against brusqueness or anger, but they get over it quickly. Their creative appetite takes precedence over problems or obstacles and their fearlessness enables them to leap without hesitation. While "look before you leap" seems like a good idea, they don't remember it too often.

Sagittarius and Career Shifting

Your energy and appreciation of new experience is certainly an asset in working with Minerva. With the sun or moon in Sagittarius, you aren't afraid of the unknown and are no doubt betting on the upside. You will probably enjoy the process for more than just its ends—learning, discussing, and critically assessing every part of the process and eventually integrating Minerva's ideas into your own philosophy. You absorb knowledge and new ideas easily.

As for transforming work, you may be confused by the number of choices you have. Your interests may take different twists and turns until you settle on one idea. As a result, your frustration level will be tested; it isn't that you can't do something, it's just that you can't do everything you want all at once. Agile, adept, and easily inspired, you may be swayed in several directions with real potential; choice is hard.

CAPRICORN

Element: Earth	*Energy: Cardinal*
Creed: I manifest.	
Ruling planet: Saturn	

Positive Qualities
Ambitious Calm Dignified
Magnetic Practical Prudent
Reverent Stable Tenacious

Challenging Qualities
Authoritative Depressed Jealous
Limited Nervous Selfish
Stingy Suspicious Tough

Notes

- Capricorn rules the knees, where one "kneels before authority."

- Capricorns are unfairly criticized for being overly ambitious while their energy, like the Capricorn Jesus, is really about making spirit into matter.

Capricorn Sun (December 22–January 19)

The sun in Capricorn endows people with a strong sense of purpose and determination to succeed in whatever goal is before them. Like mountain goats, they can work their way up a treacherous peak, all the way to the top. Some Capricorns don't feel good unless they are climbing, begging the question: How high is up? Knowing when to quit is not really a Capricorn strength. Still, in troubled times or bad weather, Capricorns can be relied upon to stay with the program.

Capricorns are therefore achievers and, as such, do best in pursuits where success can be both measured and rewarded. Structure, hierarchy, and solid ideas provide a solid foundation for them to build upon and thrive. Risk can be welcomed when their comfort level is satisfied. Sustaining losses is not difficult, but public assessment, criticism, or conjecture can be very uncomfortable for their dignified and sometimes aloof countenance.

Capricorn Moon

The internal dignity (and horror at the possibility of humiliation) of those with the moon in Capricorn keeps them playing it close to the chest. While they are productive, capable, and committed, they aren't used to taking creative risks or putting themselves publicly to the test. This makes others view them as more aloof or unfeeling than they really are, and can present them with an image problem. Their ability to keep cool during trying times is a great asset, but their reluctance to "cut loose" in public still creates an image of unapproachability.

Dealing with and sorting out others—mistakes or rewards—

is easy for these people. Justice is usually done, and their efforts at leadership are appreciated. The Capricorn energy is immensely creative when comfortable and trusting, so be aware that the environment in which they work is critical to their power and influence. Their forcefulness is tempered by both patience and an unwillingness to "let them see you sweat." Tangible, positive results ultimately bring them the greatest satisfaction; making something real is a reward in itself.

Capricorn and Career Shifts

Your drive for success is going to get you there, but the process itself may be difficult to tackle. While suns or moons in Capricorn aren't likely to be impatient, you may well question the methods and "madness" of Minerva's tactics. You won't find tangible results, rational practices, or even simple struc-ture to satisfy your preference for measurement and progress. This lack of normal curriculum is without doubt the greatest obstacle in your work with Minerva.

Otherwise, you are perfectly suited for a hardworking, goal-minded process. You are well-endowed with strength to seek and find answers, patience to allow the process to unfold, and courage and faith to pursue the path that presents itself. If you can put aside your need to make sense of how Minerva can help you, you will no doubt succeed.

AQUARIUS

Element: Air	*Energy: Fixed*
Creed: I know.	
Ruling planet: Uranus	

Positive Qualities

Humane Intuitive Knowledgeable
Patient Philosophical Pleasant
Progressive Sincere Truthful

Challenging Qualities

Cold Extremist Flighty
Gullible Long-winded Pedantic
Radical Stubborn Uncooperative

Notes

c Aquarius rules the ankles, which can suffer when under stress.
c Aquarius is the sign that rules large groups and institutions, but Aquarians hate crowds.

Aquarius Sun (January 20—February 18)

Aquarians are often thoughtful and internal people who like to accumulate knowledge and ponder the future. They are the eccentrics of the zodiac, walking to the beat of their own drummer. They might be unaware of the fact that their discoveries or preferences set trends, for once they feel "followed," they are likely to make for new territory. Aquarians tend to live a little bit ahead, into the future. As an inventive sign, they also enjoy looking for better ways to do things and new ideas or concepts to make life better.

Their biggest challenge is overcoming themselves. As a fixed sign (and in my experience the strongest "fix" of all), they are great at inventing and identifying change but find their own inertia very hard to overcome. Great advice-givers, they rarely take it. They have an intuitive knack and often know a lot about the future, but it can pass them by if they don't gather up their own energy and participate.

Aquarius Moon

The emotional life of those with the moon in Aquarius tends to be intellectualized, and in its most extreme, they can live in fantasyland. They have a great sense of compassion for the world at large, feeling deeply committed to their own causes and passions, but they are likely to think more about how they feel than just lean in to the emotions in their personal relationships. Their loyalty and commitment are strong; their stability and sense of security are taken seriously. In work situations, they are the rock, able to withstand turmoil when others panic.

Their intuitive nature and inventiveness are ideal for many different pursuits, across politics, education, science, and even astrology and other metaphysical concepts. They may be seen to be eccentric and they are probably proud of it.

Aquarius and Career Shifts

The super-fixed nature of Aquarius sun or moon makes changing anything difficult, even if it's your idea, your making, and your choice. Even when you want to do it, it can be hard to manifest. This is the paradox of your energy—you can see and shape the future very well, but since you're always living slightly ahead of the present, it's hard to be in the present long enough to make your change happen.

As a shape-shifter, you're probably the most gifted sign in the zodiac. When it's not about your own change, you're brilliant at transforming your energy, exuding compassion, and facilitating someone else's change. You're a natural teacher, better at helping others learn and being a master than being a student. To make the most of Minerva's process, consider it a game—a fun, playful project—rather than a serious, purposeful commitment. With a little humor and light, you can trick yourself into the change you want.

PISCES

Element: Water	*Energy: Mutable*
Creed: I believe.	
Ruling planet: Neptune	

Positive Qualities
Caring Focused Hospitable
Idealistic Inspiring Orderly
Peaceful Perceptive Refined

Challenging Qualities
Complex Critical Dreamy
Indecisive Negative Self-deprecating
Slow Submissive Timid

Notes

c Pisces rules the feet (so why don't we say, "Oh my achin' fish!"?).

c Pisces can find order in almost any mess.

Pisces Sun (February 19–March 20)

Pisces is the last sign of the zodiac and those born under this sign are enmeshed in mystery, hidden knowledge, and creativity. Symbolized by the fish, Pisces has no protection against its element, water, which passes through its gills and brushes up against delicate scales. Like the fish, people born under Pisces have no barriers to protect them from their environment—emotional, psychic, physical, aggressive—a constant assault on their energy. In a reaction to this constant "noise," most Pisces invent strong structure and rules to live by—it helps them make sense of the chaos. They do, however, have access to great insight and creativity, seeking bliss in all they do. Pleasure-seeking is common to Pisces energy as a way of controlling their environment.

Their mutable nature challenges them to stick to their goals, which most likely change and shift with the energy surrounding them. Working with others is fine as long as they aren't negative; working in creative, freelance situations is okay as long as they feel secure within their work flow. Risk isn't important since everything can seem like a risk to them. Stability, promise, beauty, harmony, and joy are their true goals in whatever they do.

Pisces Moon

Private, deep feelings and strong intuition are typical for those with the moon in Pisces, and modesty and shyness are often a result. They are very perceptive and sometimes pick up on the negativity others feel, even to the point of taking it upon themselves to feel criticized or put upon. Being very perceptive and intuitive does provide an enormous basis for creativity and the ability to find and create beauty in everything they do. In fact, their work involves the pursuit of emotional, personal, and professional nirvana.

All of this depth combines with their mutability to enable them to do a great job in whatever they choose to do, but it can keep them from rising higher in the ranks unless they tone down their sensitivity. Business, in its more corporate and less creative sense, has a lot of "sharks and barracudas"—some with hard-boiled Pisces moons. There is a trade-off, of course; when they purposely construct barriers to their openness and intuitive eyes, they get less information and inspiration of all kinds.

Pisces and Career Shifts

If your sun and moon are in Pisces, you have talent for insight and vision—strong assets for Minerva's methods. You have an innate ability to work with Minerva's realm of creativity—you're a natural voice to the gods and the realms of magic. Almost certainly you will see results for your efforts, but whether you actualize your plans is up to you. The amount of chaos that can be created out of a self-created career shift might be objectionable to your nature.

It is not the method that will be your challenge, but the effort of putting yourself out there to be seen, heard, and tested in a new career or creative realm. Being put on the spot or on the line is not easy—it's possible, but not something you enjoy. Furthermore, conflict that may arise, both within yourself and with those with whom you deal, might make you shy of initiating a change. For your peace-loving, bliss-seeking nature, you have to really want your prize in order to weather the shift.

EVALUATING YOUR SUN AND MOON

Once you're familiar with each sign, look in the following pages for how they combine with each other. For instance, a Gemini with an Aries moon would look under Aries and see how that sign mixes with Gemini, and then look up Gemini and see how that sign deals with Aries. If you have the same sun and moon sign, look under that sign and see how your double qualities merge.

Aries

- Aries combined with Leo or Sagittarius can act more extreme than any other combination.
- Aries combined with Gemini, Libra, or Aquarius makes for very energetic and forceful ideas, thoughts, and words.
- Aries combined with water or earth signs balances out the extremes and can provide a nice blend of creativity and practicality.

c Aries combined with Aries (both sun and moon) is especially freedom-loving but also in need of learning how to work with others. Rather than being super-aggressive, there is usually a sheltered, tender side.

Taurus

c Taurus coupled with Capricorn or Virgo can be very practical, pragmatic, and prone to worry. Risk-taking may not be easy but usually pays off.

c Taurus with water signs is greatly intuitive but can get stuck in the mud if there is any negativity around; keep emotional connections clear.

c Taurus combined with air and fire signs can be a healthy balance of productive and cautious energy with high-spirited creativity.

c A Taurus-Taurus combination can be very hard to change and fearful of risk because of money issues.

Gemini

c Gemini with Libra or Aquarius enhances the intellect but may be flighty or ungrounded.

c Gemini with fire signs is a fun-loving, high-spirited energy but, again, is challenged to be consistent and grounded.

c Gemini with water or earth signs is more balanced and cautious but may be more irritable—the pull between wanting to flit around versus being grounded or emotional.

c Gemini with itself can be super-fast and verbal but will likely suffer from nervousness and anxiety.

Cancer

c Cancer with air or fire signs makes for dynamic sensitivity; timidity and reluctance to emerge subside.

c Cancer with Scorpio or Pisces is very intuitive, creative, and emotional but may be prone to shyness or submissiveness.

c Cancer with earth signs is practical and intuitive, creative and grounded, but sometimes risk-averse.

c Cancer with itself can be very reluctant to make changes that take them away from close relationships.

Leo

c Leo is generally fueled by air signs that propel more thoughtfulness into their leadership purpose.

c With fellow fire signs, flames can get out of control through willfulness, exaggeration, or vigorous dedication.

c Leo with water or earth signs is generally tempered and acts practically and realistically, and is less likely to fall into challenging traits.

c Leo with Leo is very dignified and is in danger of being out of reach of the "common man."

Virgo

c Virgo with air signs makes for practical applications for ideas, concepts, and thoughts.

c Virgo with water signs can be very intuitive and creative but also very worried and internal.

c Virgo with fire signs makes light of worries and creates impetus to follow through on decisions.

c Virgo with earth signs is practical, concise, and productive.

c Virgo with itself creates a sharp mind and ability to sort out many difficulties but is prone to overstimulation.

Libra

c With earth and water signs, Libra leans in to its intuitive, beautiful, and bliss-loving qualities rather than intellectual ones.

c With fire signs, Libra becomes a forceful, fearless seeker of experience and problem-solving.

c With Gemini or Aquarius, Libra's intellectual capabilities are accentuated and gifts in writing and communications are prominent.

c Libra with Libra may find a lot of conflict (and resolve it well) in order to satisfy the thirst for balance.

Scorpio

c With air and fire signs, Scorpio is more removed from intensity and able to take on more risky ventures.

c With earth signs, Scorpio is grounded in reality but may find it harder to take risks.

c With water signs, Scorpio's intuitive energy is underscored but may result in a greater need of privacy.

c With itself, Scorpio is truly a strong center of creativity but will need encouragement to share it with others.

Sagittarius

c With other fire signs, Sagittarius happily and fearlessly ventures around life but may find it difficult to pay attention to others.

c With air signs, Sagittarius leans in to intellectual pursuits but can find it hard to sit still.

c With earth or water signs, Sagittarius has more insight and measured energy, making risk-taking less playful.

c With itself, Sagittarius seeks adventures but may not return to tell all the stories.

Capricorn

c With Virgo and Taurus, practical measures and solid commitments are stressed.

c With Cancer, Scorpio, or Pisces, Capricorn is a more delicate energy of practicality and idealistic insights.

- With air and fire signs Capricorn tends to be more assertive, vocal, and less organized.
- With itself, Capricorn is more quiet, internal, and set on focus and goal-achievement.

Aquarius

- With other air signs, Aquarius is a great teacher, able to guide complex ideas into the world.
- With fire signs, Aquarius has more impetus to be seen, to be a part of groups, and enjoy change.
- With water or earth signs, Aquarius is more grounded and practical but could be less vocal about interesting new (eccentric) ideas.
- With itself, Aquarius prefers thinking and considering to talking broadly to others, and is a great mentor, one-on-one.

Pisces

- With Cancer and Scorpio, Pisces is very creative, intuitive, and takes care to associate only with trustworthy people.
- With air or fire signs, Pisces is less shy, more able to vocalize and create, but can be more remote.
- With earth signs, Pisces constructs stability and order and diminishes risk as much as possible.
- With itself, Pisces creates a safe environment, both internal and external, in which to live and work.

FOUR

MAXIMIZING YOUR ASSETS

Y̶ou are now prepared for Minerva's power-building techniques. With a new or refreshed understanding of your inborn
talents and aptitudes, you are ready to enhance, invigorate, and
regenerate your career charisma. Your sun and moon signs
have prepared you to be more open to your gifts and talents;
this chapter will help you adjust your energy to your best
"charged state" to make you more magnetic, to bring the right
new roads to your view, and to entice you to walk beside
Minerva with purpose.

Your personal assets work on two levels, both positive and
negative. The positive and conscious plane allows you to choose
the skills you want to put forward, whether they are creative,
independent, practical, or pragmatic. You'll know by reading
the descriptions of your signs what makes you feel most moti-
vated. On a negative level, you have been given insight into
your inborn faults, whether it be an inclination to laziness,

indecision, or hotheaded behavior, you've probably nodded your head a few times in defining your weaknesses. We all harbor faults, but we don't consciously choose to put them forward—these traits tend to emerge whether we like them or not.

Before taking any steps to enhance your energy, you must accept who you are.

Many of my clients have been relieved to find their strengths and weaknesses defined so clearly in their astrological signs ("So that's why I'm so stubborn . . ."), but then jump to the erroneous conclusion that they can change. Change isn't the point; in fact, trying to change yourself dramatically from your inherent gifts is trying to deny who you are in the first place. Faults and talents are both critical to who you are. Accept this and you'll be much more open to personal happiness. Resist it and you'll always feel inadequate or disappointed.

One of my clients, Chris, was very frustrated in her job as an assistant to an agent for television entertainment properties. Chris considered herself smart (she is), quick to solve problems (also true), and capable of spotting trends and talent that would be marketable. As a Sagittarian, Chris was thirsty for knowledge and fearless in seeking experience; her moon in Pisces gave her an excellent intuitive capacity for topics, people, and issues that would work well on television. Chris knew she had the talent to do the job, yet she was afraid to ask her boss about how she could advance as an agent in her own right. While she expressed her desires to her colleagues, she couldn't find the words or the opportunity to talk to her boss.

With help from Minerva, Chris looked into her own power connections and found that she lacked some power in the qualities of initiative, courage, and passion—her fire element. It wasn't hard for Chris to find her spark. Afterward, she reported feeling much more excited about her future and committed to trying to establish herself as an agent. She collected some ideas and met with her boss, who was open to helping Chris and liked some of her potential projects. After her first talk with him, Chris knew it was only a matter of time before she got a break.

MINERVA'S EXERCISES FOR ASSET ENHANCEMENT

Minerva would like you to once again work with the elements to gain a fuller understanding of your powers and frailties. Before you concentrate on your sun and moon sign specifics, try a little "dance" with each element to see where you feel most comfortable. This exercise might feel awkward, since you'll be listening to the sound of your own voice, but Minerva requests that you put aside your delicate ego and proceed. Roughly translated, she wants you to get over yourself.

Exercise: Minerva's Path to Power

Tools: Tape player capable of recording and playing back.

Read the following guided meditation into a tape recorder. Read it slowly, pausing after each sentence. Take breaths in between instructions. In a safe space (where you won't be interrupted, questioned, or judged), close your eyes and listen to the tape. Allow your mind's eye to follow the story. When you're done, write down your initial reactions. *Note to the reluctant recorder:* If you simply can't record yourself or someone else onto a tape, read each passage thoroughly, one part at a time.

Close your eyes after each passage and allow yourself to experience how you respond to each element. Write down your reactions.

PART ONE

Take a deep breath and exhale slowly. Relax. You have plenty of time. Plenty of space. Lots of possibilities surround you. There is no hurry.

With eyes closed, walk along a beautiful path. Outside. The air is fresh. The surroundings are at peace. Lovely. Relaxed. The path is an easy walk. It's enjoyable. Slowly, the path begins an upward slope, still an easy walk, still beautiful, fresh, peaceful. Slowly and without strain, walk up the path. Enjoy the ease with which you walk. The path takes a turn around a bend. You're curious. There's something interesting there. It's not scary. It's not threatening. In fact, you feel even more at peace and at ease.

You round the bend and see a great fire before you, emanating beauty, warmth, and constantly changing images. You sit before the fire, unafraid. There is much power to it. You can change the fire with your will. Bend it, twist it, make it bigger, smaller. If you want, you can walk into the fire, be a part of it. Dance with its flames, unafraid. Stay with the fire. Enjoy its energy. Play in its ever-changing mystery.

[PAUSE]

When you're ready, walk away from the fire. Walk along the path for a while. Feel the warmth of the fire fade the farther away you walk. Feel yourself free of its energy. You are at peace, walking along, enjoying the beauty of your walk, the freshness, the clean air, the smooth and easy path.

PART TWO

Rounding another bend you come upon a huge rock. It's standing upright against the sky. It's big; bigger than you. Ancient and solid. Secure and strong. You take time to walk around it. To feel its immense presence.

Stand before the rock. Allow it to transform before you.

The rock is a symbol of all earth—mountains, meadows, shifting sands, sharp canyons. Feel yourself meld with the rock, feel the ancient solid knowledge it can share with you. Touch the rock. Feel its power. Enter the rock if you like, and share in the old, slow vibration of its history. The rock speaks to you in its old language—of its evolution—of time, of the earth and its slow growth and changes. The rock is solid, true, and supportive.

Stay with the rock. Enjoy its power. Feel the strength of the ages. Sit. Stay. Grow with its power in the world of earth.

[PAUSE]

When you feel ready, say good-bye to the earth and resume your walk. Look around you. Has the landscape changed? Is it the same? The path is still so easy and light, so refreshing and relaxing. Walking along, you feel the earth beneath your feet and share in its solidness.

PART THREE

As you walk, you feel the air around you start to move. A gentle breeze is blow-ing. You feel the air shift and the wind pick up ever so slightly. The breeze beck-ons you to take its hand and fly. Your feet stay on the ground at first, unsure of the promises the air is making. It's up to you. You can take off, flying with the wind as soft or as fast as you like, or you can stay on the ground, watching how the breeze dances and teases.

Air is invisible but powerful, shifting but sure. The wind can roll, gust, puff, or stream along with you. You can see it carry things in its arms. Such is air. It can be heavy, thick, and dense or crisp, cool, and assertive. Air is your friend. Play with its qualities. Share in its constancy and spaciousness.

[PAUSE]

When you are finished with air, breathe deeply and release your bond. Find the path and walk again with the breeze at your side, the earth under your feet, and the warmth of the day all around.

PART FOUR

The path takes another turn and you find yourself at a pool of water. Sit beside it.
Gaze into it. Do you feel the water's energy? Touch it. Penetrate the surface. Is it
deep? Shallow? Warm? Icy? Allow the water to tell you its secrets. Swim in it if
you like. Explore its depths. The water will let you breathe and dive as long as you
like. This water is special. It will support you for as long as you want to be in it.

Flowing, moving, current. Warm or cold, rushing or gentle. How is the
water? Is it clear or murky? Filled with life or undisturbed?

Explore water. A tiny drop. A puddle . . . a whole ocean. Water is liquid.
Swim in it; be with it. Become water.

[PAUSE]

Water is now in the air—steam, a cloud, fog. Feel water as vapor. Be with
the feeling of lightness but still water.

[PAUSE]

Water is still now. Like ice. Immovable. Still water but cold, solid, impen-
etrable. Feel the ice. Explore water as ice.

[PAUSE]

The ice melts slowly, becoming liquid. You feel the release, the warmth as it
melts. Looseness, movement, flow. Say good-bye to water. You are cleansed.

When you are ready, return to the path and walk back. Slowly become
aware of your surroundings, the room you're in, your body.

Lie still until you feel totally "back" from your trip.

POWER PATH EFFECTS

Minerva's Power Path is an intense exercise. Be sure to allow
yourself a full recovery, particularly if you use a tape recording
through all four parts without interruption. You just connected
to your elemental power source; consider yourself a lightbulb
being fueled by an entire power plant—that's how powerful this
exercise is. As a result, you might feel a little odd afterward. Take

it easy and pay attention to any reactions. Physical (queasiness, fatigue), emotional (anger, elation), or mental (forgetfulness, hyperalertness) reactions are not uncommon.

The purpose of this exercise was not only to heighten your power connection—and hence your senses and intelligence—but also to identify which elements are easy for you and which are hard. I remember doing this and feeling that water was entirely out of my league; it was complex and required me to really focus on so many of its different energies that I couldn't handle it all at once. To enhance my own connection to water, I worked with it using some of Minerva's exercises, then I did the meditation again. When I came to the part on water, after some practice, it was much easier.

It's normal to feel one or two elements are easier than others. Wherever you've had difficulties, try some of Minerva's easy techniques to fuel your power.

IMPROVING FIRE

Josie, one of my associates, was troubled by the element of fire. She could not enjoy a fire's beauty nor could she enter into its energy. While she claimed she'd never actually been in a fire or had a bad experience with it, Josie panicked and froze when she approached it in the exercise. Interestingly, Josie was having power failures in her home office (electricity connects with the fire element) and she couldn't help but see a parallel.

Josie was intent on working with her fire element since it contributes to courage and initiative—qualities she felt she lacked. At the time, she was trying to break into new areas with her work as a therapist, seeking to expand into corporate settings. While she felt confident once she got into a new situation, making the effort to actually get this new work was much more difficult than she had thought it would be.

Josie followed some of these simple exercises to become more comfortable with fire.

Minerva's Fire Empowerments

1. Introduce yourself to someone you see often but don't know personally, like your letter carrier, the school bus driver, or the security guard at the bank.
2. Do something by yourself that you don't usually do alone: Take a walk, see a movie, eat in a restaurant.
3. Try to do something new, even if you don't think you'd be good at it.
4. Volunteer to do something for a local charity.
5. If you work out, push harder, try a new method of doing something—challenge yourself.

IMPROVING EARTH

While many of us think we are perfectly comfortable in a material world, we don't all have a great connection to earth. If you found yourself wondering why you didn't really "get" the stone, feel its energy, or "know" its history, you're not alone. Earth is an element we all too often think of in terms of money; this is only a symbol of earthly matters like gold, land, food—all the things it can buy. Your relationship to earth might need more direct attention if you felt puzzled by the rock's presence.

Earth is about being sturdy, grounded, stable or shifting like sand, fallow like harvested fields. Earth is very real—under your feet—and your relationship to it has a lot to do with its power to manifest reality. You need earth to make your new career or next job real, prosperous, and supportive.

Here are some simple exercises to reestablish your connection with earth and its fundamental power.

Minerva's Earth Empowerments
1. Study a construction site and see how deeply the earth can hold a new structure.
2. Look at a sidewalk or parking lot and notice how earth and weeds can break through concrete.
3. Sit against a tree and just feel its strength.
4. Work in a garden.
5. Walk in the country and take time to study the complex life in a small patch of grass.

IMPROVING AIR

My client Richard, a Leo, didn't "get" air. He jotted down these notes:

> Air: I didn't think I'd have a problem with any element—least of all air, but that's the one I couldn't do. I felt the air all around me but didn't fly, float, or even feel much more than a breeze. No connection at all. I wonder why???

Richard looked back at the elemental qualities in chapter two and made the connection: Although he had perfectly good clarity and communication in general, Richard never felt comfortable speaking to strangers—like asking questions in a group or even in interviews. He felt awkward and clumsy when asked to make speeches or toasts.

Richard identified the part of his air element that kept him from moving into a new career—it had to do with communicating in interviews, putting himself "out there," and taking risks that would require him to speak for himself. Instead of giving over to flying and lightness, he stayed grounded and secure—and in the same place!

Awareness of the problem is the first step toward healing. Richard's recognition of his weak air connection allowed him to anticipate situations in which he'd have to speak out. He then had a few practice discussions with friends who took on the role of interviewer, and eventually his air connection grew stronger. While Richard is still not the first person to speak in a public forum, he is considerably less uncomfortable when he does.

Minerva's Air Empowerments

Try any or all of these simple methods to strengthen your relationship to the qualities of air.

1. Write down your issues and read the list out loud.
2. Practice talking to others.
3. Write practice letters and show them to people you trust for comments.
4. Take practice interviews whenever possible.
5. Face your fear—be it writing or speaking—and put yourself in situations where you can practice at a minimal risk.

IMPROVING WATER

My client Carla, a Scorpio, felt her weakest element was water. She found this odd since it was the element ruling her sun sign, but it can happen. Carla needed to find her comfort level with her own complex energy.

Here's what Carla noted about her water experience.

> I was reluctant to go into the water and only waded in up to my waist. Already I felt uncomfortable at that point, but I wanted to at least try to stay with it. Forget ice and steam—that's way too uncomfortable. I just stood there, up to my waist, and was relieved to finish the whole exercise. I don't remember what the water was like—I just didn't want to be in it.

Carla didn't know what caused her reluctance to go farther into the water until we talked, and I pointed out that water is often used in business for analogies to danger. I asked her to think about it. What she came up with was: "Getting in over your head." "Drowning in work." "Up to your ears in hot water." "Up a creek without a paddle." "Swimming with the sharks."

Carla chuckled at these phrases that were on the top of her head. She recognized that she was simply afraid of making a change. Pure and simple—fear—and she was numb. A little fear-releasing helped Carla feel more comfortable with the idea of making a change (keep in mind, Scorpio is a fixed sign and doesn't like change).

Minerva's Water Empowerments

Emotional energy around any work change is important. If it needs more power, you probably need to clear it. Here are five methods of clearing your water element that can make your feelings and intuition come more comfortably to the surface. As you feel more at ease with your own emotions, you'll notice less blockage in your relationship to water's element powers. Your emotional availability will also expand, contributing to your personal energy for change.

1. Melt an ice cube as a symbol of melting your fear.
2. Take a bath with sea salts.
3. Keep water around you—in a vase with flowers, in a bowl with seashells.
4. Allow yourself to feel angry or sad and tell someone how you feel, even if they have nothing to do with your feelings.
5. Express a pleasant or happy feeling to someone.

Your relationship to the elements can change as you continue your search. Sometimes you'll feel you need a boost in one area and then, later, in another. The more you work with the elements, the stronger and deeper your skills will be. Repeat these as often as you like.

MINERVA'S POWER MAGNET

Now it's time to take your show on the road. For those of you champing at the bit to begin moving out into the world, you're more than ready. Some of you, though, might want a little reassurance. Here is a "pocket piece" to keep you and your energy in line with your purpose. A power magnet can help you explore the world with greater ease, no matter how ready you feel.

What is a power magnet? Like a charm, amulet, or talisman, a power magnet is an object (or collection of objects) that is "charged" to serve as protection or magnetism. You can make a power magnet with anything you have handy—an old coin, a pen, a dried flower. Power magnets are not meant to last forever or be seen by others. No one has to know you're carrying it. Power magnets are highly personal, potent "pocket pieces" that allow you to trust yourself and your actions. They don't have to make sense. I have a client who carries the ID bracelet he wore in the hospital when he was born—that gives him the reassurance that he has all his inborn power. I've carried dried flower petals from arrangements I received when my books were published, another client carries a photograph of her child to remember her true heart.

If you have a number of small things—say, a coin and a few stones you like for their color—you might want to keep them together. Consider using a small bag, like a pouch or a little sack used for jewelry.

Although it doesn't matter what object you carry, it does matter how you carry it. Power magnets get not only their symbolic meaning but also their power from Minerva. She'll help you along with a little power zap from the universe in the exercise that follows.

Exercise: Minerva's Magnet Charge

Sit down and place your power magnet on your lap. Close your eyes and take some relaxing, easy breaths. Let yourself relax. Allow your mind and heart to find the power you want your magnet to hold—be it courage, desirability, intellectual clarity, confidence. Allow yourself to feel all the qualities you wish to carry with you. Breathe in this power. Feel its strength within you. Let your hands find your lap and take hold of your magnet. As you exhale, breathe the qualities you now feel into your

POWER MAGNET IDEAS

Fire (Creativity, Passion, Courage, Enterprise)

> real gold
>
> objects that are yellow, red, or orange in color

Earth (Steadiness, Sturdiness, Wealth, Fruitfulness)

> real silver and gold
>
> green stones
>
> crystals

Air (Insight, Intellect, Clarity, Ideas)

> feathers
>
> blue or purple stones
>
> crystals

Water (Intuition, Depth, Compassion, Connection)

> moonstones
>
> opals
>
> liquid silver

More Ideas for Magnets

> gold coin
>
> compass
>
> key

More Ideas for Magnets *(continued)*
    four-leaf clover
    playing card (king/queen of diamonds, lucky
        number)
    photo of hero or loved one
    medal/pin/keepsake
    letter or note written to you that holds special
        meaning

---

object. As you exhale, each breath sends those powers you want to carry with you into your object. You don't have to feel the object get charged—it will be there whether you sense it or not. When you feel as if you've completed this process and all the energy of those qualities you want to carry are infused into your power magnet, open your eyes. Allow yourself a few minutes to "come back" to yourself. Keep your power magnet with you. Don't allow others to handle it.

Power Magnet Rules

1. You must charge your own power magnet—you can't charge it for someone else nor can you accept someone else's magnet to use as your own.
2. Your power magnet works only for you.
3. If your power magnet gets lost, misplaced, or you keep forgetting to carry it, you don't need it anymore.

MINERVA'S PRACTICAL
SHAPE-SHIFTER:
GETTING OUT THERE

All career changes require some basic initiatives, like phone calls, research, letter writing—practical means to get into a new job. Few people look forward to doing this, including me. I've had to write my own bios (a very tough thing to do) as well as make cold calls to try to get a meeting or interview. I've had to write letters of introduction and even simple little notes to say How are you? or Well done! If you're like me, every one of these normal steps toward getting your new work going can be challenging. Dullness, inertia, reluctance, or just plain not knowing how can make these important steps to "get out there" feel gigantic and impossible.

Minerva will hold your hand through each of these trials, and you'll be rewarded with knowledge of your valor, integrity, and . . . results!

Most of my clients have little trouble up to this point of Minerva's process; reestablishing their talents, energizing their

gifts, and working with Minerva on an individual level is interesting and doesn't require as much start-up energy as contacting the outside world. Going within for elemental power and
astrological connection doesn't put you on the spot with new
people. If at this point you feel, well, maybe not quite ready, let
me reassure you: You are.

You are now fully prepared (even if you don't feel it) to
engage in conversations with people, but while you don't know
whether they'll be directly helpful to your career shape-shift,
these exchanges are imperative to your ultimate success.

Drew, a waiter, was hoping to be an actor. This is fairly
common in New York City, where I live. I got to know Drew
after sitting in his section of the restaurant a few times, and
he confided his ambitions. I asked him how many auditions
he attended each week and, to my surprise, he responded,
"None."

Drew felt he needed to study more before putting himself
out there, although he'd been taking acting classes for over
three years. I was shocked that he was waiting at all—I've known
actors to arrive fresh from high school graduation and start
auditioning. Drew clearly was not confident about his talent, so
I asked him to try some of Minerva's techniques.

As a Cancer, Drew was rather shy but very tuned in to emotion, hence he had acting talent. His moon in Virgo posed
more of a problem—he was very self-critical and told himself he
wasn't ready because he wasn't perfect. While Drew had what it
takes to be an actor, he didn't have the wherewithal to put himself in front of casting directors.

Minerva's techniques for getting out in the world gave
Drew a way to open some doors and take initiative toward his
goal. He needed to take some baby steps—safe, protected steps—

just to edge toward real opportunity. While Drew was adamant about not trying out for what he considered to be "serious" acting roles, he was open to getting involved in theatrical readings, workshops, and children's drama groups. Drew's personal lines were drawn to define what was acceptable public risk and what he judged to be too advanced.

With some of Minerva's energetic encouragement (see below), Drew showed up for an open meeting for a children's drama workshop. He immediately became drawn into the spirit of this nonprofit group that provided entertainment and workshops for inner-city kids. Although he was a volunteer, Drew viewed his work there as if it were a paying job. He found he really enjoyed interacting with children. While he is still waitering, he recently announced he's ready to audition—for kids-related theater groups and television programs—not quite his dream work of doing Chekhov on Broadway—but it's a start. He says he's not ready for that; still, he's grateful to Minerva for her help in preparing him to be a working actor.

Drew's experience with volunteering opened up his "success energy" in two ways. Participation in volunteer programs, even if they aren't directly related to the career shift, enhances your confidence in new situations and with new people in a low-risk setting. Among the many rewards of volunteering is meeting and working with people from different backgrounds and with different experiences. If you have any fear of meeting people or connecting to work that brings you real satisfaction, volunteering is an excellent laboratory in which to experiment, and there is virtually no personal risk involved. In fact, you'll always get something back.

Another way to "baby step" toward your new career would be to identify an approachable, accessible place to begin trying out your skills. Drew decided that children's workshops were not threatening to him. When I was trying to become a writer, I felt that magazine writing was more accessible to me than trying to write a book. I wrote several articles and pitched them to magazines—with Minerva's help they actually got read by someone on staff—and I had the good fortune of receiving personal notes of refusal instead of form letters. At the time, I thought, "Oh, this is failure," but in hindsight I realize that these articles were practice, baby steps toward my first book. I didn't have to publish a magazine article at all, but by trying to it helped me become the writer I am today.

This brings us to the next important point.

Not every step you take toward your new career will be successful or obviously relevant; but they all contribute to reaching your goal.

Minerva's guidance is still hard to see and predict. You won't find a connect-the-dot pattern that will clearly lead you to your next career. Mystery, magic, and manifestation are much more complex than that, and the story of how you get to your new career is actually being written by you, as you go along.

It's hard not to expect distinct results every time you make an effort. Ideally, you would make a phone call, get an interview, have a meeting, and land the dream job. But this isn't a predictable B-movie script—your work with Minerva is hopefully more gripping and entertaining than that.

Imagine that each step, phone call, note, meeting, conversation, even wishful thinking about your new career is putting out a little psychic energy, and that energy collects and forms in your future, contributing to the end result—your success. No step is unimportant and no result is without value, even if you don't get called back.

MINERVA'S POWER PUNCHES

With Minerva, you can contribute a little cosmic oomph to each effort you make when seeking your new career. Since Minerva's traditional domain is guiding professions, she's at home in the working world. While you're writing a letter or having a meeting, remember to have her along. She lends great invisible support.

Getting Started

Arguably, the most challenging step is the first one. Inertia is hard to overcome and your own ability to procrastinate is probably even stronger. Sure, you can make do until the spring, when it's nicer outside. Yep, you can save a little more money, concentrate on your lawn, or even just talk more about how you want to do something else, but you still have to take the first step if you actually want to get there.

Minerva's strength and force are fuel for the stagnant shape-shifter. Try her method to get yourself started. If you need to repeat it a few times to get results, you can congratulate yourself on outstanding achievement in inertia. (She won't be offended.)

Exercise: Get Going with Minerva

Tools: Your power magnet, a quiet room.

Sit with your power magnet in your hand or on your person. Close your eyes, let your breathing relax. Out loud, call in Minerva:

Minerva, please join me in blowing open doors,
windows, and pathways to opportunities. And help me
get up and go to my future.

With relaxed and easy breaths (no hyperventilating,
please), blow out through your mouth as if you are blowing
out birthday candles. Imagine your breath is strong enough
to blow open doors and windows. Imagine your breath as a
gentle energy persuading the future to be easy, open, and
energetic.

With Minerva's "Get Going" exercise, you are activating
your energy in the future. Within the next few days, feel your
ability to make a move or take a risk increase. Act on it. If you
feel looser but not yet ready to act, repeat the exercise. Be sure
to carry your power magnet with you every day.

Timing

Back in chapter two we talked about the moon and how it can
be helpful in clearing out obstacles and blockages to your personal power. Once again, the moon can be very helpful for new
endeavors and initiating contacts. Before you actually get up
and get out there, even before you write a letter or redo your
résumé, take a look at the moon. What cycle is it in? When is
the full moon? When is the new moon? If you want to pack
some punch with your first steps "out there," begin on or just
after a new moon. Whatever you do, don't start anything on a
full moon, and even avoid meetings or interviews on a full
moon if possible.

This isn't just superstition. The moon cycle really does
affect the energy it takes to get something done. Initiative and

beginnings are always new moon–related. Begin reaching out to the world in this time of growth energy and you'll be working with the forces of nature. Push yourself or someone else during a waning moon or near a full moon, and you'll need to use a lot more effort to get it done.

Even days of the week have distinct powers and associations that come from their association with their planetary rulers. Beginning with Monday, the moon's day, and ending with Sunday, the day ruled by the sun, here are the basic qualities associated with each day. You can use this as a guide to the initiatives you take with your shape-shift, but I don't recommend putting off a potentially strong meeting because it falls on an "insecure" Monday. Instead, use the quality of each day to guide you to do your best and possibly anticipate how other people might feel.

Day	Planet	Qualities
Monday	Moon	Internal, emotional, insecure, creative
Tuesday	Mars	Aggressive, passionate, ready to go
Wednesday	Mercury	Communicative, traveling, restless
Thursday	Jupiter	Risk-taking, exploring, jovial
Friday	Venus	Loving, optimistic, artful, gracious
Saturday	Saturn	Hardworking, serious, masterful
Sunday	Sun	Healing, restful, calm, relaxing

Keep in mind the qualities of the days and the phase of the moon as you move into the world. It's useful to work with these ancient influences to smooth the path to your shape-shift.

RÉSUMÉS AND LETTERS

Writing your résumé or a letter of introduction can be very difficult. Even if you're a whiz with words, it's hard to sell yourself. Some of us find it hard to "blow our own horn" and take it seriously, while others don't know the meaning of the word *humble.* Minerva can help you find the balance that's right for you.

Here are Minerva's Rules for Résumés and Letters:

1. Be sincere.
2. Be concise.
3. Ask for what you want directly.
4. Say it with Minerva's blessing.

While Minerva is not about to teach you techniques for what to say or how to say it (Minerva bows to Mercury's experts here), she does want to remind you of the basics, so that you get the best results. If you use a consultant or a written guide to help you write your résumé, be sure that you're comfortable with the tone and the content. If someone wants you to sound really aggressive or "hip," and you feel that's phony, don't do it. Minerva's power makes who you are more compelling, not some stranger's idea of who you should be.

Being sincere, concise, and direct is just plain smart. You don't want to waste anyone's time. If they want to get to know you more, they'll call you. It also saves you slaving over every sentence and word to make yourself sound interesting. Here's my favorite kind of letter.

Dear Ms. Dolnick,

I love your books and have tried some of the techniques. They work really well.

I was wondering if you take any interns or (paid) apprenticeships in your office. If you do, I'd be interested. My résumé is attached.

Sincerely,
Ms. Junior Mystic

That kind of letter is a joy to receive (praise is always welcome here) and easy to respond to. Although I didn't have work for this applicant, I sent her some ideas of how to get her own consulting business started and encouraged her to teach spell classes with my books.

While not every letter you send will be answered, you will increase your chances of being seen, heard, and helped by not complicating the process with banter or posturing.

Résumés, too, can be tiresome to read if you put too much emphasis on style to the detriment of clarity or honesty. Follow the rules above (be sincere and concise) but don't be afraid to be generous with the descriptions of your accomplishments. You can't lie (Minerva won't let you get away with it), but you can characterize your skills and achievements with pride.

Minerva will help you while you write and send your communications out.

Exercise: Minerva's Scribe

Tools: Your writing apparatus (pen/paper, typewriter, or computer), a quiet room (at least a place you can concentrate), your power magnet.

Aloud, ask Minerva to guide your writing—if you want to add another level of "Roman god expertise" to your actual prose, ask Mercury to come along, too. Here are the words I use, but you can say whatever you like.

> Minerva, please sit beside me and guide my energy and purpose into words that will be seen and heard. Mercury, please add your flair to this work. For the greater good and the purpose of my career shape-shift.

You should be saying this out loud, but it's okay to mutter if you're not alone. Begin to write the letter or résumé by simply writing out how you want to be seen—don't worry about format or style. After you've exhausted your ideas, look them over, edit them (cross out whatever you don't like) and *then* put them into the format of a letter or résumé. You can use a reference book or mentor to help you with style, but the ideas you are generating are the substance, the heart of the matter. Don't worry if it doesn't sound conventional. You can be practical later.

Here's an example of résumé notes my client Ann generated. I've made her skills less industry-specific for simplicity. She also included her dislikes to remind her what not to "sell" in her résumé.

Great at managing people who don't get along with
each other.
Love to work with creative people—have a good eye for
what works.
Capable of handling a budget but better at figuring
out how to cut costs before they get out of hand.
Good at figuring out how to get out of tight spots.
Good on my feet—covering up mistakes.
Excellent at detailed work.
Hate traveling.
Not good at thinking about long-term issues.
Really good at crisis management.

As she looked over her notes, she realized that she was best
at making things happen and being "in the whirl of it all"
instead of on the sidelines or "out there, selling." This gave her
the idea to spin her résumé with energy toward what she really
liked. Here's a simplified version of a few of her lead points.

Extensive, hands-on experience managing teams, with
an emphasis on building relationships with
"difficult" personalities.
Broad experience with creative development process
with considerable personal contacts in
production, photography, and directing.
Ability to find cost-reducing methods for high-
quality production.
Skilled with meeting deadlines and establishing
"precrisis" committees to avoid project
bottlenecks or timing issues.

With the help of a mentor who was successful in the career she was pursuing, Ann shifted some language and pushed more salient points forward to complete her résumé. She's out there right now, shopping for a job.

You need to find your own way of expressing both what you're good at and what you want to do. Sometimes you'll be heading toward a career that has no bearing on your past job skills, like my client Henry who wants to leave his job as a paste-up artist at a design firm to begin a career in antique furniture imports and sales. His résumé spun his experience with detail and design to land an interview with an antiques dealer in his town. He persuaded the owner to let him sell on weekends and, successful with that, Henry was able to propose more part-time work with bookkeeping in order to learn more about the business. His résumé grew more appropriate and impressive, and Henry is now considering making the leap into full-time antiques dealing.

Minerva's Word on Electronic Communications

If you asked Minerva if it's okay to e-mail a letter of introduction or a résumé, she'd take a conservative stand. Minerva doesn't have a big problem with electronic communication in general, but she finds it's not grounded enough for introductions and important messages. Once you've sent your letter and résumé on paper, you can use e-mail to follow them up. A "Did you receive my package?" e-mail is just fine, but unless your industry precedent is to communicate this way all the time, you're better off with paper.

Faxing is also fine these days, since most businesses have plain-paper faxes (quality is an issue) and people still consider a fax more urgent than a letter. Do, however, send a real letter by mail or messenger as well as a fax. A mailed letter with your real signature carries your power best—and if nothing else, mailing and faxing provide you with two hits, not just one.

Minerva does admit, however, that she's an old fogey about these matters and doesn't want to prevent you from trying anything you think might help break ground for your new work.

Phone Calls

Once you've established some kind of rapport with the person you want to contact, use whatever methods fit the case. If e-mail is not an option, try phone messages—but be brief. Voice mail has become a dreaded part of business life, so if you use it, be kind and short. Minerva will help you get your voice together, and given some notice, she can even help you make real contact with the person you're trying to call.

The telephone, however, is tough to use for a first contact. Cold calling puts a lot of pressure on you to make a hasty, powerful introduction and engage the person in conversation. I find myself responding with undisguised impatience when someone calls me without having been prepared for the call, as if it were an unwelcome solicitation from a telemarketer. If you insist on making a phone call, sit down (with Minerva) and script your introductions and questions. Be as short as possible and give your contact an "out." If you're lucky enough to get time on the phone with someone who can help you, you can use their advice and even their name in other solicitations.

Such as, "I spoke with Mr. Big and he recommended I contact you." With a nod to timing, try Wednesdays for cold calls.

> Introduction: Hi, Mr. Big. This is Wanna Work calling from Sister Bay, Wisconsin. I got your name from a friend and hope you don't mind spending a minute on the phone with me.
>
> Reply 1: Oh, you're busy? Is there a better time to call? I really want to have your opinion on this.
>
> Reply 2: Great.
>
> My first question is: What advice do you give to people who want to break into your business?
>
> Does my experience as a xxxx help?
>
> Who would you recommend I talk to for an interview?
>
> Would you yourself see me?
>
> Thank you. I really appreciate your advice.

Minerva isn't opposed to this route, but your power will always be most grounded on paper. Of course, this phone conversation begs for a follow-up letter using the exercise Minerva's Scribe, above.

Exercise: Calling Upon Minerva

TOOLS: Your power magnet, a quiet place to speak out loud.

First, hold your power magnet, then, out loud, ask Minerva to join you. Ask her to help you make voice contact with the person you want to reach. Ask her if she can make them answer the phone or at least call you back. If possible, ask Minerva's help the evening before you make the call. Sample:

"Minerva, please help me make phone contact with Ms. Big tomorrow and guide our conversation with wisdom."

Next, before you dial the telephone, call in Minerva (and Mercury, if you like) to help guide you through the conversation. Sample: "Minerva, please help me make this phone call successful."

Minerva can help you feel more at ease during a phone call and also help you communicate your purpose with clarity and energy. Since you'll most likely have to use the phone in many follow-up situations, it's a good idea to get in the habit of calling in Minerva right from the start. You'll see a difference.

MEETINGS WITH MINERVA

Part One: Practice

Let's say you've gotten into the office of some potentially helpful person, or even just a lightweight informational interview. How can you make sure your meeting will go well? With Minerva, you can do a bit of preparation before you get there to help the energy along, but there's no guarantee you'll ace it. You don't want to put the pressure on yourself and Minerva to make every meeting or interview stellar. Not only is it not reasonable, it's not helpful. You'll learn the most about yourself and others when you make mistakes, so practice before you really start. In fact, practice all the time.

The concept of a practice meeting is simple. You approach the day, the hour, and the actual person with the intent of doing well—leave a good impression, make a new contact—but without "make it or break it" pressure. Obviously, this is a fine balance of enthusiasm and purpose coupled with relaxed confidence and soft assertiveness.

Minerva works best with playfulness at this first stage of a career shape-shift. If you put too much stress on any one thing ("This is the 'make it or break it meeting' "), you can be certain that it won't go really well and it's not a "make it or break it" instance. Your power is more effective and attractive when you aren't obsessed with an outcome.

There's no such thing as a bad meeting.

To be able to pull off this easygoing confidence, you need to believe that nothing bad can happen. Sure, you might not get what you think you want, you might even have a bad time, but that's not a bad meeting.

My client Alec went to meet with the president of a company he really wanted to work for. He was making a leap out of accounting and into sales, and he was really excited about the prospect of working for this company. The meeting went badly, with the president going as far as to say, "You don't belong in sales. Why don't you come to work for us in accounting?," which made Alec despair. He felt pigeonholed and helpless and very disappointed.

After a few days of healing, Alec and I talked. He wasn't ready to let one person's opinion destroy his mission for a career shape-shift and I agreed he should keep going, too. That "bad meeting" actually made him angry; that anger transformed into a feisty drive to win. Previously, Alec had been reluctant to ask the company where he worked if he could be considered for a sales job. He didn't think his management would be open to that kind of career change. Yet fueled with less caution ("What can they do to me?") and help from Minerva, he set up a meeting with the VP of sales and made a case for himself. Although it was a new and unconventional request, Alec went on to further interviews and learned a lot about the kind of qualities they look for in sales staff. With this information, he was able to interview elsewhere and eventually did get into a sales job.

Exercise: Minerva's Guide for Meetings

TOOLS: A quiet place to sit, your power magnet.

Summon Minerva (out loud) before your meeting and ask her to guide you through whatever happens with success, assurance, and poise. Sample: "Minerva, please come with me and make this meeting a good one."

Minerva isn't complicated about going out and meeting people. Essentially, all you have to do is invite her and she'll be there, invisibly holding your hand and smiling upon your shape-shift.

MINERVA'S QUICK FIX

If you find yourself in a tight spot, call on Minerva to assist you. For instance, my client Tom had an interview he thought would be a simple one-stop meeting with a high-end retail fashion firm he hoped to join as a merchandising manager. Happily, his interview went very well, and because of this he was asked to stay on and meet with several other key people that same morning. Tom had prepared very well for his first meeting, doing some research on the company's background and even getting some personal background on his interviewer. He hadn't yet prepared himself to meet with these other members of the management team, all of whom had direct impact on whether he would get the job.

Tom had followed Minerva's advice for so long that now he automatically "called her in" to his meetings while he took a break in the men's room. He described it to me like this:

> I was so happy and so panicked that I'd gotten that far, I didn't want to blow it. I know that sometimes being too eager can make a person seem less desirable, especially in the fashion world. So I went to the men's room and flushed the toilet just so I could say "Minerva, please help me!" out loud. I figured she would overlook the informality of my situation. And as far as I know, she was there. I had terrific talks with every single person (some of whom, I later learned, can be difficult in interviews). Of course, they kept me hanging for a few days but I got the job!

Part Two: The Big Time

You may be more like Alec, where practice meetings lead you to the eventual goal, or like Tom, whose first interview led him all the way to the top, or you might have less opportunity to "play around" if your chosen field is narrow. For instance, Clara wanted to work for a very specific computer software company known for its tough standards, and she felt she only had one shot at getting an interview and impressing them enough to ask her back. Since Clara didn't want to go to that meeting without practice, she took interviews wherever she could find them in relevant fields. For instance, a smaller software company in her town was more approachable and she was able to meet with some people there for informational interviews regarding qualities they look for in employees—and for their opinion of the company she was targeting for a job.

Clara also got an interview at a company that sold the software her target company made, getting more information and more of a feel for what they like. She got the impression that her target company was very strict and rather male-dominated— always described as "tough," "lean," and "sharp." Someone pointed out that they didn't know of any women in the management or sales staff.

Finally, Clara got an interview with the human resources department of her dream company—her big meeting. She was not prepared for what ensued. They wanted her to work in an administrative position, not in the programming department. With Minerva's wisdom (not revealing the inner horror she was feeling), she asked what it would take to be considered for a starting position in programming. She was told that they had no positions available at that time but that they would consider her when one came up—if she took the job as an assistant to the office manager. Clara had the right education and enough experience from part-time work to make her feel worthy of an entry-level programming job and didn't like the sound of being an assistant (a secretary) in a department unrelated to her goal. She felt the "We'll consider you in the future" was a ploy to lure her into the company.

Clara was most upset and dispirited and changed her mind about wanting to work there. Instead, she went back to the first company she'd approached. Although they were small, they did interesting things and the people were nice. They even said they'd be interested in helping her become a programmer. Luckily, there was a position open.

Of course, Minerva was guiding this whole thing. Clara landed the job as a programmer and made new friends. Now her company has grown, she has stock options, and she's grateful she didn't make that first dream come true. While her ex–"dream" company is still going strong, she hears they don't pay well and they don't promote women.

Not everyone can make their dream come true, but there's something to be said for being redirected the way Clara was. Redirection is a kind way of defining "not getting what you want"—and ending up all the better for it. That's next!

TROUBLESHOOTING: MINERVA'S MANEUVERS FOR OBSTACLES AND SETBACKS

No career shape-shift goes off without a hitch. You'll naturally come across your own bumps or setbacks, whether it's cracking a lead for a job, getting an offer, or just trying to get someone to call you back. If you subscribe to the old adage "If at first you don't succeed, try, try again," then you have the right attitude, but it doesn't stop there. You can ease your own stress level and even smooth out wrinkles when you call upon the celestial powers of Minerva.

Sometimes trouble comes from everyone else—the letter and résumé returned to you marked "insufficient postage," the company that keeps saying "We want you" but doesn't extend an offer, the meetings that keep being postponed, even the jobs you "almost" get. Sure, there are a million little snags that can pollute, impede, or slow your career metamorphosis. We don't operate in a perfect world. I also think everyone has profound moments of doubt and disbelief when working on self-created change. Some call it a crisis of faith. Whatever it is, you can feel rocked to your core and face a whole bout of "giving up" before you actually get there. That, too, seems to be part of the process.

Don't be discouraged, you're in good company. Just about everyone who has made a successful career change will tell you with ample detail just how they almost failed or gave up. I remember a woman I met long ago, who was trying valiantly to shift from working as an advertising account manager to being a bond trader on Wall Street. The two careers seemed miles apart, but they were really similar in the skills needed to analyze situations and work with people. Cassie, the would-be shape-shifter, was having a hard time getting anyone to return her calls. She knew she was overqualified for an entry-level position (answering phones) and underqualified to be a trader, which demanded a track record and a list of clients. What was she to do? There seemed to be no entry point for her anywhere.

As a Scorpio with a Taurus moon, Cassie was nothing if not determined, so she never gave up her dream. Her real problem was finding a way to break through the seemingly impenetrable barrier that kept her from contacting someone who could help her. She confided to me that she wanted to give up when she just couldn't bear to call and leave one more message or get one more form letter saying "Not hiring right now." She had to find another way to get in. Though reluctant to impose on friendships and preferring to keep her aspirations private, she finally let down her own wall and asked for advice and contacts among her friends. After her regular tennis foursome, Cassie announced she was in the market for help with her career shift. After expressing surprise and interest, one of her tennis partners immediately volunteered the services of her twin sister, who sold bonds at one of Cassie's target firms. This led to several interviews (at least she got somewhere) and a lot of stalling, but she eventually got a job in a spin-off unit of that very firm.

If Cassie had asked Minerva to help her, she might have gotten there just a bit faster or perhaps with less anxiety, but she still would have had to undergo some problems. Part of the process of all career shape-shifts has to do with personal growth. While I suppose some rare people don't need to be pushed to grow, most of us do. Cassie was a rather quiet, almost secretive person. She didn't want to compromise herself or her friends by asking for favors, so she hadn't fished for contacts and help before she felt pushed to do so. What Cassie didn't realize is that those very skills—fishing for contacts and asking for help—were important qualities for being a successful bond trader. While she still fights her desire to keep to herself, she is more and more skilled at using contacts and getting information.

Your personal obstacles will no doubt be in the form of something you dread.

Two Rules for Shape-shifts

1. *You get what you resist.*
2. *Surrender often precedes victory.*

My wise friend Susan's favorite mantra (and now mine, too) is number one on the list: You get what you resist. If you consider how true that is, you'll laugh a lot more.

Cassie hated putting herself out—yet now that's what she does for a living. I hated writing long-form anything—letters, opinions, and business plans—yet now I write books. Even when I was still in advertising and working on a glamorous but strenuous account, I remember making a loud and silly proclamation: "I'll never work on a pet food account." And, of course, I later spent some of my most enjoyable and rewarding time in advertising working on the Ralston Purina dog food brands. What you resist is probably going to make you happy.

If you are prone to making big pronouncements like "I'll never work for a big company," or "I refuse to consider a position that doesn't pay me at least X," you're asking for it! When you do run into yourself, just take a deep breath, ask Minerva to guide you through it, and know that you'll end up in the right place after all.

As for surrender, this might seem a little out of place in a book that says you *can* do it. Surrender isn't about giving up your goal, it's about giving up control over how you're going to get there. Most of the people who have worked with Minerva will testify that surrender is important.

Calvin, a market researcher in between jobs, called me out of frustration. He'd been working with Minerva to make a leap out of his own independent market research work as a focus group moderator and into a position with a well-known quantitative research company where he would contribute to larger-scale studies addressing broader, noncommercial topics. He also looked forward to being part of a team with very smart, accomplished associates.

Calvin kept taking jobs for focus group work as he worked on his shape-shift but was weary of the late hours and constant travel. He'd made contact with his target "dream job" company several times and he thought it would only be a matter of time before they offered him a job. That went on for a year. Calvin kept his chin up while he waited, until, one day, he heard by chance that they'd given the job they'd discussed with him to someone else. Calvin was mortified and angered that he'd found out accidentally and was compelled to call his contact there.

Calvin called in Minerva as he dialed the telephone; he had to leave a message (he chose voice mail) and simply said he was just "checking in." Calvin wasn't surprised that his call wasn't returned for two days. When it was, he was told that they'd made other arrangements for that position but they were happy to keep him in mind in the future.

Calvin hung up and felt like a failure. Sure, he still had his market research business and he could pick and choose assignments, but his dream job had just disappeared before his eyes.

Calvin took some time before he checked in with Minerva (he won't admit it, but I think he was mad at her). He tried a different kind of exercise to work through what he only saw as the end of the road.

Minerva helped loosen up his grip on the job he "lost." Calvin was looking at his life with tunnel vision, all he saw was that job or no job at all. Once he broadened his vision, he realized that his "dream" company was not the only one that tackled broad issues, and that some were even better at analyzing and forecasting trends in his interest areas. Calvin eventually pursued and landed a position at a company that was often contracted by foreign nations interested in establishing businesses in the United States. Calvin was able to use his background as a focus group moderator to explain some simple communications techniques to clients, and he was able to enjoy fielding bigger, more comprehensive research with colleagues who had diverse backgrounds. Calvin admits that this job is better than what he'd imagined in "the one that got away."

Exercise: Minerva's Mood Eraser

This exercise is effective for clearing "mood heaviness" such as self-blame, despair, or a sense of futility. You don't need to call in Minerva for this because you are not ready for her intervention. This exercise is really just a low-key clearing to lighten your atmosphere and make you ready for more opportunities. Tools: Power magnet, saltwater, a quiet room.

Sit and relax somewhere you won't be disturbed, with a bowl of saltwater in front of you. Think about your situation. Let your anger rise to the surface. With each frustration, thought, or memory, dip your hands in the saltwater. Imagine your anger being neutralized by the water. Keep dipping while you let your feelings of disappointment rise and be expressed. Feel free to talk out loud, "exorcising" yourself of negativity. When you feel finished, toss the water out—down a drain.

MORE ON REVERSALS

Not to belabor the point, but when you're the one facing "everything falling apart," you need some strong support. I've seen and experienced many different faces of reversal and it bears more exploration.

My client Dan just went through one. He had worked hard to achieve a certain position in his real estate firm as an expert in long-term commercial leases, and was about to become a senior partner when his company unexpectedly merged with another and he lost his seniority. None of his superiors stood up for him and all of the established managing partners, who had previously supported him, unceremoniously dropped him simply to avoid any problems sorting out their own positions in the merger. Dan was angry and rightfully so. He didn't want to have to prove himself all over again somewhere else, and he didn't want to leave behind the lucrative deals he'd brought in. But there was no point staying with the firm that was so willing to overlook promises and abandon loyal and productive employees. Dan had been working with Minerva—not for a career shape-shift but to advance himself in his real estate position. Now he was at a loss.

Because the real estate business is so dynamic and Dan was having a good year with his transactions, he wanted his work to be rewarded; he realized his productivity (and success) would never be honored at this newly merged company. Hard as it was to reach this conclusion, he was willing to walk away. He spoke to rival firms that were eager to have him, but he felt skeptical about their offers. One firm offered him a better deal than his current job but without the title of senior partner. Another offered no compensation improvement though they did offer him the title he wanted. Dan's job-shopping got back to his newly merged firm and he was criticized for not being loyal. Outraged at their reaction, Dan reminded them that their lack of loyalty to him was the reason he was leaving. He walked out with his Rolodex and computer files, making the point that it was he who had the relationships with the clients.

The result of Dan's walkout disturbed the newly merged firm, whose management had fooled themselves into thinking the staff would "take what they were given." They knew Dan was a top performer with good future prospects and offered him his job back and the guarantee of senior partner in six months. He turned them down—having no faith in their promises. They offered him a better deal, but he turned them down again. Dan just didn't care anymore and that's when they offered him immediate senior partner status and better-than-average compensation.

Although he had to fight his childish desire to turn his nose up, Dan attended a meeting to discuss the terms of his return. He saw that the power of saying "no" to them twice had turned the tables to his advantage. Dan walked out of that meeting as a senior partner with a five-year contract and a guaranteed vesting of the firm's profits—something previously offered only to managing partners.

Why did this reversal suddenly become the best thing that could have happened? It often goes that way. Dan didn't even know the extent to which he could rise until he was pushed enough to push back. He realized that being able to walk away from his goal made him more powerful, not less. Management also noticed the change in him and decided that was the kind of guts a good real estate partner—like a poker player with a good hand—needed to have.

"No" is a powerful word, but it takes a lot of courage to say it with conviction. Once you get to a point in your process where you just want to let it go, walk away, or give up, you have the power to say "no." This makes you very attractive.

Once you've let go of your hold on what you want and are willing to walk away, Minerva has room to move in and make it happen.

ADVERSITY IS MINERVA'S HELPER

Frustration, delays, people going back on their word or not saying anything at all are typical shape-shift challenges. But what about the career shape-shifter who wants to leave for more entrepreneurial pursuits? Or the one who just can't find the time to look for her dream job? Minerva sometimes creates adversity just to get you going.

Paula wanted to get out of her executive assistant job at a financial services company and start a business of her own that makes and delivers gift baskets. She had some great ideas and had done some sourcing for components and for understanding the financial complexities of that business, but didn't appear ready to make a move. While her job paid well, was steady, and had great benefits, Paula began to dislike it. She felt bored—and complained loudly. Her boss noticed her work was slipping and had several talks with her to get her back on track. Finally, Paula was asked to leave because her work was insufficient. While Paula was taken off guard, she made the best of her leaving and got her business started. She apparently needed a kick in the pants.

We rarely create our own adversarial conditions, yet they seem to arise just when we need them. I remember my own career shape-shift got a big jump-start when I walked out of my last advertising job because I couldn't take the bad temper of one of my colleagues. And I had once witnessed a highly visible CEO undertake a shape-shift when she decided to walk out of a draining and less and less fulfilling position to pursue her dream of working as a media personality. You might just get asked to leave or worn down enough to walk out just in time to meet your future.

If you do experience an abrupt departure from your prior career, be sure to clean yourself off before you pursue your new road to success. Revisit chapter two and do some elemental clearings so you don't take the drudgery or negativity along with you.

WAITING . . .

Again, it's pretty common to encounter . . . nothing. No response, no answer, no where. Even if you've started the pursuit of your new career with gusto and had many doors open, somewhere along the line something's bound to get stalled. Vacations, travel schedules, budget impositions or freezes are only some of the variables that can appear like monsters and demons in a fast-moving video game, and all at once put a hold on your movement.

There's little you can do to control other people. All you can do is adjust your attitude. This is a delicate balance of "withdraw and wait" and "keep your energy up and able." If you relax too much, all the work you've done with Minerva can dissipate. If you keep pushing too hard you can get frustrated or annoying to others and crowd the space of possibility where Minerva works best.

Minerva's Room for Waiting

One of my clients, Geneva, started with Minerva only a few years ago. She readily worked through her personal and professional creative blockages and embraced her astrological assets with gusto. As a Libra with a Capricorn moon, she was a talented writer grounded in real-world issues. Her work as a writer and editor for a large-women's-clothing catalog left her little time for her love of writing essays and op-ed pieces, but she began to energize her shape-shift by exploring more news and public service media where her creative desires would be more at home. By chance (and Minerva's way of working), Geneva met with some people at her local public radio station. There was some interest in her joining as a part-time correspondent, writing news or editorial pieces about women's issues. To Geneva, this was a halfway point, blending her prior experience with writing for women and still embarking into the territory of issues and public policy. She was hopeful that this would be a stepping-stone to new experience and one day a new career.

The public radio station had stated that their budget was depleted for this year, but that in a few months they would have more money to pay her (minimally) for her services. In the meantime, they asked her to wait for their call. Geneva waited the allotted time, but still wrote some pieces on spec in hopes of being able eventually to use them. While she was slightly impatient, she was hopeful.

Geneva sensed a problem when her main contact didn't call, nor did any of the staff return her phone calls. She was puzzled and frustrated, but did the Minerva's Tranquilizer exercise, so she wouldn't give up hope. Another month went by and Geneva called again, this time her main contact took her call and advised her to keep them in mind but that there was new management in place and there was some question as to how or when they would open up to new programming ideas or talent.

This put Geneva into a tailspin; she had waited months just to get put on hold again. Since they had been so positive about working with her, she hadn't pursued any other options.

After a quick release with Minerva's Mood Eraser exercise, Geneva plunged back into her search for a place to write and be heard. Again, she canvassed friends and colleagues and found a contact at a local news weekly, a small paper that had a strong, young following. Geneva put some ideas together and took them to a meeting. There, she was able to persuade the paper to give her an assignment to do on spec; if they liked it, they could pay her.

With her work energy now focused on both her full-time job and this article, Geneva all but forgot the radio station. When they called her out of the blue, she was pleased but held back her enthusiasm in case they "disappeared off the radar" again. Sure enough, she was able to try out some ideas in a public forum they were conducting one evening and found she didn't like the immediacy of radio and feeling pressed for opinions on the spot. On the other hand, the newspaper ran her work and she has done a few more pieces. She feels it's a beginning to the long-awaited shape-shift she wants. Time lapse? Two years.

Before you hit the ceiling, be warned.

Your shape-shift will take longer than you think.

No one wants to hear this, but it's true. Minerva has all the time in the world; she's in no hurry, and you shouldn't be either. Like hunting for treasure, the thrill of the chase is part of the pleasure. If you think you don't have time, take a tranquilizer (see below) and calm down. Slow and steady wins the race.

Exercise: Minerva's Tranquilizer

TOOLS: Your power magnet, a place to sit outside where you won't be disturbed.

Sit somewhere outside where your feet are planted directly on the ground—the earth is preferable to asphalt, stones, or concrete. Hold your power magnet. Aloud, call in Minerva and sit quietly. Meditate on the feeling of the solid ground beneath your feet, the air as you breathe easily, inhaling and exhaling, and your body, which is supported by the earth and where you sit. Allow yourself to relax into a light reverie. Once relaxed, with every exhaling breath, blow light and success into your future. Know that your needs will be met, know that success is ahead of you. With each inhaling breath, feel knowledge, spaciousness, patience, and sureness—your goal already exists in your future and within you.

Take your time with this exercise. Be in that calm, knowing place as long and as often as you like.

CROSSED WIRES, SNAFUS, AND OTHER UNPREDICTABLE MESSES

Beyond the delays brought upon your career shape-shift by the outside world or the simple but painful process of waiting for the world to meet your needs, there are many other little things that can go wrong on your way to your new future. Here are some common complaints:

   c Getting a spot on a tie or suit, or a run in your stockings before a big meeting.

- **c** Getting caught in traffic, behind a slow school bus, or in an elevator on your way to an interview.
- **c** Getting to your meeting on the day after it was supposed to happen.
- **c** Forgetting someone's name.
- **c** Being clumsy (tripping, sloppy handshakes, et cetera).

While working with Minerva can help prevent some of these irritations, sometimes you might find yourself at the mercy of uncontrollable chaos. What can you do? Call Minerva in right away and ask for help. Do not lose your head and do not turn around and run home (unless you showed up on the wrong day).

The most powerful and certainly most charming people can find themselves in tight spots. I've seen executives spill coffee on themselves and even belch while giving a speech—all without losing composure.

Minerva can help you finesse some of these embarrassments, too. Just call her in and see what happens. Don't lose your head.

I recently had a big meeting with some hotshots at an Internet company. Just before the meeting I ate lunch and, quite irresponsibly, dribbled vinaigrette salad dressing on the front of my skirt. There was a *vast* stain in the most unfortunate lap area, that, when standing up, looked sort of obscene. This skirt was not washable. What could I do? There wasn't enough time to go home and there was no way out of the meeting. I was miles away from a quick "shopping fix," so I had no choice but to make the best of it. I called in Minerva (while I was in the ladies room washing my hands, so no one would hear me), and I turned my skirt around so that the stain was in the back. By pulling down on my shirt and carrying my jacket, my backward skirt was less noticeable—from the front. (But I had to make sure no one approached me from behind!)

When it was time to leave for the meeting, I quickly checked my appearance in the bathroom. In a glance of my back view I saw the stain wasn't even noticeable. By turning my skirt around, instead of a huge spot there was now only a shadow— one you had to study carefully to see. Surprised and pleased, I put my jacket on and headed toward the meeting. Afterward, when I had time to think about it, I realized the sofa where I'd been sitting had absorbed most of the stain.

The question before you now is: Would that stain have disappeared anyway, even if I hadn't called upon Minerva's services? I have no idea, and I'm not about to question it.

There are so many other kinds of little challenges that can throw you off, especially being delayed. Sometimes, even if you leave with ample travel time, you can run into trouble. Always ask Minerva for help, and always be polite. If you can call, do. If you can't, be understanding if your meeting gets postponed. And, practically speaking, if the people you are meeting with or hoping to work with don't forgive you for one mistake, you're learning something valuable: Don't work with them.

Certainly, on a second offense, people have cause for concern—about your punctuality, your grace, your ability to get it together—and, if you find that you cannot help yourself and you keep putting your foot in your mouth or tripping up in other ways, your energy probably isn't compatible. Minerva is giving you some gentle advice: You don't fit in.

My former client and now old friend Caroline has never been a graceful girl. She looks like a model and has sharp intellect and swift intuition that often startle people who think good looks preempt a good mind. Caroline's weakness has actually always been in her ankles, and her preference for very high heels adds more risk to her poise. She fondly recalls what happened to her on the way to a big interview. She was trying to make a move out of a marketing job at one bank and had secured an interview for a position in research at a well-respected rival company.

Caroline dressed for the part, wearing her navy blue suit, low-key makeup, and, of course, her trademark high heels. Being in Manhattan, Caroline didn't need a car. She opted for a cab to zip her down to the Wall Street area where she would have a half hour to spare before her meeting. Caroline's cab, however, got into an accident on the West Side Highway, the fast-moving, highly trafficked road along the Hudson River. While the cab had to wait for a cop to come and take down the accident report, Caroline didn't want to lose time. Unfortunately, she was on the river side of the drive—with no place to walk. This, by the way, was the age before cell phones, so there was no way to get in touch with anyone.

Left in this quandary, Caroline called in Minerva (though not a believer at this juncture in her career, she thought it couldn't hurt). The cab stood lamely blocking traffic in the left lane and Caroline's anxiety level mounted as the traffic piled up behind them. As soon as the police arrived, she asked if they could escort her to safety. One sympathetic officer helped her across the highway. She had about ten minutes before her interview.

Left to fend for herself in a quiet warehouse neighborhood without a cab in sight, Caroline fearlessly traipsed in her high heels to the subway a few blocks away. A train was just getting into the station and she chose to jump on instead of make the phone call to say she'd be a few minutes late. Five minutes later she climbed up from the subway, onto the pavement that just happened to be right in front of the bank. Startled by this apparent miracle, Caroline took an awkward step back and tripped, twisting her ankle on her way to the ground. In pain and slightly disheveled, Caroline limped into the bank and up to her interview.

The executive she was to meet was on a phone call when she arrived, so she quickly freshened up in the ladies room and swallowed some Tylenol in hopes her throbbing ankle would settle down. Her meeting started only ten minutes late, and Caroline established her composure during the following introductory conversation.

Caroline: How do you do, it's so nice to meet you. I'm sorry to be late.

Executive: Yes, how are you? I hope you didn't have a problem finding us here?

Caroline: Not at all. My cabdriver had a problem keeping his eye on the road, so I'm a bit delayed from a minor accident. It's not a problem at all. I'm just delighted to have a chance to speak with you. I've always had great respect for this company.

She took it from there. She focused so well on the conversation that she didn't notice her ankle at all. When she took her leave, she limped away as lightly as possible. Since she was asked back for a second interview and eventually landed the job, she likes to tell that story.

Now a senior analyst at that same bank, Caroline swears by these rules for tough spots.

1. Stay with your purpose.
2. Call on Minerva.
3. See the humor and make it a good story.

If you find that you're losing your nerve or that anxieties or fear of failure is beginning to pollute your ability to carry on a flawless meeting, go back to chapter two and repeat some clearing exercises. Sometimes circumstances can bring on a recurrence of self-criticism or insecurity, but you can banish them with Minerva's help.

Finding your humor may be a challenge. I sure didn't laugh when I got that spot on my skirt. I know Caroline didn't laugh off that interview until she actually got the job. There are times when the ending won't be happy either, but you still need to find the humor in it. Being able to laugh at yourself makes you more likable, more composed, and much more powerful. No one can laugh at you; they can only laugh with you.

Laughter heals pain. When you have less pain, you have more power.

WEARY, WORN, AND OUT OF ENERGY

It can happen. You can get so worn down and dispirited that you start to feel totally tired or numb. You've tried your best, you're out of options. You don't get excited about a new future; even disappointment doesn't feel bad. You're just going to settle for your old life. You get more sleep that way.

This isn't surrender, this is exhaustion, a place where your power can't find its fuel.

If you hit the point of fatigue, where one more phone call or effort is just too much, you need to hook up to the universal power plant and rejuice.

To get your energy back up and running takes a few steps. The first step is easy: Do nothing. Take some time off from this career shape-shift. Let things slide a bit. The slack you'll allow yourself is restful and much more healing when it's a purposeful break. No need to feel guilty or to set a short time frame. Take a solid break from the process. Know that you'll go back when the time is right and reconnect with Minerva once again.

Exercise: Reconnecting with Minerva

Tools: Power magnet, a symbol of the work you would like to do, a quiet place where you can talk to yourself.

1. Cleanse your power magnet. Select one of the following methods to clear your power magnet of lazy or toxic energy.

- Leave your power magnet in sunlight for a whole day, or
- Soak your power magnet in saltwater overnight, or
- Hold your power magnet in a brisk wind, or
- Hold your power magnet in the smoke from burning sage.

2. Reread the descriptions of your sun and moon sign.
3. Sit quietly with your power magnet and relax your breathing. When you feel ready, ask Minerva to join with you once again and help you find your way to the right career path.

Also, acknowledge your gifts and strengths. Remember to carry your power magnet with you.

Reconnecting with Minerva puts you back on track and replenishes your drive, ambition, and source of power. No matter how world-weary you might have felt, you'll soon be back on track and heading for ultimate success.

SEVEN

REACHING FOR SUCCESS

In this part of your career shape-shift Minerva helps you deal
with success.

You think you don't need help? You think it's so easy to say
"yes" to a good offer and shake hands on a deal? It's true, you
do know a lot more about yourself and how to re-create your
life. You can even make new friends and enjoy new challenges.
You're powerful. You know how to behave. But do you know
how to transition out of the search and into stability?

Do you know how to graciously say thank-you and good-
bye to Minerva? How to tie an energetic bow around your new
work so that its meaning and value don't diminish? Do you
know how to share your success with others? How to make this
new career a fully realized part of you?

Grasping success and hanging on to it is just as magical as
getting there.

WHEN SUCCESS IS NEAR

You've worked hard. You've had some ups and downs, faced yourself, and worked through fears. Now you're reaching the end of the process. You might have some sort of hunch that you're about to get what you want. Uh oh. Doesn't that mean you're about to make a big change?

It's not uncommon to back off when you come close to finishing. Success can have peculiar side effects.

SUCCESS AND ITS SIDE EFFECTS

Often, by the time you get to the end of your journey, you don't even realize you're there. You're accustomed to making calls, following up, selling yourself, sustaining disappointments—the process of a career change can become a career in itself, or at least a hobby. So how do you feel when someone says, "Okay, you can do it. Here's some money"?

I know how I felt when my editor gave me my first offer for my first book. After the immediate jolt of satisfaction and triumph, I faced a huge wall of fear. Now I had to actually do what I'd been trying to do for years, and I wondered if I really could do it, after all.

When my client Lawrence landed his first big client for financial and estate planning, he almost lost him. Lawrence felt so "on the spot" that he began to second-guess himself in their first meeting. The calm certainty and practical advice with which he had won this client seemed to evaporate; in its place was a man with a shaky backbone. Lawrence apologized for his nerves and covered with a white lie about having food poisoning. By the next meeting, Lawrence was more prepared (with Minerva's help, of course) and his client was satisfied.

Lawrence and I each had separate reactions to success, both of the same origin.

"Now that I'm here, can I really do it?"

Minerva can help you weigh anchor with your purpose so that you can enjoy the fruits of your labor and stabilize your success in your new career.

Exercise: Minerva's Anchor to Success

Tools: Your power magnet, something symbolizing your achievement (a letter with an offer, a business card, et cetera), a quiet place to sit in the dark and talk to yourself.

Sit quietly in the dark with your power magnet on top of or next to the symbol of your success. Aloud, call in Minerva and ask her to connect you to your success with calm assurance, ease, and grace. You can use these words or say it your own way.

Minerva, I call upon your guidance and powers once again to help me connect and anchor this successful career shape-shift. I claim this new work as my own, with dignity, grace, and calm assurance.

Keep yourself in a relaxed state for a few minutes so that you can really feel calm and collected with your success.

While many of us "choke" when we come to the end of the road, there is another success side effect that I believe is more rare but actually more dangerous: vanity.

Vanity rears its self-absorbed head most often in people who have started out with low self-esteem and have had to struggle to find their strengths. A monster ego can be born from weakness—it takes less work—to go from one extreme ("I'm not worth anything") to the other ("I'm the best"). It's harder work to recognize talent and self-worth while still understanding that we all have issues, weaknesses, and problems. For most of you, working with Minerva and understanding your astrological gifts and challenges can bring a balance to your self-knowledge. With Minerva, there's no such thing as good and bad, only what "is." You are your own sacred blend of "you-ness."

Conceit, an unduly high opinion of oneself, is most often found in those people who don't know that it's okay to be flawed. This vanity can initially help in a career shape-shift because it brings its own kind of exclusive, assured energy that can be very attractive to employers. Yet once an offer is made, the vulnerability masked by vanity can undo success. Insecurity can dictate some silly responses. It's easier to say "no" to a job ("It's not good enough") than to open yourself up to the possibility of being mediocre, or of failing completely. Vanity can keep you from getting where you want to go.

Everyone makes mistakes, but insecure egos don't accept them. They become blamers and fault-finders. That kind of avoidance and accusational energy will sabotage your shape-shift and dismantle your success. If you've had to work hard on your self-worth, take time to assess yourself realistically. Be confident with both your skills and your weaknesses. Ask Minerva to help.

Exercise: Minerva's Acceptance Speech

Tools: Your power magnet, a quiet room.

Sit quietly with your eyes closed. Take easy, relaxed breaths. As you exhale through your mouth, imagine impurities, fear, and judgments leaving your body. Repeat this for a minute or two. When you feel ready, say aloud: "I claim my success. I am worthy of success. I am fallible. I am successful. Minerva's wisdom is my own."

Sit with your eyes closed. With each inhalation, take in your success and your wholeness. Own and embrace both your faults and your strengths. Breathe in both good and bad, calmly, knowing you are successful with all of your qualities.

DEALING WITH SUCCESS

Minerva really likes to see you succeed, so she'll be helping you close the deal, as long as you let her in on it. Being able to accept that you're at the end of the road is only the first step to your ultimate success. Now, how about negotiating great terms for your new career?

Once you've made the shift and are accepted in your new work (or have advanced to a new level of your current career), you're almost done. There's still something you can do, which is hard to do, and that is to make a good deal. It's easy to think you're done once you get there. But what if you accept the very first thing offered? What if you find out you could have done better?

Remember the adage about the old bulls and young bulls on the hillside who see the pretty cows down in the meadow.

The young bulls run down the hill, eager to get to the prettiest cows first. The older bulls take their time, walking slowly. The young bulls are laughing, thinking the old-timers are slow and stupid for letting the young ones beat them to the best cows. The old bulls know better. The young bulls will be winded and tired by the time they get to the cows. While they recover from their run, the older bulls will show up ready and able to calmly take over.

Slow and steady wins the race. If you rush toward the first sign of interest, you might not get the best offer. Understandably, this is a common mistake.

It's hard to take your time accepting success when you've worked so hard to get there.

Sometimes being inexperienced or naive is helpful. My first advertising-job offer was at a salary $5,000 less than I had anticipated. I asked for more, not knowing how unusual it was for anyone at an entry-level job to do so. My friends told me I was crazy and that I was lucky to get an offer at all. But my employers gave me that increase and I had the satisfaction of knowing I had taken a risk (albeit, innocently) and it paid off. Minerva guided me even then.

It's really hard to negotiate for yourself; in fact, it's almost impossible. You cannot maintain objectivity in deal-making when you're talking about yourself; this puts you at a disadvantage. It's hard to ask for more when you're grateful to be offered anything at all, and you're more likely to settle for something less than perfect just to nail down the deal. But if you don't have to settle, why should you? If you get an offer or acceptance but there's one thing missing (a little more money, more vacation time, better benefits, a different title), ask for it. The worst they can say is no. The best that can happen is that you get it.

If you're bashful about asking for something, let Minerva help you. You don't have to become a tough negotiator, just find a way to say "Could you possibly meet this need?" I remember that first offer and how I blurted out, "Gee, I'd hoped for $5,000 more." My straightforward, honest request for more money was unusual. But I got it.

I also remember kicking myself when I took a new job a few years later. In that case, my salary increase seemed so great I felt like I couldn't ask for anything else, and I willingly put up with two weeks' vacation time when I could have negotiated for more. I let myself be intimidated by my own fear ("Am I worth that much money?") and unconsciously negotiated with myself ("Well, I'll work really hard and won't take much vacation— then I'll be worth it"). I learned from that.

It's tough to consider how others might see you. You've been working on yourself, getting yourself to a point where you believed this work would be possible, then getting someone else to accept you and hire you. Now that you've convinced them you can do it, don't undersell your value. Many career shape-shifters undergo a period of feeling like they "got away" with something, as if they're a fake and don't want to "get found out." That's not reality. You've earned the work and you are entitled to be well-compensated.

My client John, thirty-seven, prepared to leave his job at a brokerage firm to go back to school for a law degree. He'd done well on his entrance exams and had saved enough money to live on, although he had taken out loans to cover his tuition. When he got accepted to the university that was his first choice, he was thrilled. He didn't seem to care that he'd have a huge debt to pay off after he graduated. I pointed out that, since he'd come this far, why not apply for financial aid? Even a scholarship?

He thought I was crazy ("Who would give a scholarship to a middle-aged white guy?") and wasn't going to inquire at all, until he heard that a foundation within the school offered certain scholarships to students over thirty years old. He thought it was funny to even apply but he did, and he didn't make fun of the $10,000 scholarship he received as a result.

If you think you can't ask for more than you're offered, check in with Minerva and find the right way to state your needs.

Exercise: Minerva's Negotiator

Tools: You and your power magnet in a quiet room, pen, and paper.

List the good things you've been offered. List what you wish it would include—be reasonable. Ask Minerva to help you find the right words to ask for what you want. Close your eyes and practice asking for it out loud. Hear a positive response in your mind. Relax and feel how easy it is to ask for what you want.

One tip: You can use the moon cycle to help you. Ask for increases after a new moon, when the moon is growing in size.

WHEN SUCCESS SEEMS TOO EASY

Here's a tough one: What do you do when someone offers you your dream job right away?

How can you say no? Of course you want the job—it's what you've always wanted. So is it okay to have a happy ending so easily? Will you miss something by accepting the first thing that comes along?

I just witnessed this with my client Sylvia. She wanted to

stop working from her home office as a PR consultant and become an in-house writer for a Internet design company. Sylvia felt this was a big creative leap but got inspired by a project she did for a new website. She had writing skills from her PR job, but she didn't feel expert in the ways of the World Wide Web. Her website client put her in touch with a big Internet company that was looking for staff writers. She was offered a job within two weeks of beginning her work with Minerva.

Sylvia called me to discuss it.

Sylvia: Hi. I don't know what to do. I got a job.

Me: What do you mean, you don't know what to do? What do you mean, you got a job?

Sylvia: Just what I said.

Me: How did you feel about the place when you went to see it?

Sylvia: Great. I loved the atmosphere. Except everyone seemed twenty years younger than me. But I don't care about that—at least not that much.

Me: Are you going to be a writer?

Sylvia: Yep. A staff writer. That's the job.

Me: How's the money?

Sylvia: Okay. Not bad. And I get stock options.

Me: So what's the problem?

Sylvia: It's all happening so fast.

Me: Minerva smiled upon you. Smile back.

Sure, you're probably going to second-guess a fast offer (Why do they want me so fast? Are they sure they know what I want/what they want/what I can do? et cetera). It's natural to be nervous—after all, you are surprised. You've also been warned not to take the first thing that comes along, but what if you want to?

Here is a basic checklist if you feel unbalanced by a quick shape-shift.

1. Did the interview and the place feel good to you?
2. Were you excited about the job the whole time?
3. Do you feel you can and want to do the job?
4. Are you excited about it when you don't feel afraid?

There's no reason to turn down an offer if it's the right one. Second-guessing ("maybe I'll do better if I wait for something else") won't get you anywhere. You might do better and you might not. Here's a job you can do and you want to do. Don't pass it up.

THE RISK OF SUCCESS

Starting a new career always feels risky. Whether the work itself arrives quickly or with a long and laborious shape-shift, you'll probably ask yourself more than once if you are doing the right thing. It's important to remember that, in Minerva's eyes, there's no such thing as wrong. As long as you allow yourself to channel your creative passion into your work, you are an honorable being. When and if you want, you can change your mind and shape-shift again.

THE DONE DEAL

Now you're in the driver's seat, with a completed shape-shift to tell your friends and family about. You've transformed your creative energy into a new field, a Herculean task. How do you end the process?

Minerva now asks you to do a few things. First, give some gratitude to the world in honor of your success. Second, link your success to someone else and help others realize their dreams.

RESTARTING THE RIGHT WAY

When you begin that first day in your new work life, take your new powers with you. Keep your power magnet by your side or on your desk. Eventually, when your new work is just your career, not new anymore, you can release your power magnet and use it or lose it, as you wish.

You can also bring some closure to the shape-shifting process so that you psychically understand that you are no longer in a state of transition. A simple exercise to close (not part) with Minerva will help you finish, but beware of side effects. There can be a little sadness when you reach that long-sought-after goal.

Exercise: Closing with Minerva

TOOLS: Your power magnet, a quiet place to sit and talk out loud.

Thank Minerva for her patience and generosity in your career shape-shift and ask for her to bless and guide your new work, that you find success, creative fulfillment, and productivity. Do something in gratitude for your good fortune.

THE IMPORTANCE OF GRATITUDE

Ideally, expressing your gratitude is simply a blessing you extend to the world and the heavens (Minerva and her friends) for responding to your requests and prayers for a new creative pathway. You can say thank-you to the universe that made this career shape-shift possible. In its most pragmatic sense, gratitude is a way of ensuring that you'll appreciate and keep the blessing you've worked so hard for. Gratitude is the end, the finishing touch on your magical work with Minerva.

After my first book was published, I gave some money to a fund that helped women who needed to start their lives over. That was my gratitude ritual, so that I could share indirectly and help someone in need of a shape-shift. For every book I publish and every career breakthrough I experience, I give something back, whether it's money or time.

How to express your gratitude is up to you. Minerva has some suggestions that might inspire you.

Give time to charity or volunteer
Be a mentor or career coach
Start (and keep up) a victory garden
Start (and keep up) a victory compost heap
Participate in a fund-raiser for a favorite cause
Do someone a career favor

Gratitude rituals can start chain reactions that have very positive side effects. You set an example when you give something back.

HELPING OTHERS SUCCEED

When I was trying to become a writer, my friend Liz, an accomplished author, took me under her wing. She introduced me to my agent and she helped me develop ideas for books. She's still helping me. And she asks for nothing in return. She sets a great example, one I've tried to follow, to nurture others' careers.

After I published my first two books, I met a couple of young women who wanted to write about the experiences of pre-teen girls. They had done some research and wanted to compile a book from their notes. Understanding how hard it is to write a book, I gave them as much guidance as I could—from tips on how to organize the book to how to find a publisher and agent. I didn't do any work for them; I enabled them to do it themselves. They did finally publish their book—and that was enormously gratifying to all of us.

How to take care of and support other people's careers is not something taught in school, nor is it written into most job descriptions. Yet we all need a little off-the-record encouragement and wisdom along the way. Hopefully your shape-shift has put you primarily on the receiving end of a mentor. You've probably gained wisdom and experience by listening to others. Now you've earned the right to be the one who offers the advice.

Mentoring is a way to become a guide or counselor to

someone less experienced and probably less connected. You don't have to be in the same industry, just give your time and wisdom to someone who could use an experienced eye and a practiced opinion. Even if your company doesn't have a mentoring program, there are lots of nonprofit groups that would welcome your help.

STORYTELLING: REMEMBERING MINERVA

There will be a time in the not-too-distant future when your career won't feel "new" anymore. You won't feel as if you've just come through an enormous shift, and you'll be walking around, comfortably ensconced in your work and life once again, only happier. This is what you've been working for, the new life that feels just like regular life.

When you get to this point, don't forget Minerva. Keep her energy and power alive by telling the story of how you got here. Storytelling, especially true stories with happy endings, is a sacred form of communication and celebration. You will have many opportunities to share your story—with your family, at business functions, over dinner with friends. Don't be afraid to tell how you were able to change your life by opening yourself up to this mysterious process with Minerva.

Telling your own story, out loud, keeps your passion high and your connection to Minerva alive. And you may just inspire someone else to follow their heart into a new future.

Minerva wishes you well and hopes you'll share the magic of her myth and the reality of her power.

MOON SIGNS

12/30/1929	05:55:50	Cp	05/04/1930	16:31:41	Le	09/06/1930	21:06:24	Pi
01/01/1930	18:29:16	Aq	05/06/1930	19:10:35	Vi	09/09/1930	09:21:05	Ar
01/04/1930	07:04:27	Pi	05/08/1930	22:30:05	Li	09/11/1930	20:17:55	Ta
01/06/1930	18:27:23	Ar	05/11/1930	03:06:25	Sc	09/14/1930	05:00:53	Ge
01/09/1930	02:58:59	Ta	05/13/1930	09:38:40	Sg	09/16/1930	10:42:10	Cn
01/11/1930	07:34:29	Ge	05/15/1930	18:39:26	Cp	09/18/1930	13:18:06	Le
01/13/1930	08:34:33	Cn	05/18/1930	06:03:29	Aq	09/20/1930	13:45:09	Vi
01/15/1930	07:37:05	Le	05/20/1930	18:33:43	Pi	09/22/1930	13:43:24	Li
01/17/1930	06:56:32	Vi	05/23/1930	05:55:28	Ar	09/24/1930	15:07:17	Sc
01/19/1930	08:44:09	Li	05/25/1930	14:15:14	Ta	09/26/1930	19:34:19	Sg
01/21/1930	14:24:51	Sc	05/27/1930	19:06:50	Ge	09/29/1930	03:48:18	Cp
01/23/1930	23:56:03	Sg	05/29/1930	21:25:33	Cn	10/01/1930	15:09:05	Aq
01/26/1930	11:52:56	Cp	05/31/1930	22:45:01	Le	10/04/1930	03:47:48	Pi
01/29/1930	00:35:02	Aq	06/03/1930	00:36:52	Vi	10/06/1930	15:51:59	Ar
01/31/1930	12:58:51	Pi	06/05/1930	04:03:47	Li	10/09/1930	02:14:23	Ta
02/03/1930	00:22:42	Ar	06/07/1930	09:30:03	Sc	10/11/1930	10:29:08	Ge
02/05/1930	09:48:34	Ta	06/09/1930	16:55:57	Sg	10/13/1930	16:29:10	Cn
02/07/1930	16:08:04	Ge	06/12/1930	02:20:09	Cp	10/15/1930	20:19:19	Le
02/09/1930	18:55:13	Cn	06/14/1930	13:38:49	Aq	10/17/1930	22:25:35	Vi
02/11/1930	19:00:14	Le	06/17/1930	02:11:53	Pi	10/19/1930	23:43:10	Li
02/13/1930	18:14:02	Vi	06/19/1930	14:14:51	Ar	10/22/1930	01:32:26	Sc
02/15/1930	18:50:06	Li	06/21/1930	23:35:22	Ta	10/24/1930	05:23:17	Sg
02/17/1930	22:44:33	Sc	06/24/1930	05:00:11	Ge	10/26/1930	12:26:50	Cp
02/20/1930	06:48:31	Sg	06/26/1930	06:57:18	Cn	10/28/1930	22:53:38	Aq
02/22/1930	18:12:36	Cp	06/28/1930	07:06:10	Le	10/31/1930	11:22:42	Pi
02/25/1930	06:56:44	Aq	06/30/1930	07:28:20	Vi	11/02/1930	23:34:28	Ar
02/27/1930	19:13:03	Pi	07/02/1930	09:47:01	Li	11/05/1930	09:37:23	Ta
03/02/1930	06:08:18	Ar	07/04/1930	14:55:48	Sc	11/07/1930	16:58:21	Ge
03/04/1930	15:18:34	Ta	07/06/1930	22:49:13	Sg	11/09/1930	22:04:52	Cn
03/06/1930	22:15:46	Ge	07/09/1930	08:49:25	Cp	11/12/1930	01:45:10	Le
03/09/1930	02:34:17	Cn	07/11/1930	20:22:38	Aq	11/14/1930	04:41:39	Vi
03/11/1930	04:25:16	Le	07/14/1930	08:57:06	Pi	11/16/1930	07:26:54	Li
03/13/1930	04:53:36	Vi	07/16/1930	21:25:48	Ar	11/18/1930	10:36:08	Sc
03/15/1930	05:43:09	Li	07/19/1930	07:54:17	Ta	11/20/1930	15:00:17	Sg
03/17/1930	08:46:04	Sc	07/21/1930	14:39:05	Ge	11/22/1930	21:41:48	Cp
03/19/1930	15:23:29	Sg	07/23/1930	17:22:09	Cn	11/25/1930	07:22:40	Aq
03/22/1930	01:40:00	Cp	07/25/1930	17:18:46	Le	11/27/1930	19:32:28	Pi
03/24/1930	14:04:55	Aq	07/27/1930	16:34:12	Vi	11/30/1930	08:06:20	Ar
03/27/1930	02:23:35	Pi	07/29/1930	17:17:50	Li	12/02/1930	18:31:58	Ta
03/29/1930	12:59:46	Ar	07/31/1930	21:04:57	Sc	12/05/1930	01:31:59	Ge
03/31/1930	21:23:29	Ta	08/03/1930	04:24:10	Sg	12/07/1930	05:31:13	Cn
04/03/1930	03:42:09	Ge	08/05/1930	14:34:29	Cp	12/09/1930	07:52:35	Le
04/05/1930	08:10:56	Cn	08/08/1930	02:26:18	Aq	12/11/1930	10:04:01	Vi
04/07/1930	11:08:43	Le	08/10/1930	15:02:36	Pi	12/13/1930	13:04:59	Li
04/09/1930	13:10:44	Vi	08/13/1930	03:32:03	Ar	12/15/1930	17:19:04	Sc
04/11/1930	15:16:45	Li	08/15/1930	14:37:59	Ta	12/17/1930	22:54:19	Sg
04/13/1930	18:44:38	Sc	08/17/1930	22:45:44	Ge	12/20/1930	06:11:20	Cp
04/16/1930	00:49:10	Sg	08/20/1930	03:01:57	Cn	12/22/1930	15:43:28	Aq
04/18/1930	10:07:14	Cp	08/22/1930	03:57:41	Le	12/25/1930	03:35:25	Pi
04/20/1930	21:58:17	Aq	08/24/1930	03:13:24	Vi	12/27/1930	16:29:14	Ar
04/23/1930	10:23:16	Pi	08/26/1930	02:57:53	Li	12/30/1930	03:51:28	Ta
04/25/1930	21:09:47	Ar	08/28/1930	05:10:36	Sc	01/01/1931	11:34:12	Ge
04/28/1930	05:08:12	Ta	08/30/1930	11:04:26	Sg	01/03/1931	15:20:48	Cn
04/30/1930	10:25:55	Ge	09/01/1930	20:35:07	Cp	01/05/1931	16:32:01	Le
05/02/1930	13:53:45	Cn	09/04/1930	08:27:21	Aq	01/07/1931	17:06:01	Vi

01/09/1931	18:48:20	Li	05/22/1931	11:27:10	Le	10/01/1931	15:03:26	Ge
01/11/1931	22:40:11	Sc	05/24/1931	15:06:56	Vi	10/04/1931	00:37:36	Cn
01/14/1931	04:50:27	Sg	05/26/1931	17:50:54	Li	10/06/1931	06:49:13	Le
01/16/1931	13:01:29	Cp	05/28/1931	20:07:34	Sc	10/08/1931	09:34:02	Vi
01/18/1931	23:03:50	Aq	05/30/1931	22:47:38	Sg	10/10/1931	09:50:02	Li
01/21/1931	10:54:55	Pi	06/02/1931	03:07:12	Cp	10/12/1931	09:17:01	Sc
01/23/1931	23:54:38	Ar	06/04/1931	10:23:05	Aq	10/14/1931	09:51:00	Sg
01/26/1931	12:09:49	Ta	06/06/1931	21:00:51	Pi	10/16/1931	13:18:10	Cp
01/28/1931	21:18:12	Ge	06/09/1931	09:43:45	Ar	10/18/1931	20:38:58	Aq
01/31/1931	02:09:16	Cn	06/11/1931	21:54:14	Ta	10/21/1931	07:32:19	Pi
02/02/1931	03:24:26	Le	06/14/1931	07:21:32	Ge	10/23/1931	20:20:58	Ar
02/04/1931	02:56:29	Vi	06/16/1931	13:37:48	Cn	10/26/1931	09:11:45	Ta
02/06/1931	02:54:24	Li	06/18/1931	17:36:12	Le	10/28/1931	20:47:34	Ge
02/08/1931	05:04:22	Sc	06/20/1931	20:32:21	Vi	10/31/1931	06:26:28	Cn
02/10/1931	10:21:10	Sg	06/22/1931	23:22:34	Li	11/02/1931	13:39:22	Le
02/12/1931	18:38:51	Cp	06/25/1931	02:34:20	Sc	11/04/1931	18:07:38	Vi
02/15/1931	05:14:26	Aq	06/27/1931	06:26:18	Sg	11/06/1931	20:02:41	Li
02/17/1931	17:23:07	Pi	06/29/1931	11:34:55	Cp	11/08/1931	20:20:54	Sc
02/20/1931	06:20:37	Ar	07/01/1931	18:56:06	Aq	11/10/1931	20:38:43	Sg
02/22/1931	18:53:42	Ta	07/04/1931	05:09:29	Pi	11/12/1931	22:51:54	Cp
02/25/1931	05:13:04	Ge	07/06/1931	17:39:53	Ar	11/15/1931	04:40:03	Aq
02/27/1931	11:47:00	Cn	07/09/1931	06:13:38	Ta	11/17/1931	14:32:21	Pi
03/01/1931	14:24:56	Le	07/11/1931	16:13:52	Ge	11/20/1931	03:08:25	Ar
03/03/1931	14:20:39	Vi	07/13/1931	22:30:10	Cn	11/22/1931	15:59:46	Ta
03/05/1931	13:32:15	Li	07/16/1931	01:41:13	Le	11/25/1931	03:11:34	Ge
03/07/1931	14:02:40	Sc	07/18/1931	03:21:39	Vi	11/27/1931	12:09:10	Cn
03/09/1931	17:30:01	Sg	07/20/1931	05:05:53	Li	11/29/1931	19:05:47	Le
03/12/1931	00:38:48	Cp	07/22/1931	07:56:14	Sc	12/02/1931	00:16:21	Vi
03/14/1931	11:03:07	Aq	07/24/1931	12:18:28	Sg	12/04/1931	03:44:10	Li
03/16/1931	23:26:20	Pi	07/26/1931	18:22:07	Cp	12/06/1931	05:43:04	Sc
03/19/1931	12:23:59	Ar	07/29/1931	02:24:14	Aq	12/08/1931	07:03:54	Sg
03/22/1931	00:44:12	Ta	07/31/1931	12:45:23	Pi	12/10/1931	09:17:32	Cp
03/24/1931	11:19:02	Ge	08/03/1931	01:10:00	Ar	12/12/1931	14:09:40	Aq
03/26/1931	19:04:26	Cn	08/05/1931	14:04:52	Ta	12/14/1931	22:50:08	Pi
03/28/1931	23:28:46	Le	08/08/1931	01:01:08	Ge	12/17/1931	10:49:18	Ar
03/31/1931	00:57:35	Vi	08/10/1931	08:10:22	Cn	12/19/1931	23:45:17	Ta
04/02/1931	00:49:08	Li	08/12/1931	11:30:51	Le	12/22/1931	10:59:10	Ge
04/04/1931	00:50:20	Sc	08/14/1931	12:25:06	Vi	12/24/1931	19:21:33	Cn
04/06/1931	02:51:58	Sg	08/16/1931	12:44:54	Li	12/27/1931	01:16:09	Le
04/08/1931	08:20:19	Cp	08/18/1931	14:10:23	Sc	12/29/1931	05:40:37	Vi
04/10/1931	17:39:50	Aq	08/20/1931	17:46:55	Sg	12/31/1931	09:17:22	Li
04/13/1931	05:48:40	Pi	08/22/1931	23:58:12	Cp	01/02/1932	12:23:32	Sc
04/15/1931	18:48:00	Ar	08/25/1931	08:37:44	Aq	01/04/1932	15:15:18	Sg
04/18/1931	06:50:08	Ta	08/27/1931	19:27:13	Pi	01/06/1932	18:36:54	Cp
04/20/1931	16:55:43	Ge	08/30/1931	07:56:20	Ar	01/08/1932	23:43:30	Aq
04/23/1931	00:42:09	Cn	09/01/1931	20:59:02	Ta	01/11/1932	07:49:10	Pi
04/25/1931	06:03:40	Le	09/04/1931	08:43:12	Ge	01/13/1932	19:07:19	Ar
04/27/1931	09:09:36	Vi	09/06/1931	17:14:41	Cn	01/16/1932	08:02:18	Ta
04/29/1931	10:34:56	Li	09/08/1931	21:47:21	Le	01/18/1932	19:47:15	Ge
05/01/1931	11:25:54	Sc	09/10/1931	23:03:44	Vi	01/21/1932	04:22:21	Cn
05/03/1931	13:13:42	Sg	09/12/1931	22:42:54	Li	01/23/1932	09:39:28	Le
05/05/1931	17:35:19	Cp	09/14/1931	22:40:16	Sc	01/25/1932	12:46:34	Vi
05/08/1931	01:36:33	Aq	09/17/1931	00:39:13	Sg	01/27/1932	15:07:10	Li
05/10/1931	13:01:42	Pi	09/19/1931	05:47:33	Cp	01/29/1932	17:42:58	Sc
05/13/1931	01:56:32	Ar	09/21/1931	14:17:44	Aq	01/31/1932	21:06:39	Sg
05/15/1931	13:54:06	Ta	09/24/1931	01:28:09	Pi	02/03/1932	01:38:38	Cp
05/17/1931	23:26:23	Ge	09/26/1931	14:09:05	Ar	02/05/1932	07:48:18	Aq
05/20/1931	06:25:50	Cn	09/29/1931	03:06:43	Ta	02/07/1932	16:15:00	Pi

02/10/1932	03:17:08	Ar	06/20/1932	20:11:48	Aq	10/31/1932	04:40:01	Sg
02/12/1932	16:04:56	Ta	06/23/1932	02:25:27	Pi	11/02/1932	04:54:23	Cp
02/15/1932	04:27:28	Ge	06/25/1932	12:33:55	Ar	11/04/1932	08:05:39	Aq
02/17/1932	14:02:16	Cn	06/28/1932	01:07:37	Ta	11/06/1932	15:06:15	Pi
02/19/1932	19:48:39	Le	06/30/1932	13:34:50	Ge	11/09/1932	01:24:26	Ar
02/21/1932	22:24:41	Vi	07/03/1932	00:06:31	Cn	11/11/1932	13:33:23	Ta
02/23/1932	23:21:57	Li	07/05/1932	08:18:18	Le	11/14/1932	02:13:14	Ge
02/26/1932	00:19:47	Sc	07/07/1932	14:32:48	Vi	11/16/1932	14:31:51	Cn
02/28/1932	02:38:29	Sg	07/09/1932	19:12:24	Li	11/19/1932	01:35:20	Le
03/01/1932	07:06:26	Cp	07/11/1932	22:27:27	Sc	11/21/1932	10:08:13	Vi
03/03/1932	14:00:04	Aq	07/14/1932	00:37:41	Sg	11/23/1932	15:07:57	Li
03/05/1932	23:15:13	Pi	07/16/1932	02:35:19	Cp	11/25/1932	16:37:56	Sc
03/08/1932	10:35:08	Ar	07/18/1932	05:44:25	Aq	11/27/1932	15:58:20	Sg
03/10/1932	23:19:17	Ta	07/20/1932	11:34:08	Pi	11/29/1932	15:16:10	Cp
03/13/1932	12:02:42	Ge	07/22/1932	20:52:02	Ar	12/01/1932	16:46:17	Aq
03/15/1932	22:46:02	Cn	07/25/1932	08:54:12	Ta	12/03/1932	22:07:57	Pi
03/18/1932	05:55:43	Le	07/27/1932	21:26:03	Ge	12/06/1932	07:34:44	Ar
03/20/1932	09:18:05	Vi	07/30/1932	08:07:10	Cn	12/08/1932	19:41:15	Ta
03/22/1932	09:56:21	Li	08/01/1932	15:56:40	Le	12/11/1932	08:25:55	Ge
03/24/1932	09:34:53	Sc	08/03/1932	21:14:55	Vi	12/13/1932	20:27:55	Cn
03/26/1932	10:06:41	Sg	08/06/1932	00:55:47	Li	12/16/1932	07:12:29	Le
03/28/1932	13:07:43	Cp	08/08/1932	03:49:12	Sc	12/18/1932	16:08:49	Vi
03/30/1932	19:30:09	Aq	08/10/1932	06:31:49	Sg	12/20/1932	22:31:35	Li
04/02/1932	05:04:36	Pi	08/12/1932	09:38:08	Cp	12/23/1932	01:52:43	Sc
04/04/1932	16:53:01	Ar	08/14/1932	13:53:37	Aq	12/25/1932	02:42:05	Sg
04/07/1932	05:43:36	Ta	08/16/1932	20:13:11	Pi	12/27/1932	02:30:48	Cp
04/09/1932	18:27:00	Ge	08/19/1932	05:17:57	Ar	12/29/1932	03:22:49	Aq
04/12/1932	05:46:46	Cn	08/21/1932	16:55:43	Ta	12/31/1932	07:16:06	Pi
04/14/1932	14:21:44	Le	08/24/1932	05:33:19	Ge	01/02/1933	15:13:19	Ar
04/16/1932	19:21:26	Vi	08/26/1932	16:49:59	Cn	01/05/1933	02:36:18	Ta
04/18/1932	20:59:43	Li	08/29/1932	01:02:56	Le	01/07/1933	15:19:22	Ge
04/20/1932	20:33:21	Sc	08/31/1932	05:58:08	Vi	01/10/1933	03:16:17	Cn
04/22/1932	19:57:10	Sg	09/02/1932	08:31:38	Li	01/12/1933	13:26:29	Le
04/24/1932	21:14:42	Cp	09/04/1932	10:05:59	Sc	01/14/1933	21:41:37	Vi
04/27/1932	02:04:11	Aq	09/06/1932	11:59:35	Sg	01/17/1933	04:02:42	Li
04/29/1932	10:55:08	Pi	09/08/1932	15:11:13	Cp	01/19/1933	08:24:23	Sc
05/01/1932	22:46:13	Ar	09/10/1932	20:15:55	Aq	01/21/1933	10:54:25	Sg
05/04/1932	11:45:37	Ta	09/13/1932	03:30:37	Pi	01/23/1933	12:17:32	Cp
05/07/1932	00:19:57	Ge	09/15/1932	13:00:51	Ar	01/25/1933	13:56:29	Aq
05/09/1932	11:34:15	Cn	09/18/1932	00:33:30	Ta	01/27/1933	17:30:54	Pi
05/11/1932	20:46:33	Le	09/20/1932	13:13:37	Ge	01/30/1933	00:20:53	Ar
05/14/1932	03:13:08	Vi	09/23/1932	01:13:08	Cn	02/01/1933	10:40:03	Ta
05/16/1932	06:32:09	Li	09/25/1932	10:31:44	Le	02/03/1933	23:04:44	Ge
05/18/1932	07:14:35	Sc	09/27/1932	16:06:37	Vi	02/06/1933	11:13:11	Cn
05/20/1932	06:47:34	Sg	09/29/1932	18:21:55	Li	02/08/1933	21:16:08	Le
05/22/1932	07:12:20	Cp	10/01/1932	18:43:49	Sc	02/11/1933	04:42:58	Vi
05/24/1932	10:30:39	Aq	10/03/1932	19:02:22	Sg	02/13/1933	09:59:03	Li
05/26/1932	17:57:18	Pi	10/05/1932	20:59:56	Cp	02/15/1933	13:46:12	Sc
05/29/1932	05:08:38	Ar	10/08/1932	01:43:33	Aq	02/17/1933	16:42:16	Sg
05/31/1932	18:04:30	Ta	10/10/1932	09:26:17	Pi	02/19/1933	19:22:18	Cp
06/03/1932	06:32:08	Ge	10/12/1932	19:35:33	Ar	02/21/1933	22:28:36	Aq
06/05/1932	17:20:44	Cn	10/15/1932	07:23:40	Ta	02/24/1933	02:55:56	Pi
06/08/1932	02:14:19	Le	10/17/1932	20:02:36	Ge	02/26/1933	09:42:07	Ar
06/10/1932	09:06:18	Vi	10/20/1932	08:26:07	Cn	02/28/1933	19:19:56	Ta
06/12/1932	13:41:28	Li	10/22/1932	18:57:03	Le	03/03/1933	07:17:30	Ge
06/14/1932	15:59:36	Sc	10/25/1932	02:02:49	Vi	03/05/1933	19:42:55	Cn
06/16/1932	16:45:21	Sg	10/27/1932	05:15:23	Li	03/08/1933	06:17:43	Le
06/18/1932	17:30:54	Cp	10/29/1932	05:30:28	Sc	03/10/1933	13:41:45	Vi

03/12/1933	18:02:57	Li	07/22/1933	17:18:36	Le	12/01/1933	06:44:30	Ge
03/14/1933	20:27:19	Sc	07/25/1933	03:35:25	Vi	12/03/1933	18:52:45	Cn
03/16/1933	22:18:07	Sg	07/27/1933	11:44:05	Li	12/06/1933	07:48:38	Le
03/19/1933	00:46:48	Cp	07/29/1933	17:21:18	Sc	12/08/1933	19:59:41	Vi
03/21/1933	04:38:46	Aq	07/31/1933	20:26:34	Sg	12/11/1933	05:18:32	Li
03/23/1933	10:15:31	Pi	08/02/1933	21:40:13	Cp	12/13/1933	10:26:37	Sc
03/25/1933	17:49:24	Ar	08/04/1933	22:21:36	Aq	12/15/1933	11:48:29	Sg
03/28/1933	03:31:32	Ta	08/07/1933	00:10:26	Pi	12/17/1933	11:08:03	Cp
03/30/1933	15:13:11	Ge	08/09/1933	04:40:32	Ar	12/19/1933	10:37:08	Aq
04/02/1933	03:49:46	Cn	08/11/1933	12:44:33	Ta	12/21/1933	12:15:05	Pi
04/04/1933	15:16:25	Le	08/13/1933	23:57:11	Ge	12/23/1933	17:15:21	Ar
04/06/1933	23:32:55	Vi	08/16/1933	12:32:19	Cn	12/26/1933	01:42:29	Ta
04/09/1933	04:00:20	Li	08/19/1933	00:22:27	Le	12/28/1933	12:42:36	Ge
04/11/1933	05:31:46	Sc	08/21/1933	10:07:27	Vi	12/31/1933	01:06:30	Cn
04/13/1933	05:51:56	Sg	08/23/1933	17:29:09	Li	01/02/1934	13:56:02	Le
04/15/1933	06:53:29	Cp	08/25/1933	22:44:26	Sc	01/05/1934	02:08:50	Vi
04/17/1933	10:02:25	Aq	08/28/1933	02:21:03	Sg	01/07/1934	12:20:25	Li
04/19/1933	15:53:57	Pi	08/30/1933	04:51:40	Cp	01/09/1934	19:10:36	Sc
04/22/1933	00:14:06	Ar	09/01/1933	06:59:32	Aq	01/11/1934	22:17:37	Sg
04/24/1933	10:30:46	Ta	09/03/1933	09:43:41	Pi	01/13/1934	22:37:00	Cp
04/26/1933	22:17:57	Ge	09/05/1933	14:14:38	Ar	01/15/1934	21:56:00	Aq
04/29/1933	10:58:05	Cn	09/07/1933	21:34:45	Ta	01/17/1934	22:17:11	Pi
05/01/1933	23:06:14	Le	09/10/1933	08:00:40	Ge	01/20/1934	01:27:41	Ar
05/04/1933	08:40:35	Vi	09/12/1933	20:24:55	Cn	01/22/1934	08:26:10	Ta
05/06/1933	14:16:57	Li	09/15/1933	08:30:26	Le	01/24/1934	18:54:01	Ge
05/08/1933	16:06:30	Sc	09/17/1933	18:13:10	Vi	01/27/1934	07:23:48	Cn
05/10/1933	15:42:44	Sg	09/20/1933	00:51:11	Li	01/29/1934	20:11:35	Le
05/12/1933	15:14:53	Cp	09/22/1933	04:59:51	Sc	02/01/1934	08:00:14	Vi
05/14/1933	16:45:35	Aq	09/24/1933	07:48:34	Sg	02/03/1934	17:59:29	Li
05/16/1933	21:33:27	Pi	09/26/1933	10:22:48	Cp	02/06/1934	01:31:11	Sc
05/19/1933	05:45:08	Ar	09/28/1933	13:26:34	Aq	02/08/1934	06:14:08	Sg
05/21/1933	16:26:20	Ta	09/30/1933	17:26:43	Pi	02/10/1934	08:23:10	Cp
05/24/1933	04:31:25	Ge	10/02/1933	22:50:55	Ar	02/12/1934	08:56:58	Aq
05/26/1933	17:11:52	Cn	10/05/1933	06:17:43	Ta	02/14/1934	09:27:18	Pi
05/29/1933	05:33:06	Le	10/07/1933	16:18:01	Ge	02/16/1934	11:39:07	Ar
05/31/1933	16:05:57	Vi	10/10/1933	04:29:10	Cn	02/18/1934	17:03:21	Ta
06/02/1933	23:14:38	Li	10/12/1933	17:01:37	Le	02/21/1934	02:16:13	Ge
06/05/1933	02:24:45	Sc	10/15/1933	03:24:26	Vi	02/23/1934	14:22:22	Cn
06/07/1933	02:31:56	Sg	10/17/1933	10:07:21	Li	02/26/1934	03:13:15	Le
06/09/1933	01:32:41	Cp	10/19/1933	13:27:28	Sc	02/28/1934	14:45:59	Vi
06/11/1933	01:40:56	Aq	10/21/1933	14:53:58	Sg	03/03/1934	00:01:53	Li
06/13/1933	04:49:31	Pi	10/23/1933	16:13:18	Cp	03/05/1934	06:59:02	Sc
06/15/1933	11:50:24	Ar	10/25/1933	18:48:21	Aq	03/07/1934	11:58:11	Sg
06/17/1933	22:11:50	Ta	10/27/1933	23:17:10	Pi	03/09/1934	15:21:35	Cp
06/20/1933	10:25:27	Ge	10/30/1933	05:40:22	Ar	03/11/1934	17:35:43	Aq
06/22/1933	23:06:29	Cn	11/01/1933	13:52:37	Ta	03/13/1934	19:25:08	Pi
06/25/1933	11:16:48	Le	11/04/1933	00:01:44	Ge	03/15/1934	21:59:54	Ar
06/27/1933	22:00:56	Vi	11/06/1933	12:04:55	Cn	03/18/1934	02:45:56	Ta
06/30/1933	06:10:44	Li	11/09/1933	00:57:51	Le	03/20/1934	10:51:20	Ge
07/02/1933	10:56:35	Sc	11/11/1933	12:23:53	Vi	03/22/1934	22:12:39	Cn
07/04/1933	12:31:28	Sg	11/13/1933	20:12:29	Li	03/25/1934	11:02:42	Le
07/06/1933	12:15:10	Cp	11/15/1933	23:51:50	Sc	03/27/1934	22:44:28	Vi
07/08/1933	12:05:05	Aq	11/18/1933	00:34:30	Sg	03/30/1934	07:36:37	Li
07/10/1933	14:01:25	Pi	11/20/1933	00:23:31	Cp	04/01/1934	13:35:23	Sc
07/12/1933	19:30:57	Ar	11/22/1933	01:20:48	Aq	04/03/1934	17:36:50	Sg
07/15/1933	04:48:40	Ta	11/24/1933	04:49:37	Pi	04/05/1934	20:45:04	Cp
07/17/1933	16:44:10	Ge	11/26/1933	11:12:32	Ar	04/07/1934	23:42:37	Aq
07/20/1933	05:24:36	Cn	11/28/1933	20:02:57	Ta	04/10/1934	02:52:05	Pi

04/12/1934	06:39:51	Ar
04/14/1934	11:55:26	Ta
04/16/1934	19:41:08	Ge
04/19/1934	06:26:26	Cn
04/21/1934	19:09:57	Le
04/24/1934	07:19:42	Vi
04/26/1934	16:32:04	Li
04/28/1934	22:06:53	Sc
05/01/1934	01:01:51	Sg
05/03/1934	02:53:25	Cp
05/05/1934	05:05:51	Aq
05/07/1934	08:26:03	Pi
05/09/1934	13:08:32	Ar
05/11/1934	19:23:36	Ta
05/14/1934	03:37:54	Ge
05/16/1934	14:17:12	Cn
05/19/1934	02:54:53	Le
05/21/1934	15:35:17	Vi
05/24/1934	01:43:00	Li
05/26/1934	07:51:35	Sc
05/28/1934	10:28:23	Sg
05/30/1934	11:11:59	Cp
06/01/1934	11:55:05	Aq
06/03/1934	14:06:21	Pi
06/05/1934	18:31:23	Ar
06/08/1934	01:16:44	Ta
06/10/1934	10:13:32	Ge
06/12/1934	21:13:48	Cn
06/15/1934	09:52:36	Le
06/17/1934	22:51:16	Vi
06/20/1934	09:58:57	Li
06/22/1934	17:24:36	Sc
06/24/1934	20:49:22	Sg
06/26/1934	21:24:06	Cp
06/28/1934	21:02:09	Aq
06/30/1934	21:37:45	Pi
07/03/1934	00:38:42	Ar
07/05/1934	06:47:19	Ta
07/07/1934	15:55:14	Ge
07/10/1934	03:20:17	Cn
07/12/1934	16:07:08	Le
07/15/1934	05:06:58	Vi
07/17/1934	16:47:13	Li
07/20/1934	01:30:56	Sc
07/22/1934	06:27:40	Sg
07/24/1934	08:03:12	Cp
07/26/1934	07:43:16	Aq
07/28/1934	07:20:10	Pi
07/30/1934	08:45:31	Ar
08/01/1934	13:24:57	Ta
08/03/1934	21:48:13	Ge
08/06/1934	09:12:55	Cn
08/08/1934	22:07:41	Le
08/11/1934	10:58:47	Vi
08/13/1934	22:32:44	Li
08/16/1934	07:51:01	Sc
08/18/1934	14:11:34	Sg
08/20/1934	17:26:59	Cp

08/22/1934	18:18:04	Aq
08/24/1934	18:07:50	Pi
08/26/1934	18:43:44	Ar
08/28/1934	21:54:36	Ta
08/31/1934	04:55:09	Ge
09/02/1934	15:40:18	Cn
09/05/1934	04:31:43	Le
09/07/1934	17:16:07	Vi
09/10/1934	04:22:38	Li
09/12/1934	13:19:24	Sc
09/14/1934	20:03:19	Sg
09/17/1934	00:35:36	Cp
09/19/1934	03:06:18	Aq
09/21/1934	04:13:38	Pi
09/23/1934	05:13:01	Ar
09/25/1934	07:46:44	Ta
09/27/1934	13:33:10	Ge
09/29/1934	23:14:16	Cn
10/02/1934	11:44:12	Le
10/05/1934	00:30:38	Vi
10/07/1934	11:20:16	Li
10/09/1934	19:31:26	Sc
10/12/1934	01:31:56	Sg
10/14/1934	06:03:57	Cp
10/16/1934	09:31:56	Aq
10/18/1934	12:09:30	Pi
10/20/1934	14:28:05	Ar
10/22/1934	17:34:20	Ta
10/24/1934	22:57:35	Ge
10/27/1934	07:45:56	Cn
10/29/1934	19:42:11	Le
11/01/1934	08:35:59	Vi
11/03/1934	19:40:59	Li
11/06/1934	03:32:26	Sc
11/08/1934	08:32:55	Sg
11/10/1934	11:56:32	Cp
11/12/1934	14:51:47	Aq
11/14/1934	17:56:08	Pi
11/16/1934	21:26:05	Ar
11/19/1934	01:46:24	Ta
11/21/1934	07:47:04	Ge
11/23/1934	16:25:08	Cn
11/26/1934	03:54:01	Le
11/28/1934	16:51:44	Vi
12/01/1934	04:38:50	Li
12/03/1934	13:05:37	Sc
12/05/1934	17:52:29	Sg
12/07/1934	20:08:57	Cp
12/09/1934	21:33:40	Aq
12/11/1934	23:30:44	Pi
12/14/1934	02:51:03	Ar
12/16/1934	07:56:19	Ta
12/18/1934	14:58:04	Ge
12/21/1934	00:10:43	Cn
12/23/1934	11:37:23	Le
12/26/1934	00:31:59	Vi
12/28/1934	12:59:05	Li
12/30/1934	22:41:13	Sc

01/02/1935	04:26:47	Sg
01/04/1935	06:43:36	Cp
01/06/1935	07:03:44	Aq
01/08/1935	07:17:27	Pi
01/10/1935	09:02:41	Ar
01/12/1935	13:24:29	Ta
01/14/1935	20:42:42	Ge
01/17/1935	06:37:10	Cn
01/19/1935	18:26:56	Le
01/22/1935	07:19:22	Vi
01/24/1935	19:59:14	Li
01/27/1935	06:45:59	Sc
01/29/1935	14:10:33	Sg
01/31/1935	17:47:07	Cp
02/02/1935	18:25:43	Aq
02/04/1935	17:46:40	Pi
02/06/1935	17:48:48	Ar
02/08/1935	20:22:06	Ta
02/11/1935	02:35:12	Ge
02/13/1935	12:24:01	Cn
02/16/1935	00:35:01	Le
02/18/1935	13:33:03	Vi
02/21/1935	02:02:21	Li
02/23/1935	13:04:05	Sc
02/25/1935	21:40:05	Sg
02/28/1935	03:04:32	Cp
03/02/1935	05:16:05	Aq
03/04/1935	05:13:05	Pi
03/06/1935	04:40:23	Ar
03/08/1935	05:42:59	Ta
03/10/1935	10:11:10	Ge
03/12/1935	18:51:29	Cn
03/15/1935	06:47:51	Le
03/17/1935	19:51:19	Vi
03/20/1935	08:07:50	Li
03/22/1935	18:44:14	Sc
03/25/1935	03:23:34	Sg
03/27/1935	09:48:29	Cp
03/29/1935	13:41:21	Aq
03/31/1935	15:14:26	Pi
04/02/1935	15:31:09	Ar
04/04/1935	16:18:03	Ta
04/06/1935	19:35:05	Ge
04/09/1935	02:48:41	Cn
04/11/1935	13:51:57	Le
04/14/1935	02:46:33	Vi
04/16/1935	15:00:50	Li
04/19/1935	01:09:24	Sc
04/21/1935	09:05:55	Sg
04/23/1935	15:13:12	Cp
04/25/1935	19:43:19	Aq
04/27/1935	22:39:34	Pi
04/30/1935	00:26:18	Ar
05/02/1935	02:09:14	Ta
05/04/1935	05:25:59	Ge
05/06/1935	11:50:05	Cn
05/08/1935	21:54:56	Le
05/11/1935	10:25:39	Vi

05/13/1935	22:47:45	Li
05/16/1935	08:54:05	Sc
05/18/1935	16:12:40	Sg
05/20/1935	21:20:13	Cp
05/23/1935	01:08:22	Aq
05/25/1935	04:13:07	Pi
05/27/1935	06:58:34	Ar
05/29/1935	09:58:45	Ta
05/31/1935	14:10:49	Ge
06/02/1935	20:43:26	Cn
06/05/1935	06:19:17	Le
06/07/1935	18:25:33	Vi
06/10/1935	06:59:27	Li
06/12/1935	17:35:08	Sc
06/15/1935	00:56:50	Sg
06/17/1935	05:21:06	Cp
06/19/1935	07:55:41	Aq
06/21/1935	09:55:35	Pi
06/23/1935	12:20:56	Ar
06/25/1935	15:53:53	Ta
06/27/1935	21:06:07	Ge
06/30/1935	04:26:14	Cn
07/02/1935	14:12:44	Le
07/05/1935	02:08:19	Vi
07/07/1935	14:52:19	Li
07/10/1935	02:14:49	Sc
07/12/1935	10:27:13	Sg
07/14/1935	15:02:46	Cp
07/16/1935	16:53:14	Aq
07/18/1935	17:30:29	Pi
07/20/1935	18:32:34	Ar
07/22/1935	21:20:36	Ta
07/25/1935	02:41:41	Ge
07/27/1935	10:43:10	Cn
07/29/1935	21:03:38	Le
08/01/1935	09:06:32	Vi
08/03/1935	21:54:44	Li
08/06/1935	09:56:46	Sc
08/08/1935	19:24:41	Sg
08/11/1935	01:09:43	Cp
08/13/1935	03:21:32	Aq
08/15/1935	03:18:41	Pi
08/17/1935	02:54:51	Ar
08/19/1935	04:07:23	Ta
08/21/1935	08:25:16	Ge
08/23/1935	16:16:37	Cn
08/26/1935	03:00:18	Le
08/28/1935	15:20:20	Vi
08/31/1935	04:07:56	Li
09/02/1935	16:22:03	Sc
09/05/1935	02:48:15	Sg
09/07/1935	10:07:39	Cp
09/09/1935	13:43:55	Aq
09/11/1935	14:14:49	Pi
09/13/1935	13:20:25	Ar
09/15/1935	13:10:14	Ta
09/17/1935	15:47:51	Ge
09/19/1935	22:26:53	Cn

09/22/1935	08:49:51	Le
09/24/1935	21:18:28	Vi
09/27/1935	10:05:23	Li
09/29/1935	22:05:50	Sc
10/02/1935	08:40:49	Sg
10/04/1935	17:02:22	Cp
10/06/1935	22:20:25	Aq
10/09/1935	00:26:34	Pi
10/11/1935	00:20:04	Ar
10/12/1935	23:53:11	Ta
10/15/1935	01:17:19	Ge
10/17/1935	06:20:47	Cn
10/19/1935	15:35:07	Le
10/22/1935	03:44:05	Vi
10/24/1935	16:31:19	Li
10/27/1935	04:14:32	Sc
10/29/1935	14:17:19	Sg
10/31/1935	22:31:00	Cp
11/03/1935	04:38:05	Aq
11/05/1935	08:20:08	Pi
11/07/1935	09:53:48	Ar
11/09/1935	10:28:37	Ta
11/11/1935	11:52:09	Ge
11/13/1935	15:56:25	Cn
11/15/1935	23:50:35	Le
11/18/1935	11:10:03	Vi
11/20/1935	23:52:05	Li
11/23/1935	11:35:53	Sc
11/25/1935	21:08:26	Sg
11/28/1935	04:28:09	Cp
11/30/1935	09:59:48	Aq
12/02/1935	14:02:38	Pi
12/04/1935	16:52:42	Ar
12/06/1935	19:03:17	Ta
12/08/1935	21:36:27	Ge
12/11/1935	01:53:42	Cn
12/13/1935	09:06:37	Le
12/15/1935	19:32:33	Vi
12/18/1935	07:58:15	Li
12/20/1935	20:02:31	Sc
12/23/1935	05:44:30	Sg
12/25/1935	12:27:23	Cp
12/27/1935	16:45:43	Aq
12/29/1935	19:41:55	Pi
12/31/1935	22:15:13	Ar
01/03/1936	01:10:50	Ta
01/05/1936	05:03:52	Ge
01/07/1936	10:28:49	Cn
01/09/1936	18:01:55	Le
01/12/1936	04:04:52	Vi
01/14/1936	16:10:24	Li
01/17/1936	04:38:17	Sc
01/19/1936	15:11:08	Sg
01/21/1936	22:18:27	Cp
01/24/1936	02:02:06	Aq
01/26/1936	03:34:38	Pi
01/28/1936	04:35:45	Ar
01/30/1936	06:37:11	Ta

02/01/1936	10:38:31	Ge
02/03/1936	16:57:56	Cn
02/06/1936	01:25:53	Le
02/08/1936	11:48:03	Vi
02/10/1936	23:45:22	Li
02/13/1936	12:24:14	Sc
02/15/1936	23:56:07	Sg
02/18/1936	08:21:04	Cp
02/20/1936	12:46:26	Aq
02/22/1936	13:55:17	Pi
02/24/1936	13:34:44	Ar
02/26/1936	13:50:46	Ta
02/28/1936	16:30:03	Ge
03/01/1936	22:25:19	Cn
03/04/1936	07:20:16	Le
03/06/1936	18:17:48	Vi
03/09/1936	06:25:50	Li
03/11/1936	19:03:16	Sc
03/14/1936	07:05:47	Sg
03/16/1936	16:51:25	Cp
03/18/1936	22:52:01	Aq
03/21/1936	00:58:53	Pi
03/23/1936	00:31:14	Ar
03/24/1936	23:37:19	Ta
03/27/1936	00:31:08	Ge
03/29/1936	04:51:51	Cn
03/31/1936	13:03:29	Le
04/03/1936	00:07:13	Vi
04/05/1936	12:30:47	Li
04/08/1936	01:05:01	Sc
04/10/1936	13:02:35	Sg
04/12/1936	23:22:49	Cp
04/15/1936	06:48:57	Aq
04/17/1936	10:37:26	Pi
04/19/1936	11:20:19	Ar
04/21/1936	10:37:03	Ta
04/23/1936	10:37:20	Ge
04/25/1936	13:22:30	Cn
04/27/1936	20:03:09	Le
04/30/1936	06:21:56	Vi
05/02/1936	18:42:37	Li
05/05/1936	07:16:26	Sc
05/07/1936	18:54:01	Sg
05/10/1936	04:56:38	Cp
05/12/1936	12:47:11	Aq
05/14/1936	17:52:16	Pi
05/16/1936	20:13:41	Ar
05/18/1936	20:47:26	Ta
05/20/1936	21:11:51	Ge
05/22/1936	23:19:12	Cn
05/25/1936	04:41:14	Le
05/27/1936	13:47:35	Vi
05/30/1936	01:38:07	Li
06/01/1936	14:11:07	Sc
06/04/1936	01:37:07	Sg
06/06/1936	11:02:34	Cp
06/08/1936	18:17:12	Aq
06/10/1936	23:26:59	Pi

06/13/1936	02:46:29	Ar	10/23/1936	12:59:56	Aq	03/04/1937	04:07:57	Sg
06/15/1936	04:48:07	Ta	10/25/1936	18:27:45	Pi	03/06/1937	16:22:40	Cp
06/17/1936	06:29:27	Ge	10/27/1936	20:09:22	Ar	03/09/1937	01:35:28	Aq
06/19/1936	09:08:27	Cn	10/29/1936	19:34:04	Ta	03/11/1937	06:49:47	Pi
06/21/1936	14:05:54	Le	10/31/1936	18:49:07	Ge	03/13/1937	08:59:45	Ar
06/23/1936	22:15:20	Vi	11/02/1936	20:00:09	Cn	03/15/1937	09:53:46	Ta
06/26/1936	09:23:25	Li	11/05/1936	00:36:41	Le	03/17/1937	11:18:43	Ge
06/28/1936	21:52:26	Sc	11/07/1936	08:59:39	Vi	03/19/1937	14:25:03	Cn
07/01/1936	09:27:02	Sg	11/09/1936	20:14:41	Li	03/21/1937	19:35:23	Le
07/03/1936	18:34:00	Cp	11/12/1936	08:51:42	Sc	03/24/1937	02:43:38	Vi
07/06/1936	00:56:17	Aq	11/14/1936	21:33:19	Sg	03/26/1937	11:46:58	Li
07/08/1936	05:10:08	Pi	11/17/1936	09:20:15	Cp	03/28/1937	22:50:49	Sc
07/10/1936	08:09:52	Ar	11/19/1936	19:10:43	Aq	03/31/1937	11:32:11	Sg
07/12/1936	10:45:37	Ta	11/22/1936	02:03:59	Pi	04/03/1937	00:16:20	Cp
07/14/1936	13:38:27	Ge	11/24/1936	05:36:41	Ar	04/05/1937	10:38:29	Aq
07/16/1936	17:27:31	Cn	11/26/1936	06:28:38	Ta	04/07/1937	16:59:18	Pi
07/18/1936	22:57:38	Le	11/28/1936	06:11:28	Ge	04/09/1937	19:28:17	Ar
07/21/1936	06:53:31	Vi	11/30/1936	06:40:00	Cn	04/11/1937	19:39:10	Ta
07/23/1936	17:30:29	Li	12/02/1936	09:43:12	Le	04/13/1937	19:34:19	Ge
07/26/1936	05:53:52	Sc	12/04/1936	16:30:31	Vi	04/15/1937	21:02:28	Cn
07/28/1936	17:55:30	Sg	12/07/1936	02:55:17	Li	04/18/1937	01:11:20	Le
07/31/1936	03:23:50	Cp	12/09/1936	15:27:46	Sc	04/20/1937	08:15:40	Vi
08/02/1936	09:25:08	Aq	12/12/1936	04:07:02	Sg	04/22/1937	17:50:46	Li
08/04/1936	12:35:50	Pi	12/14/1936	15:25:13	Cp	04/25/1937	05:20:34	Sc
08/06/1936	14:21:13	Ar	12/17/1936	00:42:06	Aq	04/27/1937	18:04:49	Sg
08/08/1936	16:11:26	Ta	12/19/1936	07:43:27	Pi	04/30/1937	06:56:20	Cp
08/10/1936	19:11:42	Ge	12/21/1936	12:26:22	Ar	05/02/1937	18:08:25	Aq
08/12/1936	23:51:57	Cn	12/23/1936	15:05:25	Ta	05/05/1937	01:56:58	Pi
08/15/1936	06:19:55	Le	12/25/1936	16:24:09	Ge	05/07/1937	05:47:13	Ar
08/17/1936	14:44:25	Vi	12/27/1936	17:36:09	Cn	05/09/1937	06:31:36	Ta
08/20/1936	01:16:42	Li	12/29/1936	20:13:50	Le	05/11/1937	05:56:07	Ge
08/22/1936	13:35:58	Sc	01/01/1937	01:45:24	Vi	05/13/1937	06:00:07	Cn
08/25/1936	02:09:24	Sg	01/03/1937	10:55:02	Li	05/15/1937	08:27:07	Le
08/27/1936	12:34:50	Cp	01/05/1937	22:57:47	Sc	05/17/1937	14:18:36	Vi
08/29/1936	19:12:08	Aq	01/08/1937	11:42:44	Sg	05/19/1937	23:34:23	Li
08/31/1936	22:53:10	Pi	01/10/1937	07:43:27	Cp	05/22/1937	11:18:02	Sc
09/02/1936	22:43:01	Ar	01/13/1937	07:24:39	Aq	05/25/1937	00:10:01	Sg
09/04/1936	23:03:55	Ta	01/15/1937	13:28:13	Pi	05/27/1937	12:53:10	Cp
09/07/1936	00:54:22	Ge	01/17/1937	17:48:14	Ar	05/30/1937	00:12:58	Aq
09/09/1936	05:15:37	Cn	01/19/1937	21:06:47	Ta	06/01/1937	08:57:31	Pi
09/11/1936	12:12:57	Le	01/21/1937	23:53:30	Ge	06/03/1937	14:21:52	Ar
09/13/1936	21:19:34	Vi	01/24/1937	02:37:59	Cn	06/05/1937	16:35:56	Ta
09/16/1936	08:12:14	Li	01/26/1937	06:07:38	Le	06/07/1937	16:45:30	Ge
09/18/1936	20:32:05	Sc	01/28/1937	11:30:18	Vi	06/09/1937	16:31:13	Cn
09/21/1936	09:24:16	Sg	01/30/1937	19:49:03	Li	06/11/1937	17:44:17	Le
09/23/1936	20:52:56	Cp	02/02/1937	07:10:17	Sc	06/13/1937	22:00:58	Vi
09/26/1936	04:52:59	Aq	02/04/1937	19:58:46	Sg	06/16/1937	06:07:58	Li
09/28/1936	08:38:58	Pi	02/07/1937	07:33:47	Cp	06/18/1937	17:30:45	Sc
09/30/1936	09:09:40	Ar	02/09/1937	16:00:00	Aq	06/21/1937	06:25:19	Sg
10/02/1936	08:25:07	Ta	02/11/1937	21:09:42	Pi	06/23/1937	18:58:01	Cp
10/04/1936	08:46:47	Ge	02/14/1937	00:11:55	Ar	06/26/1937	05:53:50	Aq
10/06/1936	11:28:39	Cn	02/16/1937	02:34:27	Ta	06/28/1937	14:36:34	Pi
10/08/1936	17:44:44	Le	02/18/1937	05:22:04	Ge	06/30/1937	20:50:09	Ar
10/11/1936	03:01:09	Vi	02/20/1937	09:03:53	Cn	07/03/1937	00:34:17	Ta
10/13/1936	14:19:00	Li	02/22/1937	13:50:36	Le	07/05/1937	02:15:05	Ge
10/16/1936	02:46:33	Sc	02/24/1937	20:04:20	Vi	07/07/1937	02:53:12	Cn
10/18/1936	15:37:33	Sg	02/27/1937	04:26:12	Li	07/09/1937	03:58:59	Le
10/21/1936	03:37:19	Cp	03/01/1937	15:22:48	Sc	07/11/1937	07:15:21	Vi

07/13/1937	14:04:05	Li	11/22/1937	15:54:48	Le	04/04/1938	07:33:19	Ge
07/16/1937	00:35:58	Sc	11/24/1937	19:55:30	Vi	04/06/1938	10:07:25	Cn
07/18/1937	13:20:01	Sg	11/27/1937	03:21:30	Li	04/08/1938	13:04:06	Le
07/21/1937	01:50:15	Cp	11/29/1937	13:46:05	Sc	04/10/1938	16:50:52	Vi
07/23/1937	12:19:44	Aq	12/02/1937	02:05:07	Sg	04/12/1938	22:01:48	Li
07/25/1937	20:20:54	Pi	12/04/1937	15:07:20	Cp	04/15/1938	05:21:02	Sc
07/28/1937	02:15:06	Ar	12/07/1937	03:40:04	Aq	04/17/1938	15:19:11	Sg
07/30/1937	06:31:07	Ta	12/09/1937	14:21:15	Pi	04/20/1938	03:31:07	Cp
08/01/1937	09:29:06	Ge	12/11/1937	21:54:43	Ar	04/22/1938	16:10:32	Aq
08/03/1937	11:33:48	Cn	12/14/1937	01:49:38	Ta	04/25/1938	02:53:10	Pi
08/05/1937	13:35:17	Le	12/16/1937	02:42:12	Ge	04/27/1938	10:08:17	Ar
08/07/1937	16:53:50	Vi	12/18/1937	02:02:40	Cn	04/29/1938	14:01:29	Ta
08/09/1937	22:58:09	Li	12/20/1937	01:48:16	Le	05/01/1938	15:44:44	Ge
08/12/1937	08:36:34	Sc	12/22/1937	03:56:58	Vi	05/03/1938	16:50:30	Cn
08/14/1937	20:58:49	Sg	12/24/1937	09:52:56	Li	05/05/1938	18:41:44	Le
08/17/1937	09:37:14	Cp	12/26/1937	19:44:29	Sc	05/07/1938	22:16:45	Vi
08/19/1937	20:04:52	Aq	12/29/1937	08:11:31	Sg	05/10/1938	04:05:31	Li
08/22/1937	03:28:16	Pi	12/31/1937	21:16:38	Cp	05/12/1938	12:15:48	Sc
08/24/1937	08:23:09	Ar	01/03/1938	09:31:03	Aq	05/14/1938	22:40:25	Sg
08/26/1937	11:56:40	Ta	01/05/1938	20:06:28	Pi	05/17/1938	10:50:49	Cp
08/28/1937	15:01:23	Ge	01/08/1938	04:28:37	Ar	05/19/1938	23:37:25	Aq
08/30/1937	18:03:11	Cn	01/10/1938	10:05:45	Ta	05/22/1938	11:08:13	Pi
09/01/1937	21:21:01	Le	01/12/1938	12:49:55	Ge	05/24/1938	19:35:21	Ar
09/04/1937	01:34:22	Vi	01/14/1938	13:21:16	Cn	05/27/1938	00:16:50	Ta
09/06/1937	07:48:01	Li	01/16/1938	13:09:10	Le	05/29/1938	01:51:52	Ge
09/08/1937	16:59:15	Sc	01/18/1938	14:12:32	Vi	05/31/1938	01:52:25	Cn
09/11/1937	04:58:52	Sg	01/20/1938	18:27:05	Li	06/02/1938	02:08:33	Le
09/13/1937	17:51:25	Cp	01/23/1938	02:54:48	Sc	06/04/1938	04:21:03	Vi
09/16/1937	04:50:58	Aq	01/25/1938	14:51:11	Sg	06/06/1938	09:35:18	Li
09/18/1937	12:19:00	Pi	01/28/1938	03:57:53	Cp	06/08/1938	18:01:03	Sc
09/20/1937	16:30:44	Ar	01/30/1938	15:59:49	Aq	06/11/1938	04:57:06	Sg
09/22/1937	18:49:13	Ta	02/02/1938	01:58:16	Pi	06/13/1938	17:20:40	Cp
09/24/1937	20:45:50	Ge	02/04/1938	09:54:17	Ar	06/16/1938	06:07:09	Aq
09/26/1937	23:24:18	Cn	02/06/1938	15:58:17	Ta	06/18/1938	18:02:28	Pi
09/29/1937	03:13:55	Le	02/08/1938	20:07:31	Ge	06/21/1938	03:39:31	Ar
10/01/1937	08:28:34	Vi	02/10/1938	22:25:34	Cn	06/23/1938	09:49:31	Ta
10/03/1937	15:31:25	Li	02/12/1938	23:33:15	Le	06/25/1938	12:24:43	Ge
10/06/1937	00:54:46	Sc	02/15/1938	00:56:56	Vi	06/27/1938	12:27:06	Cn
10/08/1937	12:43:41	Sg	02/17/1938	04:27:43	Li	06/29/1938	11:45:19	Le
10/11/1937	01:46:32	Cp	02/19/1938	11:36:51	Sc	07/01/1938	12:23:38	Vi
10/13/1937	13:37:11	Aq	02/21/1938	22:33:26	Sg	07/03/1938	16:08:42	Li
10/15/1937	22:03:12	Pi	02/24/1938	11:27:58	Cp	07/05/1938	23:48:30	Sc
10/18/1937	02:32:26	Ar	02/26/1938	23:35:44	Aq	07/08/1938	10:45:14	Sg
10/20/1937	04:09:18	Ta	03/01/1938	09:13:22	Pi	07/10/1938	23:21:46	Cp
10/22/1937	04:39:53	Ge	03/03/1938	16:16:14	Ar	07/13/1938	12:05:20	Aq
10/24/1937	05:46:33	Cn	03/05/1938	21:29:16	Ta	07/15/1938	23:55:23	Pi
10/26/1937	08:42:21	Le	03/08/1938	01:33:05	Ge	07/18/1938	10:02:27	Ar
10/28/1937	14:01:28	Vi	03/10/1938	04:45:47	Cn	07/20/1938	17:30:57	Ta
10/30/1937	21:46:55	Li	03/12/1938	07:22:43	Le	07/22/1938	21:42:44	Ge
11/02/1937	07:48:14	Sc	03/14/1938	10:05:19	Vi	07/24/1938	22:54:26	Cn
11/04/1937	19:45:52	Sg	03/16/1938	14:08:04	Li	07/26/1938	22:25:38	Le
11/07/1937	08:49:55	Cp	03/18/1938	20:53:25	Sc	07/28/1938	22:16:43	Vi
11/09/1937	21:18:46	Aq	03/21/1938	07:00:52	Sg	07/31/1938	00:34:42	Li
11/12/1937	07:07:07	Pi	03/23/1938	19:31:39	Cp	08/02/1938	06:49:20	Sc
11/14/1937	12:59:22	Ar	03/26/1938	07:55:56	Aq	08/04/1938	17:01:34	Sg
11/16/1937	15:11:35	Ta	03/28/1938	17:51:40	Pi	08/07/1938	05:33:11	Cp
11/18/1937	15:09:36	Ge	03/31/1938	00:33:16	Ar	08/09/1938	18:14:49	Aq
11/20/1937	14:47:11	Cn	04/02/1938	04:42:42	Ta	08/12/1938	05:44:48	Pi

08/14/1938	15:34:10	Ar	12/24/1938	07:58:46	Aq	05/04/1939	23:10:43	Sg
08/16/1938	23:25:12	Ta	12/26/1938	20:40:55	Pi	05/07/1939	07:33:35	Cp
08/19/1938	04:51:01	Ge	12/29/1938	08:14:10	Ar	05/09/1939	18:40:59	Aq
08/21/1938	07:39:22	Cn	12/31/1938	16:47:24	Ta	05/12/1939	07:09:04	Pi
08/23/1938	08:26:40	Le	01/02/1939	21:19:18	Ge	05/14/1939	18:40:49	Ar
08/25/1938	08:42:33	Vi	01/04/1939	22:20:00	Cn	05/17/1939	03:27:59	Ta
08/27/1938	10:25:58	Li	01/06/1939	21:32:04	Le	05/19/1939	09:06:22	Ge
08/29/1938	15:25:56	Sc	01/08/1939	21:07:51	Vi	05/21/1939	12:22:37	Cn
09/01/1938	00:27:53	Sg	01/10/1939	23:10:30	Li	05/23/1939	14:33:10	Le
09/03/1938	12:29:43	Cp	01/13/1939	04:53:46	Sc	05/25/1939	16:50:35	Vi
09/06/1938	01:10:20	Aq	01/15/1939	14:09:32	Sg	05/27/1939	20:05:42	Li
09/08/1938	12:28:19	Pi	01/18/1939	01:43:27	Cp	05/30/1939	00:47:14	Sc
09/10/1938	21:40:10	Ar	01/20/1939	14:14:53	Aq	06/01/1939	07:14:59	Sg
09/13/1938	04:53:57	Ta	01/23/1939	02:51:02	Pi	06/03/1939	15:49:55	Cp
09/15/1938	10:22:45	Ge	01/25/1939	14:41:51	Ar	06/06/1939	02:40:18	Aq
09/17/1938	14:09:08	Cn	01/28/1939	00:28:55	Ta	06/08/1939	15:04:30	Pi
09/19/1938	16:25:53	Le	01/30/1939	06:50:02	Ge	06/11/1939	03:10:08	Ar
09/21/1938	18:00:53	Vi	02/01/1939	09:21:44	Cn	06/13/1939	12:42:37	Ta
09/23/1938	20:18:39	Li	02/03/1939	09:05:42	Le	06/15/1939	18:32:04	Ge
09/26/1938	00:56:32	Sc	02/05/1939	08:02:20	Vi	06/17/1939	21:06:19	Cn
09/28/1938	09:01:53	Sg	02/07/1939	08:29:29	Li	06/19/1939	21:57:48	Le
09/30/1938	20:20:08	Cp	02/09/1939	12:21:51	Sc	06/21/1939	22:56:06	Vi
10/03/1938	08:57:32	Aq	02/11/1939	20:23:42	Sg	06/24/1939	01:30:22	Li
10/05/1938	20:26:54	Pi	02/14/1939	07:41:12	Cp	06/26/1939	06:24:58	Sc
10/08/1938	05:22:23	Ar	02/16/1939	20:21:42	Aq	06/28/1939	13:39:02	Sg
10/10/1938	11:42:34	Ta	02/19/1939	08:51:47	Pi	06/30/1939	22:53:23	Cp
10/12/1938	16:10:05	Ge	02/21/1939	20:23:06	Ar	07/03/1939	09:54:00	Aq
10/14/1938	19:30:45	Cn	02/24/1939	06:18:47	Ta	07/05/1939	22:17:06	Pi
10/16/1938	22:19:27	Le	02/26/1939	13:47:07	Ge	07/08/1939	10:49:48	Ar
10/19/1938	01:08:45	Vi	02/28/1939	18:06:26	Cn	07/10/1939	21:26:42	Ta
10/21/1938	04:42:51	Li	03/02/1939	19:29:55	Le	07/13/1939	04:20:23	Ge
10/23/1938	09:59:53	Sc	03/04/1939	19:16:34	Vi	07/15/1939	07:15:40	Cn
10/25/1938	17:54:00	Sg	03/06/1939	19:25:31	Li	07/17/1939	07:30:15	Le
10/28/1938	04:38:31	Cp	03/08/1939	21:59:32	Sc	07/19/1939	07:07:27	Vi
10/30/1938	17:08:20	Aq	03/11/1939	04:22:59	Sg	07/21/1939	08:10:14	Li
11/02/1938	05:09:00	Pi	03/13/1939	14:35:20	Cp	07/23/1939	12:03:57	Sc
11/04/1938	14:34:41	Ar	03/16/1939	03:01:04	Aq	07/25/1939	19:09:33	Sg
11/06/1938	20:40:37	Ta	03/18/1939	15:31:22	Pi	07/28/1939	04:50:35	Cp
11/09/1938	00:03:16	Ge	03/21/1939	02:40:40	Ar	07/30/1939	16:14:36	Aq
11/11/1938	01:59:22	Cn	03/23/1939	11:58:19	Ta	08/02/1939	04:41:23	Pi
11/13/1938	03:49:37	Le	03/25/1939	19:14:31	Ge	08/04/1939	17:22:11	Ar
11/15/1938	06:37:46	Vi	03/28/1939	00:19:06	Cn	08/07/1939	04:47:12	Ta
11/17/1938	11:03:07	Li	03/30/1939	03:14:35	Le	08/09/1939	13:05:59	Ge
11/19/1938	17:25:33	Sc	04/01/1939	04:38:51	Vi	08/11/1939	17:20:52	Cn
11/22/1938	01:56:19	Sg	04/03/1939	05:48:28	Li	08/13/1939	18:09:08	Le
11/24/1938	12:37:28	Cp	04/05/1939	08:21:25	Sc	08/15/1939	17:19:07	Vi
11/27/1938	00:58:25	Aq	04/07/1939	13:47:16	Sg	08/17/1939	17:03:30	Li
11/29/1938	13:29:47	Pi	04/09/1939	22:46:37	Cp	08/19/1939	19:19:51	Sc
12/02/1938	00:02:15	Ar	04/12/1939	10:33:24	Aq	08/22/1939	01:13:32	Sg
12/04/1938	07:00:32	Ta	04/14/1939	23:04:25	Pi	08/24/1939	10:33:22	Cp
12/06/1938	10:18:18	Ge	04/17/1939	10:13:06	Ar	08/26/1939	22:08:57	Aq
12/08/1938	11:07:28	Cn	04/19/1939	18:56:33	Ta	08/29/1939	10:42:18	Pi
12/10/1938	11:17:15	Le	04/22/1939	01:16:07	Ge	08/31/1939	23:14:46	Ar
12/12/1938	12:37:19	Vi	04/24/1939	05:43:19	Cn	09/03/1939	10:47:11	Ta
12/14/1938	16:27:08	Li	04/26/1939	08:54:36	Le	09/05/1939	20:01:49	Ge
12/16/1938	23:12:56	Sc	04/28/1939	11:26:25	Vi	09/08/1939	01:51:47	Cn
12/19/1938	08:30:47	Sg	04/30/1939	14:01:52	Li	09/10/1939	04:11:25	Le
12/21/1938	19:38:36	Cp	05/02/1939	17:36:02	Sc	09/12/1939	04:09:04	Vi

09/14/1939	03:38:34	Li
09/16/1939	04:43:19	Sc
09/18/1939	09:01:45	Sg
09/20/1939	17:10:36	Cp
09/23/1939	04:23:52	Aq
09/25/1939	16:59:52	Pi
09/28/1939	05:22:02	Ar
09/30/1939	16:28:27	Ta
10/03/1939	01:37:57	Ge
10/05/1939	08:16:24	Cn
10/07/1939	12:09:46	Le
10/09/1939	13:45:32	Vi
10/11/1939	14:15:19	Li
10/13/1939	15:18:10	Sc
10/15/1939	18:36:00	Sg
10/18/1939	01:21:45	Cp
10/20/1939	11:39:35	Aq
10/23/1939	00:05:07	Pi
10/25/1939	12:28:06	Ar
10/27/1939	23:08:55	Ta
10/30/1939	07:30:57	Ge
11/01/1939	13:41:06	Cn
11/03/1939	18:01:07	Le
11/05/1939	20:56:42	Vi
11/07/1939	23:03:00	Li
11/10/1939	01:13:40	Sc
11/12/1939	04:41:16	Sg
11/14/1939	10:42:01	Cp
11/16/1939	20:00:04	Aq
11/19/1939	07:59:56	Pi
11/21/1939	20:35:34	Ar
11/24/1939	07:22:37	Ta
11/26/1939	15:08:56	Ge
11/28/1939	20:11:21	Cn
11/30/1939	23:33:53	Le
12/03/1939	02:22:46	Vi
12/05/1939	05:22:17	Li
12/07/1939	08:56:55	Sc
12/09/1939	13:32:07	Sg
12/11/1939	19:51:02	Cp
12/14/1939	04:42:21	Aq
12/16/1939	16:14:01	Pi
12/19/1939	05:02:41	Ar
12/21/1939	16:31:52	Ta
12/24/1939	00:37:03	Ge
12/26/1939	05:03:01	Cn
12/28/1939	07:04:55	Le
12/30/1939	08:28:40	Vi
01/01/1940	10:43:29	Li
01/03/1940	14:35:49	Sc
01/05/1940	20:12:07	Sg
01/08/1940	03:29:33	Cp
01/10/1940	12:41:46	Aq
01/13/1940	00:03:01	Pi
01/15/1940	12:55:30	Ar
01/18/1940	01:15:26	Ta
01/20/1940	10:31:44	Ge
01/22/1940	15:34:49	Cn

01/24/1940	17:10:26	Le
01/26/1940	17:11:52	Vi
01/28/1940	17:42:46	Li
01/30/1940	20:17:18	Sc
02/02/1940	01:35:43	Sg
02/04/1940	09:26:51	Cp
02/06/1940	19:21:19	Aq
02/09/1940	06:58:19	Pi
02/11/1940	19:49:13	Ar
02/14/1940	08:35:53	Ta
02/16/1940	19:09:40	Ge
02/19/1940	01:46:25	Cn
02/21/1940	04:18:57	Le
02/23/1940	04:11:26	Vi
02/25/1940	03:28:44	Li
02/27/1940	04:13:26	Sc
02/29/1940	07:54:26	Sg
03/02/1940	15:02:23	Cp
03/05/1940	01:07:10	Aq
03/07/1940	13:07:11	Pi
03/10/1940	02:00:55	Ar
03/12/1940	14:44:10	Ta
03/15/1940	01:52:35	Ge
03/17/1940	09:56:56	Cn
03/19/1940	14:14:48	Le
03/21/1940	15:20:25	Vi
03/23/1940	14:47:19	Li
03/25/1940	14:33:14	Sc
03/27/1940	16:30:54	Sg
03/29/1940	21:59:28	Cp
04/01/1940	07:13:16	Aq
04/03/1940	19:10:51	Pi
04/06/1940	08:09:58	Ar
04/08/1940	20:38:32	Ta
04/11/1940	07:32:07	Ge
04/13/1940	16:03:54	Cn
04/15/1940	21:43:44	Le
04/18/1940	00:34:28	Vi
04/20/1940	01:22:51	Li
04/22/1940	01:32:46	Sc
04/24/1940	02:48:05	Sg
04/26/1940	06:49:34	Cp
04/28/1940	14:38:54	Aq
05/01/1940	01:55:53	Pi
05/03/1940	14:51:43	Ar
05/06/1940	03:12:25	Ta
05/08/1940	13:33:31	Ge
05/10/1940	21:33:23	Cn
05/13/1940	03:22:27	Le
05/15/1940	07:17:30	Vi
05/17/1940	09:40:26	Li
05/19/1940	11:11:45	Sc
05/21/1940	12:59:52	Sg
05/23/1940	16:34:31	Cp
05/25/1940	23:18:52	Aq
05/28/1940	09:39:06	Pi
05/30/1940	22:18:16	Ar
06/02/1940	10:43:36	Ta

06/04/1940	20:49:07	Ge
06/07/1940	04:01:57	Cn
06/09/1940	09:00:23	Le
06/11/1940	12:40:45	Vi
06/13/1940	15:43:23	Li
06/15/1940	18:31:29	Sc
06/17/1940	21:33:48	Sg
06/20/1940	01:44:16	Cp
06/22/1940	08:15:00	Aq
06/24/1940	17:55:27	Pi
06/27/1940	06:13:00	Ar
06/29/1940	18:52:11	Ta
07/02/1940	05:15:07	Ge
07/04/1940	12:10:28	Cn
07/06/1940	16:12:06	Le
07/08/1940	18:44:12	Vi
07/10/1940	21:06:35	Li
07/13/1940	00:06:54	Sc
07/15/1940	04:04:34	Sg
07/17/1940	09:17:26	Cp
07/19/1940	16:21:52	Aq
07/22/1940	01:58:06	Pi
07/24/1940	14:01:31	Ar
07/27/1940	02:56:03	Ta
07/29/1940	14:03:46	Ge
07/31/1940	21:32:01	Cn
08/03/1940	01:20:01	Le
08/05/1940	02:50:23	Vi
08/07/1940	03:49:34	Li
08/09/1940	05:45:40	Sc
08/11/1940	09:28:52	Sg
08/13/1940	15:15:02	Cp
08/15/1940	23:07:05	Aq
08/18/1940	09:09:49	Pi
08/20/1940	21:13:47	Ar
08/23/1940	10:16:53	Ta
08/25/1940	22:12:55	Ge
08/28/1940	06:53:19	Cn
08/30/1940	11:31:05	Le
09/01/1940	12:56:35	Vi
09/03/1940	12:54:05	Li
09/05/1940	13:16:27	Sc
09/07/1940	15:35:59	Sg
09/09/1940	20:45:26	Cp
09/12/1940	04:51:13	Aq
09/14/1940	15:25:09	Pi
09/17/1940	03:42:58	Ar
09/19/1940	16:45:24	Ta
09/22/1940	05:05:13	Ge
09/24/1940	14:57:24	Cn
09/26/1940	21:08:56	Le
09/28/1940	23:41:27	Vi
09/30/1940	23:46:21	Li
10/02/1940	23:12:04	Sc
10/04/1940	23:53:51	Sg
10/07/1940	03:28:22	Cp
10/09/1940	10:43:44	Aq
10/11/1940	21:17:32	Pi

10/14/1940	09:49:58	Ar		02/23/1941	05:01:30	Aq		07/05/1941	16:13:08	Sg
10/16/1940	22:49:01	Ta		02/25/1941	13:18:08	Pi		07/07/1941	17:20:30	Cp
10/19/1940	10:59:18	Ge		02/27/1941	23:54:11	Ar		07/09/1941	19:35:43	Aq
10/21/1940	21:17:58	Cn		03/02/1941	12:23:14	Ta		07/12/1941	00:41:50	Pi
10/24/1940	04:50:36	Le		03/05/1941	01:11:57	Ge		07/14/1941	09:34:32	Ar
10/26/1940	09:09:30	Vi		03/07/1941	12:03:35	Cn		07/16/1941	21:29:36	Ta
10/28/1940	10:36:31	Li		03/09/1941	19:18:45	Le		07/19/1941	10:09:27	Ge
10/30/1940	10:24:37	Sc		03/11/1941	22:51:10	Vi		07/21/1941	21:15:02	Cn
11/01/1940	10:20:48	Sg		03/13/1941	23:51:23	Li		07/24/1941	05:47:47	Le
11/03/1940	12:22:22	Cp		03/16/1941	00:02:43	Sc		07/26/1941	12:03:16	Vi
11/05/1940	18:03:05	Aq		03/18/1941	01:07:33	Sg		07/28/1941	16:40:29	Li
11/08/1940	03:45:35	Pi		03/20/1941	04:24:54	Cp		07/30/1941	20:08:45	Sc
11/10/1940	16:13:01	Ar		03/22/1941	10:33:53	Aq		08/01/1941	22:49:26	Sg
11/13/1940	05:12:40	Ta		03/24/1941	19:29:58	Pi		08/04/1941	01:16:56	Cp
11/15/1940	17:00:14	Ge		03/27/1941	06:39:11	Ar		08/06/1941	04:31:49	Aq
11/18/1940	02:52:15	Cn		03/29/1941	19:13:27	Ta		08/08/1941	09:50:43	Pi
11/20/1940	10:38:22	Le		04/01/1941	08:06:21	Ge		08/10/1941	18:12:45	Ar
11/22/1940	16:10:33	Vi		04/03/1941	19:43:34	Cn		08/13/1941	05:32:00	Ta
11/24/1940	19:24:33	Li		04/06/1941	04:25:40	Le		08/15/1941	18:09:19	Ge
11/26/1940	20:44:25	Sc		04/08/1941	09:20:57	Vi		08/18/1941	05:37:21	Cn
11/28/1940	21:18:09	Sg		04/10/1941	10:54:16	Li		08/20/1941	14:15:13	Le
11/30/1940	22:50:06	Cp		04/12/1941	10:31:23	Sc		08/22/1941	19:52:42	Vi
12/03/1940	03:12:25	Aq		04/14/1941	10:07:26	Sg		08/24/1941	23:21:09	Li
12/05/1940	11:35:04	Pi		04/16/1941	11:38:29	Cp		08/27/1941	01:48:25	Sc
12/07/1940	23:26:08	Ar		04/18/1941	16:30:49	Aq		08/29/1941	04:12:44	Sg
12/10/1940	12:27:05	Ta		04/21/1941	01:06:51	Pi		08/31/1941	07:17:32	Cp
12/13/1940	00:07:33	Ge		04/23/1941	12:34:14	Ar		09/02/1941	11:38:34	Aq
12/15/1940	09:19:35	Cn		04/26/1941	01:22:29	Ta		09/04/1941	17:51:42	Pi
12/17/1940	16:16:11	Le		04/28/1941	14:10:50	Ge		09/07/1941	02:28:17	Ar
12/19/1940	21:34:43	Vi		05/01/1941	01:55:50	Cn		09/09/1941	13:31:51	Ta
12/22/1940	01:36:52	Li		05/03/1941	11:33:47	Le		09/12/1941	02:05:36	Ge
12/24/1940	04:29:46	Sc		05/05/1941	18:05:32	Vi		09/14/1941	14:08:59	Cn
12/26/1940	06:36:15	Sg		05/07/1941	21:11:13	Li		09/16/1941	23:35:50	Le
12/28/1940	08:58:04	Cp		05/09/1941	21:33:31	Sc		09/19/1941	05:28:47	Vi
12/30/1940	13:08:37	Aq		05/11/1941	20:49:25	Sg		09/21/1941	08:17:14	Li
01/01/1941	20:34:42	Pi		05/13/1941	21:03:27	Cp		09/23/1941	09:23:29	Sc
01/04/1941	07:34:16	Ar		05/16/1941	00:14:53	Aq		09/25/1941	10:24:22	Sg
01/06/1941	20:28:11	Ta		05/18/1941	07:33:23	Pi		09/27/1941	12:44:15	Cp
01/09/1941	08:26:56	Ge		05/20/1941	18:33:59	Ar		09/29/1941	17:16:40	Aq
01/11/1941	17:33:08	Cn		05/23/1941	07:26:04	Ta		10/02/1941	00:17:50	Pi
01/13/1941	23:39:08	Le		05/25/1941	20:09:57	Ge		10/04/1941	09:37:04	Ar
01/16/1941	03:45:26	Vi		05/28/1941	07:36:23	Cn		10/06/1941	20:51:39	Ta
01/18/1941	06:59:48	Li		05/30/1941	17:15:03	Le		10/09/1941	09:22:33	Ge
01/20/1941	10:03:45	Sc		06/02/1941	00:38:11	Vi		10/11/1941	21:52:37	Cn
01/22/1941	13:16:19	Sg		06/04/1941	05:17:02	Li		10/14/1941	08:28:58	Le
01/24/1941	17:00:53	Cp		06/06/1941	07:13:19	Sc		10/16/1941	15:35:56	Vi
01/26/1941	22:05:38	Aq		06/08/1941	07:23:25	Sg		10/18/1941	18:54:01	Li
01/29/1941	05:34:07	Pi		06/10/1941	07:31:31	Cp		10/20/1941	19:25:25	Sc
01/31/1941	16:01:57	Ar		06/12/1941	09:41:10	Aq		10/22/1941	19:00:18	Sg
02/03/1941	04:40:52	Ta		06/14/1941	15:33:20	Pi		10/24/1941	19:39:48	Cp
02/05/1941	17:09:13	Ge		06/17/1941	01:30:10	Ar		10/26/1941	23:02:24	Aq
02/08/1941	02:57:15	Cn		06/19/1941	14:02:38	Ta		10/29/1941	05:50:40	Pi
02/10/1941	09:07:08	Le		06/22/1941	02:44:18	Ge		10/31/1941	15:38:02	Ar
02/12/1941	12:21:06	Vi		06/24/1941	13:51:04	Cn		11/03/1941	03:18:53	Ta
02/14/1941	14:07:22	Li		06/26/1941	22:54:43	Le		11/05/1941	15:52:06	Ge
02/16/1941	15:52:17	Sc		06/29/1941	06:02:38	Vi		11/08/1941	04:25:36	Cn
02/18/1941	18:36:37	Sg		07/01/1941	11:16:49	Li		11/10/1941	15:48:42	Le
02/20/1941	22:53:31	Cp		07/03/1941	14:33:30	Sc		11/13/1941	00:28:52	Vi

11/15/1941	05:21:28	Li	03/27/1942	04:04:10	Le	08/05/1942	12:54:14	Ge
11/17/1941	06:39:49	Sc	03/29/1942	12:36:24	Vi	08/08/1942	01:30:18	Cn
11/19/1941	05:53:13	Sg	03/31/1942	17:36:18	Li	08/10/1942	13:39:20	Le
11/21/1941	05:11:24	Cp	04/02/1942	19:54:27	Sc	08/13/1942	00:08:46	Vi
11/23/1941	06:46:08	Aq	04/04/1942	21:04:09	Sg	08/15/1942	08:30:37	Li
11/25/1941	12:08:48	Pi	04/06/1942	22:41:26	Cp	08/17/1942	14:37:45	Sc
11/27/1941	21:26:15	Ar	04/09/1942	01:56:23	Aq	08/19/1942	18:34:41	Sg
11/30/1941	09:18:16	Ta	04/11/1942	07:19:14	Pi	08/21/1942	20:46:27	Cp
12/02/1941	21:59:48	Ge	04/13/1942	14:49:03	Ar	08/23/1942	22:06:58	Aq
12/05/1941	10:21:30	Cn	04/16/1942	00:17:38	Ta	08/25/1942	23:55:04	Pi
12/07/1941	21:42:42	Le	04/18/1942	11:36:31	Ge	08/28/1942	03:38:52	Ar
12/10/1941	07:12:19	Vi	04/21/1942	00:09:32	Cn	08/30/1942	10:29:03	Ta
12/12/1941	13:45:40	Li	04/23/1942	12:21:31	Le	09/01/1942	20:40:14	Ge
12/14/1941	16:51:19	Sc	04/25/1942	22:02:27	Vi	09/04/1942	09:00:09	Cn
12/16/1941	17:09:56	Sg	04/28/1942	03:49:49	Li	09/06/1942	21:15:13	Le
12/18/1941	16:26:13	Cp	04/30/1942	05:59:02	Sc	09/09/1942	07:30:38	Vi
12/20/1941	16:53:21	Aq	05/02/1942	06:02:57	Sg	09/11/1942	15:04:49	Li
12/22/1941	20:32:42	Pi	05/04/1942	06:04:26	Cp	09/13/1942	20:18:29	Sc
12/25/1941	04:23:53	Ar	05/06/1942	07:55:34	Aq	09/15/1942	23:57:45	Sg
12/27/1941	15:43:01	Ta	05/08/1942	12:43:28	Pi	09/18/1942	02:47:58	Cp
12/30/1941	04:27:02	Ge	05/10/1942	20:31:19	Ar	09/20/1942	05:27:02	Aq
01/01/1942	16:41:29	Cn	05/13/1942	06:36:50	Ta	09/22/1942	08:33:34	Pi
01/04/1942	03:32:27	Le	05/15/1942	18:14:45	Ge	09/24/1942	12:56:58	Ar
01/06/1942	12:42:08	Vi	05/18/1942	06:48:59	Cn	09/26/1942	19:34:29	Ta
01/08/1942	19:48:24	Li	05/20/1942	19:21:05	Le	09/29/1942	05:04:57	Ge
01/11/1942	00:24:03	Sc	05/23/1942	06:07:21	Vi	10/01/1942	17:03:05	Cn
01/13/1942	02:31:20	Sg	05/25/1942	13:21:49	Li	10/04/1942	05:35:07	Le
01/15/1942	03:06:55	Cp	05/27/1942	16:31:39	Sc	10/06/1942	16:13:20	Vi
01/17/1942	03:52:14	Aq	05/29/1942	16:38:42	Sg	10/08/1942	23:32:36	Li
01/19/1942	06:43:04	Pi	05/31/1942	15:43:30	Cp	10/11/1942	03:46:14	Sc
01/21/1942	13:08:03	Ar	06/02/1942	15:59:24	Aq	10/13/1942	06:10:23	Sg
01/23/1942	23:18:27	Ta	06/04/1942	19:13:45	Pi	10/15/1942	08:13:20	Cp
01/26/1942	11:43:42	Ge	06/07/1942	02:10:36	Ar	10/17/1942	11:01:00	Aq
01/29/1942	00:03:08	Cn	06/09/1942	12:15:40	Ta	10/19/1942	15:05:00	Pi
01/31/1942	10:36:46	Le	06/12/1942	00:11:27	Ge	10/21/1942	20:36:30	Ar
02/02/1942	18:57:22	Vi	06/14/1942	12:49:48	Cn	10/24/1942	03:51:57	Ta
02/05/1942	01:17:49	Li	06/17/1942	01:19:15	Le	10/26/1942	13:18:21	Ge
02/07/1942	05:55:42	Sc	06/19/1942	12:33:27	Vi	10/29/1942	01:00:00	Cn
02/09/1942	09:06:25	Sg	06/21/1942	21:04:07	Li	10/31/1942	13:48:09	Le
02/11/1942	11:18:40	Cp	06/24/1942	01:50:20	Sc	11/03/1942	01:18:50	Vi
02/13/1942	13:27:27	Aq	06/26/1942	03:08:37	Sg	11/05/1942	09:21:14	Li
02/15/1942	16:50:28	Pi	06/28/1942	02:29:40	Cp	11/07/1942	13:26:47	Sc
02/17/1942	22:46:19	Ar	06/30/1942	02:00:27	Aq	11/09/1942	14:46:59	Sg
02/20/1942	07:57:23	Ta	07/02/1942	03:45:48	Pi	11/11/1942	15:17:40	Cp
02/22/1942	19:47:06	Ge	07/04/1942	09:10:24	Ar	11/13/1942	16:48:23	Aq
02/25/1942	08:15:24	Cn	07/06/1942	18:22:26	Ta	11/15/1942	20:27:43	Pi
02/27/1942	19:05:42	Le	07/09/1942	06:10:04	Ge	11/18/1942	02:30:16	Ar
03/02/1942	03:05:43	Vi	07/11/1942	18:51:22	Cn	11/20/1942	10:37:29	Ta
03/04/1942	08:22:59	Li	07/14/1942	07:08:02	Le	11/22/1942	20:34:33	Ge
03/06/1942	11:49:57	Sc	07/16/1942	18:08:11	Vi	11/25/1942	08:16:35	Cn
03/08/1942	14:27:57	Sg	07/19/1942	03:01:52	Li	11/27/1942	21:09:18	Le
03/10/1942	17:08:22	Cp	07/21/1942	09:02:03	Sc	11/30/1942	09:29:10	Vi
03/12/1942	20:30:20	Aq	07/23/1942	11:58:04	Sg	12/02/1942	18:55:05	Li
03/15/1942	01:08:38	Pi	07/25/1942	12:37:55	Cp	12/05/1942	00:06:24	Sc
03/17/1942	07:40:39	Ar	07/27/1942	12:36:48	Aq	12/07/1942	01:33:50	Sg
03/19/1942	16:38:37	Ta	07/29/1942	13:48:46	Pi	12/09/1942	01:06:41	Cp
03/22/1942	04:00:03	Ge	07/31/1942	17:55:09	Ar	12/11/1942	00:56:36	Aq
03/24/1942	16:32:48	Cn	08/03/1942	01:47:25	Ta	12/13/1942	02:55:45	Pi

12/15/1942	08:04:05	Ar
12/17/1942	16:16:22	Ta
12/20/1942	02:45:59	Ge
12/22/1942	14:45:42	Cn
12/25/1942	03:35:21	Le
12/27/1942	16:10:07	Vi
12/30/1942	02:44:26	Li
01/01/1943	09:39:30	Sc
01/03/1943	12:33:30	Sg
01/05/1943	12:34:34	Cp
01/07/1943	11:41:49	Aq
01/09/1943	12:02:49	Pi
01/11/1943	15:20:31	Ar
01/13/1943	22:21:30	Ta
01/16/1943	08:38:38	Ge
01/18/1943	20:53:28	Cn
01/21/1943	09:43:33	Le
01/23/1943	22:02:36	Vi
01/26/1943	08:46:56	Li
01/28/1943	16:50:31	Sc
01/30/1943	21:33:49	Sg
02/01/1943	23:15:09	Cp
02/03/1943	23:10:14	Aq
02/05/1943	23:07:29	Pi
02/08/1943	01:00:09	Ar
02/10/1943	06:17:04	Ta
02/12/1943	15:24:59	Ge
02/15/1943	03:24:26	Cn
02/17/1943	16:18:20	Le
02/20/1943	04:19:52	Vi
02/22/1943	14:29:40	Li
02/24/1943	22:24:57	Sc
02/27/1943	03:58:58	Sg
03/01/1943	07:18:45	Cp
03/03/1943	08:56:06	Aq
03/05/1943	09:54:04	Pi
03/07/1943	11:41:07	Ar
03/09/1943	15:53:13	Ta
03/11/1943	23:39:00	Ge
03/14/1943	10:50:33	Cn
03/16/1943	23:41:00	Le
03/19/1943	11:42:50	Vi
03/21/1943	21:21:00	Li
03/24/1943	04:22:37	Sc
03/26/1943	09:23:16	Sg
03/28/1943	13:04:47	Cp
03/30/1943	15:57:01	Aq
04/01/1943	18:26:47	Pi
04/03/1943	21:17:24	Ar
04/06/1943	01:37:17	Ta
04/08/1943	08:41:20	Ge
04/10/1943	19:02:59	Cn
04/13/1943	07:39:29	Le
04/15/1943	19:58:58	Vi
04/18/1943	05:40:49	Li
04/20/1943	12:03:38	Sc
04/22/1943	15:56:04	Sg
04/24/1943	18:39:27	Cp

04/26/1943	21:21:00	Aq
04/29/1943	00:35:39	Pi
05/01/1943	04:39:08	Ar
05/03/1943	09:56:53	Ta
05/05/1943	17:15:39	Ge
05/08/1943	03:16:38	Cn
05/10/1943	15:38:36	Le
05/13/1943	04:21:24	Vi
05/15/1943	14:44:07	Li
05/17/1943	21:19:08	Sc
05/20/1943	00:32:53	Sg
05/22/1943	01:59:39	Cp
05/24/1943	03:22:58	Aq
05/26/1943	05:57:31	Pi
05/28/1943	10:16:12	Ar
05/30/1943	16:24:42	Ta
06/02/1943	00:29:29	Ge
06/04/1943	10:45:20	Cn
06/06/1943	23:02:58	Le
06/09/1943	12:03:06	Vi
06/11/1943	23:21:47	Li
06/14/1943	06:58:34	Sc
06/16/1943	10:35:57	Sg
06/18/1943	11:29:31	Cp
06/20/1943	11:33:30	Aq
06/22/1943	12:36:04	Pi
06/24/1943	15:52:20	Ar
06/26/1943	21:51:53	Ta
06/29/1943	06:26:45	Ge
07/01/1943	17:13:09	Cn
07/04/1943	05:39:16	Le
07/06/1943	18:44:51	Vi
07/09/1943	06:44:11	Li
07/11/1943	15:40:25	Sc
07/13/1943	20:36:43	Sg
07/15/1943	22:09:28	Cp
07/17/1943	21:45:32	Aq
07/19/1943	21:30:21	Pi
07/21/1943	23:08:04	Ar
07/24/1943	03:52:33	Ta
07/26/1943	12:03:30	Ge
07/28/1943	23:03:40	Cn
07/31/1943	11:42:57	Le
08/03/1943	00:45:03	Vi
08/05/1943	12:51:19	Li
08/07/1943	22:39:42	Sc
08/10/1943	05:08:14	Sg
08/12/1943	08:09:04	Cp
08/14/1943	08:36:21	Aq
08/16/1943	08:06:24	Pi
08/18/1943	08:32:13	Ar
08/20/1943	11:39:29	Ta
08/22/1943	18:34:09	Ge
08/25/1943	05:06:44	Cn
08/27/1943	17:49:13	Le
08/30/1943	06:46:40	Vi
09/01/1943	18:33:07	Li
09/04/1943	04:20:06	Sc

09/06/1943	11:38:28	Sg
09/08/1943	16:13:17	Cp
09/10/1943	18:17:59	Aq
09/12/1943	18:46:18	Pi
09/14/1943	19:08:29	Ar
09/16/1943	21:14:14	Ta
09/19/1943	02:42:05	Ge
09/21/1943	12:10:19	Cn
09/24/1943	00:33:47	Le
09/26/1943	13:30:20	Vi
09/29/1943	00:56:11	Li
10/01/1943	10:04:09	Sc
10/03/1943	17:02:43	Sg
10/05/1943	22:10:58	Cp
10/08/1943	01:39:21	Aq
10/10/1943	03:44:10	Pi
10/12/1943	05:11:52	Ar
10/14/1943	07:25:46	Ta
10/16/1943	12:06:44	Ge
10/18/1943	20:27:48	Cn
10/21/1943	08:12:07	Le
10/23/1943	21:09:31	Vi
10/26/1943	08:37:46	Li
10/28/1943	17:14:14	Sc
10/30/1943	23:14:21	Sg
11/02/1943	03:36:30	Cp
11/04/1943	07:09:31	Aq
11/06/1943	10:15:40	Pi
11/08/1943	13:10:22	Ar
11/10/1943	16:32:13	Ta
11/12/1943	21:31:23	Ge
11/15/1943	05:22:28	Cn
11/17/1943	16:27:22	Le
11/20/1943	05:21:20	Vi
11/22/1943	17:18:39	Li
11/25/1943	02:09:00	Sc
11/27/1943	07:34:46	Sg
11/29/1943	10:42:52	Cp
12/01/1943	13:01:04	Aq
12/03/1943	15:35:34	Pi
12/05/1943	18:59:37	Ar
12/07/1943	23:30:01	Ta
12/10/1943	05:32:19	Ge
12/12/1943	13:46:20	Cn
12/15/1943	00:36:36	Le
12/17/1943	13:22:09	Vi
12/20/1943	01:55:05	Li
12/22/1943	11:45:42	Sc
12/24/1943	17:43:40	Sg
12/26/1943	20:23:56	Cp
12/28/1943	21:20:42	Aq
12/30/1943	22:16:51	Pi
01/02/1944	00:33:46	Ar
01/04/1944	04:58:09	Ta
01/06/1944	11:44:08	Ge
01/08/1944	20:48:01	Cn
01/11/1944	07:57:30	Le
01/13/1944	20:38:13	Vi

01/16/1944	09:28:50	Li
01/18/1944	20:27:28	Sc
01/21/1944	03:53:09	Sg
01/23/1944	07:26:24	Cp
01/25/1944	08:09:25	Aq
01/27/1944	07:47:35	Pi
01/29/1944	08:14:36	Ar
01/31/1944	11:06:41	Ta
02/02/1944	17:17:10	Ge
02/05/1944	02:39:44	Cn
02/07/1944	14:19:53	Le
02/10/1944	03:07:40	Vi
02/12/1944	15:54:20	Li
02/15/1944	03:23:57	Sc
02/17/1944	12:14:47	Sg
02/19/1944	17:32:46	Cp
02/21/1944	19:26:38	Aq
02/23/1944	19:08:43	Pi
02/25/1944	18:30:49	Ar
02/27/1944	19:35:54	Ta
03/01/1944	00:05:40	Ge
03/03/1944	08:38:01	Cn
03/05/1944	20:19:25	Le
03/08/1944	09:18:14	Vi
03/10/1944	21:55:03	Li
03/13/1944	09:12:01	Sc
03/15/1944	18:30:57	Sg
03/18/1944	01:13:07	Cp
03/20/1944	04:54:53	Aq
03/22/1944	05:58:35	Pi
03/24/1944	05:41:51	Ar
03/26/1944	06:00:42	Ta
03/28/1944	08:58:16	Ge
03/30/1944	15:59:08	Cn
04/02/1944	02:54:02	Le
04/04/1944	15:48:46	Vi
04/07/1944	04:21:52	Li
04/09/1944	15:11:44	Sc
04/12/1944	00:02:08	Sg
04/14/1944	06:55:53	Cp
04/16/1944	11:45:38	Aq
04/18/1944	14:27:58	Pi
04/20/1944	15:35:22	Ar
04/22/1944	16:28:28	Ta
04/24/1944	18:58:34	Ge
04/27/1944	00:48:38	Cn
04/29/1944	10:35:55	Le
05/01/1944	23:04:17	Vi
05/04/1944	11:39:30	Li
05/06/1944	22:17:57	Sc
05/09/1944	06:26:42	Sg
05/11/1944	12:32:50	Cp
05/13/1944	17:09:54	Aq
05/15/1944	20:34:56	Pi
05/17/1944	23:03:13	Ar
05/20/1944	01:15:27	Ta
05/22/1944	04:26:17	Ge
05/24/1944	10:03:48	Cn
05/26/1944	19:04:28	Le
05/29/1944	06:58:30	Vi
05/31/1944	19:37:22	Li
06/03/1944	06:31:31	Sc
06/05/1944	14:27:15	Sg
06/07/1944	19:41:04	Cp
06/09/1944	23:12:01	Aq
06/12/1944	01:58:09	Pi
06/14/1944	04:40:36	Ar
06/16/1944	07:51:43	Ta
06/18/1944	12:10:48	Ge
06/20/1944	18:28:03	Cn
06/23/1944	03:25:26	Le
06/25/1944	14:57:47	Vi
06/28/1944	03:39:35	Li
06/30/1944	15:10:02	Sc
07/02/1944	23:38:04	Sg
07/05/1944	04:41:34	Cp
07/07/1944	07:13:45	Aq
07/09/1944	08:38:36	Pi
07/11/1944	10:18:17	Ar
07/13/1944	13:16:12	Ta
07/15/1944	18:11:13	Ge
07/18/1944	01:21:27	Cn
07/20/1944	10:50:47	Le
07/22/1944	22:24:14	Vi
07/25/1944	11:07:44	Li
07/27/1944	23:16:11	Sc
07/30/1944	08:49:55	Sg
08/01/1944	14:42:04	Cp
08/03/1944	17:10:09	Aq
08/05/1944	17:34:48	Pi
08/07/1944	17:43:12	Ar
08/09/1944	19:19:25	Ta
08/11/1944	23:38:12	Ge
08/14/1944	07:03:24	Cn
08/16/1944	17:08:02	Le
08/19/1944	05:00:26	Vi
08/21/1944	17:45:03	Li
08/24/1944	06:13:02	Sc
08/26/1944	16:51:35	Sg
08/29/1944	00:12:18	Cp
08/31/1944	03:44:07	Aq
09/02/1944	04:14:25	Pi
09/04/1944	03:27:04	Ar
09/06/1944	03:28:22	Ta
09/08/1944	06:13:31	Ge
09/10/1944	12:46:45	Cn
09/12/1944	22:50:16	Le
09/15/1944	11:00:22	Vi
09/17/1944	23:47:48	Li
09/20/1944	12:11:00	Sc
09/22/1944	23:16:14	Sg
09/25/1944	07:55:28	Cp
09/27/1944	13:09:49	Aq
09/29/1944	14:57:36	Pi
10/01/1944	14:29:37	Ar
10/03/1944	13:45:44	Ta
10/05/1944	14:59:22	Ge
10/07/1944	19:56:09	Cn
10/10/1944	05:03:02	Le
10/12/1944	17:04:27	Vi
10/15/1944	05:55:05	Li
10/17/1944	18:03:21	Sc
10/20/1944	04:49:56	Sg
10/22/1944	13:48:19	Cp
10/24/1944	20:18:56	Aq
10/26/1944	23:53:05	Pi
10/29/1944	00:53:41	Ar
10/31/1944	00:44:59	Ta
11/02/1944	01:28:12	Ge
11/04/1944	05:04:13	Cn
11/06/1944	12:44:04	Le
11/08/1944	23:58:55	Vi
11/11/1944	12:44:33	Li
11/14/1944	00:47:33	Sc
11/16/1944	11:01:40	Sg
11/18/1944	19:19:49	Cp
11/21/1944	01:46:58	Aq
11/23/1944	06:18:13	Pi
11/25/1944	08:56:49	Ar
11/27/1944	10:22:08	Ta
11/29/1944	11:54:47	Ge
12/01/1944	15:16:30	Cn
12/03/1944	21:52:51	Le
12/06/1944	08:03:45	Vi
12/08/1944	20:28:27	Li
12/11/1944	08:41:56	Sc
12/13/1944	18:50:04	Sg
12/16/1944	02:21:39	Cp
12/18/1944	07:43:56	Aq
12/20/1944	11:39:07	Pi
12/22/1944	14:42:06	Ar
12/24/1944	17:24:06	Ta
12/26/1944	20:25:48	Ge
12/29/1944	00:43:36	Cn
12/31/1944	07:19:06	Le
01/02/1945	16:48:51	Vi
01/05/1945	04:43:51	Li
01/07/1945	17:12:53	Sc
01/10/1945	03:55:12	Sg
01/12/1945	11:27:41	Cp
01/14/1945	15:56:42	Aq
01/16/1945	18:27:05	Pi
01/18/1945	20:20:33	Ar
01/20/1945	22:47:38	Ta
01/23/1945	02:34:32	Ge
01/25/1945	08:04:54	Cn
01/27/1945	15:32:35	Le
01/30/1945	01:08:47	Vi
02/01/1945	12:45:37	Li
02/04/1945	01:22:11	Sc
02/06/1945	12:57:26	Sg
02/08/1945	21:29:13	Cp
02/11/1945	02:12:01	Aq
02/13/1945	03:52:27	Pi

02/15/1945	04:12:13	Ar	06/27/1945	15:36:23	Aq	11/06/1945	11:18:03	Sg
02/17/1945	05:04:48	Ta	06/29/1945	20:51:12	Pi	11/08/1945	23:35:09	Cp
02/19/1945	08:00:57	Ge	07/02/1945	00:29:07	Ar	11/11/1945	09:58:47	Aq
02/21/1945	13:42:25	Cn	07/04/1945	03:04:26	Ta	11/13/1945	17:04:50	Pi
02/23/1945	21:58:23	Le	07/06/1945	05:19:33	Ge	11/15/1945	20:24:09	Ar
02/26/1945	08:13:27	Vi	07/08/1945	08:10:23	Cn	11/17/1945	20:47:38	Ta
02/28/1945	19:56:45	Li	07/10/1945	12:43:13	Le	11/19/1945	20:02:22	Ge
03/03/1945	08:32:24	Sc	07/12/1945	19:57:44	Vi	11/21/1945	20:13:36	Cn
03/05/1945	20:44:38	Sg	07/15/1945	06:12:40	Li	11/23/1945	23:11:56	Le
03/08/1945	06:37:19	Cp	07/17/1945	18:28:34	Sc	11/26/1945	05:59:07	Vi
03/10/1945	12:39:37	Aq	07/20/1945	06:35:46	Sg	11/28/1945	16:18:24	Li
03/12/1945	14:49:42	Pi	07/22/1945	16:28:34	Cp	12/01/1945	04:43:01	Sc
03/14/1945	14:32:04	Ar	07/24/1945	23:16:14	Aq	12/03/1945	17:29:46	Sg
03/16/1945	13:54:22	Ta	07/27/1945	03:26:29	Pi	12/06/1945	05:23:23	Cp
03/18/1945	15:04:26	Ge	07/29/1945	06:07:09	Ar	12/08/1945	15:34:03	Aq
03/20/1945	19:31:20	Cn	07/31/1945	08:28:38	Ta	12/10/1945	23:20:17	Pi
03/23/1945	03:31:30	Le	08/02/1945	11:23:03	Ge	12/13/1945	04:15:06	Ar
03/25/1945	14:10:50	Vi	08/04/1945	15:22:32	Cn	12/15/1945	06:29:38	Ta
03/28/1945	02:14:57	Li	08/06/1945	20:52:29	Le	12/17/1945	07:02:30	Ge
03/30/1945	14:49:49	Sc	08/09/1945	04:23:39	Vi	12/19/1945	07:27:17	Cn
04/02/1945	03:07:32	Sg	08/11/1945	14:20:58	Li	12/21/1945	09:30:25	Le
04/04/1945	13:51:29	Cp	08/14/1945	02:24:29	Sc	12/23/1945	14:43:38	Vi
04/06/1945	21:28:04	Aq	08/16/1945	14:55:44	Sg	12/25/1945	23:44:53	Li
04/09/1945	01:10:11	Pi	08/19/1945	01:30:34	Cp	12/28/1945	11:42:45	Sc
04/11/1945	01:37:43	Ar	08/21/1945	08:32:09	Aq	12/31/1945	00:32:15	Sg
04/13/1945	00:39:35	Ta	08/23/1945	12:04:57	Pi	01/02/1946	12:10:57	Cp
04/15/1945	00:31:03	Ge	08/25/1945	13:29:54	Ar	01/04/1946	21:37:40	Aq
04/17/1945	03:13:33	Cn	08/27/1945	14:33:29	Ta	01/07/1946	04:46:42	Pi
04/19/1945	09:52:00	Le	08/29/1945	16:46:46	Ge	01/09/1946	09:55:34	Ar
04/21/1945	20:03:03	Vi	08/31/1945	20:59:43	Cn	01/11/1946	13:25:11	Ta
04/24/1945	08:14:35	Li	09/03/1945	03:19:33	Le	01/13/1946	15:42:23	Ge
04/26/1945	20:52:07	Sc	09/05/1945	11:36:23	Vi	01/15/1946	17:32:10	Cn
04/29/1945	08:55:48	Sg	09/07/1945	21:48:11	Li	01/17/1946	20:03:29	Le
05/01/1945	19:39:46	Cp	09/10/1945	09:47:43	Sc	01/20/1946	00:40:17	Vi
05/04/1945	04:05:37	Aq	09/12/1945	22:37:24	Sg	01/22/1946	08:31:26	Li
05/06/1945	09:20:57	Pi	09/15/1945	10:11:20	Cp	01/24/1946	19:39:51	Sc
05/08/1945	11:24:46	Ar	09/17/1945	18:19:26	Aq	01/27/1946	08:27:08	Sg
05/10/1945	11:24:09	Ta	09/19/1945	22:18:47	Pi	01/29/1946	20:17:48	Cp
05/12/1945	11:11:50	Ge	09/21/1945	23:10:32	Ar	02/01/1946	05:23:26	Aq
05/14/1945	12:50:51	Cn	09/23/1945	22:53:09	Ta	02/03/1946	11:32:22	Pi
05/16/1945	17:56:54	Le	09/25/1945	23:31:30	Ge	02/05/1946	15:37:56	Ar
05/19/1945	02:25:56	Vi	09/28/1945	02:38:21	Cn	02/07/1946	18:46:33	Ta
05/21/1945	14:42:50	Li	09/30/1945	08:46:53	Le	02/09/1946	21:45:12	Ge
05/24/1945	03:20:32	Sc	10/02/1945	17:33:46	Vi	02/12/1946	00:58:39	Cn
05/26/1945	15:11:05	Sg	10/05/1945	04:16:31	Li	02/14/1946	04:50:05	Le
05/29/1945	01:24:03	Cp	10/07/1945	16:23:46	Sc	02/16/1946	10:02:49	Vi
05/31/1945	09:34:58	Aq	10/10/1945	05:17:27	Sg	02/18/1946	17:36:01	Li
06/02/1945	15:25:06	Pi	10/12/1945	17:32:49	Cp	02/21/1946	04:04:38	Sc
06/04/1945	18:50:34	Ar	10/15/1945	03:06:32	Aq	02/23/1946	16:41:00	Sg
06/06/1945	20:23:06	Ta	10/17/1945	08:33:41	Pi	02/26/1946	05:01:25	Cp
06/08/1945	21:14:35	Ge	10/19/1945	10:08:50	Ar	02/28/1946	14:34:22	Aq
06/10/1945	23:01:44	Cn	10/21/1945	09:30:06	Ta	03/02/1946	20:24:57	Pi
06/13/1945	03:19:49	Le	10/23/1945	08:49:26	Ge	03/04/1946	23:23:23	Ar
06/15/1945	11:07:11	Vi	10/25/1945	10:10:54	Cn	03/07/1946	01:08:11	Ta
06/17/1945	22:06:15	Li	10/27/1945	14:55:06	Le	03/09/1946	03:11:38	Ge
06/20/1945	10:35:57	Sc	10/29/1945	23:12:00	Vi	03/11/1946	06:28:27	Cn
06/22/1945	22:27:05	Sg	11/01/1945	10:07:44	Li	03/13/1946	11:14:15	Le
06/25/1945	08:14:15	Cp	11/03/1945	22:29:21	Sc	03/15/1946	17:32:07	Vi

03/18/1946	01:40:13	Li		07/28/1946	03:57:02	Le		12/07/1946	16:29:37	Ge
03/20/1946	12:04:20	Sc		07/30/1946	06:32:26	Vi		12/09/1946	15:49:41	Cn
03/23/1946	00:30:13	Sg		08/01/1946	12:04:40	Li		12/11/1946	15:46:24	Le
03/25/1946	13:17:35	Cp		08/03/1946	21:22:35	Sc		12/13/1946	18:08:49	Vi
03/27/1946	23:50:36	Aq		08/06/1946	09:36:15	Sg		12/16/1946	00:07:12	Li
03/30/1946	06:26:00	Pi		08/08/1946	22:23:22	Cp		12/18/1946	09:42:58	Sc
04/01/1946	09:16:06	Ar		08/11/1946	09:23:30	Aq		12/20/1946	21:48:27	Sg
04/03/1946	09:56:14	Ta		08/13/1946	17:40:50	Pi		12/23/1946	10:50:09	Cp
04/05/1946	10:24:59	Ge		08/15/1946	23:36:58	Ar		12/25/1946	23:29:29	Aq
04/07/1946	12:20:53	Cn		08/18/1946	03:59:07	Ta		12/28/1946	10:43:20	Pi
04/09/1946	16:37:09	Le		08/20/1946	07:22:18	Ge		12/30/1946	19:31:00	Ar
04/11/1946	23:20:02	Vi		08/22/1946	10:06:05	Cn		01/02/1947	01:05:50	Ta
04/14/1946	08:13:12	Li		08/24/1946	12:37:47	Le		01/04/1947	03:25:53	Ge
04/16/1946	19:03:07	Sc		08/26/1946	15:53:49	Vi		01/06/1947	03:27:42	Cn
04/19/1946	07:29:42	Sg		08/28/1946	21:14:57	Li		01/08/1947	02:53:03	Le
04/21/1946	20:28:12	Cp		08/31/1946	05:49:17	Sc		01/10/1947	03:44:32	Vi
04/24/1946	07:56:19	Aq		09/02/1946	17:31:02	Sg		01/12/1947	07:53:55	Li
04/26/1946	15:54:05	Pi		09/05/1946	06:23:37	Cp		01/14/1947	16:15:23	Sc
04/28/1946	19:45:23	Ar		09/07/1946	17:41:07	Aq		01/17/1947	04:02:54	Sg
04/30/1946	20:30:43	Ta		09/10/1946	01:45:45	Pi		01/19/1947	17:10:15	Cp
05/02/1946	20:03:10	Ge		09/12/1946	06:48:50	Ar		01/22/1947	05:36:55	Aq
05/04/1946	20:22:36	Cn		09/14/1946	10:03:27	Ta		01/24/1947	16:22:53	Pi
05/06/1946	23:04:26	Le		09/16/1946	12:45:27	Ge		01/27/1947	01:10:22	Ar
05/09/1946	04:57:01	Vi		09/18/1946	15:41:45	Cn		01/29/1947	07:45:25	Ta
05/11/1946	13:53:19	Li		09/20/1946	19:12:34	Le		01/31/1947	11:51:52	Ge
05/14/1946	01:08:26	Sc		09/22/1946	23:37:58	Vi		02/02/1947	13:38:20	Cn
05/16/1946	13:45:55	Sg		09/25/1946	05:39:59	Li		02/04/1947	14:01:18	Le
05/19/1946	02:41:45	Cp		09/27/1946	14:12:04	Sc		02/06/1947	14:41:47	Vi
05/21/1946	14:31:16	Aq		09/30/1946	01:32:25	Sg		02/08/1947	17:39:21	Li
05/23/1946	23:38:42	Pi		10/02/1946	14:29:10	Cp		02/11/1947	00:28:03	Sc
05/26/1946	05:04:39	Ar		10/05/1946	02:27:02	Aq		02/13/1947	11:15:28	Sg
05/28/1946	07:03:28	Ta		10/07/1946	11:08:51	Pi		02/16/1947	00:11:51	Cp
05/30/1946	06:54:23	Ge		10/09/1946	16:04:48	Ar		02/18/1947	12:38:27	Aq
06/01/1946	06:28:33	Cn		10/11/1946	18:20:21	Ta		02/20/1947	22:57:14	Pi
06/03/1946	07:39:23	Le		10/13/1946	19:36:31	Ge		02/23/1947	06:57:30	Ar
06/05/1946	11:56:39	Vi		10/15/1946	21:22:54	Cn		02/25/1947	13:07:36	Ta
06/07/1946	19:56:50	Li		10/18/1946	00:35:01	Le		02/27/1947	17:46:43	Ge
06/10/1946	07:04:22	Sc		10/20/1946	05:35:25	Vi		03/01/1947	20:58:37	Cn
06/12/1946	19:50:27	Sg		10/22/1946	12:33:06	Li		03/03/1947	22:59:54	Le
06/15/1946	08:39:18	Cp		10/24/1946	21:40:35	Sc		03/06/1947	00:46:21	Vi
06/17/1946	20:15:48	Aq		10/27/1946	09:03:04	Sg		03/08/1947	03:50:44	Li
06/20/1946	05:42:46	Pi		10/29/1946	21:59:22	Cp		03/10/1947	09:50:47	Sc
06/22/1946	12:19:19	Ar		11/01/1946	10:36:14	Aq		03/12/1947	19:33:48	Sg
06/24/1946	15:55:43	Ta		11/03/1946	20:31:52	Pi		03/15/1947	08:00:06	Cp
06/26/1946	17:07:07	Ge		11/06/1946	02:27:55	Ar		03/17/1947	20:35:16	Aq
06/28/1946	17:10:17	Cn		11/08/1946	04:48:47	Ta		03/20/1947	06:57:23	Pi
06/30/1946	17:47:26	Le		11/10/1946	05:07:13	Ge		03/22/1947	14:22:44	Ar
07/02/1946	20:44:52	Vi		11/12/1946	05:15:25	Cn		03/24/1947	19:28:55	Ta
07/05/1946	03:20:47	Li		11/14/1946	06:52:39	Le		03/26/1947	23:15:40	Ge
07/07/1946	13:41:20	Sc		11/16/1946	11:04:39	Vi		03/29/1947	02:25:45	Cn
07/10/1946	02:20:14	Sg		11/18/1946	18:12:20	Li		03/31/1947	05:21:59	Le
07/12/1946	15:05:21	Cp		11/21/1946	03:57:54	Sc		04/02/1947	08:30:12	Vi
07/15/1946	02:16:44	Aq		11/23/1946	15:43:39	Sg		04/04/1947	12:39:21	Li
07/17/1946	11:15:11	Pi		11/26/1946	04:39:31	Cp		04/06/1947	18:56:27	Sc
07/19/1946	17:58:43	Ar		11/28/1946	17:29:46	Aq		04/09/1947	04:12:10	Sg
07/21/1946	22:35:07	Ta		12/01/1946	04:29:33	Pi		04/11/1947	16:08:23	Cp
07/24/1946	01:18:26	Ge		12/03/1946	12:05:03	Ar		04/14/1947	04:51:09	Aq
07/26/1946	02:43:30	Cn		12/05/1946	15:48:16	Ta		04/16/1947	15:47:01	Pi

04/18/1947	23:25:27	Ar	08/28/1947	14:18:03	Aq	01/07/1948	04:40:31	Sg
04/21/1947	03:55:36	Ta	08/31/1947	02:03:20	Pi	01/09/1948	15:40:55	Cp
04/23/1947	06:27:31	Ge	09/02/1947	12:02:27	Ar	01/12/1948	03:53:58	Aq
04/25/1947	08:22:09	Cn	09/04/1947	20:10:10	Ta	01/14/1948	16:35:13	Pi
04/27/1947	10:43:57	Le	09/07/1947	02:18:08	Ge	01/17/1948	04:43:41	Ar
04/29/1947	14:15:02	Vi	09/09/1947	06:12:01	Cn	01/19/1948	14:42:24	Ta
05/01/1947	19:23:40	Li	09/11/1947	08:02:52	Le	01/21/1948	21:01:14	Ge
05/04/1947	02:35:11	Sc	09/13/1947	08:50:34	Vi	01/23/1948	23:23:13	Cn
05/06/1947	12:09:06	Sg	09/15/1947	10:16:01	Li	01/25/1948	22:59:37	Le
05/08/1947	23:54:44	Cp	09/17/1947	14:10:35	Sc	01/27/1948	21:55:56	Vi
05/11/1947	12:40:47	Aq	09/19/1947	21:49:21	Sg	01/29/1948	22:29:01	Li
05/14/1947	00:20:11	Pi	09/22/1947	08:57:28	Cp	02/01/1948	02:27:11	Sc
05/16/1947	08:56:16	Ar	09/24/1947	21:37:31	Aq	02/03/1948	10:25:44	Sg
05/18/1947	13:51:20	Ta	09/27/1947	09:24:27	Pi	02/05/1948	21:29:32	Cp
05/20/1947	15:51:09	Ge	09/29/1947	18:58:06	Ar	02/08/1948	09:58:57	Aq
05/22/1947	16:26:42	Cn	10/02/1947	02:15:03	Ta	02/10/1948	22:36:49	Pi
05/24/1947	17:17:57	Le	10/04/1947	07:43:31	Ge	02/13/1948	10:37:16	Ar
05/26/1947	19:49:39	Vi	10/06/1947	11:46:54	Cn	02/15/1948	21:08:01	Ta
05/29/1947	00:53:50	Li	10/08/1947	14:41:25	Le	02/18/1948	04:55:41	Ge
05/31/1947	08:42:07	Sc	10/10/1947	16:56:48	Vi	02/20/1948	09:08:40	Cn
06/02/1947	18:54:01	Sg	10/12/1947	19:31:22	Li	02/22/1948	10:06:45	Le
06/05/1947	06:51:24	Cp	10/14/1947	23:45:26	Sc	02/24/1948	09:22:14	Vi
06/07/1947	19:37:54	Aq	10/17/1947	06:52:39	Sg	02/26/1948	09:05:07	Li
06/10/1947	07:46:55	Pi	10/19/1947	17:13:57	Cp	02/28/1948	11:23:46	Sc
06/12/1947	17:33:46	Ar	10/22/1947	05:38:48	Aq	03/01/1948	17:41:12	Sg
06/14/1947	23:45:15	Ta	10/24/1947	17:45:27	Pi	03/04/1948	03:50:26	Cp
06/17/1947	02:21:27	Ge	10/27/1947	03:30:42	Ar	03/06/1948	16:14:02	Aq
06/19/1947	02:32:14	Cn	10/29/1947	10:16:01	Ta	03/09/1948	04:53:02	Pi
06/21/1947	02:06:25	Le	10/31/1947	14:35:40	Ge	03/11/1948	16:32:54	Ar
06/23/1947	03:01:02	Vi	11/02/1947	17:31:53	Cn	03/14/1948	02:40:07	Ta
06/25/1947	06:51:07	Li	11/04/1947	20:03:17	Le	03/16/1948	10:45:10	Ge
06/27/1947	14:16:32	Sc	11/06/1947	22:54:46	Vi	03/18/1948	16:13:48	Cn
06/30/1947	00:45:58	Sg	11/09/1947	02:42:20	Li	03/20/1948	18:57:45	Le
07/02/1947	13:02:35	Cp	11/11/1947	08:02:29	Sc	03/22/1948	19:42:22	Vi
07/05/1947	01:49:35	Aq	11/13/1947	15:33:20	Sg	03/24/1948	20:01:23	Li
07/07/1947	14:02:54	Pi	11/16/1947	01:36:57	Cp	03/26/1948	21:49:26	Sc
07/10/1947	00:34:21	Ar	11/18/1947	13:45:01	Aq	03/29/1948	02:46:27	Sg
07/12/1947	08:11:58	Ta	11/21/1947	02:16:06	Pi	03/31/1948	11:33:39	Cp
07/14/1947	12:16:28	Ge	11/23/1947	12:53:00	Ar	04/02/1948	23:18:23	Aq
07/16/1947	13:14:19	Cn	11/25/1947	20:05:43	Ta	04/05/1948	11:55:51	Pi
07/18/1947	12:34:08	Le	11/27/1947	23:55:06	Ge	04/07/1948	23:28:09	Ar
07/20/1947	12:19:01	Vi	11/30/1947	01:30:52	Cn	04/10/1948	08:58:28	Ta
07/22/1947	14:33:18	Li	12/02/1947	02:29:58	Le	04/12/1948	16:19:48	Ge
07/24/1947	20:40:49	Sc	12/04/1947	04:23:25	Vi	04/14/1948	21:41:20	Cn
07/27/1947	06:40:12	Sg	12/06/1947	08:13:40	Li	04/17/1948	01:15:59	Le
07/29/1947	19:01:24	Cp	12/08/1947	14:24:16	Sc	04/19/1948	03:30:17	Vi
08/01/1947	07:49:40	Aq	12/10/1947	22:49:21	Sg	04/21/1948	05:16:11	Li
08/03/1947	19:48:58	Pi	12/13/1947	09:13:53	Cp	04/23/1948	07:49:04	Sc
08/06/1947	06:19:32	Ar	12/15/1947	21:15:34	Aq	04/25/1948	12:31:09	Sg
08/08/1947	14:43:11	Ta	12/18/1947	09:58:50	Pi	04/27/1948	20:21:32	Cp
08/10/1947	20:17:25	Ge	12/20/1947	21:36:45	Ar	04/30/1948	07:15:55	Aq
08/12/1947	22:49:26	Cn	12/23/1947	06:11:03	Ta	05/02/1948	19:43:45	Pi
08/14/1947	23:06:02	Le	12/25/1947	10:46:59	Ge	05/05/1948	07:28:07	Ar
08/16/1947	22:48:36	Vi	12/27/1947	12:02:50	Cn	05/07/1948	16:47:51	Ta
08/19/1947	00:03:51	Li	12/29/1947	11:41:14	Le	05/09/1948	23:19:47	Ge
08/21/1947	04:44:23	Sc	12/31/1947	11:46:51	Vi	05/12/1948	03:38:17	Cn
08/23/1947	13:34:13	Sg	01/02/1948	14:09:52	Li	05/14/1948	06:38:56	Le
08/26/1947	01:30:38	Cp	01/04/1948	19:50:55	Sc	05/16/1948	09:14:14	Vi

05/18/1948	12:06:56	Li
05/20/1948	15:55:31	Sc
05/22/1948	21:21:48	Sg
05/25/1948	05:07:40	Cp
05/27/1948	15:30:44	Aq
05/30/1948	03:45:56	Pi
06/01/1948	15:54:44	Ar
06/04/1948	01:43:22	Ta
06/06/1948	08:06:05	Ge
06/08/1948	11:28:22	Cn
06/10/1948	13:11:25	Le
06/12/1948	14:48:30	Vi
06/14/1948	17:33:03	Li
06/16/1948	22:03:14	Sc
06/19/1948	04:28:19	Sg
06/21/1948	12:50:44	Cp
06/23/1948	23:15:00	Aq
06/26/1948	11:23:08	Pi
06/28/1948	23:55:43	Ar
07/01/1948	10:39:50	Ta
07/03/1948	17:47:38	Ge
07/05/1948	21:06:35	Cn
07/07/1948	21:52:55	Le
07/09/1948	22:03:28	Vi
07/11/1948	23:30:36	Li
07/14/1948	03:27:49	Sc
07/16/1948	10:11:00	Sg
07/18/1948	19:13:17	Cp
07/21/1948	06:02:11	Aq
07/23/1948	18:12:50	Pi
07/26/1948	06:57:17	Ar
07/28/1948	18:33:59	Ta
07/31/1948	03:01:10	Ge
08/02/1948	07:20:05	Cn
08/04/1948	08:13:11	Le
08/06/1948	07:32:23	Vi
08/08/1948	07:29:35	Li
08/10/1948	09:56:29	Sc
08/12/1948	15:49:01	Sg
08/15/1948	00:51:24	Cp
08/17/1948	12:02:30	Aq
08/20/1948	00:22:58	Pi
08/22/1948	13:05:18	Ar
08/25/1948	01:03:20	Ta
08/27/1948	10:39:53	Ge
08/29/1948	16:33:46	Cn
08/31/1948	18:40:59	Le
09/02/1948	18:20:20	Vi
09/04/1948	17:35:27	Li
09/06/1948	18:34:03	Sc
09/08/1948	22:51:35	Sg
09/11/1948	06:56:20	Cp
09/13/1948	17:58:23	Aq
09/16/1948	06:26:42	Pi
09/18/1948	19:01:39	Ar
09/21/1948	06:45:20	Ta
09/23/1948	16:40:00	Ge
09/25/1948	23:45:49	Cn

09/28/1948	03:34:45	Le
09/30/1948	04:40:10	Vi
10/02/1948	04:29:57	Li
10/04/1948	04:58:17	Sc
10/06/1948	07:54:56	Sg
10/08/1948	14:30:48	Cp
10/11/1948	00:42:03	Aq
10/13/1948	13:03:05	Pi
10/16/1948	01:36:07	Ar
10/18/1948	12:53:51	Ta
10/20/1948	22:14:29	Ge
10/23/1948	05:21:20	Cn
10/25/1948	10:09:36	Le
10/27/1948	12:53:10	Vi
10/29/1948	14:15:44	Li
10/31/1948	15:31:03	Sc
11/02/1948	18:10:25	Sg
11/04/1948	23:39:31	Cp
11/07/1948	08:41:11	Aq
11/09/1948	20:33:29	Pi
11/12/1948	09:12:05	Ar
11/14/1948	20:23:59	Ta
11/17/1948	05:01:53	Ge
11/19/1948	11:11:01	Cn
11/21/1948	15:32:10	Le
11/23/1948	18:48:16	Vi
11/25/1948	21:32:50	Li
11/28/1948	00:18:30	Sc
11/30/1948	03:51:44	Sg
12/02/1948	09:16:22	Cp
12/04/1948	17:31:50	Aq
12/07/1948	04:45:42	Pi
12/09/1948	17:29:42	Ar
12/12/1948	05:08:33	Ta
12/14/1948	13:44:01	Ge
12/16/1948	19:00:46	Cn
12/18/1948	22:02:54	Le
12/21/1948	00:18:51	Vi
12/23/1948	02:59:04	Li
12/25/1948	06:38:33	Sc
12/27/1948	11:28:43	Sg
12/29/1948	17:46:29	Cp
01/01/1949	02:07:20	Aq
01/03/1949	12:58:11	Pi
01/06/1949	01:40:29	Ar
01/08/1949	14:02:47	Ta
01/10/1949	23:30:35	Ge
01/13/1949	04:56:35	Cn
01/15/1949	07:07:34	Le
01/17/1949	07:51:59	Vi
01/19/1949	09:02:55	Li
01/21/1949	11:59:23	Sc
01/23/1949	17:08:49	Sg
01/26/1949	00:21:31	Cp
01/28/1949	09:26:25	Aq
01/30/1949	20:26:03	Pi
02/02/1949	09:04:15	Ar
02/04/1949	21:56:59	Ta

02/07/1949	08:40:11	Ge
02/09/1949	15:22:14	Cn
02/11/1949	18:00:26	Le
02/13/1949	18:05:18	Vi
02/15/1949	17:43:41	Li
02/17/1949	18:52:54	Sc
02/19/1949	22:49:12	Sg
02/22/1949	05:50:07	Cp
02/24/1949	15:25:47	Aq
02/27/1949	02:53:49	Pi
03/01/1949	15:35:33	Ar
03/04/1949	04:32:51	Ta
03/06/1949	16:05:08	Ge
03/09/1949	00:21:27	Cn
03/11/1949	04:33:05	Le
03/13/1949	05:23:54	Vi
03/15/1949	04:39:47	Li
03/17/1949	04:25:08	Sc
03/19/1949	06:30:31	Sg
03/21/1949	12:04:23	Cp
03/23/1949	21:10:03	Aq
03/26/1949	08:49:44	Pi
03/28/1949	21:41:19	Ar
03/31/1949	10:29:07	Ta
04/02/1949	22:02:38	Ge
04/05/1949	07:09:57	Cn
04/07/1949	12:59:11	Le
04/09/1949	15:31:30	Vi
04/11/1949	15:47:35	Li
04/13/1949	15:27:15	Sc
04/15/1949	16:23:14	Sg
04/17/1949	20:15:46	Cp
04/20/1949	03:59:08	Aq
04/22/1949	15:07:38	Pi
04/25/1949	04:00:43	Ar
04/27/1949	16:40:47	Ta
04/30/1949	03:47:39	Ge
05/02/1949	12:43:04	Cn
05/04/1949	19:11:11	Le
05/06/1949	23:11:18	Vi
05/09/1949	01:06:46	Li
05/11/1949	01:53:32	Sc
05/13/1949	02:56:55	Sg
05/15/1949	05:56:58	Cp
05/17/1949	12:18:55	Aq
05/19/1949	22:25:59	Pi
05/22/1949	11:01:38	Ar
05/24/1949	23:41:34	Ta
05/27/1949	10:26:50	Ge
05/29/1949	18:38:30	Cn
06/01/1949	00:35:52	Le
06/03/1949	04:53:23	Vi
06/05/1949	07:57:29	Li
06/07/1949	10:13:09	Sc
06/09/1949	12:23:31	Sg
06/11/1949	15:39:41	Cp
06/13/1949	21:26:09	Aq
06/16/1949	06:38:25	Pi

06/18/1949	18:44:36	Ar	10/28/1949	07:50:00	Aq	03/09/1950	16:37:19	Sg
06/21/1949	07:30:01	Ta	10/30/1949	17:21:18	Pi	03/11/1950	20:06:39	Cp
06/23/1949	18:19:36	Ge	11/02/1949	05:34:21	Ar	03/14/1950	01:52:07	Aq
06/26/1949	02:01:23	Cn	11/04/1949	18:36:31	Ta	03/16/1950	09:59:17	Pi
06/28/1949	07:00:31	Le	11/07/1949	06:54:58	Ge	03/18/1950	20:20:53	Ar
06/30/1949	10:26:28	Vi	11/09/1949	17:34:57	Cn	03/21/1950	08:31:58	Ta
07/02/1949	13:21:55	Li	11/12/1949	02:00:18	Le	03/23/1950	21:27:50	Ge
07/04/1949	16:21:44	Sc	11/14/1949	07:42:17	Vi	03/26/1950	09:16:48	Cn
07/06/1949	19:44:53	Sg	11/16/1949	10:35:28	Li	03/28/1950	18:04:25	Le
07/09/1949	00:02:11	Cp	11/18/1949	11:18:23	Sc	03/30/1950	23:00:40	Vi
07/11/1949	06:08:53	Aq	11/20/1949	11:15:17	Sg	04/02/1950	00:40:29	Li
07/13/1949	15:01:19	Pi	11/22/1949	12:19:31	Cp	04/04/1950	00:35:23	Sc
07/16/1949	02:42:45	Ar	11/24/1949	16:24:12	Aq	04/06/1950	00:36:54	Sg
07/18/1949	15:35:39	Ta	11/27/1949	00:35:06	Pi	04/08/1950	02:29:21	Cp
07/21/1949	02:56:58	Ge	11/29/1949	12:17:54	Ar	04/10/1950	07:24:15	Aq
07/23/1949	10:51:51	Cn	12/02/1949	01:21:44	Ta	04/12/1950	15:37:55	Pi
07/25/1949	15:18:46	Le	12/04/1949	13:28:26	Ge	04/15/1950	02:31:34	Ar
07/27/1949	17:35:49	Vi	12/06/1949	23:31:13	Cn	04/17/1950	14:59:30	Ta
07/29/1949	19:19:38	Li	12/09/1949	07:27:28	Le	04/20/1950	03:54:03	Ge
07/31/1949	21:43:49	Sc	12/11/1949	13:31:04	Vi	04/22/1950	16:01:46	Cn
08/03/1949	01:24:50	Sg	12/13/1949	17:44:51	Li	04/25/1950	01:57:18	Le
08/05/1949	06:36:00	Cp	12/15/1949	20:13:17	Sc	04/27/1950	08:29:49	Vi
08/07/1949	13:33:44	Aq	12/17/1949	21:31:51	Sg	04/29/1950	11:24:55	Li
08/09/1949	22:45:24	Pi	12/19/1949	22:59:46	Cp	05/01/1950	11:37:17	Sc
08/12/1949	10:19:49	Ar	12/22/1949	02:24:21	Aq	05/03/1950	10:50:31	Sg
08/14/1949	23:17:53	Ta	12/24/1949	09:19:46	Pi	05/05/1950	11:07:58	Cp
08/17/1949	11:22:31	Ge	12/26/1949	20:04:34	Ar	05/07/1950	14:21:55	Aq
08/19/1949	20:14:46	Cn	12/29/1949	08:57:53	Ta	05/09/1950	21:33:32	Pi
08/22/1949	01:07:31	Le	12/31/1949	21:12:43	Ge	05/12/1950	08:17:59	Ar
08/24/1949	02:55:32	Vi	01/03/1950	06:56:01	Cn	05/14/1950	20:58:41	Ta
08/26/1949	03:24:02	Li	01/05/1950	13:57:43	Le	05/17/1950	09:52:17	Ge
08/28/1949	04:19:29	Sc	01/07/1950	19:05:47	Vi	05/19/1950	21:50:25	Cn
08/30/1949	07:00:18	Sg	01/09/1950	23:08:13	Li	05/22/1950	08:06:04	Le
09/01/1949	12:04:42	Cp	01/12/1950	02:27:38	Sc	05/24/1950	15:50:29	Vi
09/03/1949	19:36:57	Aq	01/14/1950	05:15:57	Sg	05/26/1950	20:26:00	Li
09/06/1949	05:25:58	Pi	01/16/1950	08:06:16	Cp	05/28/1950	22:00:49	Sc
09/08/1949	17:12:58	Ar	01/18/1950	12:06:48	Aq	05/30/1950	21:43:23	Sg
09/11/1949	06:12:01	Ta	01/20/1950	18:41:06	Pi	06/01/1950	21:26:44	Cp
09/13/1949	18:46:37	Ge	01/23/1950	04:37:29	Ar	06/03/1950	23:17:54	Aq
09/16/1949	04:51:31	Cn	01/25/1950	17:07:52	Ta	06/06/1950	04:57:00	Pi
09/18/1949	11:04:24	Le	01/28/1950	05:42:54	Ge	06/08/1950	14:43:50	Ar
09/20/1949	13:33:42	Vi	01/30/1950	15:49:43	Cn	06/11/1950	03:12:06	Ta
09/22/1949	13:41:29	Li	02/01/1950	22:33:33	Le	06/13/1950	16:04:54	Ge
09/24/1949	13:20:30	Sc	02/04/1950	02:36:32	Vi	06/16/1950	03:44:49	Cn
09/26/1949	14:21:03	Sg	02/06/1950	05:18:51	Li	06/18/1950	13:37:08	Le
09/28/1949	18:06:45	Cp	02/08/1950	07:50:02	Sc	06/20/1950	21:31:15	Vi
10/01/1949	01:13:04	Aq	02/10/1950	10:51:03	Sg	06/23/1950	03:09:21	Li
10/03/1949	11:19:28	Pi	02/12/1950	14:44:32	Cp	06/25/1950	06:18:44	Sc
10/05/1949	23:27:10	Ar	02/14/1950	19:57:21	Aq	06/27/1950	07:25:37	Sg
10/08/1949	12:26:15	Ta	02/17/1950	03:10:46	Pi	06/29/1950	07:48:08	Cp
10/11/1949	01:02:12	Ge	02/19/1950	13:00:36	Ar	07/01/1950	09:19:16	Aq
10/13/1949	11:50:49	Cn	02/22/1950	01:11:35	Ta	07/03/1950	13:51:22	Pi
10/15/1949	19:34:48	Le	02/24/1950	14:02:41	Ge	07/05/1950	22:24:13	Ar
10/17/1949	23:42:20	Vi	02/27/1950	01:02:58	Cn	07/08/1950	10:13:25	Ta
10/20/1949	00:47:42	Li	03/01/1950	08:30:03	Le	07/10/1950	23:01:34	Ge
10/22/1949	00:18:19	Sc	03/03/1950	12:24:18	Vi	07/13/1950	10:33:30	Cn
10/24/1949	00:07:43	Sg	03/05/1950	14:00:03	Li	07/15/1950	19:52:19	Le
10/26/1949	02:10:20	Cp	03/07/1950	14:55:13	Sc	07/18/1950	03:05:19	Vi

07/20/1950	08:33:40	Li	11/29/1950	12:01:55	Le	04/10/1951	00:40:31	Ge
07/22/1950	12:26:38	Sc	12/01/1950	21:53:27	Vi	04/12/1951	13:04:11	Cn
07/24/1950	14:55:11	Sg	12/04/1950	04:28:51	Li	04/15/1951	01:17:48	Le
07/26/1950	16:39:07	Cp	12/06/1950	07:19:09	Sc	04/17/1951	11:06:56	Vi
07/28/1950	18:55:12	Aq	12/08/1950	07:16:50	Sg	04/19/1951	17:13:13	Li
07/30/1950	23:18:34	Pi	12/10/1950	06:16:07	Cp	04/21/1951	19:54:45	Sc
08/02/1950	07:02:36	Ar	12/12/1950	06:34:06	Aq	04/23/1951	20:39:33	Sg
08/04/1950	18:05:38	Ta	12/14/1950	10:10:29	Pi	04/25/1951	21:19:28	Cp
08/07/1950	06:43:56	Ge	12/16/1950	17:58:11	Ar	04/27/1951	23:32:09	Aq
08/09/1950	18:26:50	Cn	12/19/1950	05:09:29	Ta	04/30/1951	04:12:58	Pi
08/12/1950	03:36:14	Le	12/21/1950	17:49:17	Ge	05/02/1951	11:26:04	Ar
08/14/1950	10:03:06	Vi	12/24/1950	06:17:36	Cn	05/04/1951	20:46:31	Ta
08/16/1950	14:30:40	Li	12/26/1950	17:45:05	Le	05/07/1951	07:50:41	Ge
08/18/1950	17:48:56	Sc	12/29/1950	03:41:02	Vi	05/09/1951	20:12:52	Cn
08/20/1950	20:35:37	Sg	12/31/1950	11:19:56	Li	05/12/1951	08:49:20	Le
08/22/1950	23:22:55	Cp	01/02/1951	15:57:44	Sc	05/14/1951	19:43:53	Vi
08/25/1950	02:52:45	Aq	01/04/1951	17:38:06	Sg	05/17/1951	03:04:58	Li
08/27/1950	08:01:38	Pi	01/06/1951	17:31:41	Cp	05/19/1951	06:22:57	Sc
08/29/1950	15:44:29	Ar	01/08/1951	17:35:20	Aq	05/21/1951	06:43:39	Sg
09/01/1950	02:18:38	Ta	01/10/1951	19:55:41	Pi	05/23/1951	06:07:03	Cp
09/03/1950	14:45:18	Ge	01/13/1951	02:05:05	Ar	05/25/1951	06:41:24	Aq
09/06/1950	02:53:29	Cn	01/15/1951	12:10:21	Ta	05/27/1951	10:05:00	Pi
09/08/1950	12:33:54	Le	01/18/1951	00:35:49	Ge	05/29/1951	16:53:11	Ar
09/10/1950	18:54:47	Vi	01/20/1951	13:05:55	Cn	06/01/1951	02:33:10	Ta
09/12/1950	22:27:36	Li	01/23/1951	00:11:31	Le	06/03/1951	14:02:38	Ge
09/15/1950	00:26:43	Sc	01/25/1951	09:25:49	Vi	06/06/1951	02:31:01	Cn
09/17/1950	02:12:03	Sg	01/27/1951	16:45:50	Li	06/08/1951	15:11:38	Le
09/19/1950	04:48:38	Cp	01/29/1951	22:03:41	Sc	06/11/1951	02:46:31	Vi
09/21/1950	08:59:28	Aq	02/01/1951	01:16:14	Sg	06/13/1951	11:30:43	Li
09/23/1950	15:09:08	Pi	02/03/1951	02:52:26	Cp	06/15/1951	16:16:38	Sc
09/25/1950	23:31:34	Ar	02/05/1951	04:03:40	Aq	06/17/1951	17:25:59	Sg
09/28/1950	10:08:01	Ta	02/07/1951	06:28:43	Pi	06/19/1951	16:37:39	Cp
09/30/1950	22:26:29	Ge	02/09/1951	11:42:37	Ar	06/21/1951	16:03:43	Aq
10/03/1950	10:59:03	Cn	02/11/1951	20:33:08	Ta	06/23/1951	17:49:04	Pi
10/05/1950	21:39:52	Le	02/14/1951	08:18:03	Ge	06/25/1951	23:13:04	Ar
10/08/1950	04:53:32	Vi	02/16/1951	20:51:12	Cn	06/28/1951	08:17:06	Ta
10/10/1950	08:28:43	Li	02/19/1951	08:00:45	Le	06/30/1951	19:51:12	Ge
10/12/1950	09:30:55	Sc	02/21/1951	16:42:33	Vi	07/03/1951	08:27:21	Cn
10/14/1950	09:43:54	Sg	02/23/1951	23:00:59	Li	07/05/1951	21:00:23	Le
10/16/1950	10:55:01	Cp	02/26/1951	03:30:55	Sc	07/08/1951	08:35:45	Vi
10/18/1950	14:26:33	Aq	02/28/1951	06:49:12	Sg	07/10/1951	18:04:16	Li
10/20/1950	20:52:57	Pi	03/02/1951	09:29:23	Cp	07/13/1951	00:18:40	Sc
10/23/1950	05:58:36	Ar	03/04/1951	12:10:34	Aq	07/15/1951	03:02:49	Sg
10/25/1950	17:02:36	Ta	03/06/1951	15:45:24	Pi	07/17/1951	03:14:05	Cp
10/28/1950	05:22:11	Ge	03/08/1951	21:15:56	Ar	07/19/1951	02:41:13	Aq
10/30/1950	18:03:11	Cn	03/11/1951	05:32:32	Ta	07/21/1951	03:28:35	Pi
11/02/1950	05:37:54	Le	03/13/1951	16:36:00	Ge	07/23/1951	07:21:17	Ar
11/04/1950	14:20:49	Vi	03/16/1951	05:05:53	Cn	07/25/1951	15:06:41	Ta
11/06/1950	19:09:58	Li	03/18/1951	16:44:21	Le	07/28/1951	02:07:29	Ge
11/08/1950	20:28:32	Sc	03/21/1951	01:38:50	Vi	07/30/1951	14:42:04	Cn
11/10/1950	19:51:06	Sg	03/23/1951	07:20:53	Li	08/02/1951	03:07:30	Le
11/12/1950	19:25:15	Cp	03/25/1951	10:35:33	Sc	08/04/1951	14:18:01	Vi
11/14/1950	21:14:19	Aq	03/27/1951	12:40:17	Sg	08/06/1951	23:34:08	Li
11/17/1950	02:38:25	Pi	03/29/1951	14:50:51	Cp	08/09/1951	06:23:46	Sc
11/19/1950	11:39:18	Ar	03/31/1951	18:02:04	Aq	08/11/1951	10:30:50	Sg
11/21/1950	23:07:34	Ta	04/02/1951	22:44:30	Pi	08/13/1951	12:18:04	Cp
11/24/1950	11:38:25	Ge	04/05/1951	05:15:38	Ar	08/15/1951	12:52:54	Aq
11/27/1950	00:13:01	Cn	04/07/1951	13:52:03	Ta	08/17/1951	13:52:22	Pi

08/19/1951	16:58:23	Ar	12/30/1951	01:35:42	Aq	05/10/1952	14:50:24	Sg
08/21/1951	23:26:29	Ta	01/01/1952	02:10:06	Pi	05/12/1952	17:08:52	Cp
08/24/1951	09:27:16	Ge	01/03/1952	05:41:37	Ar	05/14/1952	19:14:02	Aq
08/26/1951	21:44:09	Cn	01/05/1952	12:43:07	Ta	05/16/1952	22:05:26	Pi
08/29/1951	10:09:38	Le	01/07/1952	22:42:09	Ge	05/19/1952	02:06:55	Ar
08/31/1951	20:59:45	Vi	01/10/1952	10:34:00	Cn	05/21/1952	07:29:15	Ta
09/03/1951	05:31:48	Li	01/12/1952	23:19:02	Le	05/23/1952	14:37:07	Ge
09/05/1951	11:48:38	Sc	01/15/1952	12:00:15	Vi	05/26/1952	00:05:53	Cn
09/07/1951	16:10:59	Sg	01/17/1952	23:19:12	Li	05/28/1952	11:59:19	Le
09/09/1951	19:06:01	Cp	01/20/1952	07:43:59	Sc	05/31/1952	00:56:57	Vi
09/11/1951	21:11:17	Aq	01/22/1952	12:21:54	Sg	06/02/1952	12:25:39	Li
09/13/1951	23:21:26	Pi	01/24/1952	13:38:46	Cp	06/04/1952	20:19:14	Sc
09/16/1951	02:47:09	Ar	01/26/1952	13:06:20	Aq	06/07/1952	00:20:36	Sg
09/18/1951	08:41:13	Ta	01/28/1952	12:45:18	Pi	06/09/1952	01:46:05	Cp
09/20/1951	17:46:42	Ge	01/30/1952	14:32:35	Ar	06/11/1952	02:26:30	Aq
09/23/1951	05:34:08	Cn	02/01/1952	19:50:37	Ta	06/13/1952	04:00:27	Pi
09/25/1951	18:07:30	Le	02/04/1952	04:54:56	Ge	06/15/1952	07:28:40	Ar
09/28/1951	05:05:26	Vi	02/06/1952	16:43:53	Cn	06/17/1952	13:10:35	Ta
09/30/1951	13:08:20	Li	02/09/1952	05:35:54	Le	06/19/1952	21:03:19	Ge
10/02/1951	18:23:09	Sc	02/11/1952	18:01:39	Vi	06/22/1952	07:03:48	Cn
10/04/1951	21:48:03	Sg	02/14/1952	05:00:01	Li	06/24/1952	19:02:20	Le
10/07/1951	00:29:54	Cp	02/16/1952	13:44:48	Sc	06/27/1952	08:06:10	Vi
10/09/1951	03:18:55	Aq	02/18/1952	19:42:18	Sg	06/29/1952	20:18:03	Li
10/11/1951	06:46:17	Pi	02/20/1952	22:49:25	Cp	07/02/1952	05:25:08	Sc
10/13/1951	11:19:21	Ar	02/22/1952	23:48:15	Aq	07/04/1952	10:26:33	Sg
10/15/1951	17:36:58	Ta	02/25/1952	00:00:58	Pi	07/06/1952	12:02:13	Cp
10/18/1951	02:21:57	Ge	02/27/1952	01:11:29	Ar	07/08/1952	11:54:14	Aq
10/20/1951	13:42:31	Cn	02/29/1952	05:01:36	Ta	07/10/1952	11:59:07	Pi
10/23/1951	02:24:39	Le	03/02/1952	12:36:09	Ge	07/12/1952	13:55:58	Ar
10/25/1951	14:01:18	Vi	03/04/1952	23:40:19	Cn	07/14/1952	18:45:01	Ta
10/27/1951	22:25:06	Li	03/07/1952	12:30:01	Le	07/17/1952	02:37:25	Ge
10/30/1951	03:09:17	Sc	03/10/1952	00:51:21	Vi	07/19/1952	13:04:40	Cn
11/01/1951	05:19:41	Sg	03/12/1952	11:16:11	Li	07/22/1952	01:20:02	Le
11/03/1951	06:39:45	Cp	03/14/1952	19:20:24	Sc	07/24/1952	14:24:27	Vi
11/05/1951	08:42:47	Aq	03/17/1952	01:15:03	Sg	07/27/1952	02:53:53	Li
11/07/1951	12:22:57	Pi	03/19/1952	05:19:08	Cp	07/29/1952	13:04:08	Sc
11/09/1951	17:52:29	Ar	03/21/1952	07:54:39	Aq	07/31/1952	19:37:06	Sg
11/12/1951	01:07:19	Ta	03/23/1952	09:38:42	Pi	08/02/1952	22:27:14	Cp
11/14/1951	10:15:12	Ge	03/25/1952	11:33:57	Ar	08/04/1952	22:40:59	Aq
11/16/1951	21:27:27	Cn	03/27/1952	15:05:16	Ta	08/06/1952	22:04:41	Pi
11/19/1951	10:11:59	Le	03/29/1952	21:35:38	Ge	08/08/1952	22:33:17	Ar
11/21/1951	22:35:27	Vi	04/01/1952	07:38:46	Cn	08/11/1952	01:45:32	Ta
11/24/1951	08:08:38	Li	04/03/1952	20:09:42	Le	08/13/1952	08:36:12	Ge
11/26/1951	13:31:46	Sc	04/06/1952	08:40:03	Vi	08/15/1952	18:52:00	Cn
11/28/1951	15:19:53	Sg	04/08/1952	18:55:42	Li	08/18/1952	07:18:43	Le
11/30/1951	15:22:13	Cp	04/11/1952	02:13:11	Sc	08/20/1952	20:22:12	Vi
12/02/1951	15:44:44	Aq	04/13/1952	07:07:44	Sg	08/23/1952	08:41:28	Li
12/04/1951	18:07:53	Pi	04/15/1952	10:41:21	Cp	08/25/1952	19:10:02	Sc
12/06/1951	23:17:47	Ar	04/17/1952	13:43:05	Aq	08/28/1952	02:53:03	Sg
12/09/1951	07:04:19	Ta	04/19/1952	16:40:10	Pi	08/30/1952	07:23:33	Cp
12/11/1951	16:53:48	Ge	04/21/1952	19:56:12	Ar	09/01/1952	09:02:33	Aq
12/14/1951	04:22:11	Cn	04/24/1952	00:14:36	Ta	09/03/1952	08:59:44	Pi
12/16/1951	17:04:36	Le	04/26/1952	06:40:16	Ge	09/05/1952	08:57:08	Ar
12/19/1951	05:52:01	Vi	04/28/1952	16:05:40	Cn	09/07/1952	10:47:45	Ta
12/21/1951	16:40:30	Li	05/01/1952	04:12:14	Le	09/09/1952	16:05:57	Ge
12/23/1951	23:38:30	Sc	05/03/1952	16:57:21	Vi	09/12/1952	01:23:44	Cn
12/26/1951	02:26:53	Sg	05/06/1952	03:38:46	Li	09/14/1952	13:38:11	Le
12/28/1951	02:23:54	Cp	05/08/1952	10:48:47	Sc	09/17/1952	02:41:30	Vi

09/19/1952	14:41:10	Li
09/22/1952	00:42:59	Sc
09/24/1952	08:32:40	Sg
09/26/1952	14:05:56	Cp
09/28/1952	17:24:09	Aq
09/30/1952	18:52:22	Pi
10/02/1952	19:33:46	Ar
10/04/1952	21:05:23	Ta
10/07/1952	01:14:48	Ge
10/09/1952	09:15:50	Cn
10/11/1952	20:49:58	Le
10/14/1952	09:50:41	Vi
10/16/1952	21:44:17	Li
10/19/1952	07:09:52	Sc
10/21/1952	14:11:48	Sg
10/23/1952	19:28:20	Cp
10/25/1952	23:27:51	Aq
10/28/1952	02:22:40	Pi
10/30/1952	04:34:18	Ar
11/01/1952	06:58:10	Ta
11/03/1952	11:01:55	Ge
11/05/1952	18:12:19	Cn
11/08/1952	04:56:11	Le
11/10/1952	17:46:54	Vi
11/13/1952	05:57:02	Li
11/15/1952	15:18:22	Sc
11/17/1952	21:33:08	Sg
11/20/1952	01:40:06	Cp
11/22/1952	04:51:40	Aq
11/24/1952	07:54:41	Pi
11/26/1952	11:09:04	Ar
11/28/1952	14:54:01	Ta
11/30/1952	19:52:52	Ge
12/03/1952	03:08:31	Cn
12/05/1952	13:22:43	Le
12/08/1952	01:57:19	Vi
12/10/1952	14:35:02	Li
12/13/1952	00:38:39	Sc
12/15/1952	06:59:40	Sg
12/17/1952	10:17:01	Cp
12/19/1952	12:02:01	Aq
12/21/1952	13:45:28	Pi
12/23/1952	16:29:47	Ar
12/25/1952	20:45:39	Ta
12/28/1952	02:47:51	Ge
12/30/1952	10:53:13	Cn
01/01/1953	21:17:06	Le
01/04/1953	09:40:50	Vi
01/06/1953	22:36:25	Li
01/09/1953	09:43:42	Sc
01/11/1953	17:13:58	Sg
01/13/1953	20:54:50	Cp
01/15/1953	21:57:06	Aq
01/17/1953	22:06:52	Pi
01/19/1953	23:08:15	Ar
01/22/1953	02:20:10	Ta
01/24/1953	08:20:55	Ge
01/26/1953	17:06:31	Cn

01/29/1953	04:05:58	Le
01/31/1953	16:35:15	Vi
02/03/1953	05:31:20	Li
02/05/1953	17:20:36	Sc
02/08/1953	02:20:01	Sg
02/10/1953	07:31:49	Cp
02/12/1953	09:16:29	Aq
02/14/1953	08:57:55	Pi
02/16/1953	08:30:31	Ar
02/18/1953	09:50:34	Ta
02/20/1953	14:26:55	Ge
02/22/1953	22:47:27	Cn
02/25/1953	10:05:16	Le
02/27/1953	22:50:51	Vi
03/02/1953	11:40:47	Li
03/04/1953	23:30:48	Sc
03/07/1953	09:19:48	Sg
03/09/1953	16:09:54	Cp
03/11/1953	19:37:06	Aq
03/13/1953	20:16:35	Pi
03/15/1953	19:38:35	Ar
03/17/1953	19:44:19	Ta
03/19/1953	22:34:59	Ge
03/22/1953	05:29:08	Cn
03/24/1953	16:14:02	Le
03/27/1953	05:03:44	Vi
03/29/1953	17:51:17	Li
04/01/1953	05:19:16	Sc
04/03/1953	14:58:18	Sg
04/05/1953	22:28:56	Cp
04/08/1953	03:27:11	Aq
04/10/1953	05:49:04	Pi
04/12/1953	06:18:56	Ar
04/14/1953	06:31:13	Ta
04/16/1953	08:26:43	Ge
04/18/1953	13:52:49	Cn
04/20/1953	23:26:49	Le
04/23/1953	11:52:31	Vi
04/26/1953	00:40:12	Li
04/28/1953	11:51:48	Sc
04/30/1953	20:52:07	Sg
05/03/1953	03:54:30	Cp
05/05/1953	09:12:20	Aq
05/07/1953	12:46:14	Pi
05/09/1953	14:48:52	Ar
05/11/1953	16:11:55	Ta
05/13/1953	18:26:33	Ge
05/15/1953	23:16:04	Cn
05/18/1953	07:46:57	Le
05/20/1953	19:30:48	Vi
05/23/1953	08:15:48	Li
05/25/1953	19:32:08	Sc
05/28/1953	04:07:59	Sg
05/30/1953	10:16:40	Cp
06/01/1953	14:44:59	Aq
06/03/1953	18:11:49	Pi
06/05/1953	21:01:09	Ar
06/07/1953	23:41:04	Ta

06/10/1953	03:02:39	Ge
06/12/1953	08:17:18	Cn
06/14/1953	16:27:07	Le
06/17/1953	03:36:34	Vi
06/19/1953	16:16:15	Li
06/22/1953	03:57:13	Sc
06/24/1953	12:47:30	Sg
06/26/1953	18:28:35	Cp
06/28/1953	21:51:21	Aq
07/01/1953	00:08:23	Pi
07/03/1953	02:23:27	Ar
07/05/1953	05:23:02	Ta
07/07/1953	09:42:16	Ge
07/09/1953	15:54:04	Cn
07/12/1953	00:27:47	Le
07/14/1953	11:28:20	Vi
07/17/1953	00:03:36	Li
07/19/1953	12:16:37	Sc
07/21/1953	21:58:55	Sg
07/24/1953	04:06:29	Cp
07/26/1953	07:02:40	Aq
07/28/1953	08:06:47	Pi
07/30/1953	08:55:34	Ar
08/01/1953	10:56:41	Ta
08/03/1953	15:10:18	Ge
08/05/1953	21:59:29	Cn
08/08/1953	07:15:47	Le
08/10/1953	18:33:05	Vi
08/13/1953	07:08:02	Li
08/15/1953	19:43:24	Sc
08/18/1953	06:29:47	Sg
08/20/1953	13:52:51	Cp
08/22/1953	17:28:36	Aq
08/24/1953	18:11:43	Pi
08/26/1953	17:45:58	Ar
08/28/1953	18:10:00	Ta
08/30/1953	21:06:31	Ge
09/02/1953	03:29:37	Cn
09/04/1953	13:04:34	Le
09/07/1953	00:47:00	Vi
09/09/1953	13:27:09	Li
09/12/1953	02:05:17	Sc
09/14/1953	13:31:42	Sg
09/16/1953	22:20:39	Cp
09/19/1953	03:29:46	Aq
09/21/1953	05:06:18	Pi
09/23/1953	04:30:20	Ar
09/25/1953	03:44:50	Ta
09/27/1953	05:00:36	Ge
09/29/1953	09:56:21	Cn
10/01/1953	18:53:08	Le
10/04/1953	06:40:13	Vi
10/06/1953	19:27:57	Li
10/09/1953	07:55:59	Sc
10/11/1953	19:19:10	Sg
10/14/1953	04:51:23	Cp
10/16/1953	11:34:10	Aq
10/18/1953	14:54:58	Pi

10/20/1953	15:26:48	Ar	03/02/1954	02:06:47	Aq	07/11/1954	19:18:29	Sg
10/22/1953	14:46:35	Ta	03/04/1954	04:32:11	Pi	07/14/1954	05:39:47	Cp
10/24/1953	15:04:07	Ge	03/06/1954	04:40:00	Ar	07/16/1954	13:19:02	Aq
10/26/1953	18:23:44	Cn	03/08/1954	04:32:19	Ta	07/18/1954	18:32:40	Pi
10/29/1953	01:54:43	Le	03/10/1954	06:06:04	Ge	07/20/1954	22:07:12	Ar
10/31/1953	13:04:15	Vi	03/12/1954	10:37:20	Cn	07/23/1954	00:52:12	Ta
11/03/1953	01:50:55	Li	03/14/1954	18:16:45	Le	07/25/1954	03:30:11	Ge
11/05/1953	14:11:48	Sc	03/17/1954	04:21:05	Vi	07/27/1954	06:40:59	Cn
11/08/1953	01:06:26	Sg	03/19/1954	15:57:20	Li	07/29/1954	11:10:22	Le
11/10/1953	10:18:22	Cp	03/22/1954	04:25:56	Sc	07/31/1954	17:49:31	Vi
11/12/1953	17:30:37	Aq	03/24/1954	16:55:58	Sg	08/03/1954	03:13:53	Li
11/14/1953	22:17:05	Pi	03/27/1954	03:55:02	Cp	08/05/1954	15:02:36	Sc
11/17/1953	00:35:08	Ar	03/29/1954	11:37:12	Aq	08/08/1954	03:32:11	Sg
11/19/1953	01:14:52	Ta	03/31/1954	15:16:17	Pi	08/10/1954	14:20:00	Cp
11/21/1953	01:54:31	Ge	04/02/1954	15:39:55	Ar	08/12/1954	21:54:08	Aq
11/23/1953	04:31:29	Cn	04/04/1954	14:42:35	Ta	08/15/1954	02:16:48	Pi
11/25/1953	10:40:29	Le	04/06/1954	14:39:56	Ge	08/17/1954	04:37:29	Ar
11/27/1953	20:40:47	Vi	04/08/1954	17:28:35	Cn	08/19/1954	06:25:48	Ta
11/30/1953	09:05:41	Li	04/11/1954	00:05:19	Le	08/21/1954	08:56:01	Ge
12/02/1953	21:30:16	Sc	04/13/1954	10:02:40	Vi	08/23/1954	12:49:48	Cn
12/05/1953	08:08:35	Sg	04/15/1954	21:57:31	Li	08/25/1954	18:22:06	Le
12/07/1953	16:32:50	Cp	04/18/1954	10:32:03	Sc	08/28/1954	01:43:32	Vi
12/09/1953	22:59:03	Aq	04/20/1954	22:54:51	Sg	08/30/1954	11:11:56	Li
12/12/1953	03:46:03	Pi	04/23/1954	10:11:06	Cp	09/01/1954	22:48:30	Sc
12/14/1953	07:05:58	Ar	04/25/1954	19:02:00	Aq	09/04/1954	11:32:10	Sg
12/16/1953	09:22:17	Ta	04/28/1954	00:21:01	Pi	09/06/1954	23:09:54	Cp
12/18/1953	11:27:14	Ge	04/30/1954	02:08:27	Ar	09/09/1954	07:30:49	Aq
12/20/1953	14:39:43	Cn	05/02/1954	01:42:24	Ta	09/11/1954	11:54:50	Pi
12/22/1953	20:22:42	Le	05/04/1954	01:06:25	Ge	09/13/1954	13:22:03	Ar
12/25/1953	05:23:56	Vi	05/06/1954	02:30:00	Cn	09/15/1954	13:44:08	Ta
12/27/1953	17:10:50	Li	05/08/1954	07:28:41	Le	09/17/1954	14:54:39	Ge
12/30/1953	05:42:51	Sc	05/10/1954	16:22:30	Vi	09/19/1954	18:12:46	Cn
01/01/1954	16:39:20	Sg	05/13/1954	04:03:13	Li	09/22/1954	00:03:43	Le
01/04/1954	00:45:27	Cp	05/15/1954	16:41:48	Sc	09/24/1954	08:10:37	Vi
01/06/1954	06:08:59	Aq	05/18/1954	04:53:16	Sg	09/26/1954	18:10:50	Li
01/08/1954	09:42:51	Pi	05/20/1954	15:48:49	Cp	09/29/1954	05:51:54	Sc
01/10/1954	12:26:49	Ar	05/23/1954	00:48:05	Aq	10/01/1954	18:41:09	Sg
01/12/1954	15:09:39	Ta	05/25/1954	07:08:20	Pi	10/04/1954	07:04:14	Cp
01/14/1954	18:29:05	Ge	05/27/1954	10:31:32	Ar	10/06/1954	16:45:15	Aq
01/16/1954	23:00:42	Cn	05/29/1954	11:33:18	Ta	10/08/1954	22:16:41	Pi
01/19/1954	05:24:05	Le	05/31/1954	11:40:31	Ge	10/10/1954	23:58:02	Ar
01/21/1954	14:13:49	Vi	06/02/1954	12:45:37	Cn	10/12/1954	23:31:46	Ta
01/24/1954	01:29:55	Li	06/04/1954	16:34:10	Le	10/14/1954	23:09:40	Ge
01/26/1954	14:03:18	Sc	06/07/1954	00:06:09	Vi	10/17/1954	00:49:41	Cn
01/29/1954	01:42:21	Sg	06/09/1954	10:58:53	Li	10/19/1954	05:40:57	Le
01/31/1954	10:26:26	Cp	06/11/1954	23:29:30	Sc	10/21/1954	13:44:23	Vi
02/02/1954	15:37:41	Aq	06/14/1954	11:37:10	Sg	10/24/1954	00:11:57	Li
02/04/1954	18:03:08	Pi	06/16/1954	22:05:00	Cp	10/26/1954	12:10:35	Sc
02/06/1954	19:14:10	Ar	06/19/1954	06:25:52	Aq	10/29/1954	00:58:37	Sg
02/08/1954	20:46:55	Ta	06/21/1954	12:36:37	Pi	10/31/1954	13:36:05	Cp
02/10/1954	23:54:05	Ge	06/23/1954	16:43:29	Ar	11/03/1954	00:21:58	Aq
02/13/1954	05:09:53	Cn	06/25/1954	19:08:50	Ta	11/05/1954	07:34:11	Pi
02/15/1954	12:35:16	Le	06/27/1954	20:41:23	Ge	11/07/1954	10:42:20	Ar
02/17/1954	22:00:14	Vi	06/29/1954	22:35:21	Cn	11/09/1954	10:48:22	Ta
02/20/1954	09:14:02	Li	07/02/1954	02:16:22	Le	11/11/1954	09:50:31	Ge
02/22/1954	21:43:15	Sc	07/04/1954	08:55:48	Vi	11/13/1954	09:59:22	Cn
02/25/1954	10:00:05	Sg	07/06/1954	18:53:03	Li	11/15/1954	13:02:54	Le
02/27/1954	19:57:41	Cp	07/09/1954	07:03:36	Sc	11/17/1954	19:52:13	Vi

11/20/1954	06:02:07	Li	04/01/1955	08:20:26	Le	08/11/1955	23:33:22	Ge
11/22/1954	18:12:51	Sc	04/03/1955	14:30:50	Vi	08/14/1955	01:50:17	Cn
11/25/1954	07:01:21	Sg	04/05/1955	22:33:31	Li	08/16/1955	03:33:55	Le
11/27/1954	19:23:52	Cp	04/08/1955	08:37:52	Sc	08/18/1955	05:57:21	Vi
11/30/1954	06:18:59	Aq	04/10/1955	20:41:17	Sg	08/20/1955	10:33:45	Li
12/02/1954	14:38:07	Pi	04/13/1955	09:40:24	Cp	08/22/1955	18:37:11	Sc
12/04/1954	19:34:56	Ar	04/15/1955	21:19:48	Aq	08/25/1955	06:03:16	Sg
12/06/1954	21:22:38	Ta	04/18/1955	05:28:05	Pi	08/27/1955	18:56:31	Cp
12/08/1954	21:16:11	Ge	04/20/1955	09:29:09	Ar	08/30/1955	06:35:02	Aq
12/10/1954	21:06:06	Cn	04/22/1955	10:29:09	Ta	09/01/1955	15:22:40	Pi
12/12/1954	22:48:17	Le	04/24/1955	10:23:43	Ge	09/03/1955	21:23:44	Ar
12/15/1954	03:53:43	Vi	04/26/1955	11:08:46	Cn	09/06/1955	01:36:21	Ta
12/17/1954	12:51:07	Li	04/28/1955	14:08:28	Le	09/08/1955	04:58:03	Ge
12/20/1954	00:43:13	Sc	04/30/1955	19:57:30	Vi	09/10/1955	08:00:46	Cn
12/22/1954	13:34:48	Sg	05/03/1955	04:25:46	Li	09/12/1955	11:01:51	Le
12/25/1954	01:40:18	Cp	05/05/1955	15:03:40	Sc	09/14/1955	14:32:59	Vi
12/27/1954	12:00:13	Aq	05/08/1955	03:18:32	Sg	09/16/1955	19:35:01	Li
12/29/1954	20:09:09	Pi	05/10/1955	16:18:33	Cp	09/19/1955	03:18:29	Sc
01/01/1955	01:55:57	Ar	05/13/1955	04:29:00	Aq	09/21/1955	14:11:11	Sg
01/03/1955	05:24:00	Ta	05/15/1955	13:53:00	Pi	09/24/1955	03:00:45	Cp
01/05/1955	07:04:08	Ge	05/17/1955	19:20:33	Ar	09/26/1955	15:07:17	Aq
01/07/1955	08:00:09	Cn	05/19/1955	21:11:34	Ta	09/29/1955	00:12:23	Pi
01/09/1955	09:41:05	Le	05/21/1955	20:56:19	Ge	10/01/1955	05:46:24	Ar
01/11/1955	13:42:43	Vi	05/23/1955	20:32:42	Cn	10/03/1955	08:51:35	Ta
01/13/1955	21:14:50	Li	05/25/1955	21:52:30	Le	10/05/1955	10:59:05	Ge
01/16/1955	08:14:30	Sc	05/28/1955	02:15:40	Vi	10/07/1955	13:22:34	Cn
01/18/1955	21:01:16	Sg	05/30/1955	10:07:33	Li	10/09/1955	16:41:06	Le
01/21/1955	09:09:04	Cp	06/01/1955	20:53:39	Sc	10/11/1955	21:11:13	Vi
01/23/1955	18:58:21	Aq	06/04/1955	09:23:32	Sg	10/14/1955	03:13:21	Li
01/26/1955	02:10:54	Pi	06/06/1955	22:20:44	Cp	10/16/1955	11:23:19	Sc
01/28/1955	07:19:23	Ar	06/09/1955	10:29:42	Aq	10/18/1955	22:07:25	Sg
01/30/1955	11:05:57	Ta	06/11/1955	20:31:55	Pi	10/21/1955	10:51:31	Cp
02/01/1955	14:02:23	Ge	06/14/1955	03:23:42	Ar	10/23/1955	23:32:34	Aq
02/03/1955	16:36:07	Cn	06/16/1955	06:49:46	Ta	10/26/1955	09:37:01	Pi
02/05/1955	19:28:11	Le	06/18/1955	07:36:25	Ge	10/28/1955	15:45:59	Ar
02/07/1955	23:42:49	Vi	06/20/1955	07:14:59	Cn	10/30/1955	18:29:35	Ta
02/10/1955	06:33:17	Li	06/22/1955	07:36:11	Le	11/01/1955	19:22:35	Ge
02/12/1955	16:38:19	Sc	06/24/1955	10:26:00	Vi	11/03/1955	20:11:07	Cn
02/15/1955	05:07:01	Sg	06/26/1955	16:55:16	Li	11/05/1955	22:19:41	Le
02/17/1955	17:34:19	Cp	06/29/1955	03:04:22	Sc	11/08/1955	02:36:24	Vi
02/20/1955	03:32:55	Aq	07/01/1955	15:33:59	Sg	11/10/1955	09:15:09	Li
02/22/1955	10:09:16	Pi	07/04/1955	04:29:16	Cp	11/12/1955	18:12:03	Sc
02/24/1955	14:05:58	Ar	07/06/1955	16:18:08	Aq	11/15/1955	05:16:52	Sg
02/26/1955	16:46:14	Ta	07/09/1955	02:08:28	Pi	11/17/1955	17:58:54	Cp
02/28/1955	19:23:53	Ge	07/11/1955	09:32:55	Ar	11/20/1955	06:58:27	Aq
03/02/1955	22:39:35	Cn	07/13/1955	14:20:03	Ta	11/22/1955	18:10:14	Pi
03/05/1955	02:48:28	Le	07/15/1955	16:42:50	Ge	11/25/1955	01:47:19	Ar
03/07/1955	08:08:38	Vi	07/17/1955	17:29:41	Cn	11/27/1955	05:26:44	Ta
03/09/1955	15:19:44	Li	07/19/1955	18:03:07	Le	11/29/1955	06:10:50	Ge
03/12/1955	01:04:04	Sc	07/21/1955	20:06:13	Vi	12/01/1955	05:46:17	Cn
03/14/1955	13:13:07	Sg	07/24/1955	01:15:59	Li	12/03/1955	06:07:13	Le
03/17/1955	02:01:18	Cp	07/26/1955	10:18:36	Sc	12/05/1955	08:49:42	Vi
03/19/1955	12:46:31	Aq	07/28/1955	22:23:54	Sg	12/07/1955	14:48:04	Li
03/21/1955	19:44:48	Pi	07/31/1955	11:18:27	Cp	12/09/1955	23:59:23	Sc
03/23/1955	23:09:02	Ar	08/02/1955	22:51:37	Aq	12/12/1955	11:33:33	Sg
03/26/1955	00:31:16	Ta	08/05/1955	08:03:57	Pi	12/15/1955	00:23:16	Cp
03/28/1955	01:41:40	Ge	08/07/1955	14:59:28	Ar	12/17/1955	13:19:12	Aq
03/30/1955	04:05:00	Cn	08/09/1955	20:02:50	Ta	12/20/1955	01:01:50	Pi

12/22/1955	10:05:17	Ar	05/02/1956	01:27:23	Aq	09/10/1956	10:45:50	Sg
12/24/1955	15:32:56	Ta	05/04/1956	13:15:19	Pi	09/12/1956	21:45:34	Cp
12/26/1955	17:32:58	Ge	05/06/1956	22:05:25	Ar	09/15/1956	10:27:53	Aq
12/28/1955	17:17:14	Cn	05/09/1956	03:23:55	Ta	09/17/1956	22:33:32	Pi
12/30/1955	16:36:01	Le	05/11/1956	06:00:15	Ge	09/20/1956	08:47:24	Ar
01/01/1956	17:30:39	Vi	05/13/1956	07:20:47	Cn	09/22/1956	17:00:54	Ta
01/03/1956	21:43:57	Li	05/15/1956	08:51:43	Le	09/24/1956	23:24:41	Ge
01/06/1956	05:59:44	Sc	05/17/1956	11:39:46	Vi	09/27/1956	03:59:43	Cn
01/08/1956	17:32:28	Sg	05/19/1956	16:25:22	Li	09/29/1956	06:48:33	Le
01/11/1956	06:33:26	Cp	05/21/1956	23:26:28	Sc	10/01/1956	08:24:13	Vi
01/13/1956	19:19:17	Aq	05/24/1956	08:46:15	Sg	10/03/1956	10:01:10	Li
01/16/1956	06:47:07	Pi	05/26/1956	20:10:59	Cp	10/05/1956	13:18:59	Sc
01/18/1956	16:16:58	Ar	05/29/1956	08:51:38	Aq	10/07/1956	19:45:50	Sg
01/20/1956	23:11:00	Ta	05/31/1956	21:09:24	Pi	10/10/1956	05:47:45	Cp
01/23/1956	03:05:29	Ge	06/03/1956	07:04:27	Ar	10/12/1956	18:09:12	Aq
01/25/1956	04:19:41	Cn	06/05/1956	13:21:43	Ta	10/15/1956	06:24:34	Pi
01/27/1956	04:06:17	Le	06/07/1956	16:09:17	Ge	10/17/1956	16:35:11	Ar
01/29/1956	04:17:14	Vi	06/09/1956	16:41:53	Cn	10/20/1956	00:07:09	Ta
01/31/1956	06:55:39	Li	06/11/1956	16:44:40	Le	10/22/1956	05:28:27	Ge
02/02/1956	13:33:02	Sc	06/13/1956	18:03:18	Vi	10/24/1956	09:23:13	Cn
02/05/1956	00:12:47	Sg	06/15/1956	21:58:23	Li	10/26/1956	12:26:54	Le
02/07/1956	13:08:10	Cp	06/18/1956	05:02:40	Sc	10/28/1956	15:09:22	Vi
02/10/1956	01:51:50	Aq	06/20/1956	14:55:12	Sg	10/30/1956	18:09:44	Li
02/12/1956	12:51:40	Pi	06/23/1956	02:42:55	Cp	11/01/1956	22:24:20	Sc
02/14/1956	21:48:04	Ar	06/25/1956	15:25:28	Aq	11/04/1956	04:56:15	Sg
02/17/1956	04:48:20	Ta	06/28/1956	03:54:18	Pi	11/06/1956	14:23:58	Cp
02/19/1956	09:50:23	Ge	06/30/1956	14:42:44	Ar	11/09/1956	02:19:22	Aq
02/21/1956	12:49:32	Cn	07/02/1956	22:25:32	Ta	11/11/1956	14:50:39	Pi
02/23/1956	14:10:19	Le	07/05/1956	02:25:45	Ge	11/14/1956	01:36:10	Ar
02/25/1956	15:04:44	Vi	07/07/1956	03:19:41	Cn	11/16/1956	09:12:18	Ta
02/27/1956	17:20:22	Li	07/09/1956	02:41:56	Le	11/18/1956	13:44:53	Ge
02/29/1956	22:44:48	Sc	07/11/1956	02:34:20	Vi	11/20/1956	16:17:27	Cn
03/03/1956	08:09:18	Sg	07/13/1956	04:54:11	Li	11/22/1956	18:09:53	Le
03/05/1956	20:32:22	Cp	07/15/1956	10:56:22	Sc	11/24/1956	20:31:48	Vi
03/08/1956	09:19:05	Aq	07/17/1956	20:37:38	Sg	11/27/1956	00:10:56	Li
03/10/1956	20:11:22	Pi	07/20/1956	08:40:29	Cp	11/29/1956	05:34:21	Sc
03/13/1956	04:26:00	Ar	07/22/1956	21:28:13	Aq	12/01/1956	12:58:48	Sg
03/15/1956	10:31:57	Ta	07/25/1956	09:50:06	Pi	12/03/1956	22:35:56	Cp
03/17/1956	15:11:28	Ge	07/27/1956	20:53:33	Ar	12/06/1956	10:16:05	Aq
03/19/1956	18:47:09	Cn	07/30/1956	05:40:06	Ta	12/08/1956	22:56:38	Pi
03/21/1956	21:30:44	Le	08/01/1956	11:15:51	Ge	12/11/1956	10:36:47	Ar
03/23/1956	23:52:52	Vi	08/03/1956	13:32:05	Cn	12/13/1956	19:15:26	Ta
03/26/1956	02:59:38	Li	08/05/1956	13:26:44	Le	12/16/1956	00:06:02	Ge
03/28/1956	08:18:30	Sc	08/07/1956	12:49:37	Vi	12/18/1956	01:51:49	Cn
03/30/1956	16:55:34	Sg	08/09/1956	13:50:31	Li	12/20/1956	02:10:58	Le
04/02/1956	04:37:26	Cp	08/11/1956	18:20:10	Sc	12/22/1956	02:55:32	Vi
04/04/1956	17:24:16	Aq	08/14/1956	02:59:42	Sg	12/24/1956	05:38:47	Li
04/07/1956	04:37:04	Pi	08/16/1956	14:47:24	Cp	12/26/1956	11:08:39	Sc
04/09/1956	12:46:24	Ar	08/19/1956	03:37:37	Aq	12/28/1956	19:19:48	Sg
04/11/1956	18:03:00	Ta	08/21/1956	15:47:06	Pi	12/31/1956	05:36:47	Cp
04/13/1956	21:30:28	Ge	08/24/1956	02:29:29	Ar	01/02/1957	17:24:28	Aq
04/16/1956	00:14:36	Cn	08/26/1956	11:23:20	Ta	01/05/1957	06:04:16	Pi
04/18/1956	03:00:16	Le	08/28/1956	17:59:15	Ge	01/07/1957	18:22:31	Ar
04/20/1956	06:16:42	Vi	08/30/1956	21:51:10	Cn	01/10/1957	04:26:29	Ta
04/22/1956	10:36:13	Li	09/01/1956	23:13:55	Le	01/12/1957	10:43:35	Ge
04/24/1956	16:44:16	Sc	09/03/1956	23:20:16	Vi	01/14/1957	13:05:27	Cn
04/27/1956	01:25:14	Sg	09/06/1956	00:04:17	Li	01/16/1957	12:50:21	Le
04/29/1956	12:44:11	Cp	09/08/1956	03:26:35	Sc	01/18/1957	12:03:23	Vi

01/20/1957	12:54:58	Li	06/02/1957	04:45:03	Le	10/12/1957	13:00:37	Ge
01/22/1957	17:02:25	Sc	06/04/1957	06:59:04	Vi	10/14/1957	20:54:11	Cn
01/25/1957	00:51:53	Sg	06/06/1957	09:45:29	Li	10/17/1957	01:59:16	Le
01/27/1957	11:32:02	Cp	06/08/1957	13:40:43	Sc	10/19/1957	04:23:26	Vi
01/29/1957	23:41:44	Aq	06/10/1957	19:09:14	Sg	10/21/1957	05:03:01	Li
02/01/1957	12:20:23	Pi	06/13/1957	02:36:18	Cp	10/23/1957	05:30:52	Sc
02/04/1957	00:41:50	Ar	06/15/1957	12:23:06	Aq	10/25/1957	07:33:12	Sg
02/06/1957	11:37:02	Ta	06/18/1957	00:14:43	Pi	10/27/1957	12:40:57	Cp
02/08/1957	19:34:22	Ge	06/20/1957	12:45:33	Ar	10/29/1957	21:32:04	Aq
02/10/1957	23:38:39	Cn	06/22/1957	23:38:04	Ta	11/01/1957	09:18:14	Pi
02/13/1957	00:18:29	Le	06/25/1957	07:06:37	Ge	11/03/1957	21:59:52	Ar
02/14/1957	23:16:46	Vi	06/27/1957	11:00:30	Cn	11/06/1957	09:37:40	Ta
02/16/1957	22:49:35	Li	06/29/1957	12:30:54	Le	11/08/1957	19:08:49	Ge
02/19/1957	01:05:44	Sc	07/01/1957	13:23:24	Vi	11/11/1957	02:23:30	Cn
02/21/1957	07:22:46	Sg	07/03/1957	15:15:57	Li	11/13/1957	07:35:59	Le
02/23/1957	17:26:37	Cp	07/05/1957	19:09:49	Sc	11/15/1957	11:06:56	Vi
02/26/1957	05:42:22	Aq	07/08/1957	01:20:13	Sg	11/17/1957	13:25:08	Li
02/28/1957	18:24:57	Pi	07/10/1957	09:34:55	Cp	11/19/1957	15:17:11	Sc
03/03/1957	06:30:38	Ar	07/12/1957	19:42:42	Aq	11/21/1957	17:51:32	Sg
03/05/1957	17:20:16	Ta	07/15/1957	07:32:05	Pi	11/23/1957	22:29:10	Cp
03/08/1957	02:03:18	Ge	07/17/1957	20:14:16	Ar	11/26/1957	06:15:59	Aq
03/10/1957	07:44:44	Cn	07/20/1957	07:57:40	Ta	11/28/1957	17:15:49	Pi
03/12/1957	10:11:33	Le	07/22/1957	16:33:43	Ge	12/01/1957	05:56:20	Ar
03/14/1957	10:19:50	Vi	07/24/1957	21:04:56	Cn	12/03/1957	17:47:41	Ta
03/16/1957	09:58:38	Li	07/26/1957	22:16:23	Le	12/06/1957	03:00:13	Ge
03/18/1957	11:14:40	Sc	07/28/1957	21:59:09	Vi	12/08/1957	09:15:51	Cn
03/20/1957	15:53:35	Sg	07/30/1957	22:19:50	Li	12/10/1957	13:23:06	Le
03/23/1957	00:34:00	Cp	08/02/1957	01:00:29	Sc	12/12/1957	16:28:16	Vi
03/25/1957	12:17:04	Aq	08/04/1957	06:47:10	Sg	12/14/1957	19:22:35	Li
03/28/1957	00:59:38	Pi	08/06/1957	15:23:14	Cp	12/16/1957	22:35:27	Sc
03/30/1957	12:54:39	Ar	08/09/1957	02:01:28	Aq	12/19/1957	02:30:28	Sg
04/01/1957	23:10:54	Ta	08/11/1957	14:01:47	Pi	12/21/1957	07:46:43	Cp
04/04/1957	07:30:03	Ge	08/14/1957	02:45:55	Ar	12/23/1957	15:18:38	Aq
04/06/1957	13:37:14	Cn	08/16/1957	15:00:19	Ta	12/26/1957	01:40:56	Pi
04/08/1957	17:24:04	Le	08/19/1957	00:51:14	Ge	12/28/1957	14:12:35	Ar
04/10/1957	19:12:51	Vi	08/21/1957	06:48:18	Cn	12/31/1957	02:37:02	Ta
04/12/1957	20:08:15	Li	08/23/1957	08:50:54	Le	01/02/1958	12:21:14	Ge
04/14/1957	21:45:11	Sc	08/25/1957	08:25:42	Vi	01/04/1958	18:21:32	Cn
04/17/1957	01:42:46	Sg	08/27/1957	07:41:22	Li	01/06/1958	21:21:23	Le
04/19/1957	09:08:00	Cp	08/29/1957	08:45:27	Sc	01/08/1958	22:58:49	Vi
04/21/1957	19:53:29	Aq	08/31/1957	13:07:00	Sg	01/11/1958	00:51:32	Li
04/24/1957	08:22:46	Pi	09/02/1957	21:05:14	Cp	01/13/1958	04:01:59	Sc
04/26/1957	20:21:42	Ar	09/05/1957	07:49:48	Aq	01/15/1958	08:49:22	Sg
04/29/1957	06:17:33	Ta	09/07/1957	20:03:48	Pi	01/17/1958	15:12:34	Cp
05/01/1957	13:46:35	Ge	09/10/1957	08:44:43	Ar	01/19/1958	23:22:12	Aq
05/03/1957	19:07:58	Cn	09/12/1957	20:57:01	Ta	01/22/1958	09:41:32	Pi
05/05/1957	22:53:29	Le	09/15/1957	07:26:02	Ge	01/24/1958	22:02:56	Ar
05/08/1957	01:36:38	Vi	09/17/1957	14:49:27	Cn	01/27/1958	10:56:26	Ta
05/10/1957	03:57:12	Li	09/19/1957	18:30:38	Le	01/29/1958	21:47:08	Ge
05/12/1957	06:48:03	Sc	09/21/1957	19:11:01	Vi	02/01/1958	04:40:29	Cn
05/14/1957	11:13:25	Sg	09/23/1957	18:32:34	Li	02/03/1958	07:37:25	Le
05/16/1957	18:13:25	Cp	09/25/1957	18:40:12	Sc	02/05/1958	08:10:33	Vi
05/19/1957	04:12:11	Aq	09/27/1957	21:27:06	Sg	02/07/1958	08:23:14	Li
05/21/1957	16:20:04	Pi	09/30/1957	03:59:04	Cp	02/09/1958	10:02:58	Sc
05/24/1957	04:33:43	Ar	10/02/1957	14:03:49	Aq	02/11/1958	14:11:13	Sg
05/26/1957	14:42:55	Ta	10/05/1957	02:17:18	Pi	02/13/1958	20:55:05	Cp
05/28/1957	21:46:47	Ge	10/07/1957	14:56:53	Ar	02/16/1958	05:51:10	Aq
05/31/1957	02:05:30	Cn	10/10/1957	02:47:40	Ta	02/18/1958	16:39:12	Pi

02/21/1958	05:01:41	Ar	07/02/1958	19:44:26	Aq	11/12/1958	01:02:55	Sg
02/23/1958	18:04:39	Ta	07/05/1958	03:56:53	Pi	11/14/1958	01:54:14	Cp
02/26/1958	05:52:18	Ge	07/07/1958	15:17:46	Ar	11/16/1958	05:52:52	Aq
02/28/1958	14:16:38	Cn	07/10/1958	04:08:55	Ta	11/18/1958	13:56:20	Pi
03/02/1958	18:26:42	Le	07/12/1958	15:46:24	Ge	11/21/1958	01:28:16	Ar
03/04/1958	19:14:50	Vi	07/15/1958	00:15:24	Cn	11/23/1958	14:30:20	Ta
03/06/1958	18:35:13	Li	07/17/1958	05:30:48	Le	11/26/1958	03:00:19	Ge
03/08/1958	18:34:20	Sc	07/19/1958	08:41:54	Vi	11/28/1958	13:51:00	Cn
03/10/1958	20:56:18	Sg	07/21/1958	11:11:28	Li	11/30/1958	22:40:39	Le
03/13/1958	02:36:17	Cp	07/23/1958	13:57:13	Sc	12/03/1958	05:17:46	Vi
03/15/1958	11:27:51	Aq	07/25/1958	17:25:27	Sg	12/05/1958	09:30:34	Li
03/17/1958	22:41:12	Pi	07/27/1958	21:52:47	Cp	12/07/1958	11:27:57	Sc
03/20/1958	11:16:56	Ar	07/30/1958	03:52:08	Aq	12/09/1958	12:01:37	Sg
03/23/1958	00:15:32	Ta	08/01/1958	12:11:27	Pi	12/11/1958	12:46:14	Cp
03/25/1958	12:19:32	Ge	08/03/1958	23:14:14	Ar	12/13/1958	15:37:38	Aq
03/27/1958	21:52:45	Cn	08/06/1958	12:04:07	Ta	12/15/1958	22:11:53	Pi
03/30/1958	03:45:27	Le	08/09/1958	00:16:11	Ge	12/18/1958	08:45:24	Ar
04/01/1958	06:00:52	Vi	08/11/1958	09:24:58	Cn	12/20/1958	21:37:31	Ta
04/03/1958	05:53:42	Li	08/13/1958	14:43:20	Le	12/23/1958	10:08:49	Ge
04/05/1958	05:16:26	Sc	08/15/1958	17:06:51	Vi	12/25/1958	20:32:43	Cn
04/07/1958	06:06:46	Sg	08/17/1958	18:16:53	Li	12/28/1958	04:33:06	Le
04/09/1958	10:00:32	Cp	08/19/1958	19:49:31	Sc	12/30/1958	10:40:34	Vi
04/11/1958	17:41:19	Aq	08/21/1958	22:47:51	Sg	01/01/1959	15:21:01	Li
04/14/1958	04:38:21	Pi	08/24/1958	03:38:09	Cp	01/03/1959	18:41:46	Sc
04/16/1958	17:22:45	Ar	08/26/1958	10:27:37	Aq	01/05/1959	20:55:29	Sg
04/19/1958	06:16:13	Ta	08/28/1958	19:24:51	Pi	01/07/1959	22:49:45	Cp
04/21/1958	18:02:53	Ge	08/31/1958	06:35:00	Ar	01/10/1959	01:51:31	Aq
04/24/1958	03:46:13	Cn	09/02/1958	19:23:46	Ta	01/12/1959	07:39:29	Pi
04/26/1958	10:43:37	Le	09/05/1958	08:06:36	Ge	01/14/1959	17:09:29	Ar
04/28/1958	14:40:26	Vi	09/07/1958	18:21:57	Cn	01/17/1959	05:32:34	Ta
04/30/1958	16:06:20	Li	09/10/1958	00:41:31	Le	01/19/1959	18:15:32	Ge
05/02/1958	16:13:58	Sc	09/12/1958	03:19:21	Vi	01/22/1959	04:46:35	Cn
05/04/1958	16:43:17	Sg	09/14/1958	03:44:18	Li	01/24/1959	12:13:06	Le
05/06/1958	19:20:38	Cp	09/16/1958	03:49:18	Sc	01/26/1959	17:13:16	Vi
05/09/1958	01:29:17	Aq	09/18/1958	05:15:58	Sg	01/28/1959	20:54:02	Li
05/11/1958	11:26:48	Pi	09/20/1958	09:12:36	Cp	01/31/1959	00:05:16	Sc
05/13/1958	23:57:41	Ar	09/22/1958	16:03:10	Aq	02/02/1959	03:10:29	Sg
05/16/1958	12:49:41	Ta	09/25/1958	01:33:06	Pi	02/04/1959	06:28:37	Cp
05/19/1958	00:13:40	Ge	09/27/1958	13:07:23	Ar	02/06/1959	10:40:17	Aq
05/21/1958	09:22:51	Cn	09/30/1958	01:57:54	Ta	02/08/1959	16:50:03	Pi
05/23/1958	16:14:27	Le	10/02/1958	14:50:21	Ge	02/11/1959	01:54:32	Ar
05/25/1958	20:59:47	Vi	10/05/1958	02:00:02	Cn	02/13/1959	13:47:02	Ta
05/27/1958	23:55:15	Li	10/07/1958	09:50:28	Le	02/16/1959	02:39:19	Ge
05/30/1958	01:33:09	Sc	10/09/1958	13:49:20	Vi	02/18/1959	13:50:26	Cn
06/01/1958	02:53:28	Sg	10/11/1958	14:43:33	Li	02/20/1959	21:37:40	Le
06/03/1958	05:22:37	Cp	10/13/1958	14:11:27	Sc	02/23/1959	02:05:45	Vi
06/05/1958	10:33:38	Aq	10/15/1958	14:08:49	Sg	02/25/1959	04:28:37	Li
06/07/1958	19:23:42	Pi	10/17/1958	16:22:42	Cp	02/27/1959	06:14:29	Sc
06/10/1958	07:20:20	Ar	10/19/1958	22:03:52	Aq	03/01/1959	08:32:48	Sg
06/12/1958	20:12:16	Ta	10/22/1958	07:19:28	Pi	03/03/1959	12:05:28	Cp
06/15/1958	07:30:50	Ge	10/24/1958	19:10:24	Ar	03/05/1959	17:16:04	Aq
06/17/1958	16:03:38	Cn	10/27/1958	08:07:25	Ta	03/08/1959	00:25:20	Pi
06/19/1958	22:03:52	Le	10/29/1958	20:49:25	Ge	03/10/1959	09:53:30	Ar
06/22/1958	02:21:55	Vi	11/01/1958	08:08:38	Cn	03/12/1959	21:36:33	Ta
06/24/1958	05:42:07	Li	11/03/1958	17:02:28	Le	03/15/1959	10:30:29	Ge
06/26/1958	08:30:25	Sc	11/05/1958	22:45:25	Vi	03/17/1959	22:27:45	Cn
06/28/1958	11:11:29	Sg	11/08/1958	01:16:16	Li	03/20/1959	07:22:20	Le
06/30/1958	14:32:07	Cp	11/10/1958	01:29:34	Sc	03/22/1959	12:27:34	Vi

03/24/1959	14:26:51	Li
03/26/1959	14:53:32	Sc
03/28/1959	15:31:18	Sg
03/30/1959	17:48:44	Cp
04/01/1959	22:41:26	Aq
04/04/1959	06:22:58	Pi
04/06/1959	16:32:39	Ar
04/09/1959	04:31:38	Ta
04/11/1959	17:24:43	Ge
04/14/1959	05:47:38	Cn
04/16/1959	15:54:49	Le
04/18/1959	22:27:26	Vi
04/21/1959	01:18:45	Li
04/23/1959	01:33:38	Sc
04/25/1959	00:58:49	Sg
04/27/1959	01:32:24	Cp
04/29/1959	04:55:23	Aq
05/01/1959	11:58:21	Pi
05/03/1959	22:18:44	Ar
05/06/1959	10:38:51	Ta
05/08/1959	23:34:13	Ge
05/11/1959	11:56:30	Cn
05/13/1959	22:40:22	Le
05/16/1959	06:37:38	Vi
05/18/1959	11:06:18	Li
05/20/1959	12:24:09	Sc
05/22/1959	11:50:41	Sg
05/24/1959	11:23:51	Cp
05/26/1959	13:09:25	Aq
05/28/1959	18:42:10	Pi
05/31/1959	04:18:13	Ar
06/02/1959	16:36:49	Ta
06/05/1959	05:35:12	Ge
06/07/1959	17:43:36	Cn
06/10/1959	04:18:46	Le
06/12/1959	12:50:00	Vi
06/14/1959	18:41:45	Li
06/16/1959	21:38:03	Sc
06/18/1959	22:14:22	Sg
06/20/1959	22:01:09	Cp
06/22/1959	23:00:25	Aq
06/25/1959	03:09:07	Pi
06/27/1959	11:27:34	Ar
06/29/1959	23:10:48	Ta
07/02/1959	12:05:22	Ge
07/05/1959	00:03:16	Cn
07/07/1959	10:07:51	Le
07/09/1959	18:15:06	Vi
07/12/1959	00:26:18	Li
07/14/1959	04:33:01	Sc
07/16/1959	06:41:40	Sg
07/18/1959	07:41:27	Cp
07/20/1959	09:04:38	Aq
07/22/1959	12:40:54	Pi
07/24/1959	19:53:24	Ar
07/27/1959	06:43:05	Ta
07/29/1959	19:23:23	Ge
08/01/1959	07:23:32	Cn
08/03/1959	17:09:00	Le
08/06/1959	00:29:27	Vi
08/08/1959	05:56:16	Li
08/10/1959	09:59:29	Sc
08/12/1959	12:58:04	Sg
08/14/1959	15:18:28	Cp
08/16/1959	17:53:16	Aq
08/18/1959	21:59:14	Pi
08/21/1959	04:51:27	Ar
08/23/1959	14:58:12	Ta
08/26/1959	03:18:22	Ge
08/28/1959	15:33:21	Cn
08/31/1959	01:33:14	Le
09/02/1959	08:30:43	Vi
09/04/1959	12:56:24	Li
09/06/1959	15:52:51	Sc
09/08/1959	18:20:08	Sg
09/10/1959	21:04:28	Cp
09/13/1959	00:43:08	Aq
09/15/1959	05:53:56	Pi
09/17/1959	13:16:02	Ar
09/19/1959	23:12:12	Ta
09/22/1959	11:15:58	Ge
09/24/1959	23:49:06	Cn
09/27/1959	10:36:03	Le
09/29/1959	18:03:55	Vi
10/01/1959	22:08:15	Li
10/03/1959	23:53:53	Sc
10/06/1959	00:53:58	Sg
10/08/1959	02:38:18	Cp
10/10/1959	06:12:11	Aq
10/12/1959	12:05:52	Pi
10/14/1959	20:19:49	Ar
10/17/1959	06:39:49	Ta
10/19/1959	18:39:56	Ge
10/22/1959	07:22:21	Cn
10/24/1959	19:03:16	Le
10/27/1959	03:48:24	Vi
10/29/1959	08:41:21	Li
10/31/1959	10:13:53	Sc
11/02/1959	10:01:39	Sg
11/04/1959	10:04:50	Cp
11/06/1959	12:13:51	Aq
11/08/1959	17:35:29	Pi
11/11/1959	02:09:52	Ar
11/13/1959	13:04:07	Ta
11/16/1959	01:16:22	Ge
11/18/1959	13:56:30	Cn
11/21/1959	02:03:51	Le
11/23/1959	12:07:48	Vi
11/25/1959	18:41:03	Li
11/27/1959	21:21:25	Sc
11/29/1959	21:11:33	Sg
12/01/1959	20:10:46	Cp
12/03/1959	20:34:45	Aq
12/06/1959	00:16:12	Pi
12/08/1959	07:59:23	Ar
12/10/1959	18:55:47	Ta
12/13/1959	07:24:00	Ge
12/15/1959	20:00:22	Cn
12/18/1959	07:57:38	Le
12/20/1959	18:29:30	Vi
12/23/1959	02:28:35	Li
12/25/1959	07:00:30	Sc
12/27/1959	08:15:27	Sg
12/29/1959	07:37:37	Cp
12/31/1959	07:14:44	Aq
01/02/1960	09:18:52	Pi
01/04/1960	15:21:12	Ar
01/07/1960	01:22:23	Ta
01/09/1960	13:44:59	Ge
01/12/1960	02:23:16	Cn
01/14/1960	13:59:02	Le
01/17/1960	00:03:16	Vi
01/19/1960	08:14:07	Li
01/21/1960	13:59:05	Sc
01/23/1960	17:02:26	Sg
01/25/1960	17:59:28	Cp
01/27/1960	18:18:46	Aq
01/29/1960	19:56:25	Pi
02/01/1960	00:38:57	Ar
02/03/1960	09:15:59	Ta
02/05/1960	20:58:24	Ge
02/08/1960	09:37:02	Cn
02/10/1960	21:08:00	Le
02/13/1960	06:34:39	Vi
02/15/1960	13:55:14	Li
02/17/1960	19:23:37	Sc
02/19/1960	23:11:35	Sg
02/22/1960	01:39:22	Cp
02/24/1960	03:32:24	Aq
02/26/1960	06:03:37	Pi
02/28/1960	10:37:29	Ar
03/01/1960	18:18:24	Ta
03/04/1960	05:07:40	Ge
03/06/1960	17:36:35	Cn
03/09/1960	05:24:53	Le
03/11/1960	14:47:20	Vi
03/13/1960	21:19:26	Li
03/16/1960	01:36:57	Sc
03/18/1960	04:37:17	Sg
03/20/1960	07:14:06	Cp
03/22/1960	10:09:59	Aq
03/24/1960	14:01:55	Pi
03/26/1960	19:29:27	Ar
03/29/1960	03:13:00	Ta
03/31/1960	13:31:45	Ge
04/03/1960	01:45:43	Cn
04/05/1960	14:00:53	Le
04/08/1960	00:01:44	Vi
04/10/1960	06:35:26	Li
04/12/1960	10:00:58	Sc
04/14/1960	11:37:25	Sg
04/16/1960	13:00:54	Cp
04/18/1960	15:31:48	Aq
04/20/1960	19:55:27	Pi

04/23/1960	02:22:48	Ar	09/02/1960	12:34:57	Aq	01/13/1961	02:40:19	Sg
04/25/1960	10:50:27	Ta	09/04/1960	13:50:45	Pi	01/15/1961	03:41:03	Cp
04/27/1960	21:16:12	Ge	09/06/1960	16:25:46	Ar	01/17/1961	02:55:25	Aq
04/30/1960	09:22:24	Cn	09/08/1960	21:44:23	Ta	01/19/1961	02:31:50	Pi
05/02/1960	21:58:36	Le	09/11/1960	06:30:57	Ge	01/21/1961	04:26:23	Ar
05/05/1960	08:58:49	Vi	09/13/1960	18:10:22	Cn	01/23/1961	09:51:16	Ta
05/07/1960	16:29:56	Li	09/16/1960	06:46:24	Le	01/25/1961	18:49:48	Ge
05/09/1960	20:06:30	Sc	09/18/1960	18:06:57	Vi	01/28/1961	06:21:49	Cn
05/11/1960	20:54:56	Sg	09/21/1960	02:58:14	Li	01/30/1961	19:04:59	Le
05/13/1960	20:50:15	Cp	09/23/1960	09:17:39	Sc	02/02/1961	07:48:10	Vi
05/15/1960	21:51:00	Aq	09/25/1960	13:41:39	Sg	02/04/1961	19:26:54	Li
05/18/1960	01:23:20	Pi	09/27/1960	16:53:51	Cp	02/07/1961	04:50:36	Sc
05/20/1960	07:55:05	Ar	09/29/1960	19:32:16	Aq	02/09/1961	11:01:02	Sg
05/22/1960	16:59:53	Ta	10/01/1960	22:14:00	Pi	02/11/1961	13:50:24	Cp
05/25/1960	03:54:44	Ge	10/04/1960	01:46:11	Ar	02/13/1961	14:14:23	Aq
05/27/1960	16:06:11	Cn	10/06/1960	07:08:43	Ta	02/15/1961	13:52:47	Pi
05/30/1960	04:50:19	Le	10/08/1960	15:16:28	Ge	02/17/1961	14:40:40	Ar
06/01/1960	16:37:53	Vi	10/11/1960	02:18:07	Cn	02/19/1961	18:21:09	Ta
06/04/1960	01:31:05	Li	10/13/1960	14:54:51	Le	02/22/1961	01:51:22	Ge
06/06/1960	06:19:43	Sc	10/16/1960	02:39:58	Vi	02/24/1961	12:48:36	Cn
06/08/1960	07:30:45	Sg	10/18/1960	11:32:15	Li	02/27/1961	01:34:21	Le
06/10/1960	06:47:38	Cp	10/20/1960	17:05:41	Sc	03/01/1961	14:11:51	Vi
06/12/1960	06:22:55	Aq	10/22/1960	20:15:38	Sg	03/04/1961	01:20:56	Li
06/14/1960	08:17:27	Pi	10/24/1960	22:27:59	Cp	03/06/1961	10:23:32	Sc
06/16/1960	13:42:20	Ar	10/27/1960	00:57:17	Aq	03/08/1961	17:03:36	Sg
06/18/1960	22:33:08	Ta	10/29/1960	04:26:07	Pi	03/10/1961	21:18:42	Cp
06/21/1960	09:45:54	Ge	10/31/1960	09:11:04	Ar	03/12/1961	23:28:51	Aq
06/23/1960	22:09:35	Cn	11/02/1960	15:27:19	Ta	03/15/1961	00:26:01	Pi
06/26/1960	10:51:23	Le	11/04/1960	23:44:21	Ge	03/17/1961	01:32:10	Ar
06/28/1960	22:52:38	Vi	11/07/1960	10:25:57	Cn	03/19/1961	04:25:21	Ta
07/01/1960	08:46:04	Li	11/09/1960	22:59:18	Le	03/21/1961	10:32:05	Ge
07/03/1960	15:08:22	Sc	11/12/1960	11:23:51	Vi	03/23/1961	20:22:12	Cn
07/05/1960	17:42:13	Sg	11/14/1960	21:07:22	Li	03/26/1961	08:48:24	Le
07/07/1960	17:34:07	Cp	11/17/1960	02:53:01	Sc	03/28/1961	21:29:33	Vi
07/09/1960	16:42:56	Aq	11/19/1960	05:16:34	Sg	03/31/1961	08:20:59	Li
07/11/1960	17:18:56	Pi	11/21/1960	06:01:59	Cp	04/02/1961	16:36:26	Sc
07/13/1960	21:06:54	Ar	11/23/1960	07:04:24	Aq	04/04/1961	22:33:48	Sg
07/16/1960	04:48:07	Ta	11/25/1960	09:49:18	Pi	04/07/1961	02:51:53	Cp
07/18/1960	15:40:19	Ge	11/27/1960	14:50:33	Ar	04/09/1961	06:02:35	Aq
07/21/1960	04:08:49	Cn	11/29/1960	21:59:32	Ta	04/11/1961	08:31:19	Pi
07/23/1960	16:45:40	Le	12/02/1960	07:00:32	Ge	04/13/1961	10:55:07	Ar
07/26/1960	04:31:12	Vi	12/04/1960	17:52:01	Cn	04/15/1961	14:16:25	Ta
07/28/1960	14:33:02	Li	12/07/1960	06:20:59	Le	04/17/1961	19:54:50	Ge
07/30/1960	21:54:49	Sc	12/09/1960	19:13:13	Vi	04/20/1961	04:49:49	Cn
08/02/1960	02:04:03	Sg	12/12/1960	06:10:09	Li	04/22/1961	16:42:55	Le
08/04/1960	03:25:26	Cp	12/14/1960	13:12:56	Sc	04/25/1961	05:30:51	Vi
08/06/1960	03:20:37	Aq	12/16/1960	16:06:45	Sg	04/27/1961	16:34:17	Li
08/08/1960	03:41:58	Pi	12/18/1960	16:16:02	Cp	04/30/1961	00:26:54	Sc
08/10/1960	06:21:21	Ar	12/20/1960	15:48:35	Aq	05/02/1961	05:24:45	Sg
08/12/1960	12:35:33	Ta	12/22/1960	16:47:14	Pi	05/04/1961	08:39:30	Cp
08/14/1960	22:29:11	Ge	12/24/1960	20:34:26	Ar	05/06/1961	11:23:51	Aq
08/17/1960	10:42:43	Cn	12/27/1960	03:30:03	Ta	05/08/1961	14:22:32	Pi
08/19/1960	23:17:33	Le	12/29/1960	13:01:16	Ge	05/10/1961	17:55:40	Ar
08/22/1960	10:41:22	Vi	01/01/1961	00:21:33	Cn	05/12/1961	22:24:56	Ta
08/24/1960	20:09:09	Li	01/03/1961	12:53:46	Le	05/15/1961	04:34:13	Ge
08/27/1960	03:23:27	Sc	01/06/1961	01:47:59	Vi	05/17/1961	13:16:33	Cn
08/29/1960	08:18:58	Sg	01/08/1961	13:30:57	Li	05/20/1961	00:44:51	Le
08/31/1960	11:08:35	Cp	01/10/1961	22:08:32	Sc	05/22/1961	13:38:07	Vi

05/25/1961	01:17:34	Li
05/27/1961	09:34:18	Sc
05/29/1961	14:10:46	Sg
05/31/1961	16:19:59	Cp
06/02/1961	17:44:36	Aq
06/04/1961	19:50:11	Pi
06/06/1961	23:23:22	Ar
06/09/1961	04:37:39	Ta
06/11/1961	11:40:14	Ge
06/13/1961	20:49:31	Cn
06/16/1961	08:15:36	Le
06/18/1961	21:11:51	Vi
06/21/1961	09:31:45	Li
06/23/1961	18:50:40	Sc
06/26/1961	00:05:23	Sg
06/28/1961	01:59:37	Cp
06/30/1961	02:17:45	Aq
07/02/1961	02:52:28	Pi
07/04/1961	05:11:44	Ar
07/06/1961	10:01:27	Ta
07/08/1961	17:27:07	Ge
07/11/1961	03:12:54	Cn
07/13/1961	14:56:17	Le
07/16/1961	03:54:32	Vi
07/18/1961	16:38:32	Li
07/21/1961	03:04:30	Sc
07/23/1961	09:41:45	Sg
07/25/1961	12:28:26	Cp
07/27/1961	12:41:15	Aq
07/29/1961	12:12:41	Pi
07/31/1961	12:55:40	Ar
08/02/1961	16:18:40	Ta
08/04/1961	23:03:52	Ge
08/07/1961	08:56:23	Cn
08/09/1961	20:59:04	Le
08/12/1961	10:00:11	Vi
08/14/1961	22:43:30	Li
08/17/1961	09:44:14	Sc
08/19/1961	17:43:39	Sg
08/21/1961	22:07:02	Cp
08/23/1961	23:25:15	Aq
08/25/1961	23:02:18	Pi
08/27/1961	22:48:38	Ar
08/30/1961	00:36:35	Ta
09/01/1961	05:52:28	Ge
09/03/1961	15:00:03	Cn
09/06/1961	03:00:42	Le
09/08/1961	16:04:53	Vi
09/11/1961	04:33:11	Li
09/13/1961	15:22:41	Sc
09/15/1961	23:54:17	Sg
09/18/1961	05:41:47	Cp
09/20/1961	08:42:59	Aq
09/22/1961	09:35:50	Pi
09/24/1961	09:39:47	Ar
09/26/1961	10:41:49	Ta
09/28/1961	14:31:30	Ge
09/30/1961	22:18:58	Cn

10/03/1961	09:43:27	Le
10/05/1961	22:45:28	Vi
10/08/1961	11:03:38	Li
10/10/1961	21:18:57	Sc
10/13/1961	05:20:41	Sg
10/15/1961	11:23:34	Cp
10/17/1961	15:36:57	Aq
10/19/1961	18:09:45	Pi
10/21/1961	19:35:28	Ar
10/23/1961	21:06:39	Ta
10/26/1961	00:24:24	Ge
10/28/1961	07:02:46	Cn
10/30/1961	17:29:32	Le
11/02/1961	06:17:25	Vi
11/04/1961	18:42:15	Li
11/07/1961	04:40:19	Sc
11/09/1961	11:50:43	Sg
11/11/1961	16:59:20	Cp
11/13/1961	20:59:02	Aq
11/16/1961	00:18:18	Pi
11/18/1961	03:10:06	Ar
11/20/1961	06:02:47	Ta
11/22/1961	09:58:51	Ge
11/24/1961	16:20:18	Cn
11/27/1961	02:01:12	Le
11/29/1961	14:24:57	Vi
12/02/1961	03:07:53	Li
12/04/1961	13:29:44	Sc
12/06/1961	20:24:30	Sg
12/09/1961	00:30:33	Cp
12/11/1961	03:11:16	Aq
12/13/1961	05:41:24	Pi
12/15/1961	08:43:57	Ar
12/17/1961	12:38:35	Ta
12/19/1961	17:47:18	Ge
12/22/1961	00:49:34	Cn
12/24/1961	10:25:39	Le
12/26/1961	22:29:17	Vi
12/29/1961	11:26:11	Li
12/31/1961	22:41:47	Sc
01/03/1962	06:22:59	Sg
01/05/1962	10:23:51	Cp
01/07/1962	11:59:54	Aq
01/09/1962	12:53:09	Pi
01/11/1962	14:33:44	Ar
01/13/1962	18:01:14	Ta
01/15/1962	23:41:46	Ge
01/18/1962	07:39:28	Cn
01/20/1962	17:49:41	Le
01/23/1962	05:53:25	Vi
01/25/1962	18:51:52	Li
01/28/1962	06:54:02	Sc
01/30/1962	15:59:09	Sg
02/01/1962	21:09:27	Cp
02/03/1962	22:56:39	Aq
02/05/1962	22:52:41	Pi
02/07/1962	22:50:21	Ar
02/10/1962	00:34:36	Ta

02/12/1962	05:18:08	Ge
02/14/1962	13:19:38	Cn
02/17/1962	00:03:37	Le
02/19/1962	12:26:30	Vi
02/22/1962	01:21:28	Li
02/24/1962	13:36:15	Sc
02/26/1962	23:46:11	Sg
03/01/1962	06:37:55	Cp
03/03/1962	09:51:36	Aq
03/05/1962	10:16:18	Pi
03/07/1962	09:31:48	Ar
03/09/1962	09:39:55	Ta
03/11/1962	12:35:02	Ge
03/13/1962	19:25:28	Cn
03/16/1962	05:55:45	Le
03/18/1962	18:32:45	Vi
03/21/1962	07:28:10	Li
03/23/1962	19:28:29	Sc
03/26/1962	05:48:30	Sg
03/28/1962	13:45:30	Cp
03/30/1962	18:43:03	Aq
04/01/1962	20:42:12	Pi
04/03/1962	20:40:57	Ar
04/05/1962	20:24:54	Ta
04/07/1962	21:59:36	Ge
04/10/1962	03:11:57	Cn
04/12/1962	12:35:59	Le
04/15/1962	00:56:41	Vi
04/17/1962	13:53:32	Li
04/20/1962	01:36:51	Sc
04/22/1962	11:26:48	Sg
04/24/1962	19:19:40	Cp
04/27/1962	01:07:49	Aq
04/29/1962	04:39:53	Pi
05/01/1962	06:11:54	Ar
05/03/1962	06:48:54	Ta
05/05/1962	08:16:15	Ge
05/07/1962	12:27:49	Cn
05/09/1962	20:35:25	Le
05/12/1962	08:11:05	Vi
05/14/1962	21:02:30	Li
05/17/1962	08:42:50	Sc
05/19/1962	18:02:22	Sg
05/22/1962	01:07:57	Cp
05/24/1962	06:30:37	Aq
05/26/1962	10:29:20	Pi
05/28/1962	13:14:43	Ar
05/30/1962	15:16:32	Ta
06/01/1962	17:40:18	Ge
06/03/1962	21:56:22	Cn
06/06/1962	05:23:05	Le
06/08/1962	16:12:00	Vi
06/11/1962	04:50:29	Li
06/13/1962	16:44:40	Sc
06/16/1962	02:03:26	Sg
06/18/1962	08:29:40	Cp
06/20/1962	12:48:47	Aq
06/22/1962	15:58:30	Pi

06/24/1962	18:42:52	Ar
06/26/1962	21:34:16	Ta
06/29/1962	01:09:16	Ge
07/01/1962	06:18:32	Cn
07/03/1962	13:55:25	Le
07/06/1962	00:21:57	Vi
07/08/1962	12:47:37	Li
07/11/1962	01:05:10	Sc
07/13/1962	11:00:06	Sg
07/15/1962	17:31:52	Cp
07/17/1962	21:07:05	Aq
07/19/1962	23:00:04	Pi
07/22/1962	00:33:32	Ar
07/24/1962	02:56:40	Ta
07/26/1962	06:56:37	Ge
07/28/1962	13:00:11	Cn
07/30/1962	21:20:40	Le
08/02/1962	07:57:16	Vi
08/04/1962	20:17:28	Li
08/07/1962	08:55:34	Sc
08/09/1962	19:47:58	Sg
08/12/1962	03:17:31	Cp
08/14/1962	07:07:13	Aq
08/16/1962	08:16:32	Pi
08/18/1962	08:25:07	Ar
08/20/1962	09:19:44	Ta
08/22/1962	12:27:44	Ge
08/24/1962	18:33:31	Cn
08/27/1962	03:29:49	Le
08/29/1962	14:35:30	Vi
09/01/1962	03:00:46	Li
09/03/1962	15:46:15	Sc
09/06/1962	03:25:57	Sg
09/08/1962	12:19:44	Cp
09/10/1962	17:26:01	Aq
09/12/1962	19:01:36	Pi
09/14/1962	18:32:32	Ar
09/16/1962	18:00:33	Ta
09/18/1962	19:28:49	Ge
09/21/1962	00:25:36	Cn
09/23/1962	09:06:42	Le
09/25/1962	20:30:46	Vi
09/28/1962	09:07:51	Li
09/30/1962	21:48:37	Sc
10/03/1962	09:39:43	Sg
10/05/1962	19:34:56	Cp
10/08/1962	02:21:29	Aq
10/10/1962	05:28:36	Pi
10/12/1962	05:40:26	Ar
10/14/1962	04:43:08	Ta
10/16/1962	04:50:14	Ge
10/18/1962	08:04:38	Cn
10/20/1962	15:30:06	Le
10/23/1962	02:30:57	Vi
10/25/1962	15:13:30	Li
10/28/1962	03:48:32	Sc
10/30/1962	15:19:26	Sg
11/02/1962	01:17:06	Cp
11/04/1962	09:02:09	Aq
11/06/1962	13:52:07	Pi
11/08/1962	15:45:15	Ar
11/10/1962	15:44:47	Ta
11/12/1962	15:43:23	Ge
11/14/1962	17:48:43	Cn
11/16/1962	23:39:47	Le
11/19/1962	09:33:08	Vi
11/21/1962	21:57:48	Li
11/24/1962	10:33:14	Sc
11/26/1962	21:43:11	Sg
11/29/1962	07:00:17	Cp
12/01/1962	14:25:36	Aq
12/03/1962	19:53:24	Pi
12/05/1962	23:17:02	Ar
12/08/1962	00:59:10	Ta
12/10/1962	02:07:20	Ge
12/12/1962	04:21:04	Cn
12/14/1962	09:20:13	Le
12/16/1962	17:59:17	Vi
12/19/1962	05:40:58	Li
12/21/1962	18:17:48	Sc
12/24/1962	05:32:32	Sg
12/26/1962	14:18:34	Cp
12/28/1962	20:42:16	Aq
12/31/1962	01:20:13	Pi
01/02/1963	04:47:32	Ar
01/04/1963	07:33:27	Ta
01/06/1963	10:13:49	Ge
01/08/1963	13:41:15	Cn
01/10/1963	19:00:46	Le
01/13/1963	03:06:55	Vi
01/15/1963	14:04:33	Li
01/18/1963	02:35:26	Sc
01/20/1963	14:20:25	Sg
01/22/1963	23:23:28	Cp
01/25/1963	05:13:35	Aq
01/27/1963	08:34:50	Pi
01/29/1963	10:43:35	Ar
01/31/1963	12:54:37	Ta
02/02/1963	16:02:52	Ge
02/04/1963	20:40:16	Cn
02/07/1963	03:05:43	Le
02/09/1963	11:35:54	Vi
02/11/1963	22:17:57	Li
02/14/1963	10:38:18	Sc
02/16/1963	22:56:56	Sg
02/19/1963	09:00:04	Cp
02/21/1963	15:23:15	Aq
02/23/1963	18:17:04	Pi
02/25/1963	19:04:54	Ar
02/27/1963	19:38:16	Ta
03/01/1963	21:38:31	Ge
03/04/1963	02:07:40	Cn
03/06/1963	09:14:51	Le
03/08/1963	18:33:41	Vi
03/11/1963	05:34:49	Li
03/13/1963	17:51:14	Sc
03/16/1963	06:26:46	Sg
03/18/1963	17:34:32	Cp
03/21/1963	01:21:05	Aq
03/23/1963	05:04:06	Pi
03/25/1963	05:37:28	Ar
03/27/1963	04:56:40	Ta
03/29/1963	05:12:52	Ge
03/31/1963	08:13:31	Cn
04/02/1963	14:45:23	Le
04/05/1963	00:20:21	Vi
04/07/1963	11:49:27	Li
04/10/1963	00:13:33	Sc
04/12/1963	12:47:52	Sg
04/15/1963	00:26:55	Cp
04/17/1963	09:33:56	Aq
04/19/1963	14:53:13	Pi
04/21/1963	16:29:40	Ar
04/23/1963	15:50:36	Ta
04/25/1963	15:06:06	Ge
04/27/1963	16:27:02	Cn
04/29/1963	21:24:54	Le
05/02/1963	06:12:50	Vi
05/04/1963	17:42:07	Li
05/07/1963	06:15:44	Sc
05/09/1963	18:42:20	Sg
05/12/1963	06:13:17	Cp
05/14/1963	15:51:14	Aq
05/16/1963	22:31:44	Pi
05/19/1963	01:47:32	Ar
05/21/1963	02:21:11	Ta
05/23/1963	01:53:21	Ge
05/25/1963	02:28:32	Cn
05/27/1963	05:58:31	Le
05/29/1963	13:21:32	Vi
06/01/1963	00:08:54	Li
06/03/1963	12:38:28	Sc
06/06/1963	01:00:35	Sg
06/08/1963	12:06:34	Cp
06/10/1963	21:21:47	Aq
06/13/1963	04:20:29	Pi
06/15/1963	08:46:16	Ar
06/17/1963	10:54:20	Ta
06/19/1963	11:43:35	Ge
06/21/1963	12:46:15	Cn
06/23/1963	15:43:59	Le
06/25/1963	21:56:11	Vi
06/28/1963	07:40:36	Li
06/30/1963	19:47:35	Sc
07/03/1963	08:11:06	Sg
07/05/1963	19:02:53	Cp
07/08/1963	03:36:03	Aq
07/10/1963	09:52:49	Pi
07/12/1963	14:15:59	Ar
07/14/1963	17:14:49	Ta
07/16/1963	19:26:59	Ge
07/18/1963	21:44:44	Cn
07/21/1963	01:14:52	Le
07/23/1963	07:06:28	Vi

07/25/1963	16:02:14	Li
07/28/1963	03:38:21	Sc
07/30/1963	16:07:48	Sg
08/02/1963	03:12:11	Cp
08/04/1963	11:25:24	Aq
08/06/1963	16:45:34	Pi
08/08/1963	20:06:31	Ar
08/10/1963	22:37:22	Ta
08/13/1963	01:15:37	Ge
08/15/1963	04:39:19	Cn
08/17/1963	09:16:37	Le
08/19/1963	15:40:13	Vi
08/22/1963	00:25:20	Li
08/24/1963	11:38:50	Sc
08/27/1963	00:15:00	Sg
08/29/1963	11:57:08	Cp
08/31/1963	20:37:07	Aq
09/03/1963	01:37:01	Pi
09/05/1963	03:51:55	Ar
09/07/1963	05:01:59	Ta
09/09/1963	06:45:30	Ge
09/11/1963	10:07:36	Cn
09/13/1963	15:29:42	Le
09/15/1963	22:47:23	Vi
09/18/1963	07:59:36	Li
09/20/1963	19:10:24	Sc
09/23/1963	07:49:55	Sg
09/25/1963	20:15:20	Cp
09/28/1963	06:03:09	Aq
09/30/1963	11:46:20	Pi
10/02/1963	13:47:48	Ar
10/04/1963	13:49:37	Ta
10/06/1963	13:58:05	Ge
10/08/1963	16:00:39	Cn
10/10/1963	20:53:56	Le
10/13/1963	04:34:04	Vi
10/15/1963	14:24:05	Li
10/18/1963	01:52:29	Sc
10/20/1963	14:32:21	Sg
10/23/1963	03:20:39	Cp
10/25/1963	14:19:59	Aq
10/27/1963	21:35:56	Pi
10/30/1963	00:39:52	Ar
11/01/1963	00:42:20	Ta
11/02/1963	23:47:59	Ge
11/05/1963	00:08:06	Cn
11/07/1963	03:23:46	Le
11/09/1963	10:13:53	Vi
11/11/1963	20:07:29	Li
11/14/1963	07:56:39	Sc
11/16/1963	20:39:42	Sg
11/19/1963	09:22:42	Cp
11/21/1963	20:51:21	Aq
11/24/1963	05:32:09	Pi
11/26/1963	10:24:53	Ar
11/28/1963	11:48:55	Ta
11/30/1963	11:14:29	Ge
12/02/1963	10:44:33	Cn

12/04/1963	12:19:49	Le
12/06/1963	17:26:12	Vi
12/09/1963	02:21:22	Li
12/11/1963	14:04:11	Sc
12/14/1963	02:53:16	Sg
12/16/1963	15:21:11	Cp
12/19/1963	02:28:45	Aq
12/21/1963	11:28:23	Pi
12/23/1963	17:40:48	Ar
12/25/1963	20:57:19	Ta
12/27/1963	21:58:08	Ge
12/29/1963	22:06:43	Cn
12/31/1963	23:08:53	Le
01/03/1964	02:47:46	Vi
01/05/1964	10:09:50	Li
01/07/1964	21:03:39	Sc
01/10/1964	09:49:05	Sg
01/12/1964	22:13:39	Cp
01/15/1964	08:47:40	Aq
01/17/1964	17:03:52	Pi
01/19/1964	23:10:06	Ar
01/22/1964	03:23:09	Ta
01/24/1964	06:04:29	Ge
01/26/1964	07:51:11	Cn
01/28/1964	09:44:57	Le
01/30/1964	13:08:45	Vi
02/01/1964	19:25:07	Li
02/04/1964	05:12:27	Sc
02/06/1964	17:35:19	Sg
02/09/1964	06:10:37	Cp
02/11/1964	16:39:13	Aq
02/14/1964	00:08:47	Pi
02/16/1964	05:09:40	Ar
02/18/1964	08:44:52	Ta
02/20/1964	11:47:51	Ge
02/22/1964	14:49:11	Cn
02/24/1964	18:10:47	Le
02/26/1964	22:29:54	Vi
02/29/1964	04:46:05	Li
03/02/1964	13:53:53	Sc
03/05/1964	01:46:43	Sg
03/07/1964	14:35:14	Cp
03/10/1964	01:35:28	Aq
03/12/1964	09:05:01	Pi
03/14/1964	13:15:12	Ar
03/16/1964	15:29:59	Ta
03/18/1964	17:25:51	Ge
03/20/1964	20:11:23	Cn
03/23/1964	00:14:42	Le
03/25/1964	05:41:45	Vi
03/27/1964	12:47:38	Li
03/29/1964	22:03:22	Sc
04/01/1964	09:40:38	Sg
04/03/1964	22:36:00	Cp
04/06/1964	10:24:10	Aq
04/08/1964	18:46:44	Pi
04/10/1964	23:08:16	Ar
04/13/1964	00:36:44	Ta

04/15/1964	01:05:50	Ge
04/17/1964	02:23:24	Cn
04/19/1964	05:39:44	Le
04/21/1964	11:17:21	Vi
04/23/1964	19:07:56	Li
04/26/1964	05:00:36	Sc
04/28/1964	16:45:47	Sg
05/01/1964	05:42:21	Cp
05/03/1964	18:06:19	Aq
05/06/1964	03:43:05	Pi
05/08/1964	09:15:26	Ar
05/10/1964	11:08:50	Ta
05/12/1964	11:01:22	Ge
05/14/1964	10:53:22	Cn
05/16/1964	12:31:11	Le
05/18/1964	17:02:15	Vi
05/21/1964	00:41:07	Li
05/23/1964	10:57:47	Sc
05/25/1964	23:02:59	Sg
05/28/1964	11:59:58	Cp
05/31/1964	00:32:24	Aq
06/02/1964	11:01:11	Pi
06/04/1964	18:02:43	Ar
06/06/1964	21:19:45	Ta
06/08/1964	21:49:52	Ge
06/10/1964	21:16:21	Cn
06/12/1964	21:34:50	Le
06/15/1964	00:27:07	Vi
06/17/1964	06:53:49	Li
06/19/1964	16:48:58	Sc
06/22/1964	05:03:11	Sg
06/24/1964	18:01:48	Cp
06/27/1964	06:21:30	Aq
06/29/1964	16:56:02	Pi
07/02/1964	00:52:15	Ar
07/04/1964	05:42:22	Ta
07/06/1964	07:42:45	Ge
07/08/1964	07:56:49	Cn
07/10/1964	08:00:54	Le
07/12/1964	09:44:04	Vi
07/14/1964	14:41:09	Li
07/16/1964	23:32:19	Sc
07/19/1964	11:27:54	Sg
07/22/1964	00:26:45	Cp
07/24/1964	12:30:27	Aq
07/26/1964	22:35:33	Pi
07/29/1964	06:25:14	Ar
07/31/1964	12:00:22	Ta
08/02/1964	15:28:00	Ge
08/04/1964	17:12:48	Cn
08/06/1964	18:10:52	Le
08/08/1964	19:49:57	Vi
08/10/1964	23:51:26	Li
08/13/1964	07:31:20	Sc
08/15/1964	18:44:11	Sg
08/18/1964	07:37:57	Cp
08/20/1964	19:38:57	Aq
08/23/1964	05:13:20	Pi

08/25/1964	12:15:09	Ar	01/04/1965	09:04:08	Aq	05/15/1965	22:31:37	Sg
08/27/1964	17:23:29	Ta	01/06/1965	21:06:01	Pi	05/18/1965	09:19:34	Cp
08/29/1964	21:15:53	Ge	01/09/1965	07:07:54	Ar	05/20/1965	21:50:28	Aq
09/01/1964	00:13:08	Cn	01/11/1965	14:10:20	Ta	05/23/1965	10:14:11	Pi
09/03/1964	02:36:21	Le	01/13/1965	17:48:08	Ge	05/25/1965	20:18:29	Ar
09/05/1964	05:12:22	Vi	01/15/1965	18:34:42	Cn	05/28/1965	02:48:17	Ta
09/07/1964	09:19:07	Li	01/17/1965	17:57:22	Le	05/30/1965	05:58:21	Ge
09/09/1964	16:19:34	Sc	01/19/1965	17:54:38	Vi	06/01/1965	07:05:12	Cn
09/12/1964	02:47:18	Sg	01/21/1965	20:27:43	Li	06/03/1965	07:46:32	Le
09/14/1964	15:30:02	Cp	01/24/1965	03:00:54	Sc	06/05/1965	09:33:01	Vi
09/17/1964	03:47:17	Aq	01/26/1965	13:31:58	Sg	06/07/1965	13:29:26	Li
09/19/1964	13:22:07	Pi	01/29/1965	02:21:11	Cp	06/09/1965	20:03:41	Sc
09/21/1964	19:43:44	Ar	01/31/1965	15:17:28	Aq	06/12/1965	05:09:41	Sg
09/23/1964	23:46:03	Ta	02/03/1965	02:55:35	Pi	06/14/1965	16:20:14	Cp
09/26/1964	02:45:56	Ge	02/05/1965	12:43:14	Ar	06/17/1965	04:51:11	Aq
09/28/1964	05:39:27	Cn	02/07/1965	20:23:44	Ta	06/19/1965	17:28:52	Pi
09/30/1964	08:52:29	Le	02/10/1965	01:36:01	Ge	06/22/1965	04:28:57	Ar
10/02/1964	12:42:11	Vi	02/12/1965	04:13:41	Cn	06/24/1965	12:16:04	Ta
10/04/1964	17:44:26	Li	02/14/1965	04:54:15	Le	06/26/1965	16:18:00	Ge
10/07/1964	00:56:35	Sc	02/16/1965	05:05:17	Vi	06/28/1965	17:19:50	Cn
10/09/1964	11:02:09	Sg	02/18/1965	06:44:56	Li	06/30/1965	16:58:45	Le
10/11/1964	23:31:43	Cp	02/20/1965	11:45:20	Sc	07/02/1965	17:11:03	Vi
10/14/1964	12:15:24	Aq	02/22/1965	20:56:57	Sg	07/04/1965	19:42:44	Li
10/16/1964	22:32:37	Pi	02/25/1965	09:16:53	Cp	07/07/1965	01:37:48	Sc
10/19/1964	05:04:42	Ar	02/27/1965	22:14:21	Aq	07/09/1965	10:53:21	Sg
10/21/1964	08:24:16	Ta	03/02/1965	09:38:13	Pi	07/11/1965	22:28:46	Cp
10/23/1964	10:03:18	Ge	03/04/1965	18:44:36	Ar	07/14/1965	11:07:50	Aq
10/25/1964	11:37:24	Cn	03/07/1965	01:49:21	Ta	07/16/1965	23:44:41	Pi
10/27/1964	14:13:55	Le	03/09/1965	07:13:56	Ge	07/19/1965	11:12:34	Ar
10/29/1964	18:25:17	Vi	03/11/1965	11:02:43	Cn	07/21/1965	20:13:53	Ta
11/01/1964	00:24:08	Li	03/13/1965	13:22:47	Le	07/24/1965	01:47:54	Ge
11/03/1964	08:24:42	Sc	03/15/1965	14:55:21	Vi	07/26/1965	03:53:00	Cn
11/05/1964	18:43:11	Sg	03/17/1965	17:03:51	Li	07/28/1965	03:37:08	Le
11/08/1964	07:05:39	Cp	03/19/1965	21:31:54	Sc	07/30/1965	02:54:41	Vi
11/10/1964	20:08:09	Aq	03/22/1965	05:36:39	Sg	08/01/1965	03:54:03	Li
11/13/1964	07:28:13	Pi	03/24/1965	17:06:53	Cp	08/03/1965	08:20:14	Sc
11/15/1964	15:10:07	Ar	03/27/1965	05:58:46	Aq	08/05/1965	16:48:53	Sg
11/17/1964	18:56:39	Ta	03/29/1965	17:31:44	Pi	08/08/1965	04:22:14	Cp
11/19/1964	19:58:27	Ge	04/01/1965	02:18:41	Ar	08/10/1965	17:09:01	Aq
11/21/1964	20:03:46	Cn	04/03/1965	08:28:32	Ta	08/13/1965	05:37:26	Pi
11/23/1964	20:58:35	Le	04/05/1965	12:54:33	Ge	08/15/1965	16:56:44	Ar
11/26/1964	00:02:29	Vi	04/07/1965	16:24:09	Cn	08/18/1965	02:27:14	Ta
11/28/1964	05:54:06	Li	04/09/1965	19:23:28	Le	08/20/1965	09:20:26	Ge
11/30/1964	14:30:36	Sc	04/11/1965	22:14:17	Vi	08/22/1965	13:04:08	Cn
12/03/1964	01:23:48	Sg	04/14/1965	01:38:18	Li	08/24/1965	14:01:02	Le
12/05/1964	13:53:12	Cp	04/16/1965	06:41:53	Sc	08/26/1965	13:36:05	Vi
12/08/1964	02:57:15	Aq	04/18/1965	14:31:13	Sg	08/28/1965	13:52:06	Li
12/10/1964	14:59:40	Pi	04/21/1965	01:23:53	Cp	08/30/1965	16:53:45	Sc
12/13/1964	00:12:00	Ar	04/23/1965	14:03:58	Aq	09/01/1965	23:59:35	Sg
12/15/1964	05:32:31	Ta	04/26/1965	02:02:00	Pi	09/04/1965	10:51:09	Cp
12/17/1964	07:21:04	Ge	04/28/1965	11:11:51	Ar	09/06/1965	23:33:33	Aq
12/19/1964	07:02:21	Cn	04/30/1965	17:03:29	Ta	09/09/1965	11:56:30	Pi
12/21/1964	06:30:40	Le	05/02/1965	20:26:31	Ge	09/11/1965	22:49:41	Ar
12/23/1964	07:41:30	Vi	05/04/1965	22:38:45	Cn	09/14/1965	07:55:55	Ta
12/25/1964	12:04:22	Li	05/07/1965	00:49:29	Le	09/16/1965	15:06:05	Ge
12/27/1964	20:11:02	Sc	05/09/1965	03:47:02	Vi	09/18/1965	20:00:45	Cn
12/30/1964	07:20:27	Sg	05/11/1965	08:04:02	Li	09/20/1965	22:34:55	Le
01/01/1965	20:06:21	Cp	05/13/1965	14:09:31	Sc	09/22/1965	23:29:43	Vi

09/25/1965	00:15:25	Li
09/27/1965	02:46:46	Sc
09/29/1965	08:41:56	Sg
10/01/1965	18:28:45	Cp
10/04/1965	06:48:00	Aq
10/06/1965	19:13:53	Pi
10/09/1965	05:53:50	Ar
10/11/1965	14:16:23	Ta
10/13/1965	20:39:39	Ge
10/16/1965	01:26:42	Cn
10/18/1965	04:51:00	Le
10/20/1965	07:13:02	Vi
10/22/1965	09:20:50	Li
10/24/1965	12:31:23	Sc
10/26/1965	18:08:59	Sg
10/29/1965	03:04:47	Cp
10/31/1965	14:49:25	Aq
11/03/1965	03:22:34	Pi
11/05/1965	14:21:25	Ar
11/07/1965	22:29:27	Ta
11/10/1965	03:54:22	Ge
11/12/1965	07:29:19	Cn
11/14/1965	10:13:27	Le
11/16/1965	12:54:30	Vi
11/18/1965	16:09:57	Li
11/20/1965	20:36:42	Sc
11/23/1965	02:56:29	Sg
11/25/1965	11:45:25	Cp
11/27/1965	23:03:16	Aq
11/30/1965	11:39:41	Pi
12/02/1965	23:22:23	Ar
12/05/1965	08:10:59	Ta
12/07/1965	13:27:22	Ge
12/09/1965	15:56:45	Cn
12/11/1965	17:07:57	Le
12/13/1965	18:35:29	Vi
12/15/1965	21:33:23	Li
12/18/1965	02:40:09	Sc
12/20/1965	10:01:00	Sg
12/22/1965	19:26:39	Cp
12/25/1965	06:43:58	Aq
12/27/1965	19:17:20	Pi
12/30/1965	07:39:37	Ar
01/01/1966	17:45:58	Ta
01/04/1966	00:06:05	Ge
01/06/1966	02:40:12	Cn
01/08/1966	02:49:41	Le
01/10/1966	02:34:15	Vi
01/12/1966	03:52:52	Li
01/14/1966	08:08:26	Sc
01/16/1966	15:39:26	Sg
01/19/1966	01:44:42	Cp
01/21/1966	13:25:54	Aq
01/24/1966	01:58:24	Pi
01/26/1966	14:32:51	Ar
01/29/1966	01:42:47	Ta
01/31/1966	09:43:19	Ge
02/02/1966	13:40:49	Cn
02/04/1966	14:13:37	Le
02/06/1966	13:11:13	Vi
02/08/1966	12:50:15	Li
02/10/1966	15:14:38	Sc
02/12/1966	21:32:57	Sg
02/15/1966	07:25:36	Cp
02/17/1966	19:25:29	Aq
02/20/1966	08:04:57	Pi
02/22/1966	20:30:00	Ar
02/25/1966	07:53:05	Ta
02/27/1966	17:02:35	Ge
03/01/1966	22:47:50	Cn
03/04/1966	00:56:32	Le
03/06/1966	00:36:25	Vi
03/07/1966	23:48:28	Li
03/10/1966	00:46:48	Sc
03/12/1966	05:18:06	Sg
03/14/1966	13:55:19	Cp
03/17/1966	01:34:33	Aq
03/19/1966	14:18:30	Pi
03/22/1966	02:33:18	Ar
03/24/1966	13:31:35	Ta
03/26/1966	22:41:20	Ge
03/29/1966	05:23:15	Cn
03/31/1966	09:11:51	Le
04/02/1966	10:30:49	Vi
04/04/1966	10:39:30	Li
04/06/1966	11:29:54	Sc
04/08/1966	14:53:37	Sg
04/10/1966	22:01:39	Cp
04/13/1966	08:41:54	Aq
04/15/1966	21:13:14	Pi
04/18/1966	09:27:08	Ar
04/20/1966	20:00:21	Ta
04/23/1966	04:26:52	Ge
04/25/1966	10:47:34	Cn
04/27/1966	15:09:16	Le
04/29/1966	17:49:34	Vi
05/01/1966	19:30:53	Li
05/03/1966	21:23:18	Sc
05/06/1966	00:52:04	Sg
05/08/1966	07:12:23	Cp
05/10/1966	16:51:42	Aq
05/13/1966	04:54:44	Pi
05/15/1966	17:15:12	Ar
05/18/1966	03:48:55	Ta
05/20/1966	11:39:35	Ge
05/22/1966	16:59:58	Cn
05/24/1966	20:36:49	Le
05/26/1966	23:21:53	Vi
05/29/1966	01:59:53	Li
05/31/1966	05:10:56	Sc
06/02/1966	09:38:26	Sg
06/04/1966	16:10:02	Cp
06/07/1966	01:20:47	Aq
06/09/1966	12:56:49	Pi
06/12/1966	01:26:05	Ar
06/14/1966	12:29:28	Ta
06/16/1966	20:25:54	Ge
06/19/1966	01:04:58	Cn
06/21/1966	03:28:53	Le
06/23/1966	05:07:46	Vi
06/25/1966	07:22:31	Li
06/27/1966	11:03:46	Sc
06/29/1966	16:31:04	Sg
07/01/1966	23:51:13	Cp
07/04/1966	09:14:11	Aq
07/06/1966	20:39:20	Pi
07/09/1966	09:15:38	Ar
07/11/1966	21:03:25	Ta
07/14/1966	05:51:18	Ge
07/16/1966	10:44:10	Cn
07/18/1966	12:27:24	Le
07/20/1966	12:46:33	Vi
07/22/1966	13:38:08	Li
07/24/1966	16:31:38	Sc
07/26/1966	22:04:28	Sg
07/29/1966	06:04:17	Cp
07/31/1966	16:01:39	Aq
08/03/1966	03:35:30	Pi
08/05/1966	16:14:36	Ar
08/08/1966	04:37:39	Ta
08/10/1966	14:38:16	Ge
08/12/1966	20:41:25	Cn
08/14/1966	22:49:59	Le
08/16/1966	22:34:50	Vi
08/18/1966	22:05:10	Li
08/20/1966	23:23:53	Sc
08/23/1966	03:50:44	Sg
08/25/1966	11:36:51	Cp
08/27/1966	21:55:50	Aq
08/30/1966	09:48:04	Pi
09/01/1966	22:27:25	Ar
09/04/1966	10:59:08	Ta
09/06/1966	21:52:16	Ge
09/09/1966	05:26:23	Cn
09/11/1966	09:00:46	Le
09/13/1966	09:25:27	Vi
09/15/1966	08:32:53	Li
09/17/1966	08:33:59	Sc
09/19/1966	11:21:14	Sg
09/21/1966	17:52:28	Cp
09/24/1966	03:47:51	Aq
09/26/1966	15:48:28	Pi
09/29/1966	04:29:17	Ar
10/01/1966	16:46:50	Ta
10/04/1966	03:43:16	Ge
10/06/1966	12:12:22	Cn
10/08/1966	17:24:36	Le
10/10/1966	19:26:46	Vi
10/12/1966	19:29:09	Li
10/14/1966	19:21:01	Sc
10/16/1966	20:59:05	Sg
10/19/1966	01:55:24	Cp
10/21/1966	10:40:31	Aq
10/23/1966	22:20:16	Pi

10/26/1966	11:03:02	Ar	03/07/1967	02:03:25	Aq	07/17/1967	09:22:01	Sg
10/28/1966	23:05:28	Ta	03/09/1967	12:41:04	Pi	07/19/1967	12:59:06	Cp
10/31/1966	09:27:49	Ge	03/12/1967	00:52:47	Ar	07/21/1967	17:59:19	Aq
11/02/1966	17:42:34	Cn	03/14/1967	13:53:51	Ta	07/24/1967	01:27:59	Pi
11/04/1966	23:35:58	Le	03/17/1967	02:18:53	Ge	07/26/1967	11:59:57	Ar
11/07/1966	03:09:36	Vi	03/19/1967	12:09:47	Cn	07/29/1967	00:40:25	Ta
11/09/1966	04:53:55	Li	03/21/1967	18:03:35	Le	07/31/1967	13:00:24	Ge
11/11/1966	05:53:05	Sc	03/23/1967	20:08:01	Vi	08/02/1967	22:31:38	Cn
11/13/1966	07:35:59	Sg	03/25/1967	19:49:53	Li	08/05/1967	04:25:58	Le
11/15/1966	11:36:42	Cp	03/27/1967	19:10:26	Sc	08/07/1967	07:35:53	Vi
11/17/1966	19:03:01	Aq	03/29/1967	20:08:09	Sg	08/09/1967	09:34:26	Li
11/20/1966	05:52:49	Pi	04/01/1967	00:10:32	Cp	08/11/1967	11:43:56	Sc
11/22/1966	18:30:55	Ar	04/03/1967	07:48:40	Aq	08/13/1967	14:52:10	Sg
11/25/1966	06:36:43	Ta	04/05/1967	18:28:30	Pi	08/15/1967	19:17:56	Cp
11/27/1966	16:30:35	Ge	04/08/1967	06:56:40	Ar	08/18/1967	01:16:38	Aq
11/29/1966	23:49:32	Cn	04/10/1967	19:56:02	Ta	08/20/1967	09:17:43	Pi
12/02/1966	05:01:35	Le	04/13/1967	08:14:38	Ge	08/22/1967	19:47:26	Ar
12/04/1966	08:47:58	Vi	04/15/1967	18:36:40	Cn	08/25/1967	08:21:14	Ta
12/06/1966	11:43:06	Li	04/18/1967	01:54:03	Le	08/27/1967	21:08:05	Ge
12/08/1966	14:17:37	Sc	04/20/1967	05:42:28	Vi	08/30/1967	07:34:22	Cn
12/10/1966	17:12:58	Sg	04/22/1967	06:41:08	Li	09/01/1967	14:08:04	Le
12/12/1966	21:30:18	Cp	04/24/1967	06:18:48	Sc	09/03/1967	17:07:13	Vi
12/15/1966	04:18:58	Aq	04/26/1967	06:26:45	Sg	09/05/1967	18:02:56	Li
12/17/1966	14:17:11	Pi	04/28/1967	08:53:51	Cp	09/07/1967	18:43:55	Sc
12/20/1966	02:39:18	Ar	04/30/1967	14:57:21	Aq	09/09/1967	20:39:40	Sg
12/22/1966	15:07:08	Ta	05/03/1967	00:46:51	Pi	09/12/1967	00:42:31	Cp
12/25/1966	01:13:33	Ge	05/05/1967	13:09:37	Ar	09/14/1967	07:08:15	Aq
12/27/1966	07:58:06	Cn	05/08/1967	02:09:21	Ta	09/16/1967	15:52:48	Pi
12/29/1966	11:57:13	Le	05/10/1967	14:08:10	Ge	09/19/1967	02:46:04	Ar
12/31/1966	14:33:01	Vi	05/13/1967	00:10:31	Cn	09/21/1967	15:20:24	Ta
01/02/1967	17:03:37	Li	05/15/1967	07:48:49	Le	09/24/1967	04:21:06	Ge
01/04/1967	20:15:59	Sc	05/17/1967	12:51:51	Vi	09/26/1967	15:45:11	Cn
01/07/1967	00:27:49	Sg	05/19/1967	15:30:45	Li	09/28/1967	23:41:09	Le
01/09/1967	05:53:13	Cp	05/21/1967	16:29:39	Sc	10/01/1967	03:38:17	Vi
01/11/1967	13:05:24	Aq	05/23/1967	17:05:47	Sg	10/03/1967	04:34:10	Li
01/13/1967	22:44:30	Pi	05/25/1967	18:58:01	Cp	10/05/1967	04:14:04	Sc
01/16/1967	10:47:48	Ar	05/27/1967	23:43:41	Aq	10/07/1967	04:31:55	Sg
01/18/1967	23:39:16	Ta	05/30/1967	08:18:04	Pi	10/09/1967	07:03:37	Cp
01/21/1967	10:38:09	Ge	06/01/1967	20:06:34	Ar	10/11/1967	12:44:58	Aq
01/23/1967	17:50:53	Cn	06/04/1967	09:04:04	Ta	10/13/1967	21:37:36	Pi
01/25/1967	21:20:21	Le	06/06/1967	20:51:59	Ge	10/16/1967	08:57:32	Ar
01/27/1967	22:36:02	Vi	06/09/1967	06:17:34	Cn	10/18/1967	21:40:59	Ta
01/29/1967	23:32:37	Li	06/11/1967	13:18:45	Le	10/21/1967	10:38:05	Ge
02/01/1967	01:43:38	Sc	06/13/1967	18:23:31	Vi	10/23/1967	22:27:01	Cn
02/03/1967	05:55:26	Sg	06/15/1967	21:58:13	Li	10/26/1967	07:39:57	Le
02/05/1967	12:10:03	Cp	06/18/1967	00:25:04	Sc	10/28/1967	13:19:04	Vi
02/07/1967	20:16:48	Aq	06/20/1967	02:19:49	Sg	10/30/1967	15:31:08	Li
02/10/1967	06:18:46	Pi	06/22/1967	04:46:20	Cp	11/01/1967	15:26:05	Sc
02/12/1967	18:16:44	Ar	06/24/1967	09:10:50	Aq	11/03/1967	14:51:05	Sg
02/15/1967	07:18:36	Ta	06/26/1967	16:49:27	Pi	11/05/1967	15:43:55	Cp
02/17/1967	19:15:31	Ge	06/29/1967	03:52:34	Ar	11/07/1967	19:45:23	Aq
02/20/1967	03:47:37	Cn	07/01/1967	16:42:37	Ta	11/10/1967	03:42:22	Pi
02/22/1967	08:04:07	Le	07/04/1967	04:38:34	Ge	11/12/1967	14:58:20	Ar
02/24/1967	09:03:49	Vi	07/06/1967	13:47:23	Cn	11/15/1967	03:52:09	Ta
02/26/1967	08:44:21	Li	07/08/1967	19:58:27	Le	11/17/1967	16:39:55	Ge
02/28/1967	09:09:25	Sc	07/11/1967	00:07:21	Vi	11/20/1967	04:12:47	Cn
03/02/1967	11:52:46	Sg	07/13/1967	03:19:33	Li	11/22/1967	13:46:53	Le
03/04/1967	17:34:58	Cp	07/15/1967	06:17:23	Sc	11/24/1967	20:45:36	Vi

11/27/1967	00:48:04	Li	04/07/1968	05:28:16	Le	08/16/1968	15:51:01	Ge
11/29/1967	02:13:18	Sc	04/09/1968	12:03:45	Vi	08/19/1968	04:15:10	Cn
12/01/1967	02:10:00	Sg	04/11/1968	15:00:42	Li	08/21/1968	14:39:42	Le
12/03/1967	02:24:39	Cp	04/13/1968	15:31:49	Sc	08/23/1968	22:20:52	Vi
12/05/1967	04:56:46	Aq	04/15/1968	15:23:00	Sg	08/26/1968	03:44:33	Li
12/07/1967	11:19:08	Pi	04/17/1968	16:22:39	Cp	08/28/1968	07:38:08	Sc
12/09/1967	21:43:12	Ar	04/19/1968	19:56:52	Aq	08/30/1968	10:40:25	Sg
12/12/1967	10:31:36	Ta	04/22/1968	02:45:31	Pi	09/01/1968	13:21:40	Cp
12/14/1967	23:17:51	Ge	04/24/1968	12:32:05	Ar	09/03/1968	16:19:06	Aq
12/17/1967	10:22:38	Cn	04/27/1968	00:22:01	Ta	09/05/1968	20:27:10	Pi
12/19/1967	19:20:47	Le	04/29/1968	13:10:58	Ge	09/08/1968	02:48:54	Ar
12/22/1967	02:20:58	Vi	05/02/1968	01:49:39	Cn	09/10/1968	12:05:35	Ta
12/24/1967	07:26:42	Li	05/04/1968	12:53:47	Le	09/12/1968	23:54:21	Ge
12/26/1967	10:35:50	Sc	05/06/1968	20:58:10	Vi	09/15/1968	12:28:16	Cn
12/28/1967	12:09:01	Sg	05/09/1968	01:20:37	Li	09/17/1968	23:25:06	Le
12/30/1967	13:10:49	Cp	05/11/1968	02:29:36	Sc	09/20/1968	07:15:28	Vi
01/01/1968	15:23:35	Aq	05/13/1968	01:53:15	Sg	09/22/1968	11:59:47	Li
01/03/1968	20:35:24	Pi	05/15/1968	01:30:36	Cp	09/24/1968	14:38:35	Sc
01/06/1968	05:45:18	Ar	05/17/1968	03:21:49	Aq	09/26/1968	16:30:13	Sg
01/08/1968	18:02:28	Ta	05/19/1968	08:52:31	Pi	09/28/1968	18:44:15	Cp
01/11/1968	06:54:09	Ge	05/21/1968	18:14:07	Ar	09/30/1968	22:10:36	Aq
01/13/1968	17:53:33	Cn	05/24/1968	06:15:26	Ta	10/03/1968	03:20:42	Pi
01/16/1968	02:09:21	Le	05/26/1968	19:12:00	Ge	10/05/1968	10:35:12	Ar
01/18/1968	08:10:50	Vi	05/29/1968	07:42:36	Cn	10/07/1968	20:06:31	Ta
01/20/1968	12:47:15	Li	05/31/1968	18:53:13	Le	10/10/1968	07:43:27	Ge
01/22/1968	16:27:46	Sc	06/03/1968	03:52:03	Vi	10/12/1968	20:23:18	Cn
01/24/1968	19:23:23	Sg	06/05/1968	09:49:07	Li	10/15/1968	08:08:03	Le
01/26/1968	21:56:49	Cp	06/07/1968	12:30:13	Sc	10/17/1968	16:58:26	Vi
01/29/1968	01:05:50	Aq	06/09/1968	12:42:08	Sg	10/19/1968	22:05:04	Li
01/31/1968	06:15:50	Pi	06/11/1968	12:05:21	Cp	10/22/1968	00:05:32	Sc
02/02/1968	14:39:24	Ar	06/13/1968	12:46:23	Aq	10/24/1968	00:32:11	Sg
02/05/1968	02:14:56	Ta	06/15/1968	16:41:57	Pi	10/26/1968	01:13:21	Cp
02/07/1968	15:08:44	Ge	06/18/1968	00:49:43	Ar	10/28/1968	03:42:44	Aq
02/10/1968	02:34:11	Cn	06/20/1968	12:24:51	Ta	10/30/1968	08:54:04	Pi
02/12/1968	10:49:46	Le	06/23/1968	01:21:58	Ge	11/01/1968	16:50:35	Ar
02/14/1968	16:02:29	Vi	06/25/1968	13:42:52	Cn	11/04/1968	03:01:09	Ta
02/16/1968	19:21:07	Li	06/28/1968	00:30:20	Le	11/06/1968	14:47:35	Ge
02/18/1968	21:59:40	Sc	06/30/1968	09:25:48	Vi	11/09/1968	03:26:27	Cn
02/21/1968	00:47:42	Sg	07/02/1968	16:09:48	Li	11/11/1968	15:44:34	Le
02/23/1968	04:11:49	Cp	07/04/1968	20:20:11	Sc	11/14/1968	01:54:39	Vi
02/25/1968	08:36:42	Aq	07/06/1968	22:04:33	Sg	11/16/1968	08:26:10	Li
02/27/1968	14:42:11	Pi	07/08/1968	22:23:41	Cp	11/18/1968	11:05:45	Sc
02/29/1968	23:14:24	Ar	07/10/1968	23:03:10	Aq	11/20/1968	11:03:50	Sg
03/03/1968	10:27:29	Ta	07/13/1968	02:02:50	Pi	11/22/1968	10:19:37	Cp
03/05/1968	23:16:45	Ge	07/15/1968	08:51:29	Ar	11/24/1968	11:02:03	Aq
03/08/1968	11:21:15	Cn	07/17/1968	19:30:26	Ta	11/26/1968	14:52:28	Pi
03/10/1968	20:27:00	Le	07/20/1968	08:12:37	Ge	11/28/1968	22:25:42	Ar
03/13/1968	01:51:18	Vi	07/22/1968	20:30:54	Cn	12/01/1968	08:57:34	Ta
03/15/1968	04:22:54	Li	07/25/1968	06:54:44	Le	12/03/1968	21:05:39	Ge
03/17/1968	05:33:03	Sc	07/27/1968	15:09:41	Vi	12/06/1968	09:43:16	Cn
03/19/1968	06:53:33	Sg	07/29/1968	21:32:03	Li	12/08/1968	22:02:24	Le
03/21/1968	09:34:28	Cp	08/01/1968	02:11:02	Sc	12/11/1968	08:59:26	Vi
03/23/1968	14:16:25	Aq	08/03/1968	05:10:34	Sg	12/13/1968	17:08:25	Li
03/25/1968	21:15:01	Pi	08/05/1968	06:57:16	Cp	12/15/1968	21:31:14	Sc
03/28/1968	06:31:46	Ar	08/07/1968	08:37:13	Aq	12/17/1968	22:27:29	Sg
03/30/1968	17:54:49	Ta	08/09/1968	11:45:30	Pi	12/19/1968	21:32:19	Cp
04/02/1968	06:40:14	Ge	08/11/1968	17:52:55	Ar	12/21/1968	20:59:23	Aq
04/04/1968	19:12:35	Cn	08/14/1968	03:35:49	Ta	12/23/1968	23:00:40	Pi

12/26/1968	05:01:52	Ar
12/28/1968	14:56:45	Ta
12/31/1968	03:10:53	Ge
01/02/1969	15:52:33	Cn
01/05/1969	03:54:29	Le
01/07/1969	14:42:00	Vi
01/09/1969	23:32:23	Li
01/12/1969	05:31:48	Sc
01/14/1969	08:18:42	Sg
01/16/1969	08:38:55	Cp
01/18/1969	08:16:39	Aq
01/20/1969	09:20:32	Pi
01/22/1969	13:43:24	Ar
01/24/1969	22:12:42	Ta
01/27/1969	09:53:06	Ge
01/29/1969	22:36:14	Cn
02/01/1969	10:28:43	Le
02/03/1969	20:40:27	Vi
02/06/1969	05:00:07	Li
02/08/1969	11:18:05	Sc
02/10/1969	15:23:02	Sg
02/12/1969	17:28:12	Cp
02/14/1969	18:30:26	Aq
02/16/1969	20:02:53	Pi
02/18/1969	23:48:28	Ar
02/21/1969	07:01:35	Ta
02/23/1969	17:41:10	Ge
02/26/1969	06:11:00	Cn
02/28/1969	18:11:38	Le
03/03/1969	04:06:41	Vi
03/05/1969	11:33:50	Li
03/07/1969	16:56:13	Sc
03/09/1969	20:47:43	Sg
03/11/1969	23:40:08	Cp
03/14/1969	02:09:04	Aq
03/16/1969	05:03:38	Pi
03/18/1969	09:26:48	Ar
03/20/1969	16:20:19	Ta
03/23/1969	02:12:24	Ge
03/25/1969	14:18:24	Cn
03/28/1969	02:36:38	Le
03/30/1969	12:53:32	Vi
04/01/1969	20:03:03	Li
04/04/1969	00:22:19	Sc
04/06/1969	02:57:17	Sg
04/08/1969	05:04:26	Cp
04/10/1969	07:45:53	Aq
04/12/1969	11:40:56	Pi
04/14/1969	17:13:01	Ar
04/17/1969	00:42:52	Ta
04/19/1969	10:28:18	Ge
04/21/1969	22:16:50	Cn
04/24/1969	10:50:44	Le
04/26/1969	21:56:43	Vi
04/29/1969	05:43:27	Li
05/01/1969	09:49:28	Sc
05/03/1969	11:18:47	Sg
05/05/1969	11:56:41	Cp
05/07/1969	13:27:36	Aq
05/09/1969	17:03:50	Pi
05/11/1969	23:08:48	Ar
05/14/1969	07:28:17	Ta
05/16/1969	17:41:19	Ge
05/19/1969	05:30:21	Cn
05/21/1969	18:12:09	Le
05/24/1969	06:06:39	Vi
05/26/1969	15:07:19	Li
05/28/1969	20:04:48	Sc
05/30/1969	21:29:52	Sg
06/01/1969	21:06:34	Cp
06/03/1969	21:03:31	Aq
06/05/1969	23:13:04	Pi
06/08/1969	04:36:25	Ar
06/10/1969	13:05:48	Ta
06/12/1969	23:48:25	Ge
06/15/1969	11:52:03	Cn
06/18/1969	00:35:03	Le
06/20/1969	12:53:24	Vi
06/22/1969	23:03:27	Li
06/25/1969	05:30:47	Sc
06/27/1969	07:59:38	Sg
06/29/1969	07:44:09	Cp
07/01/1969	06:49:06	Aq
07/03/1969	07:26:13	Pi
07/05/1969	11:16:19	Ar
07/07/1969	18:52:48	Ta
07/10/1969	05:31:04	Ge
07/12/1969	17:47:03	Cn
07/15/1969	06:28:59	Le
07/17/1969	18:41:54	Vi
07/20/1969	05:19:39	Li
07/22/1969	13:03:47	Sc
07/24/1969	17:10:18	Sg
07/26/1969	18:09:02	Cp
07/28/1969	17:34:30	Aq
07/30/1969	17:30:30	Pi
08/01/1969	19:54:35	Ar
08/04/1969	02:01:36	Ta
08/06/1969	11:49:16	Ge
08/08/1969	23:57:09	Cn
08/11/1969	12:38:14	Le
08/14/1969	00:32:26	Vi
08/16/1969	10:50:41	Li
08/18/1969	18:53:47	Sc
08/21/1969	00:12:00	Sg
08/23/1969	02:48:39	Cp
08/25/1969	03:35:37	Aq
08/27/1969	04:03:18	Pi
08/29/1969	05:57:21	Ar
08/31/1969	10:49:57	Ta
09/02/1969	19:23:26	Ge
09/05/1969	06:56:51	Cn
09/07/1969	19:35:59	Le
09/10/1969	07:20:18	Vi
09/12/1969	17:01:28	Li
09/15/1969	00:24:48	Sc
09/17/1969	05:41:56	Sg
09/19/1969	09:13:41	Cp
09/21/1969	11:30:56	Aq
09/23/1969	13:22:10	Pi
09/25/1969	15:55:27	Ar
09/27/1969	20:28:50	Ta
09/30/1969	04:05:30	Ge
10/02/1969	14:51:57	Cn
10/05/1969	03:24:50	Le
10/07/1969	15:21:15	Vi
10/10/1969	00:48:19	Li
10/12/1969	07:18:35	Sc
10/14/1969	11:32:51	Sg
10/16/1969	14:35:17	Cp
10/18/1969	17:20:54	Aq
10/20/1969	20:25:37	Pi
10/23/1969	00:17:06	Ar
10/25/1969	05:32:23	Ta
10/27/1969	13:00:15	Ge
10/29/1969	23:12:40	Cn
11/01/1969	11:34:32	Le
11/04/1969	00:00:07	Vi
11/06/1969	09:58:45	Li
11/08/1969	16:17:41	Sc
11/10/1969	19:29:50	Sg
11/12/1969	21:08:23	Cp
11/14/1969	22:52:44	Aq
11/17/1969	01:51:55	Pi
11/19/1969	06:31:43	Ar
11/21/1969	12:52:02	Ta
11/23/1969	20:58:38	Ge
11/26/1969	07:10:13	Cn
11/28/1969	19:21:53	Le
12/01/1969	08:13:38	Vi
12/03/1969	19:16:48	Li
12/06/1969	02:30:07	Sc
12/08/1969	05:42:31	Sg
12/10/1969	06:20:11	Cp
12/12/1969	06:27:06	Aq
12/14/1969	07:56:17	Pi
12/16/1969	11:55:41	Ar
12/18/1969	18:35:04	Ta
12/21/1969	03:27:42	Ge
12/23/1969	14:08:30	Cn
12/26/1969	02:21:04	Le
12/28/1969	15:20:04	Vi
12/31/1969	03:17:52	Li
01/02/1970	12:03:14	Sc
01/04/1970	16:32:47	Sg
01/06/1970	17:29:46	Cp
01/08/1970	16:47:23	Aq
01/10/1970	16:36:35	Pi
01/12/1970	18:47:49	Ar
01/15/1970	00:20:18	Ta
01/17/1970	09:06:49	Ge
01/19/1970	20:13:26	Cn
01/22/1970	08:39:58	Le
01/24/1970	21:32:42	Vi

01/27/1970	09:42:14	Li	06/07/1970	21:16:35	Le	10/17/1970	13:43:15	Ge
01/29/1970	19:34:00	Sc	06/10/1970	10:01:51	Vi	10/19/1970	19:58:41	Cn
02/01/1970	01:49:41	Sg	06/12/1970	22:27:33	Li	10/22/1970	06:12:06	Le
02/03/1970	04:21:30	Cp	06/15/1970	08:01:24	Sc	10/24/1970	18:56:55	Vi
02/05/1970	04:19:20	Aq	06/17/1970	13:38:46	Sg	10/27/1970	07:36:50	Li
02/07/1970	03:37:11	Pi	06/19/1970	16:04:28	Cp	10/29/1970	18:14:48	Sc
02/09/1970	04:17:02	Ar	06/21/1970	17:00:28	Aq	11/01/1970	02:23:58	Sg
02/11/1970	07:58:56	Ta	06/23/1970	18:11:27	Pi	11/03/1970	08:32:21	Cp
02/13/1970	15:28:54	Ge	06/25/1970	20:51:49	Ar	11/05/1970	13:10:50	Aq
02/16/1970	02:16:40	Cn	06/28/1970	01:34:33	Ta	11/07/1970	16:32:44	Pi
02/18/1970	14:53:06	Le	06/30/1970	08:24:04	Ge	11/09/1970	18:51:33	Ar
02/21/1970	03:41:35	Vi	07/02/1970	17:20:45	Cn	11/11/1970	20:49:51	Ta
02/23/1970	15:29:38	Li	07/05/1970	04:25:46	Le	11/13/1970	23:48:09	Ge
02/26/1970	01:23:12	Sc	07/07/1970	17:10:56	Vi	11/16/1970	05:22:55	Cn
02/28/1970	08:38:06	Sg	07/10/1970	06:02:29	Li	11/18/1970	14:35:41	Le
03/02/1970	12:53:57	Cp	07/12/1970	16:40:35	Sc	11/21/1970	02:49:45	Vi
03/04/1970	14:34:22	Aq	07/14/1970	23:25:38	Sg	11/23/1970	15:39:00	Li
03/06/1970	14:48:40	Pi	07/17/1970	02:19:00	Cp	11/26/1970	02:24:35	Sc
03/08/1970	15:16:01	Ar	07/19/1970	02:44:22	Aq	11/28/1970	10:02:10	Sg
03/10/1970	17:43:25	Ta	07/21/1970	02:36:23	Pi	11/30/1970	15:05:29	Cp
03/12/1970	23:36:33	Ge	07/23/1970	03:42:22	Ar	12/02/1970	18:44:40	Aq
03/15/1970	09:18:23	Cn	07/25/1970	07:17:54	Ta	12/04/1970	21:55:16	Pi
03/17/1970	21:39:27	Le	07/27/1970	13:52:43	Ge	12/07/1970	01:03:12	Ar
03/20/1970	10:29:36	Vi	07/29/1970	23:13:45	Cn	12/09/1970	04:24:09	Ta
03/22/1970	21:56:32	Li	08/01/1970	10:43:55	Le	12/11/1970	08:33:06	Ge
03/25/1970	07:09:51	Sc	08/03/1970	23:34:07	Vi	12/13/1970	14:32:00	Cn
03/27/1970	14:06:29	Sg	08/06/1970	12:32:31	Li	12/15/1970	23:21:24	Le
03/29/1970	19:00:01	Cp	08/08/1970	23:56:36	Sc	12/18/1970	11:04:28	Vi
03/31/1970	22:08:07	Aq	08/11/1970	08:06:58	Sg	12/21/1970	00:01:06	Li
04/03/1970	00:00:33	Pi	08/13/1970	12:24:37	Cp	12/23/1970	11:26:49	Sc
04/05/1970	01:31:38	Ar	08/15/1970	13:30:45	Aq	12/25/1970	19:27:28	Sg
04/07/1970	04:01:51	Ta	08/17/1970	13:00:58	Pi	12/28/1970	00:01:15	Cp
04/09/1970	09:01:46	Ge	08/19/1970	12:50:04	Ar	12/30/1970	02:23:35	Aq
04/11/1970	17:33:10	Cn	08/21/1970	14:45:50	Ta	01/01/1971	04:07:43	Pi
04/14/1970	05:15:30	Le	08/23/1970	20:03:16	Ge	01/03/1971	06:26:20	Ar
04/16/1970	18:06:52	Vi	08/26/1970	04:57:48	Cn	01/05/1971	10:00:04	Ta
04/19/1970	05:34:49	Li	08/28/1970	16:37:58	Le	01/07/1971	15:08:14	Ge
04/21/1970	14:15:16	Sc	08/31/1970	05:35:42	Vi	01/09/1971	22:08:41	Cn
04/23/1970	20:14:40	Sg	09/02/1970	18:25:20	Li	01/12/1971	07:23:57	Le
04/26/1970	00:26:12	Cp	09/05/1970	05:54:16	Sc	01/14/1971	18:57:27	Vi
04/28/1970	03:42:55	Aq	09/07/1970	14:57:57	Sg	01/17/1971	07:53:00	Li
04/30/1970	06:37:23	Pi	09/09/1970	20:51:21	Cp	01/19/1971	20:03:48	Sc
05/02/1970	09:32:18	Ar	09/11/1970	23:33:28	Aq	01/22/1971	05:15:27	Sg
05/04/1970	13:04:48	Ta	09/13/1970	23:56:50	Pi	01/24/1971	10:32:24	Cp
05/06/1970	18:17:20	Ge	09/15/1970	23:34:55	Ar	01/26/1971	12:35:48	Aq
05/09/1970	02:16:42	Cn	09/18/1970	00:20:48	Ta	01/28/1971	13:01:29	Pi
05/11/1970	13:21:47	Le	09/20/1970	04:01:49	Ge	01/30/1971	13:35:54	Ar
05/14/1970	02:10:28	Vi	09/22/1970	11:40:46	Cn	02/01/1971	15:48:33	Ta
05/16/1970	14:02:25	Li	09/24/1970	22:54:09	Le	02/03/1971	20:34:24	Ge
05/18/1970	22:49:13	Sc	09/27/1970	11:53:23	Vi	02/06/1971	04:06:40	Cn
05/21/1970	04:10:52	Sg	09/30/1970	00:33:02	Li	02/08/1971	14:06:13	Le
05/23/1970	07:12:55	Cp	10/02/1970	11:35:13	Sc	02/11/1971	01:57:42	Vi
05/25/1970	09:25:26	Aq	10/04/1970	20:31:09	Sg	02/13/1971	14:50:00	Li
05/27/1970	11:58:32	Pi	10/07/1970	03:10:06	Cp	02/16/1971	03:21:34	Sc
05/29/1970	15:26:36	Ar	10/09/1970	07:25:41	Aq	02/18/1971	13:45:24	Sg
05/31/1970	20:03:05	Ta	10/11/1970	09:29:55	Pi	02/20/1971	20:36:44	Cp
06/03/1970	02:09:32	Ge	10/13/1970	10:11:52	Ar	02/22/1971	23:42:48	Aq
06/05/1970	10:25:12	Cn	10/15/1970	10:59:39	Ta	02/25/1971	00:05:11	Pi

02/26/1971	23:29:33	Ar	07/09/1971	11:26:23	Aq	11/18/1971	11:29:38	Sg
02/28/1971	23:53:58	Ta	07/11/1971	14:14:12	Pi	11/20/1971	21:36:14	Cp
03/03/1971	03:01:23	Ge	07/13/1971	16:32:06	Ar	11/23/1971	05:52:04	Aq
03/05/1971	09:47:17	Cn	07/15/1971	19:10:18	Ta	11/25/1971	11:47:36	Pi
03/07/1971	19:55:15	Le	07/17/1971	22:46:36	Ge	11/27/1971	15:03:27	Ar
03/10/1971	08:10:16	Vi	07/20/1971	03:56:27	Cn	11/29/1971	16:08:00	Ta
03/12/1971	21:05:38	Li	07/22/1971	11:16:26	Le	12/01/1971	16:25:04	Ge
03/15/1971	09:31:05	Sc	07/24/1971	21:09:10	Vi	12/03/1971	17:50:51	Cn
03/17/1971	20:23:25	Sg	07/27/1971	09:11:36	Li	12/05/1971	22:16:45	Le
03/20/1971	04:37:17	Cp	07/29/1971	21:50:01	Sc	12/08/1971	06:40:26	Vi
03/22/1971	09:28:27	Aq	08/01/1971	08:49:21	Sg	12/10/1971	18:18:59	Li
03/24/1971	11:07:16	Pi	08/03/1971	16:31:47	Cp	12/13/1971	07:01:27	Sc
03/26/1971	10:45:17	Ar	08/05/1971	20:46:30	Aq	12/15/1971	18:37:14	Sg
03/28/1971	10:15:31	Ta	08/07/1971	22:34:13	Pi	12/18/1971	04:07:11	Cp
03/30/1971	11:43:31	Ge	08/09/1971	23:26:40	Ar	12/20/1971	11:32:28	Aq
04/01/1971	16:50:38	Cn	08/12/1971	00:55:15	Ta	12/22/1971	17:09:47	Pi
04/04/1971	02:05:19	Le	08/14/1971	04:10:28	Ge	12/24/1971	21:09:05	Ar
04/06/1971	14:16:06	Vi	08/16/1971	09:49:34	Cn	12/26/1971	23:44:58	Ta
04/09/1971	03:16:45	Li	08/18/1971	17:57:26	Le	12/29/1971	01:38:12	Ge
04/11/1971	15:27:45	Sc	08/21/1971	04:18:31	Vi	12/31/1971	04:01:09	Cn
04/14/1971	02:02:48	Sg	08/23/1971	16:22:23	Li	01/02/1972	08:21:47	Le
04/16/1971	10:38:03	Cp	08/26/1971	05:08:51	Sc	01/04/1972	15:50:09	Vi
04/18/1971	16:45:33	Aq	08/28/1971	16:56:30	Sg	01/07/1972	02:32:55	Li
04/20/1971	20:07:29	Pi	08/31/1971	01:54:13	Cp	01/09/1972	15:03:10	Sc
04/22/1971	21:08:13	Ar	09/02/1971	07:03:47	Aq	01/12/1972	02:57:14	Sg
04/24/1971	21:06:26	Ta	09/04/1971	08:50:35	Pi	01/14/1972	12:25:44	Cp
04/26/1971	21:58:16	Ge	09/06/1971	08:43:10	Ar	01/16/1972	19:03:39	Aq
04/29/1971	01:43:16	Cn	09/08/1971	08:37:25	Ta	01/18/1972	23:27:48	Pi
05/01/1971	09:34:27	Le	09/10/1971	10:24:46	Ge	01/21/1972	02:35:09	Ar
05/03/1971	21:02:49	Vi	09/12/1971	15:20:38	Cn	01/23/1972	05:17:01	Ta
05/06/1971	09:59:04	Li	09/14/1971	23:37:35	Le	01/25/1972	08:13:40	Ge
05/08/1971	22:03:22	Sc	09/17/1971	10:28:45	Vi	01/27/1972	12:01:28	Cn
05/11/1971	08:07:33	Sg	09/19/1971	22:46:53	Li	01/29/1972	17:21:15	Le
05/13/1971	16:08:49	Cp	09/22/1971	11:32:50	Sc	02/01/1972	00:55:37	Vi
05/15/1971	22:19:23	Aq	09/24/1971	23:43:09	Sg	02/03/1972	11:06:31	Li
05/18/1971	02:39:10	Pi	09/27/1971	09:52:31	Cp	02/05/1972	23:17:37	Sc
05/20/1971	05:10:53	Ar	09/29/1971	16:38:35	Aq	02/08/1972	11:37:46	Sg
05/22/1971	06:31:10	Ta	10/01/1971	19:36:26	Pi	02/10/1972	21:49:51	Cp
05/24/1971	08:00:52	Ge	10/03/1971	19:40:23	Ar	02/13/1972	04:36:03	Aq
05/26/1971	11:25:56	Cn	10/05/1971	18:41:47	Ta	02/15/1972	08:10:46	Pi
05/28/1971	18:16:14	Le	10/07/1971	18:52:59	Ge	02/17/1972	09:50:36	Ar
05/31/1971	04:47:56	Vi	10/09/1971	22:10:27	Cn	02/19/1972	11:11:20	Ta
06/02/1971	17:26:16	Li	10/12/1971	05:30:13	Le	02/21/1972	13:35:26	Ge
06/05/1971	05:35:56	Sc	10/14/1971	16:16:02	Vi	02/23/1972	17:52:02	Cn
06/07/1971	15:27:59	Sg	10/17/1971	04:47:18	Li	02/26/1972	00:14:45	Le
06/09/1971	22:44:52	Cp	10/19/1971	17:30:39	Sc	02/28/1972	08:39:07	Vi
06/12/1971	04:02:36	Aq	10/22/1971	05:31:24	Sg	03/01/1972	18:59:54	Li
06/14/1971	08:01:16	Pi	10/24/1971	16:05:07	Cp	03/04/1972	07:00:07	Sc
06/16/1971	11:05:37	Ar	10/27/1971	00:11:03	Aq	03/06/1972	19:36:27	Sg
06/18/1971	13:38:37	Ta	10/29/1971	04:56:32	Pi	03/09/1972	06:49:24	Cp
06/20/1971	16:23:37	Ge	10/31/1971	06:25:52	Ar	03/11/1972	14:42:26	Aq
06/22/1971	20:29:54	Cn	11/02/1971	05:55:08	Ta	03/13/1972	18:39:11	Pi
06/25/1971	03:11:59	Le	11/04/1971	05:27:08	Ge	03/15/1972	19:36:52	Ar
06/27/1971	13:06:06	Vi	11/06/1971	07:14:45	Cn	03/17/1972	19:27:24	Ta
06/30/1971	01:22:17	Li	11/08/1971	12:56:26	Le	03/19/1972	20:12:25	Ge
07/02/1971	13:45:47	Sc	11/10/1971	22:43:56	Vi	03/21/1972	23:26:11	Cn
07/04/1971	23:58:36	Sg	11/13/1971	11:05:23	Li	03/24/1972	05:45:51	Le
07/07/1971	07:03:04	Cp	11/15/1971	23:49:23	Sc	03/26/1972	14:47:32	Vi

03/29/1972	01:41:44	Li	08/07/1972	23:55:57	Le	12/18/1972	12:24:12	Ge
03/31/1972	13:48:19	Sc	08/10/1972	05:22:37	Vi	12/20/1972	11:56:36	Cn
04/03/1972	02:26:54	Sg	08/12/1972	13:27:20	Li	12/22/1972	12:34:07	Le
04/05/1972	14:20:31	Cp	08/15/1972	00:19:27	Sc	12/24/1972	16:02:36	Vi
04/07/1972	23:37:20	Aq	08/17/1972	12:48:49	Sg	12/26/1972	23:21:26	Li
04/10/1972	04:57:34	Pi	08/20/1972	00:37:36	Cp	12/29/1972	10:09:58	Sc
04/12/1972	06:32:04	Ar	08/22/1972	09:42:55	Aq	12/31/1972	22:51:21	Sg
04/14/1972	05:54:25	Ta	08/24/1972	15:28:24	Pi	01/03/1973	11:30:04	Cp
04/16/1972	05:16:29	Ge	08/26/1972	18:40:23	Ar	01/05/1973	22:46:52	Aq
04/18/1972	06:45:57	Cn	08/28/1972	20:42:42	Ta	01/08/1973	08:02:32	Pi
04/20/1972	11:46:30	Le	08/30/1972	22:55:31	Ge	01/10/1973	14:57:21	Ar
04/22/1972	20:24:11	Vi	09/02/1972	02:11:23	Cn	01/12/1973	19:24:19	Ta
04/25/1972	07:34:16	Li	09/04/1972	06:53:36	Le	01/14/1973	21:40:47	Ge
04/27/1972	19:55:36	Sc	09/06/1972	13:15:01	Vi	01/16/1973	22:38:32	Cn
04/30/1972	08:30:31	Sg	09/08/1972	21:36:26	Li	01/18/1973	23:40:03	Le
05/02/1972	20:28:33	Cp	09/11/1972	08:15:16	Sc	01/21/1973	02:23:28	Vi
05/05/1972	06:35:05	Aq	09/13/1972	20:42:06	Sg	01/23/1973	08:16:08	Li
05/07/1972	13:27:35	Pi	09/16/1972	09:07:22	Cp	01/25/1973	17:51:52	Sc
05/09/1972	16:34:40	Ar	09/18/1972	19:04:27	Aq	01/28/1973	06:10:16	Sg
05/11/1972	16:47:13	Ta	09/21/1972	01:08:59	Pi	01/30/1973	18:53:55	Cp
05/13/1972	15:57:01	Ge	09/23/1972	03:44:20	Ar	02/02/1973	05:55:12	Aq
05/15/1972	16:15:59	Cn	09/25/1972	04:27:27	Ta	02/04/1973	14:22:04	Pi
05/17/1972	19:37:39	Le	09/27/1972	05:14:17	Ge	02/06/1973	20:28:42	Ar
05/20/1972	02:55:48	Vi	09/29/1972	07:38:33	Cn	02/09/1973	00:53:26	Ta
05/22/1972	13:36:12	Li	10/01/1972	12:25:08	Le	02/11/1973	04:09:47	Ge
05/25/1972	02:00:46	Sc	10/03/1972	19:30:41	Vi	02/13/1973	06:44:11	Cn
05/27/1972	14:33:06	Sg	10/06/1972	04:34:36	Li	02/15/1973	09:11:54	Le
05/30/1972	02:12:31	Cp	10/08/1972	15:26:55	Sc	02/17/1973	12:31:04	Vi
06/01/1972	12:14:58	Aq	10/11/1972	03:52:24	Sg	02/19/1973	17:58:03	Li
06/03/1972	19:51:49	Pi	10/13/1972	16:43:59	Cp	02/22/1973	02:34:57	Sc
06/06/1972	00:27:24	Ar	10/16/1972	03:51:03	Aq	02/24/1973	14:14:16	Sg
06/08/1972	02:14:29	Ta	10/18/1972	11:12:16	Pi	02/27/1973	03:03:40	Cp
06/10/1972	02:24:09	Ge	10/20/1972	14:22:19	Ar	03/01/1973	14:22:04	Aq
06/12/1972	02:44:34	Cn	10/22/1972	14:37:01	Ta	03/03/1973	22:30:56	Pi
06/14/1972	05:09:37	Le	10/24/1972	14:02:07	Ge	03/06/1973	03:36:50	Ar
06/16/1972	11:03:03	Vi	10/26/1972	14:44:21	Cn	03/08/1973	06:50:35	Ta
06/18/1972	20:38:39	Li	10/28/1972	18:14:15	Le	03/10/1973	09:30:40	Ge
06/21/1972	08:42:32	Sc	10/31/1972	00:59:03	Vi	03/12/1973	12:28:53	Cn
06/23/1972	21:14:12	Sg	11/02/1972	10:26:55	Li	03/14/1973	16:07:18	Le
06/26/1972	08:36:15	Cp	11/04/1972	21:46:10	Sc	03/16/1973	20:41:54	Vi
06/28/1972	18:02:24	Aq	11/07/1972	10:16:22	Sg	03/19/1973	02:47:51	Li
07/01/1972	01:18:24	Pi	11/09/1972	23:10:53	Cp	03/21/1973	11:15:20	Sc
07/03/1972	06:21:57	Ar	11/12/1972	11:02:19	Aq	03/23/1973	22:26:02	Sg
07/05/1972	09:24:39	Ta	11/14/1972	19:56:06	Pi	03/26/1973	11:15:41	Cp
07/07/1972	11:04:30	Ge	11/17/1972	00:43:56	Ar	03/28/1973	23:12:21	Aq
07/09/1972	12:29:09	Cn	11/19/1972	01:52:46	Ta	03/31/1973	07:54:41	Pi
07/11/1972	15:05:08	Le	11/21/1972	01:04:51	Ge	04/02/1973	12:47:54	Ar
07/13/1972	20:15:57	Vi	11/23/1972	00:30:48	Cn	04/04/1973	14:58:05	Ta
07/16/1972	04:48:41	Li	11/25/1972	02:11:34	Le	04/06/1973	16:11:46	Ge
07/18/1972	16:15:11	Sc	11/27/1972	07:24:17	Vi	04/08/1973	18:04:18	Cn
07/21/1972	04:46:08	Sg	11/29/1972	16:14:51	Li	04/10/1973	21:31:05	Le
07/23/1972	16:09:57	Cp	12/02/1972	03:42:12	Sc	04/13/1973	02:46:31	Vi
07/26/1972	01:06:58	Aq	12/04/1972	16:22:26	Sg	04/15/1973	09:49:48	Li
07/28/1972	07:28:47	Pi	12/07/1972	05:06:26	Cp	04/17/1973	18:50:59	Sc
07/30/1972	11:50:07	Ar	12/09/1972	16:53:23	Aq	04/20/1973	06:01:35	Sg
08/01/1972	14:57:22	Ta	12/12/1972	02:32:29	Pi	04/22/1973	18:48:57	Cp
08/03/1972	17:33:14	Ge	12/14/1972	08:59:16	Ar	04/25/1973	07:20:54	Aq
08/05/1972	20:17:38	Cn	12/16/1972	11:58:50	Ta	04/27/1973	17:09:28	Pi

04/29/1973	22:53:11	Ar	09/08/1973	16:30:19	Aq	01/18/1974	03:11:50	Sg
05/02/1973	01:01:20	Ta	09/11/1973	02:40:04	Pi	01/20/1974	15:47:11	Cp
05/04/1973	01:15:42	Ge	09/13/1973	09:55:46	Ar	01/23/1974	04:49:37	Aq
05/06/1973	01:34:53	Cn	09/15/1973	14:58:49	Ta	01/25/1974	17:00:25	Pi
05/08/1973	03:36:07	Le	09/17/1973	18:47:40	Ge	01/28/1974	03:31:40	Ar
05/10/1973	08:12:41	Vi	09/19/1973	22:00:48	Cn	01/30/1974	11:41:15	Ta
05/12/1973	15:30:42	Li	09/22/1973	00:56:16	Le	02/01/1974	16:53:02	Ge
05/15/1973	01:09:03	Sc	09/24/1973	03:58:17	Vi	02/03/1974	19:05:27	Cn
05/17/1973	12:41:24	Sg	09/26/1973	08:00:18	Li	02/05/1974	19:11:25	Le
05/20/1973	01:29:52	Cp	09/28/1973	14:18:00	Sc	02/07/1974	18:51:39	Vi
05/22/1973	14:17:08	Aq	09/30/1973	23:47:15	Sg	02/09/1974	20:10:00	Li
05/25/1973	01:05:11	Pi	10/03/1973	12:02:05	Cp	02/12/1974	00:57:43	Sc
05/27/1973	08:14:19	Ar	10/06/1973	00:48:30	Aq	02/14/1974	10:00:50	Sg
05/29/1973	11:27:31	Ta	10/08/1973	11:23:14	Pi	02/16/1974	22:15:38	Cp
05/31/1973	11:52:31	Ge	10/10/1973	18:28:42	Ar	02/19/1974	11:20:32	Aq
06/02/1973	11:20:50	Cn	10/12/1973	22:35:47	Ta	02/21/1974	23:15:02	Pi
06/04/1973	11:49:03	Le	10/15/1973	01:08:38	Ge	02/24/1974	09:12:19	Ar
06/06/1973	14:51:14	Vi	10/17/1973	03:28:24	Cn	02/26/1974	17:11:06	Ta
06/08/1973	21:15:38	Li	10/19/1973	06:24:39	Le	02/28/1974	23:10:06	Ge
06/11/1973	06:51:36	Sc	10/21/1973	10:18:35	Vi	03/03/1974	02:59:27	Cn
06/13/1973	18:42:43	Sg	10/23/1973	15:28:03	Li	03/05/1974	04:48:38	Le
06/16/1973	07:36:37	Cp	10/25/1973	22:27:42	Sc	03/07/1974	05:33:00	Vi
06/18/1973	20:18:50	Aq	10/28/1973	07:57:30	Sg	03/09/1974	06:51:39	Li
06/21/1973	07:28:40	Pi	10/30/1973	19:56:55	Cp	03/11/1974	10:39:39	Sc
06/23/1973	15:48:11	Ar	11/02/1973	08:58:06	Aq	03/13/1974	18:19:49	Sg
06/25/1973	20:36:58	Ta	11/04/1973	20:25:46	Pi	03/16/1974	05:41:05	Cp
06/27/1973	22:17:39	Ge	11/07/1973	04:19:01	Ar	03/18/1974	18:38:12	Aq
06/29/1973	22:08:03	Cn	11/09/1973	08:25:18	Ta	03/21/1974	06:33:20	Pi
07/01/1973	21:55:20	Le	11/11/1973	09:59:25	Ge	03/23/1974	16:02:23	Ar
07/03/1973	23:30:48	Vi	11/13/1973	10:46:21	Cn	03/25/1974	23:09:24	Ta
07/06/1973	04:23:27	Li	11/15/1973	12:19:44	Le	03/28/1974	04:32:46	Ge
07/08/1973	13:05:08	Sc	11/17/1973	15:40:51	Vi	03/30/1974	08:39:35	Cn
07/11/1973	00:47:34	Sg	11/19/1973	21:15:24	Li	04/01/1974	11:40:26	Le
07/13/1973	13:45:22	Cp	11/22/1973	05:06:29	Sc	04/03/1974	13:56:19	Vi
07/16/1973	02:14:41	Aq	11/24/1973	15:10:34	Sg	04/05/1974	16:22:27	Li
07/18/1973	13:07:11	Pi	11/27/1973	03:12:33	Cp	04/07/1974	20:24:45	Sc
07/20/1973	21:43:26	Ar	11/29/1973	16:17:06	Aq	04/10/1974	03:27:06	Sg
07/23/1973	03:40:39	Ta	12/02/1973	04:31:51	Pi	04/12/1974	13:56:16	Cp
07/25/1973	06:58:01	Ge	12/04/1973	13:49:55	Ar	04/15/1974	02:33:56	Aq
07/27/1973	08:09:59	Cn	12/06/1973	19:08:18	Ta	04/17/1974	14:44:08	Pi
07/29/1973	08:28:56	Le	12/08/1973	20:57:44	Ge	04/20/1974	00:20:00	Ar
07/31/1973	09:34:31	Vi	12/10/1973	20:51:43	Cn	04/22/1974	06:53:23	Ta
08/02/1973	13:12:09	Li	12/12/1973	20:44:15	Le	04/24/1974	11:10:45	Ge
08/04/1973	20:35:28	Sc	12/14/1973	22:20:26	Vi	04/26/1974	14:17:20	Cn
08/07/1973	07:36:41	Sg	12/17/1973	02:53:17	Li	04/28/1974	17:03:15	Le
08/09/1973	20:29:32	Cp	12/19/1973	10:43:38	Sc	04/30/1974	20:00:18	Vi
08/12/1973	08:52:09	Aq	12/21/1973	21:19:38	Sg	05/02/1974	23:38:49	Li
08/14/1973	19:13:51	Pi	12/24/1973	09:41:12	Cp	05/05/1974	04:42:56	Sc
08/17/1973	03:15:30	Ar	12/26/1973	22:42:39	Aq	05/07/1974	12:05:09	Sg
08/19/1973	09:13:38	Ta	12/29/1973	11:09:43	Pi	05/09/1974	22:14:51	Cp
08/21/1973	13:26:05	Ge	12/31/1973	21:33:46	Ar	05/12/1974	10:34:08	Aq
08/23/1973	16:07:33	Cn	01/03/1974	04:37:40	Ta	05/14/1974	23:02:56	Pi
08/25/1973	17:48:45	Le	01/05/1974	07:59:38	Ge	05/17/1974	09:19:29	Ar
08/27/1973	19:33:02	Vi	01/07/1974	08:28:10	Cn	05/19/1974	16:10:00	Ta
08/29/1973	22:52:15	Li	01/09/1974	07:42:00	Le	05/21/1974	19:53:51	Ge
09/01/1973	05:17:26	Sc	01/11/1974	07:41:29	Vi	05/23/1974	21:45:37	Cn
09/03/1973	15:24:15	Sg	01/13/1974	10:21:12	Li	05/25/1974	23:11:47	Le
09/06/1973	04:00:49	Cp	01/15/1974	16:53:51	Sc	05/28/1974	01:25:20	Vi

05/30/1974	05:15:46	Li
06/01/1974	11:10:17	Sc
06/03/1974	19:21:21	Sg
06/06/1974	05:48:14	Cp
06/08/1974	18:01:55	Aq
06/11/1974	06:43:21	Pi
06/13/1974	17:52:19	Ar
06/16/1974	01:46:23	Ta
06/18/1974	05:58:41	Ge
06/20/1974	07:21:04	Cn
06/22/1974	07:29:37	Le
06/24/1974	08:11:08	Vi
06/26/1974	10:57:05	Li
06/28/1974	16:39:57	Sc
07/01/1974	01:20:26	Sg
07/03/1974	12:18:55	Cp
07/06/1974	00:41:10	Aq
07/08/1974	13:25:27	Pi
07/11/1974	01:10:11	Ar
07/13/1974	10:20:57	Ta
07/15/1974	15:53:53	Ge
07/17/1974	17:55:59	Cn
07/19/1974	17:42:53	Le
07/21/1974	17:09:41	Vi
07/23/1974	18:18:44	Li
07/25/1974	22:45:25	Sc
07/28/1974	06:59:34	Sg
07/30/1974	18:10:37	Cp
08/02/1974	06:46:04	Aq
08/04/1974	19:26:27	Pi
08/07/1974	07:14:54	Ar
08/09/1974	17:12:32	Ta
08/12/1974	00:14:50	Ge
08/14/1974	03:48:31	Cn
08/16/1974	04:26:13	Le
08/18/1974	03:42:29	Vi
08/20/1974	03:44:41	Li
08/22/1974	06:36:58	Sc
08/24/1974	13:33:50	Sg
08/27/1974	00:14:55	Cp
08/29/1974	12:52:31	Aq
09/01/1974	01:29:02	Pi
09/03/1974	12:57:46	Ar
09/05/1974	22:50:06	Ta
09/08/1974	06:36:02	Ge
09/10/1974	11:39:27	Cn
09/12/1974	13:53:57	Le
09/14/1974	14:11:47	Vi
09/16/1974	14:16:47	Li
09/18/1974	16:13:48	Sc
09/20/1974	21:46:13	Sg
09/23/1974	07:21:33	Cp
09/25/1974	19:38:17	Aq
09/28/1974	08:14:31	Pi
09/30/1974	19:25:21	Ar
10/03/1974	04:39:07	Ta
10/05/1974	12:00:26	Ge
10/07/1974	17:29:56	Cn

10/09/1974	21:02:30	Le
10/11/1974	22:55:49	Vi
10/14/1974	00:10:39	Li
10/16/1974	02:23:07	Sc
10/18/1974	07:14:19	Sg
10/20/1974	15:43:46	Cp
10/23/1974	03:19:53	Aq
10/25/1974	15:56:39	Pi
10/28/1974	03:13:16	Ar
10/30/1974	11:59:48	Ta
11/01/1974	18:22:47	Ge
11/03/1974	23:00:49	Cn
11/06/1974	02:29:54	Le
11/08/1974	05:17:55	Vi
11/10/1974	07:58:27	Li
11/12/1974	11:23:16	Sc
11/14/1974	16:38:44	Sg
11/17/1974	00:41:41	Cp
11/19/1974	11:38:40	Aq
11/22/1974	00:11:13	Pi
11/24/1974	11:58:47	Ar
11/26/1974	21:04:37	Ta
11/29/1974	02:57:46	Ge
12/01/1974	06:21:38	Cn
12/03/1974	08:31:13	Le
12/05/1974	10:39:47	Vi
12/07/1974	13:42:24	Li
12/09/1974	18:13:18	Sc
12/12/1974	00:34:20	Sg
12/14/1974	09:03:43	Cp
12/16/1974	19:47:53	Aq
12/19/1974	08:11:47	Pi
12/21/1974	20:35:01	Ar
12/24/1974	06:44:33	Ta
12/26/1974	13:15:21	Ge
12/28/1974	16:15:22	Cn
12/30/1974	17:04:38	Le
01/01/1975	17:32:28	Vi
01/03/1975	19:21:23	Li
01/05/1975	23:38:30	Sc
01/08/1975	06:38:59	Sg
01/10/1975	15:58:03	Cp
01/13/1975	03:02:58	Aq
01/15/1975	15:23:12	Pi
01/18/1975	04:03:28	Ar
01/20/1975	15:21:01	Ta
01/22/1975	23:22:41	Ge
01/25/1975	03:20:09	Cn
01/27/1975	03:59:59	Le
01/29/1975	03:13:39	Vi
01/31/1975	03:13:16	Li
02/02/1975	05:53:01	Sc
02/04/1975	12:09:58	Sg
02/06/1975	21:42:06	Cp
02/09/1975	09:16:17	Aq
02/11/1975	21:45:03	Pi
02/14/1975	10:22:06	Ar
02/16/1975	22:08:57	Ta

02/19/1975	07:34:36	Ge
02/21/1975	13:18:17	Cn
02/23/1975	15:12:53	Le
02/25/1975	14:36:47	Vi
02/27/1975	13:38:20	Li
03/01/1975	14:33:32	Sc
03/03/1975	19:05:23	Sg
03/06/1975	03:39:26	Cp
03/08/1975	15:09:25	Aq
03/11/1975	03:48:50	Pi
03/13/1975	16:18:15	Ar
03/16/1975	03:52:15	Ta
03/18/1975	13:42:58	Ge
03/20/1975	20:48:13	Cn
03/23/1975	00:31:03	Le
03/25/1975	01:20:49	Vi
03/27/1975	00:51:14	Li
03/29/1975	01:07:37	Sc
03/31/1975	04:09:35	Sg
04/02/1975	11:08:08	Cp
04/04/1975	21:44:56	Aq
04/07/1975	10:16:41	Pi
04/09/1975	22:43:59	Ar
04/12/1975	09:53:14	Ta
04/14/1975	19:14:06	Ge
04/17/1975	02:26:56	Cn
04/19/1975	07:14:08	Le
04/21/1975	09:42:19	Vi
04/23/1975	10:41:24	Li
04/25/1975	11:39:27	Sc
04/27/1975	14:19:42	Sg
04/29/1975	20:08:23	Cp
05/02/1975	05:33:40	Aq
05/04/1975	17:34:08	Pi
05/07/1975	06:02:39	Ar
05/09/1975	17:03:17	Ta
05/12/1975	01:44:08	Ge
05/14/1975	08:07:35	Cn
05/16/1975	12:38:13	Le
05/18/1975	15:45:26	Vi
05/20/1975	18:04:48	Li
05/22/1975	20:25:25	Sc
05/24/1975	23:51:19	Sg
05/27/1975	05:30:39	Cp
05/29/1975	14:09:18	Aq
06/01/1975	01:32:01	Pi
06/03/1975	14:01:10	Ar
06/06/1975	01:18:37	Ta
06/08/1975	09:49:09	Ge
06/10/1975	15:21:26	Cn
06/12/1975	18:45:04	Le
06/14/1975	21:10:35	Vi
06/16/1975	23:40:42	Li
06/19/1975	02:58:52	Sc
06/21/1975	07:34:25	Sg
06/23/1975	13:55:47	Cp
06/25/1975	22:32:45	Aq
06/28/1975	09:33:04	Pi

06/30/1975	22:01:57	Ar
07/03/1975	09:53:58	Ta
07/05/1975	18:58:21	Ge
07/08/1975	00:22:59	Cn
07/10/1975	02:50:05	Le
07/12/1975	03:55:20	Vi
07/14/1975	05:21:08	Li
07/16/1975	08:22:47	Sc
07/18/1975	13:31:51	Sg
07/20/1975	20:45:41	Cp
07/23/1975	05:55:39	Aq
07/25/1975	16:58:17	Pi
07/28/1975	05:27:04	Ar
07/30/1975	17:53:21	Ta
08/02/1975	04:02:02	Ge
08/04/1975	10:16:48	Cn
08/06/1975	12:43:33	Le
08/08/1975	12:53:21	Vi
08/10/1975	12:50:51	Li
08/12/1975	14:29:56	Sc
08/14/1975	18:59:16	Sg
08/17/1975	02:24:49	Cp
08/19/1975	12:09:03	Aq
08/21/1975	23:32:02	Pi
08/24/1975	12:02:27	Ar
08/27/1975	00:44:38	Ta
08/29/1975	11:53:17	Ge
08/31/1975	19:34:48	Cn
09/02/1975	23:07:49	Le
09/04/1975	23:29:15	Vi
09/06/1975	22:37:43	Li
09/08/1975	22:45:39	Sc
09/11/1975	01:40:40	Sg
09/13/1975	08:10:51	Cp
09/15/1975	17:51:01	Aq
09/18/1975	05:31:44	Pi
09/20/1975	18:06:53	Ar
09/23/1975	06:43:11	Ta
09/25/1975	18:12:51	Ge
09/28/1975	03:06:48	Cn
09/30/1975	08:20:15	Le
10/02/1975	10:03:00	Vi
10/04/1975	09:38:38	Li
10/06/1975	09:08:36	Sc
10/08/1975	10:35:32	Sg
10/10/1975	15:28:44	Cp
10/13/1975	00:09:35	Aq
10/15/1975	11:40:03	Pi
10/18/1975	00:20:04	Ar
10/20/1975	12:43:04	Ta
10/22/1975	23:51:05	Ge
10/25/1975	08:57:02	Cn
10/27/1975	15:19:39	Le
10/29/1975	18:46:34	Vi
10/31/1975	19:54:59	Li
11/02/1975	20:07:25	Sc
11/04/1975	21:09:51	Sg
11/07/1975	00:45:05	Cp
11/09/1975	07:59:08	Aq
11/11/1975	18:41:44	Pi
11/14/1975	07:17:12	Ar
11/16/1975	19:37:34	Ta
11/19/1975	06:14:00	Ge
11/21/1975	14:36:06	Cn
11/23/1975	20:47:52	Le
11/26/1975	01:04:19	Vi
11/28/1975	03:47:38	Li
11/30/1975	05:36:30	Sc
12/02/1975	07:33:02	Sg
12/04/1975	10:58:17	Cp
12/06/1975	17:11:55	Aq
12/09/1975	02:51:34	Pi
12/11/1975	15:06:08	Ar
12/14/1975	03:38:54	Ta
12/16/1975	14:12:10	Ge
12/18/1975	21:48:47	Cn
12/21/1975	02:53:30	Le
12/23/1975	06:27:31	Vi
12/25/1975	09:27:12	Li
12/27/1975	12:27:44	Sc
12/29/1975	15:52:43	Sg
12/31/1975	20:16:15	Cp
01/03/1976	02:32:44	Aq
01/05/1976	11:34:52	Pi
01/07/1976	23:20:46	Ar
01/10/1976	12:09:31	Ta
01/12/1976	23:19:19	Ge
01/15/1976	07:00:15	Cn
01/17/1976	11:15:00	Le
01/19/1976	13:24:56	Vi
01/21/1976	15:10:29	Li
01/23/1976	17:47:54	Sc
01/25/1976	21:51:01	Sg
01/28/1976	03:23:55	Cp
01/30/1976	10:33:51	Aq
02/01/1976	19:46:31	Pi
02/04/1976	07:17:05	Ar
02/06/1976	20:13:12	Ta
02/09/1976	08:15:48	Ge
02/11/1976	16:58:32	Cn
02/13/1976	21:32:24	Le
02/15/1976	22:58:48	Vi
02/17/1976	23:13:49	Li
02/20/1976	00:13:33	Sc
02/22/1976	03:18:01	Sg
02/24/1976	08:54:04	Cp
02/26/1976	16:48:24	Aq
02/29/1976	02:41:31	Pi
03/02/1976	14:22:09	Ar
03/05/1976	03:17:58	Ta
03/07/1976	15:55:39	Ge
03/10/1976	01:58:39	Cn
03/12/1976	07:55:13	Le
03/14/1976	09:58:32	Vi
03/16/1976	09:44:14	Li
03/18/1976	09:17:37	Sc
03/20/1976	10:33:39	Sg
03/22/1976	14:48:11	Cp
03/24/1976	22:19:21	Aq
03/27/1976	08:33:42	Pi
03/29/1976	20:36:58	Ar
04/01/1976	09:33:48	Ta
04/03/1976	22:15:19	Ge
04/06/1976	09:06:25	Cn
04/08/1976	16:36:25	Le
04/10/1976	20:15:44	Vi
04/12/1976	20:54:12	Li
04/14/1976	20:14:17	Sc
04/16/1976	20:14:53	Sg
04/18/1976	22:43:18	Cp
04/21/1976	04:47:20	Aq
04/23/1976	14:27:35	Pi
04/26/1976	02:36:37	Ar
04/28/1976	15:37:26	Ta
05/01/1976	04:04:52	Ge
05/03/1976	14:53:14	Cn
05/05/1976	23:09:09	Le
05/08/1976	04:20:58	Vi
05/10/1976	06:39:17	Li
05/12/1976	07:02:35	Sc
05/14/1976	07:04:00	Sg
05/16/1976	08:31:26	Cp
05/18/1976	13:02:29	Aq
05/20/1976	21:26:37	Pi
05/23/1976	09:06:47	Ar
05/25/1976	22:07:00	Ta
05/28/1976	10:21:58	Ge
05/30/1976	20:38:51	Cn
06/02/1976	04:37:22	Le
06/04/1976	10:20:48	Vi
06/06/1976	13:59:40	Li
06/08/1976	15:58:02	Sc
06/10/1976	17:06:29	Sg
06/12/1976	18:45:14	Cp
06/14/1976	22:30:59	Aq
06/17/1976	05:43:28	Pi
06/19/1976	16:32:13	Ar
06/22/1976	05:21:19	Ta
06/24/1976	17:36:40	Ge
06/27/1976	03:28:58	Cn
06/29/1976	10:39:26	Le
07/01/1976	15:46:05	Vi
07/03/1976	19:34:19	Li
07/05/1976	22:33:22	Sc
07/08/1976	01:05:17	Sg
07/10/1976	03:49:12	Cp
07/12/1976	07:53:06	Aq
07/14/1976	14:35:56	Pi
07/17/1976	00:39:45	Ar
07/19/1976	13:11:09	Ta
07/22/1976	01:40:15	Ge
07/24/1976	11:39:12	Cn
07/26/1976	18:18:32	Le
07/28/1976	22:23:14	Vi

07/31/1976	01:13:23	Li	12/10/1976	10:11:53	Le	04/21/1977	02:37:06	Ge
08/02/1976	03:55:15	Sc	12/12/1976	17:54:57	Vi	04/23/1977	15:24:58	Cn
08/04/1976	07:03:13	Sg	12/14/1976	23:13:02	Li	04/26/1977	02:42:55	Le
08/06/1976	10:54:23	Cp	12/17/1976	02:01:19	Sc	04/28/1977	10:51:51	Vi
08/08/1976	15:56:56	Aq	12/19/1976	02:53:44	Sg	04/30/1977	15:12:25	Li
08/10/1976	23:00:26	Pi	12/21/1976	03:11:34	Cp	05/02/1977	16:23:29	Sc
08/13/1976	08:48:55	Ar	12/23/1976	04:48:14	Aq	05/04/1977	15:58:44	Sg
08/15/1976	21:05:12	Ta	12/25/1976	09:35:52	Pi	05/06/1977	15:54:08	Cp
08/18/1976	09:53:50	Ge	12/27/1976	18:31:43	Ar	05/08/1977	17:59:40	Aq
08/20/1976	20:33:40	Cn	12/30/1976	06:43:08	Ta	05/10/1977	23:28:49	Pi
08/23/1976	03:30:32	Le	01/01/1977	19:42:38	Ge	05/13/1977	08:29:26	Ar
08/25/1976	07:03:32	Vi	01/04/1977	07:12:12	Cn	05/15/1977	20:04:04	Ta
08/27/1976	08:41:35	Li	01/06/1977	16:20:25	Le	05/18/1977	08:50:11	Ge
08/29/1976	10:04:51	Sc	01/08/1977	23:23:02	Vi	05/20/1977	21:35:18	Cn
08/31/1976	12:28:08	Sg	01/11/1977	04:47:39	Li	05/23/1977	09:13:10	Le
09/02/1976	16:28:57	Cp	01/13/1977	08:44:07	Sc	05/25/1977	18:30:58	Vi
09/04/1976	22:19:52	Aq	01/15/1977	11:17:45	Sg	05/28/1977	00:28:18	Li
09/07/1976	06:11:23	Pi	01/17/1977	13:01:42	Cp	05/30/1977	02:56:31	Sc
09/09/1976	16:17:57	Ar	01/19/1977	15:11:52	Aq	06/01/1977	02:53:42	Sg
09/12/1976	04:29:55	Ta	01/21/1977	19:30:01	Pi	06/03/1977	02:07:06	Cp
09/14/1976	17:32:10	Ge	01/24/1977	03:19:31	Ar	06/05/1977	02:43:39	Aq
09/17/1976	05:06:32	Cn	01/26/1977	14:40:58	Ta	06/07/1977	06:35:25	Pi
09/19/1976	13:10:27	Le	01/29/1977	03:36:54	Ge	06/09/1977	14:34:08	Ar
09/21/1976	17:15:56	Vi	01/31/1977	15:19:48	Cn	06/12/1977	01:56:27	Ta
09/23/1976	18:27:40	Li	02/03/1977	00:11:20	Le	06/14/1977	14:49:40	Ge
09/25/1976	18:33:34	Sc	02/05/1977	06:17:03	Vi	06/17/1977	03:28:20	Cn
09/27/1976	19:21:27	Sg	02/07/1977	10:35:56	Li	06/19/1977	14:53:12	Le
09/29/1976	22:13:02	Cp	02/09/1977	14:03:56	Sc	06/22/1977	00:28:44	Vi
10/02/1976	03:49:07	Aq	02/11/1977	17:10:51	Sg	06/24/1977	07:35:19	Li
10/04/1976	12:09:43	Pi	02/13/1977	20:13:39	Cp	06/26/1977	11:41:46	Sc
10/06/1976	22:49:39	Ar	02/15/1977	23:44:43	Aq	06/28/1977	13:01:41	Sg
10/09/1976	11:11:03	Ta	02/18/1977	04:44:40	Pi	06/30/1977	12:48:00	Cp
10/12/1976	00:14:20	Ge	02/20/1977	12:22:27	Ar	07/02/1977	12:56:05	Aq
10/14/1976	12:23:51	Cn	02/22/1977	23:06:02	Ta	07/04/1977	15:31:06	Pi
10/16/1976	21:49:12	Le	02/25/1977	11:49:45	Ge	07/06/1977	22:03:09	Ar
10/19/1976	03:24:39	Vi	02/28/1977	00:02:10	Cn	07/09/1977	08:32:44	Ta
10/21/1976	05:26:18	Li	03/02/1977	09:24:44	Le	07/11/1977	21:14:47	Ge
10/23/1976	05:16:46	Sc	03/04/1977	15:18:37	Vi	07/14/1977	09:49:32	Cn
10/25/1976	04:48:38	Sg	03/06/1977	18:34:25	Li	07/16/1977	20:51:10	Le
10/27/1976	05:55:20	Cp	03/08/1977	20:36:45	Sc	07/19/1977	05:58:16	Vi
10/29/1976	10:05:14	Aq	03/10/1977	22:41:39	Sg	07/21/1977	13:09:16	Li
10/31/1976	17:53:09	Pi	03/13/1977	01:39:35	Cp	07/23/1977	18:13:14	Sc
11/03/1976	04:45:36	Ar	03/15/1977	05:59:46	Aq	07/25/1977	21:04:24	Sg
11/05/1976	17:22:53	Ta	03/17/1977	12:05:33	Pi	07/27/1977	22:14:40	Cp
11/08/1976	06:20:52	Ge	03/19/1977	20:22:53	Ar	07/29/1977	23:04:19	Aq
11/10/1976	18:27:44	Cn	03/22/1977	07:05:25	Ta	08/01/1977	01:23:27	Pi
11/13/1976	04:36:02	Le	03/24/1977	19:38:38	Ge	08/03/1977	06:54:18	Ar
11/15/1976	11:46:10	Vi	03/27/1977	08:16:28	Cn	08/05/1977	16:17:52	Ta
11/17/1976	15:33:47	Li	03/29/1977	18:40:20	Le	08/08/1977	04:29:17	Ge
11/19/1976	16:31:27	Sc	04/01/1977	01:24:44	Vi	08/10/1977	17:03:52	Cn
11/21/1976	16:03:19	Sg	04/03/1977	04:38:45	Li	08/13/1977	03:56:42	Le
11/23/1976	16:03:27	Cp	04/05/1977	05:39:38	Sc	08/15/1977	12:25:40	Vi
11/25/1976	18:29:47	Aq	04/07/1977	06:08:33	Sg	08/17/1977	18:48:48	Li
11/28/1976	00:47:21	Pi	04/09/1977	07:40:17	Cp	08/19/1977	23:35:10	Sc
11/30/1976	11:01:20	Ar	04/11/1977	11:23:39	Aq	08/22/1977	03:02:38	Sg
12/02/1976	23:41:14	Ta	04/13/1977	17:49:23	Pi	08/24/1977	05:30:13	Cp
12/05/1976	12:38:01	Ge	04/16/1977	02:51:44	Ar	08/26/1977	07:40:39	Aq
12/08/1976	00:20:49	Cn	04/18/1977	14:02:20	Ta	08/28/1977	10:46:26	Pi

08/30/1977	16:11:27	Ar
09/02/1977	00:51:41	Ta
09/04/1977	12:26:50	Ge
09/07/1977	01:02:45	Cn
09/09/1977	12:13:33	Le
09/11/1977	20:34:20	Vi
09/14/1977	02:07:28	Li
09/16/1977	05:45:18	Sc
09/18/1977	08:27:59	Sg
09/20/1977	11:04:06	Cp
09/22/1977	14:11:57	Aq
09/24/1977	18:29:37	Pi
09/27/1977	00:40:20	Ar
09/29/1977	09:21:17	Ta
10/01/1977	20:33:24	Ge
10/04/1977	09:08:46	Cn
10/06/1977	20:57:32	Le
10/09/1977	05:58:33	Vi
10/11/1977	11:29:24	Li
10/13/1977	14:10:41	Sc
10/15/1977	15:27:07	Sg
10/17/1977	16:50:36	Cp
10/19/1977	19:35:53	Aq
10/22/1977	00:26:20	Pi
10/24/1977	07:34:00	Ar
10/26/1977	16:52:51	Ta
10/29/1977	04:07:46	Ge
10/31/1977	16:39:54	Cn
11/03/1977	05:02:59	Le
11/05/1977	15:16:31	Vi
11/07/1977	21:50:57	Li
11/10/1977	00:41:48	Sc
11/12/1977	01:03:29	Sg
11/14/1977	00:50:23	Cp
11/16/1977	01:59:51	Aq
11/18/1977	05:58:26	Pi
11/20/1977	13:13:00	Ar
11/22/1977	23:09:19	Ta
11/25/1977	10:48:20	Ge
11/27/1977	23:19:55	Cn
11/30/1977	11:52:45	Le
12/02/1977	23:05:16	Vi
12/05/1977	07:17:29	Li
12/07/1977	11:32:53	Sc
12/09/1977	12:21:35	Sg
12/11/1977	11:25:47	Cp
12/13/1977	10:59:27	Aq
12/15/1977	13:09:10	Pi
12/17/1977	19:11:08	Ar
12/20/1977	04:53:50	Ta
12/22/1977	16:51:12	Ge
12/25/1977	05:29:41	Cn
12/27/1977	17:51:32	Le
12/30/1977	05:13:23	Vi
01/01/1978	14:31:15	Li
01/03/1978	20:34:53	Sc
01/05/1978	23:03:27	Sg
01/07/1978	22:54:38	Cp
01/09/1978	22:04:58	Aq
01/11/1978	22:50:22	Pi
01/14/1978	03:04:48	Ar
01/16/1978	11:30:18	Ta
01/18/1978	23:06:25	Ge
01/21/1978	11:50:20	Cn
01/24/1978	00:02:01	Le
01/26/1978	10:55:46	Vi
01/28/1978	20:07:36	Li
01/31/1978	03:03:30	Sc
02/02/1978	07:13:17	Sg
02/04/1978	08:49:46	Cp
02/06/1978	09:04:12	Aq
02/08/1978	09:47:30	Pi
02/10/1978	12:56:22	Ar
02/12/1978	19:50:21	Ta
02/15/1978	06:24:10	Ge
02/17/1978	18:55:36	Cn
02/20/1978	07:09:28	Le
02/22/1978	17:39:24	Vi
02/25/1978	02:03:15	Li
02/27/1978	08:27:54	Sc
03/01/1978	13:01:50	Sg
03/03/1978	15:57:45	Cp
03/05/1978	17:50:32	Aq
03/07/1978	19:45:31	Pi
03/09/1978	23:08:05	Ar
03/12/1978	05:17:46	Ta
03/14/1978	14:48:17	Ge
03/17/1978	02:48:50	Cn
03/19/1978	15:12:06	Le
03/22/1978	01:49:24	Vi
03/24/1978	09:41:21	Li
03/26/1978	15:01:00	Sc
03/28/1978	18:37:10	Sg
03/30/1978	21:23:23	Cp
04/02/1978	00:04:49	Aq
04/04/1978	03:20:21	Pi
04/06/1978	07:50:48	Ar
04/08/1978	14:21:27	Ta
04/10/1978	23:27:22	Ge
04/13/1978	10:58:53	Cn
04/15/1978	23:30:15	Le
04/18/1978	10:43:50	Vi
04/20/1978	18:52:47	Li
04/22/1978	23:38:57	Sc
04/25/1978	02:00:07	Sg
04/27/1978	03:27:27	Cp
04/29/1978	05:27:49	Aq
05/01/1978	08:59:41	Pi
05/03/1978	14:26:44	Ar
05/05/1978	21:52:11	Ta
05/08/1978	07:18:17	Ge
05/10/1978	18:41:20	Cn
05/13/1978	07:16:44	Le
05/15/1978	19:14:47	Vi
05/18/1978	04:24:15	Li
05/20/1978	09:38:35	Sc
05/22/1978	11:30:50	Sg
05/24/1978	11:41:18	Cp
05/26/1978	12:09:46	Aq
05/28/1978	14:36:26	Pi
05/30/1978	19:52:09	Ar
06/02/1978	03:50:07	Ta
06/04/1978	13:53:27	Ge
06/07/1978	01:29:58	Cn
06/09/1978	14:07:14	Le
06/12/1978	02:34:41	Vi
06/14/1978	12:55:21	Li
06/16/1978	19:28:19	Sc
06/18/1978	22:00:49	Sg
06/20/1978	21:51:44	Cp
06/22/1978	21:07:27	Aq
06/24/1978	21:56:43	Pi
06/27/1978	01:52:45	Ar
06/29/1978	09:20:51	Ta
07/01/1978	19:37:28	Ge
07/04/1978	07:33:12	Cn
07/06/1978	20:12:46	Le
07/09/1978	08:44:23	Vi
07/11/1978	19:48:00	Li
07/14/1978	03:46:42	Sc
07/16/1978	07:49:36	Sg
07/18/1978	08:32:58	Cp
07/20/1978	07:41:30	Aq
07/22/1978	07:26:02	Pi
07/24/1978	09:45:45	Ar
07/26/1978	15:50:22	Ta
07/29/1978	01:30:33	Ge
07/31/1978	13:28:01	Cn
08/03/1978	02:10:10	Le
08/05/1978	14:28:51	Vi
08/08/1978	01:29:35	Li
08/10/1978	10:11:16	Sc
08/12/1978	15:42:41	Sg
08/14/1978	18:02:51	Cp
08/16/1978	18:14:46	Aq
08/18/1978	18:04:28	Pi
08/20/1978	19:29:20	Ar
08/23/1978	00:05:34	Ta
08/25/1978	08:31:05	Ge
08/27/1978	19:58:54	Cn
08/30/1978	08:39:35	Le
09/01/1978	20:46:15	Vi
09/04/1978	07:15:23	Li
09/06/1978	15:37:55	Sc
09/08/1978	21:39:11	Sg
09/11/1978	01:19:38	Cp
09/13/1978	03:08:30	Aq
09/15/1978	04:09:15	Pi
09/17/1978	05:49:48	Ar
09/19/1978	09:42:53	Ta
09/21/1978	16:55:59	Ge
09/24/1978	03:31:11	Cn
09/26/1978	16:01:30	Le
09/29/1978	04:11:02	Vi

10/01/1978	14:16:35	Li	02/10/1979	04:25:17	Le	06/21/1979	23:22:34	Ge
10/03/1978	21:47:44	Sc	02/12/1979	17:17:36	Vi	06/24/1979	07:24:30	Cn
10/06/1978	03:06:28	Sg	02/15/1979	05:36:54	Li	06/26/1979	17:46:51	Le
10/08/1978	06:52:16	Cp	02/17/1979	16:11:46	Sc	06/29/1979	06:13:48	Vi
10/10/1978	09:42:26	Aq	02/19/1979	23:50:50	Sg	07/01/1979	19:07:50	Li
10/12/1978	12:12:18	Pi	02/22/1979	04:00:25	Cp	07/04/1979	05:56:58	Sc
10/14/1978	15:05:45	Ar	02/24/1979	05:12:00	Aq	07/06/1979	12:55:27	Sg
10/16/1978	19:21:53	Ta	02/26/1979	04:52:12	Pi	07/08/1979	16:07:13	Cp
10/19/1978	02:05:15	Ge	02/28/1979	04:53:58	Ar	07/10/1979	16:58:45	Aq
10/21/1978	11:52:26	Cn	03/02/1979	07:09:06	Ta	07/12/1979	17:22:37	Pi
10/24/1978	00:03:53	Le	03/04/1979	12:58:04	Ge	07/14/1979	18:56:54	Ar
10/26/1978	12:31:41	Vi	03/06/1979	22:34:06	Cn	07/16/1979	22:42:41	Ta
10/28/1978	22:50:48	Li	03/09/1979	10:47:16	Le	07/19/1979	04:59:31	Ge
10/31/1978	05:52:30	Sc	03/11/1979	23:42:25	Vi	07/21/1979	13:40:12	Cn
11/02/1978	10:03:18	Sg	03/14/1979	11:41:30	Li	07/24/1979	00:29:49	Le
11/04/1978	12:40:27	Cp	03/16/1979	21:49:02	Sc	07/26/1979	13:01:08	Vi
11/06/1978	15:03:35	Aq	03/19/1979	05:37:59	Sg	07/29/1979	02:05:59	Li
11/08/1978	18:05:56	Pi	03/21/1979	10:56:13	Cp	07/31/1979	13:46:11	Sc
11/10/1978	22:11:25	Ar	03/23/1979	13:51:47	Aq	08/02/1979	22:05:23	Sg
11/13/1978	03:34:50	Ta	03/25/1979	15:04:25	Pi	08/05/1979	02:22:39	Cp
11/15/1978	10:44:33	Ge	03/27/1979	15:47:15	Ar	08/07/1979	03:28:09	Aq
11/17/1978	20:15:59	Cn	03/29/1979	17:36:10	Ta	08/09/1979	03:05:24	Pi
11/20/1978	08:08:46	Le	03/31/1979	22:08:16	Ge	08/11/1979	03:09:55	Ar
11/22/1978	20:57:06	Vi	04/03/1979	06:23:42	Cn	08/13/1979	05:21:21	Ta
11/25/1978	08:06:52	Li	04/05/1979	17:57:34	Le	08/15/1979	10:41:07	Ge
11/27/1978	15:38:26	Sc	04/08/1979	06:51:44	Vi	08/17/1979	19:17:02	Cn
11/29/1978	19:23:14	Sg	04/10/1979	18:44:44	Li	08/20/1979	06:28:28	Le
12/01/1978	20:43:58	Cp	04/13/1979	04:15:36	Sc	08/22/1979	19:11:08	Vi
12/03/1978	21:35:21	Aq	04/15/1979	11:18:00	Sg	08/25/1979	08:13:25	Li
12/05/1978	23:36:08	Pi	04/17/1979	16:22:44	Cp	08/27/1979	20:12:28	Sc
12/08/1978	03:39:31	Ar	04/19/1979	20:02:06	Aq	08/30/1979	05:39:12	Sg
12/10/1978	09:50:20	Ta	04/21/1979	22:41:00	Pi	09/01/1979	11:33:27	Cp
12/12/1978	17:54:25	Ge	04/24/1979	00:50:59	Ar	09/03/1979	13:58:59	Aq
12/15/1978	03:49:41	Cn	04/26/1979	03:27:09	Ta	09/05/1979	14:02:41	Pi
12/17/1978	15:37:24	Le	04/28/1979	07:48:32	Ge	09/07/1979	13:28:47	Ar
12/20/1978	04:34:06	Vi	04/30/1979	15:11:18	Cn	09/09/1979	14:12:20	Ta
12/22/1978	16:39:54	Li	05/03/1979	01:56:26	Le	09/11/1979	17:54:01	Ge
12/25/1978	01:32:04	Sc	05/05/1979	14:41:12	Vi	09/14/1979	01:26:45	Cn
12/27/1978	06:07:20	Sg	05/08/1979	02:47:28	Li	09/16/1979	12:25:09	Le
12/29/1978	07:15:25	Cp	05/10/1979	12:09:45	Sc	09/19/1979	01:15:24	Vi
12/31/1978	06:52:51	Aq	05/12/1979	18:24:39	Sg	09/21/1979	14:10:36	Li
01/02/1979	07:07:56	Pi	05/14/1979	22:25:28	Cp	09/24/1979	01:53:48	Sc
01/04/1979	09:41:12	Ar	05/17/1979	01:25:29	Aq	09/26/1979	11:35:36	Sg
01/06/1979	15:17:26	Ta	05/19/1979	04:18:18	Pi	09/28/1979	18:39:44	Cp
01/08/1979	23:42:28	Ge	05/21/1979	07:30:01	Ar	09/30/1979	22:48:47	Aq
01/11/1979	10:14:10	Cn	05/23/1979	11:20:17	Ta	10/03/1979	00:23:00	Pi
01/13/1979	22:16:06	Le	05/25/1979	16:27:51	Ge	10/05/1979	00:28:03	Ar
01/16/1979	11:10:05	Vi	05/27/1979	23:50:35	Cn	10/07/1979	00:44:35	Ta
01/18/1979	23:40:21	Li	05/30/1979	10:07:51	Le	10/09/1979	03:07:05	Ge
01/21/1979	09:50:39	Sc	06/01/1979	22:40:38	Vi	10/11/1979	09:08:57	Cn
01/23/1979	16:07:43	Sg	06/04/1979	11:11:32	Li	10/13/1979	19:11:32	Le
01/25/1979	18:27:21	Cp	06/06/1979	21:04:44	Sc	10/16/1979	07:51:10	Vi
01/27/1979	18:11:54	Aq	06/09/1979	03:14:32	Sg	10/18/1979	20:44:19	Li
01/29/1979	17:25:11	Pi	06/11/1979	06:23:17	Cp	10/21/1979	08:02:05	Sc
01/31/1979	18:11:17	Ar	06/13/1979	08:06:07	Aq	10/23/1979	17:08:58	Sg
02/02/1979	22:02:53	Ta	06/15/1979	09:55:52	Pi	10/26/1979	00:11:02	Cp
02/05/1979	05:32:55	Ge	06/17/1979	12:52:10	Ar	10/28/1979	05:16:30	Aq
02/07/1979	16:05:32	Cn	06/19/1979	17:18:07	Ta	10/30/1979	08:28:44	Pi

Date	Time	Sign
11/01/1979	10:08:42	Ar
11/03/1979	11:15:43	Ta
11/05/1979	13:25:32	Ge
11/07/1979	18:23:35	Cn
11/10/1979	03:14:22	Le
11/12/1979	15:20:12	Vi
11/15/1979	04:16:20	Li
11/17/1979	15:29:25	Sc
11/19/1979	23:56:24	Sg
11/22/1979	06:01:22	Cp
11/24/1979	10:36:33	Aq
11/26/1979	14:17:05	Pi
11/28/1979	17:16:34	Ar
11/30/1979	19:54:20	Ta
12/02/1979	23:01:58	Ge
12/05/1979	04:01:28	Cn
12/07/1979	12:08:47	Le
12/09/1979	23:32:40	Vi
12/12/1979	12:28:53	Li
12/15/1979	00:07:53	Sc
12/17/1979	08:36:25	Sg
12/19/1979	13:54:31	Cp
12/21/1979	17:12:33	Aq
12/23/1979	19:50:00	Pi
12/25/1979	22:40:01	Ar
12/28/1979	02:07:33	Ta
12/30/1979	06:31:55	Ge
01/01/1980	11:24:03	Cn
01/03/1980	20:47:05	Le
01/06/1980	07:48:22	Vi
01/08/1980	20:37:43	Li
01/11/1980	08:55:11	Sc
01/13/1980	18:17:05	Sg
01/15/1980	23:51:12	Cp
01/18/1980	02:24:45	Aq
01/20/1980	03:32:57	Pi
01/22/1980	04:51:32	Ar
01/24/1980	07:31:25	Ta
01/26/1980	12:10:47	Ge
01/28/1980	19:02:25	Cn
01/31/1980	04:08:11	Le
02/02/1980	15:21:07	Vi
02/05/1980	04:04:06	Li
02/07/1980	16:45:49	Sc
02/10/1980	03:19:05	Sg
02/12/1980	10:11:43	Cp
02/14/1980	13:19:24	Aq
02/16/1980	13:53:55	Pi
02/18/1980	13:42:32	Ar
02/20/1980	14:34:49	Ta
02/22/1980	17:58:04	Ge
02/25/1980	00:34:19	Cn
02/27/1980	10:10:06	Le
02/29/1980	21:53:05	Vi
03/03/1980	10:39:52	Li
03/05/1980	23:22:27	Sc
03/08/1980	10:38:24	Sg
03/10/1980	19:01:43	Cp
03/12/1980	23:45:08	Aq
03/15/1980	01:10:28	Pi
03/17/1980	00:40:53	Ar
03/19/1980	00:12:50	Ta
03/21/1980	01:47:14	Ge
03/23/1980	06:55:23	Cn
03/25/1980	15:58:23	Le
03/28/1980	03:51:49	Vi
03/30/1980	16:48:41	Li
04/02/1980	05:21:12	Sc
04/04/1980	16:34:31	Sg
04/07/1980	01:42:34	Cp
04/09/1980	07:59:32	Aq
04/11/1980	11:06:36	Pi
04/13/1980	11:39:56	Ar
04/15/1980	11:10:35	Ta
04/17/1980	11:41:03	Ge
04/19/1980	15:11:30	Cn
04/21/1980	22:51:49	Le
04/24/1980	10:11:53	Vi
04/26/1980	23:09:13	Li
04/29/1980	11:34:41	Sc
05/01/1980	22:21:36	Sg
05/04/1980	07:14:06	Cp
05/06/1980	14:03:28	Aq
05/08/1980	18:33:14	Pi
05/10/1980	20:44:20	Ar
05/12/1980	21:24:03	Ta
05/14/1980	22:07:24	Ge
05/17/1980	00:51:53	Cn
05/19/1980	07:14:20	Le
05/21/1980	17:32:26	Vi
05/24/1980	06:10:48	Li
05/26/1980	18:36:35	Sc
05/29/1980	05:04:35	Sg
05/31/1980	13:14:27	Cp
06/02/1980	19:29:20	Aq
06/05/1980	00:09:38	Pi
06/07/1980	03:23:16	Ar
06/09/1980	05:29:28	Ta
06/11/1980	07:22:23	Ge
06/13/1980	10:29:18	Cn
06/15/1980	16:21:54	Le
06/18/1980	01:47:01	Vi
06/20/1980	13:55:07	Li
06/23/1980	02:26:17	Sc
06/25/1980	13:01:30	Sg
06/27/1980	20:45:52	Cp
06/30/1980	02:03:35	Aq
07/02/1980	05:48:16	Pi
07/04/1980	08:46:11	Ar
07/06/1980	11:30:07	Ta
07/08/1980	14:33:28	Ge
07/10/1980	18:44:26	Cn
07/13/1980	01:02:30	Le
07/15/1980	10:11:11	Vi
07/17/1980	21:54:51	Li
07/20/1980	10:33:01	Sc
07/22/1980	21:41:58	Sg
07/25/1980	05:44:32	Cp
07/27/1980	10:34:29	Aq
07/29/1980	13:10:39	Pi
07/31/1980	14:53:04	Ar
08/02/1980	16:54:44	Ta
08/04/1980	20:09:38	Ge
08/07/1980	01:12:06	Cn
08/09/1980	08:23:24	Le
08/11/1980	17:54:13	Vi
08/14/1980	05:31:56	Li
08/16/1980	18:14:52	Sc
08/19/1980	06:07:32	Sg
08/21/1980	15:11:08	Cp
08/23/1980	20:32:27	Aq
08/25/1980	22:43:14	Pi
08/27/1980	23:10:44	Ar
08/29/1980	23:40:54	Ta
09/01/1980	01:49:48	Ge
09/03/1980	06:39:17	Cn
09/05/1980	14:22:08	Le
09/08/1980	00:30:43	Vi
09/10/1980	12:22:00	Li
09/13/1980	01:05:51	Sc
09/15/1980	13:27:43	Sg
09/17/1980	23:45:00	Cp
09/20/1980	06:30:26	Aq
09/22/1980	09:27:00	Pi
09/24/1980	09:37:08	Ar
09/26/1980	08:53:00	Ta
09/28/1980	09:20:49	Ge
09/30/1980	12:46:27	Cn
10/02/1980	19:56:45	Le
10/05/1980	06:18:49	Vi
10/07/1980	18:30:09	Li
10/10/1980	07:14:38	Sc
10/12/1980	19:37:18	Sg
10/15/1980	06:36:41	Cp
10/17/1980	14:53:32	Aq
10/19/1980	19:31:07	Pi
10/21/1980	20:42:47	Ar
10/23/1980	19:55:11	Ta
10/25/1980	19:16:42	Ge
10/27/1980	20:59:57	Cn
10/30/1980	02:38:29	Le
11/01/1980	12:18:28	Vi
11/04/1980	00:31:14	Li
11/06/1980	13:18:54	Sc
11/09/1980	01:25:27	Sg
11/11/1980	12:15:00	Cp
11/13/1980	21:10:11	Aq
11/16/1980	03:20:45	Pi
11/18/1980	06:21:29	Ar
11/20/1980	06:50:41	Ta
11/22/1980	06:27:01	Ge
11/24/1980	07:18:33	Cn
11/26/1980	11:23:07	Le
11/28/1980	19:37:20	Vi

12/01/1980	07:13:07	Li	04/12/1981	02:36:21	Le	08/22/1981	15:18:07	Ge
12/03/1980	20:00:06	Sc	04/14/1981	10:56:15	Vi	08/24/1981	18:16:35	Cn
12/06/1980	07:57:18	Sg	04/16/1981	21:37:45	Li	08/26/1981	22:09:54	Le
12/08/1980	18:11:44	Cp	04/19/1981	09:38:46	Sc	08/29/1981	03:31:30	Vi
12/11/1980	02:35:39	Aq	04/21/1981	22:14:36	Sg	08/31/1981	11:02:27	Li
12/13/1980	09:03:13	Pi	04/24/1981	10:31:02	Cp	09/02/1981	21:10:05	Sc
12/15/1980	13:21:08	Ar	04/26/1981	20:56:52	Aq	09/05/1981	09:23:35	Sg
12/17/1980	15:36:05	Ta	04/29/1981	03:56:05	Pi	09/07/1981	21:48:16	Cp
12/19/1980	16:39:21	Ge	05/01/1981	06:57:08	Ar	09/10/1981	07:58:30	Aq
12/21/1980	18:02:58	Cn	05/03/1981	06:59:06	Ta	09/12/1981	14:33:47	Pi
12/23/1980	21:33:33	Le	05/05/1981	06:01:01	Ge	09/14/1981	17:55:25	Ar
12/26/1980	04:32:14	Vi	05/07/1981	06:17:40	Cn	09/16/1981	19:30:04	Ta
12/28/1980	15:04:41	Li	05/09/1981	09:40:06	Le	09/18/1981	20:58:47	Ge
12/31/1980	03:36:00	Sc	05/11/1981	16:55:00	Vi	09/20/1981	23:39:26	Cn
01/02/1981	15:41:41	Sg	05/14/1981	03:24:04	Li	09/23/1981	04:08:17	Le
01/05/1981	01:40:59	Cp	05/16/1981	15:37:17	Sc	09/25/1981	10:28:39	Vi
01/07/1981	09:12:25	Aq	05/19/1981	04:13:50	Sg	09/27/1981	18:40:05	Li
01/09/1981	14:41:57	Pi	05/21/1981	16:19:52	Cp	09/30/1981	04:52:37	Sc
01/11/1981	18:43:27	Ar	05/24/1981	03:00:28	Aq	10/02/1981	16:59:33	Sg
01/13/1981	21:44:51	Ta	05/26/1981	11:05:15	Pi	10/05/1981	05:48:52	Cp
01/16/1981	00:17:11	Ge	05/28/1981	15:43:36	Ar	10/07/1981	17:00:58	Aq
01/18/1981	03:07:35	Cn	05/30/1981	17:10:10	Ta	10/10/1981	00:32:25	Pi
01/20/1981	07:20:42	Le	06/01/1981	16:48:11	Ge	10/12/1981	04:00:51	Ar
01/22/1981	14:02:14	Vi	06/03/1981	16:38:27	Cn	10/14/1981	04:43:12	Ta
01/24/1981	23:45:05	Li	06/05/1981	18:42:43	Le	10/16/1981	04:41:11	Ge
01/27/1981	11:48:35	Sc	06/08/1981	00:25:27	Vi	10/18/1981	05:52:26	Cn
01/30/1981	00:11:30	Sg	06/10/1981	09:54:54	Li	10/20/1981	09:34:21	Le
02/01/1981	10:36:51	Cp	06/12/1981	21:54:13	Sc	10/22/1981	16:04:39	Vi
02/03/1981	17:54:57	Aq	06/15/1981	10:31:19	Sg	10/25/1981	00:56:30	Li
02/05/1981	22:21:22	Pi	06/17/1981	22:20:52	Cp	10/27/1981	11:38:00	Sc
02/08/1981	01:01:18	Ar	06/20/1981	08:35:54	Aq	10/29/1981	23:48:23	Sg
02/10/1981	03:10:29	Ta	06/22/1981	16:44:00	Pi	11/01/1981	12:46:00	Cp
02/12/1981	05:50:52	Ge	06/24/1981	22:18:07	Ar	11/04/1981	00:50:40	Aq
02/14/1981	09:42:34	Cn	06/27/1981	01:16:13	Ta	11/06/1981	09:52:04	Pi
02/16/1981	15:10:00	Le	06/29/1981	02:21:06	Ge	11/08/1981	14:38:27	Ar
02/18/1981	22:33:59	Vi	07/01/1981	02:56:48	Cn	11/10/1981	15:44:16	Ta
02/21/1981	08:12:05	Li	07/03/1981	04:47:01	Le	11/12/1981	14:59:18	Ge
02/23/1981	19:54:23	Sc	07/05/1981	09:26:05	Vi	11/14/1981	14:36:38	Cn
02/26/1981	08:29:00	Sg	07/07/1981	17:42:05	Li	11/16/1981	16:32:33	Le
02/28/1981	19:46:16	Cp	07/10/1981	05:01:36	Sc	11/18/1981	21:52:44	Vi
03/03/1981	03:50:34	Aq	07/12/1981	17:34:48	Sg	11/21/1981	06:32:49	Li
03/05/1981	08:11:58	Pi	07/15/1981	05:19:10	Cp	11/23/1981	17:36:29	Sc
03/07/1981	09:48:09	Ar	07/17/1981	15:01:42	Aq	11/26/1981	06:00:23	Sg
03/09/1981	10:22:30	Ta	07/19/1981	22:25:34	Pi	11/28/1981	18:52:38	Cp
03/11/1981	11:42:07	Ge	07/22/1981	03:43:26	Ar	12/01/1981	07:08:57	Aq
03/13/1981	15:05:30	Cn	07/24/1981	07:18:13	Ta	12/03/1981	17:15:55	Pi
03/15/1981	21:02:27	Le	07/26/1981	09:41:37	Ge	12/05/1981	23:48:43	Ar
03/18/1981	05:19:37	Vi	07/28/1981	11:40:43	Cn	12/08/1981	02:31:17	Ta
03/20/1981	15:30:38	Li	07/30/1981	14:20:16	Le	12/10/1981	02:30:04	Ge
03/23/1981	03:13:50	Sc	08/01/1981	18:54:22	Vi	12/12/1981	01:40:28	Cn
03/25/1981	15:50:44	Sg	08/04/1981	02:23:52	Li	12/14/1981	02:08:21	Le
03/28/1981	03:52:14	Cp	08/06/1981	12:58:11	Sc	12/16/1981	05:37:54	Vi
03/30/1981	13:15:25	Aq	08/09/1981	01:22:16	Sg	12/18/1981	12:57:54	Li
04/01/1981	18:40:47	Pi	08/11/1981	13:20:04	Cp	12/20/1981	23:38:48	Sc
04/03/1981	20:24:59	Ar	08/13/1981	22:56:10	Aq	12/23/1981	12:11:02	Sg
04/05/1981	20:04:08	Ta	08/16/1981	05:34:27	Pi	12/26/1981	00:59:09	Cp
04/07/1981	19:47:08	Ge	08/18/1981	09:49:00	Ar	12/28/1981	12:53:29	Aq
04/09/1981	21:33:33	Cn	08/20/1981	12:43:23	Ta	12/30/1981	23:00:49	Pi

01/02/1982	06:32:44	Ar
01/04/1982	11:02:07	Ta
01/06/1982	12:48:27	Ge
01/08/1982	13:01:02	Cn
01/10/1982	13:20:57	Le
01/12/1982	15:37:03	Vi
01/14/1982	21:16:46	Li
01/17/1982	06:46:11	Sc
01/19/1982	19:00:04	Sg
01/22/1982	07:50:36	Cp
01/24/1982	19:24:38	Aq
01/27/1982	04:49:15	Pi
01/29/1982	11:58:23	Ar
01/31/1982	17:03:12	Ta
02/02/1982	20:19:57	Ge
02/04/1982	22:17:48	Cn
02/06/1982	23:49:58	Le
02/09/1982	02:14:55	Vi
02/11/1982	07:01:55	Li
02/13/1982	15:15:44	Sc
02/16/1982	02:44:47	Sg
02/18/1982	15:35:48	Cp
02/21/1982	03:14:53	Aq
02/23/1982	12:08:48	Pi
02/25/1982	18:16:57	Ar
02/27/1982	22:31:37	Ta
03/02/1982	01:49:46	Ge
03/04/1982	04:48:21	Cn
03/06/1982	07:50:07	Le
03/08/1982	11:26:40	Vi
03/10/1982	16:33:43	Li
03/13/1982	00:16:36	Sc
03/15/1982	11:03:11	Sg
03/17/1982	23:46:51	Cp
03/20/1982	11:52:55	Aq
03/22/1982	21:01:16	Pi
03/25/1982	02:36:51	Ar
03/27/1982	05:39:31	Ta
03/29/1982	07:43:46	Ge
03/31/1982	10:08:56	Cn
04/02/1982	13:36:26	Le
04/04/1982	18:18:09	Vi
04/07/1982	00:26:28	Li
04/09/1982	08:32:51	Sc
04/11/1982	19:06:37	Sg
04/14/1982	07:41:15	Cp
04/16/1982	20:17:52	Aq
04/19/1982	06:19:32	Pi
04/21/1982	12:22:41	Ar
04/23/1982	14:58:36	Ta
04/25/1982	15:48:05	Ge
04/27/1982	16:43:22	Cn
04/29/1982	19:09:11	Le
05/01/1982	23:44:54	Vi
05/04/1982	06:32:27	Li
05/06/1982	15:23:57	Sc
05/09/1982	02:16:31	Sg
05/11/1982	14:49:32	Cp
05/14/1982	03:44:07	Aq
05/16/1982	14:46:13	Pi
05/18/1982	22:04:00	Ar
05/21/1982	01:21:43	Ta
05/23/1982	01:54:30	Ge
05/25/1982	01:38:17	Cn
05/27/1982	02:26:45	Le
05/29/1982	05:43:06	Vi
05/31/1982	12:02:20	Li
06/02/1982	21:11:40	Sc
06/05/1982	08:31:11	Sg
06/07/1982	21:11:47	Cp
06/10/1982	10:07:42	Aq
06/12/1982	21:43:57	Pi
06/15/1982	06:20:05	Ar
06/17/1982	11:06:37	Ta
06/19/1982	12:33:59	Ge
06/21/1982	12:12:34	Cn
06/23/1982	11:56:39	Le
06/25/1982	13:36:00	Vi
06/27/1982	18:30:09	Li
06/30/1982	03:01:32	Sc
07/02/1982	14:25:14	Sg
07/05/1982	03:14:55	Cp
07/07/1982	16:02:45	Aq
07/10/1982	03:35:10	Pi
07/12/1982	12:49:02	Ar
07/14/1982	18:59:46	Ta
07/16/1982	22:03:07	Ge
07/18/1982	22:45:48	Cn
07/20/1982	22:35:18	Le
07/22/1982	23:19:52	Vi
07/25/1982	02:44:53	Li
07/27/1982	09:57:58	Sc
07/29/1982	20:47:34	Sg
08/01/1982	09:36:03	Cp
08/03/1982	22:17:02	Aq
08/06/1982	09:23:25	Pi
08/08/1982	18:20:32	Ar
08/11/1982	01:00:03	Ta
08/13/1982	05:21:55	Ge
08/15/1982	07:40:24	Cn
08/17/1982	08:39:52	Le
08/19/1982	09:39:40	Vi
08/21/1982	12:21:56	Li
08/23/1982	18:20:46	Sc
08/26/1982	04:10:57	Sg
08/28/1982	16:41:33	Cp
08/31/1982	05:23:27	Aq
09/02/1982	16:10:38	Pi
09/05/1982	00:23:39	Ar
09/07/1982	06:26:45	Ta
09/09/1982	10:57:17	Ge
09/11/1982	14:18:06	Cn
09/13/1982	16:45:52	Le
09/15/1982	18:57:10	Vi
09/17/1982	22:02:44	Li
09/20/1982	03:32:26	Sc
09/22/1982	12:30:12	Sg
09/25/1982	00:31:23	Cp
09/27/1982	13:21:17	Aq
09/30/1982	00:18:22	Pi
10/02/1982	08:05:39	Ar
10/04/1982	13:08:39	Ta
10/06/1982	16:38:45	Ge
10/08/1982	19:39:24	Cn
10/10/1982	22:44:00	Le
10/13/1982	02:08:46	Vi
10/15/1982	06:22:30	Li
10/17/1982	12:20:32	Sc
10/19/1982	21:02:24	Sg
10/22/1982	08:37:48	Cp
10/24/1982	21:35:39	Aq
10/27/1982	09:12:18	Pi
10/29/1982	17:24:55	Ar
10/31/1982	22:03:37	Ta
11/03/1982	00:22:31	Ge
11/05/1982	01:58:40	Cn
11/07/1982	04:10:01	Le
11/09/1982	07:39:44	Vi
11/11/1982	12:45:36	Li
11/13/1982	19:42:12	Sc
11/16/1982	04:51:35	Sg
11/18/1982	16:21:17	Cp
11/21/1982	05:20:24	Aq
11/23/1982	17:42:32	Pi
11/26/1982	03:06:55	Ar
11/28/1982	08:31:23	Ta
11/30/1982	10:35:37	Ge
12/02/1982	10:57:32	Cn
12/04/1982	11:26:10	Le
12/06/1982	13:32:12	Vi
12/08/1982	18:10:33	Li
12/11/1982	01:34:31	Sc
12/13/1982	11:26:41	Sg
12/15/1982	23:15:14	Cp
12/18/1982	12:12:17	Aq
12/21/1982	00:55:47	Pi
12/23/1982	11:34:00	Ar
12/25/1982	18:36:37	Ta
12/27/1982	21:48:30	Ge
12/29/1982	22:11:51	Cn
12/31/1982	21:32:52	Le
01/02/1983	21:49:20	Vi
01/05/1983	00:44:18	Li
01/07/1983	07:16:08	Sc
01/09/1983	17:13:32	Sg
01/12/1983	05:25:42	Cp
01/14/1983	18:26:12	Aq
01/17/1983	07:02:16	Pi
01/19/1983	18:07:51	Ar
01/22/1983	02:35:42	Ta
01/24/1983	07:39:48	Ge
01/26/1983	09:28:18	Cn
01/28/1983	09:09:53	Le
01/30/1983	08:34:35	Vi

02/01/1983	09:46:56	Li	06/13/1983	22:21:17	Le	10/24/1983	09:09:58	Ge
02/03/1983	14:32:10	Sc	06/15/1983	23:37:47	Vi	10/26/1983	14:46:52	Cn
02/05/1983	23:28:27	Sg	06/18/1983	02:36:23	Li	10/28/1983	18:50:18	Le
02/08/1983	11:33:26	Cp	06/20/1983	07:59:20	Sc	10/30/1983	21:32:47	Vi
02/11/1983	00:40:21	Aq	06/22/1983	15:55:05	Sg	11/01/1983	23:30:32	Li
02/13/1983	13:01:36	Pi	06/25/1983	02:08:10	Cp	11/04/1983	01:53:01	Sc
02/15/1983	23:45:45	Ar	06/27/1983	14:06:31	Aq	11/06/1983	06:08:50	Sg
02/18/1983	08:30:28	Ta	06/30/1983	02:51:38	Pi	11/08/1983	13:31:13	Cp
02/20/1983	14:51:41	Ge	07/02/1983	14:47:28	Ar	11/11/1983	00:10:23	Aq
02/22/1983	18:30:59	Cn	07/05/1983	00:05:12	Ta	11/13/1983	12:40:38	Pi
02/24/1983	19:46:31	Le	07/07/1983	05:40:54	Ge	11/16/1983	00:36:21	Ar
02/26/1983	19:49:04	Vi	07/09/1983	07:50:12	Cn	11/18/1983	10:06:09	Ta
02/28/1983	20:30:01	Li	07/11/1983	07:53:38	Le	11/20/1983	16:44:58	Ge
03/02/1983	23:50:38	Sc	07/13/1983	07:42:50	Vi	11/22/1983	21:10:26	Cn
03/05/1983	07:14:43	Sg	07/15/1983	09:10:04	Li	11/25/1983	00:19:23	Le
03/07/1983	18:28:57	Cp	07/17/1983	13:38:03	Sc	11/27/1983	03:01:49	Vi
03/10/1983	07:29:49	Aq	07/19/1983	21:31:18	Sg	11/29/1983	05:56:40	Li
03/12/1983	19:47:04	Pi	07/22/1983	08:10:51	Cp	12/01/1983	09:40:32	Sc
03/15/1983	06:00:04	Ar	07/24/1983	20:26:24	Aq	12/03/1983	14:56:04	Sg
03/17/1983	14:04:24	Ta	07/27/1983	09:11:08	Pi	12/05/1983	22:28:01	Cp
03/19/1983	20:19:38	Ge	07/29/1983	21:20:37	Ar	12/08/1983	08:39:17	Aq
03/22/1983	00:52:20	Cn	08/01/1983	07:36:49	Ta	12/10/1983	20:52:57	Pi
03/24/1983	03:42:54	Le	08/03/1983	14:42:50	Ge	12/13/1983	09:16:34	Ar
03/26/1983	05:17:55	Vi	08/05/1983	18:08:39	Cn	12/15/1983	19:32:40	Ta
03/28/1983	06:48:17	Li	08/07/1983	18:36:57	Le	12/18/1983	02:23:29	Ge
03/30/1983	09:56:42	Sc	08/09/1983	17:48:46	Vi	12/20/1983	06:02:15	Cn
04/01/1983	16:19:40	Sg	08/11/1983	17:51:26	Li	12/22/1983	07:43:36	Le
04/04/1983	02:29:35	Cp	08/13/1983	20:43:47	Sc	12/24/1983	09:01:25	Vi
04/06/1983	15:06:05	Aq	08/16/1983	03:33:28	Sg	12/26/1983	11:18:20	Li
04/09/1983	03:30:20	Pi	08/18/1983	13:59:19	Cp	12/28/1983	15:26:34	Sc
04/11/1983	13:36:59	Ar	08/21/1983	02:25:30	Aq	12/30/1983	21:43:47	Sg
04/13/1983	20:58:46	Ta	08/23/1983	15:09:39	Pi	01/02/1984	06:07:19	Cp
04/16/1983	02:14:38	Ge	08/26/1983	03:07:57	Ar	01/04/1984	16:30:29	Aq
04/18/1983	06:13:42	Cn	08/28/1983	13:37:51	Ta	01/07/1984	04:34:09	Pi
04/20/1983	09:26:10	Le	08/30/1983	21:48:41	Ge	01/09/1984	17:15:08	Ar
04/22/1983	12:11:30	Vi	09/02/1983	02:52:38	Cn	01/12/1984	04:36:03	Ta
04/24/1983	15:03:41	Li	09/04/1983	04:47:04	Le	01/14/1984	12:40:16	Ge
04/26/1983	19:04:21	Sc	09/06/1983	04:35:58	Vi	01/16/1984	16:47:23	Cn
04/29/1983	01:28:07	Sg	09/08/1983	04:13:13	Li	01/18/1984	17:49:28	Le
05/01/1983	11:01:13	Cp	09/10/1983	05:49:07	Sc	01/20/1984	17:35:10	Vi
05/03/1983	23:09:00	Aq	09/12/1983	11:07:41	Sg	01/22/1984	18:06:44	Li
05/06/1983	11:43:27	Pi	09/14/1983	20:33:31	Cp	01/24/1984	21:03:58	Sc
05/08/1983	22:16:26	Ar	09/17/1983	08:45:28	Aq	01/27/1984	03:12:17	Sg
05/11/1983	05:35:50	Ta	09/19/1983	21:29:50	Pi	01/29/1984	12:12:21	Cp
05/13/1983	10:03:15	Ge	09/22/1983	09:10:16	Ar	01/31/1984	23:11:01	Aq
05/15/1983	12:47:43	Cn	09/24/1983	19:12:22	Ta	02/03/1984	11:21:50	Pi
05/17/1983	15:00:52	Le	09/27/1983	03:24:16	Ge	02/06/1984	00:03:38	Ar
05/19/1983	17:36:30	Vi	09/29/1983	09:24:25	Cn	02/08/1984	12:05:20	Ta
05/21/1983	21:11:22	Li	10/01/1983	12:54:19	Le	02/10/1984	21:39:12	Ge
05/24/1983	02:17:03	Sc	10/03/1983	14:15:00	Vi	02/13/1984	03:20:18	Cn
05/26/1983	09:27:17	Sg	10/05/1983	14:41:37	Li	02/15/1984	05:09:05	Le
05/28/1983	19:06:36	Cp	10/07/1983	16:05:54	Sc	02/17/1984	04:31:51	Vi
05/31/1983	06:59:34	Aq	10/09/1983	20:20:37	Sg	02/19/1984	03:39:19	Li
06/02/1983	19:41:41	Pi	10/12/1983	04:30:08	Cp	02/21/1984	04:44:29	Sc
06/05/1983	06:59:04	Ar	10/14/1983	15:59:52	Aq	02/23/1984	09:22:11	Sg
06/07/1983	15:04:39	Ta	10/17/1983	04:41:10	Pi	02/25/1984	17:49:23	Cp
06/09/1983	19:37:10	Ge	10/19/1983	16:18:18	Ar	02/28/1984	05:02:01	Aq
06/11/1983	21:32:16	Cn	10/22/1983	01:47:20	Ta	03/01/1984	17:29:16	Pi

03/04/1984	06:06:49	Ar
03/06/1984	18:08:39	Ta
03/09/1984	04:29:32	Ge
03/11/1984	11:47:47	Cn
03/13/1984	15:20:51	Le
03/15/1984	15:46:47	Vi
03/17/1984	14:51:27	Li
03/19/1984	14:48:42	Sc
03/21/1984	17:41:05	Sg
03/24/1984	00:36:02	Cp
03/26/1984	11:08:42	Aq
03/28/1984	23:37:02	Pi
03/31/1984	12:13:52	Ar
04/02/1984	23:55:20	Ta
04/05/1984	10:04:25	Ge
04/07/1984	17:59:26	Cn
04/09/1984	23:01:16	Le
04/12/1984	01:10:57	Vi
04/14/1984	01:29:15	Li
04/16/1984	01:41:00	Sc
04/18/1984	03:43:40	Sg
04/20/1984	09:10:25	Cp
04/22/1984	18:27:03	Aq
04/25/1984	06:26:08	Pi
04/27/1984	19:02:29	Ar
04/30/1984	06:30:26	Ta
05/02/1984	16:01:39	Ge
05/04/1984	23:25:45	Cn
05/07/1984	04:42:55	Le
05/09/1984	08:01:49	Vi
05/11/1984	09:54:03	Li
05/13/1984	11:21:52	Sc
05/15/1984	13:49:45	Sg
05/17/1984	18:43:09	Cp
05/20/1984	02:55:33	Aq
05/22/1984	14:08:33	Pi
05/25/1984	02:39:22	Ar
05/27/1984	14:13:27	Ta
05/29/1984	23:22:54	Ge
06/01/1984	05:53:32	Cn
06/03/1984	10:18:54	Le
06/05/1984	13:27:03	Vi
06/07/1984	16:03:08	Li
06/09/1984	18:48:12	Sc
06/11/1984	22:26:13	Sg
06/14/1984	03:48:00	Cp
06/16/1984	11:40:57	Aq
06/18/1984	22:18:05	Pi
06/21/1984	10:40:08	Ar
06/23/1984	22:37:50	Ta
06/26/1984	08:03:48	Ge
06/28/1984	14:09:03	Cn
06/30/1984	17:29:54	Le
07/02/1984	19:27:31	Vi
07/04/1984	21:26:33	Li
07/07/1984	00:28:17	Sc
07/09/1984	05:02:58	Sg
07/11/1984	11:22:47	Cp
07/13/1984	19:41:13	Aq
07/16/1984	06:10:17	Pi
07/18/1984	18:25:50	Ar
07/21/1984	06:52:23	Ta
07/23/1984	17:09:58	Ge
07/25/1984	23:43:55	Cn
07/28/1984	02:41:14	Le
07/30/1984	03:29:01	Vi
08/01/1984	04:02:49	Li
08/03/1984	06:03:57	Sc
08/05/1984	10:29:35	Sg
08/07/1984	17:24:29	Cp
08/10/1984	02:25:16	Aq
08/12/1984	13:12:36	Pi
08/15/1984	01:27:51	Ar
08/17/1984	14:13:15	Ta
08/20/1984	01:31:15	Ge
08/22/1984	09:20:09	Cn
08/24/1984	12:59:55	Le
08/26/1984	13:32:11	Vi
08/28/1984	12:56:55	Li
08/30/1984	13:23:02	Sc
09/01/1984	16:29:35	Sg
09/03/1984	22:54:38	Cp
09/06/1984	08:11:28	Aq
09/08/1984	19:24:19	Pi
09/11/1984	07:46:31	Ar
09/13/1984	20:33:00	Ta
09/16/1984	08:25:36	Ge
09/18/1984	17:35:43	Cn
09/20/1984	22:48:38	Le
09/23/1984	00:19:00	Vi
09/24/1984	23:41:00	Li
09/26/1984	23:03:56	Sc
09/29/1984	00:31:50	Sg
10/01/1984	05:27:46	Cp
10/03/1984	14:03:09	Aq
10/06/1984	01:19:11	Pi
10/08/1984	13:50:39	Ar
10/11/1984	02:28:08	Ta
10/13/1984	14:13:47	Ge
10/16/1984	00:00:03	Cn
10/18/1984	06:41:01	Le
10/20/1984	09:55:41	Vi
10/22/1984	10:31:30	Li
10/24/1984	10:07:40	Sc
10/26/1984	10:43:01	Sg
10/28/1984	14:04:41	Cp
10/30/1984	21:13:05	Aq
11/02/1984	07:49:32	Pi
11/04/1984	20:20:20	Ar
11/07/1984	08:53:11	Ta
11/09/1984	20:10:11	Ge
11/12/1984	05:31:07	Cn
11/14/1984	12:33:32	Le
11/16/1984	17:07:37	Vi
11/18/1984	19:29:19	Li
11/20/1984	20:30:29	Sc
11/22/1984	21:34:02	Sg
11/25/1984	00:17:19	Cp
11/27/1984	06:05:59	Aq
11/29/1984	15:33:11	Pi
12/02/1984	03:41:53	Ar
12/04/1984	16:20:23	Ta
12/07/1984	03:23:35	Ge
12/09/1984	11:56:24	Cn
12/11/1984	18:08:16	Le
12/13/1984	22:35:08	Vi
12/16/1984	01:51:42	Li
12/18/1984	04:27:14	Sc
12/20/1984	06:58:10	Sg
12/22/1984	10:20:37	Cp
12/24/1984	15:47:11	Aq
12/27/1984	00:18:06	Pi
12/29/1984	11:49:28	Ar
01/01/1985	00:36:10	Ta
01/03/1985	12:00:04	Ge
01/05/1985	20:17:33	Cn
01/08/1985	01:28:04	Le
01/10/1985	04:39:31	Vi
01/12/1985	07:13:18	Li
01/14/1985	10:07:25	Sc
01/16/1985	13:48:02	Sg
01/18/1985	18:28:47	Cp
01/21/1985	00:38:10	Aq
01/23/1985	09:01:58	Pi
01/25/1985	20:05:06	Ar
01/28/1985	08:53:16	Ta
01/30/1985	21:00:31	Ge
02/02/1985	05:58:54	Cn
02/04/1985	11:01:39	Le
02/06/1985	13:09:09	Vi
02/08/1985	14:10:23	Li
02/10/1985	15:48:48	Sc
02/12/1985	19:08:39	Sg
02/15/1985	00:26:53	Cp
02/17/1985	07:36:07	Aq
02/19/1985	16:37:47	Pi
02/22/1985	03:42:30	Ar
02/24/1985	16:27:22	Ta
02/27/1985	05:11:09	Ge
03/01/1985	15:23:26	Cn
03/03/1985	21:28:01	Le
03/05/1985	23:42:34	Vi
03/07/1985	23:47:16	Li
03/09/1985	23:47:00	Sc
03/12/1985	01:28:52	Sg
03/14/1985	05:54:29	Cp
03/16/1985	13:10:54	Aq
03/18/1985	22:50:12	Pi
03/21/1985	10:20:09	Ar
03/23/1985	23:06:23	Ta
03/26/1985	12:01:56	Ge
03/28/1985	23:13:20	Cn
03/31/1985	06:51:24	Le
04/02/1985	10:24:43	Vi

04/04/1985	10:53:31	Li	08/14/1985	16:56:59	Le	12/24/1985	08:44:57	Ge
04/06/1985	10:10:22	Sc	08/16/1985	21:14:51	Vi	12/26/1985	20:44:01	Cn
04/08/1985	10:17:34	Sg	08/18/1985	23:43:38	Li	12/29/1985	06:44:14	Le
04/10/1985	12:56:55	Cp	08/21/1985	01:51:05	Sc	12/31/1985	14:43:27	Vi
04/12/1985	19:03:47	Aq	08/23/1985	04:35:59	Sg	01/02/1986	20:45:17	Li
04/15/1985	04:30:26	Pi	08/25/1985	08:24:20	Cp	01/05/1986	00:44:01	Sc
04/17/1985	16:18:14	Ar	08/27/1985	13:31:12	Aq	01/07/1986	02:46:49	Sg
04/20/1985	05:12:21	Ta	08/29/1985	20:24:38	Pi	01/09/1986	03:41:47	Cp
04/22/1985	18:00:30	Ge	09/01/1985	05:41:38	Ar	01/11/1986	05:01:22	Aq
04/25/1985	05:26:05	Cn	09/03/1985	17:27:38	Ta	01/13/1986	08:39:00	Pi
04/27/1985	14:10:04	Le	09/06/1985	06:27:00	Ge	01/15/1986	16:03:03	Ar
04/29/1985	19:24:02	Vi	09/08/1985	18:10:09	Cn	01/18/1986	03:13:32	Ta
05/01/1985	21:21:55	Li	09/11/1985	02:27:20	Le	01/20/1986	16:11:51	Ge
05/03/1985	21:16:59	Sc	09/13/1985	06:52:22	Vi	01/23/1986	04:14:29	Cn
05/05/1985	20:55:46	Sg	09/15/1985	08:33:40	Li	01/25/1986	13:47:10	Le
05/07/1985	22:11:25	Cp	09/17/1985	09:17:01	Sc	01/27/1986	20:50:59	Vi
05/10/1985	02:37:49	Aq	09/19/1985	10:40:20	Sg	01/30/1986	02:09:53	Li
05/12/1985	10:55:40	Pi	09/21/1985	13:49:09	Cp	02/01/1986	06:19:04	Sc
05/14/1985	22:25:21	Ar	09/23/1985	19:11:25	Aq	02/03/1986	09:31:25	Sg
05/17/1985	11:23:24	Ta	09/26/1985	02:50:24	Pi	02/05/1986	12:01:28	Cp
05/20/1985	00:00:54	Ge	09/28/1985	12:42:29	Ar	02/07/1986	14:34:48	Aq
05/22/1985	11:04:35	Cn	10/01/1985	00:34:42	Ta	02/09/1986	18:32:09	Pi
05/24/1985	19:53:49	Le	10/03/1985	13:36:28	Ge	02/12/1986	01:20:34	Ar
05/27/1985	02:06:22	Vi	10/06/1985	01:59:03	Cn	02/14/1986	11:38:05	Ta
05/29/1985	05:40:30	Li	10/08/1985	11:33:24	Le	02/17/1986	00:16:54	Ge
05/31/1985	07:07:07	Sc	10/10/1985	17:09:22	Vi	02/19/1986	12:38:52	Cn
06/02/1985	07:33:22	Sg	10/12/1985	19:11:58	Li	02/21/1986	22:24:37	Le
06/04/1985	08:33:51	Cp	10/14/1985	19:12:44	Sc	02/24/1986	04:57:48	Vi
06/06/1985	11:51:56	Aq	10/16/1985	19:05:30	Sg	02/26/1986	09:07:03	Li
06/08/1985	18:46:31	Pi	10/18/1985	20:35:02	Cp	02/28/1986	12:05:52	Sc
06/11/1985	05:23:57	Ar	10/21/1985	00:54:26	Aq	03/02/1986	14:51:24	Sg
06/13/1985	18:11:19	Ta	10/23/1985	08:27:17	Pi	03/04/1986	17:55:44	Cp
06/16/1985	06:45:10	Ge	10/25/1985	18:47:11	Ar	03/06/1986	21:42:29	Aq
06/18/1985	17:21:41	Cn	10/28/1985	06:59:10	Ta	03/09/1986	02:48:02	Pi
06/21/1985	01:31:56	Le	10/30/1985	19:59:01	Ge	03/11/1986	10:03:09	Ar
06/23/1985	07:32:25	Vi	11/02/1985	08:30:51	Cn	03/13/1986	20:03:46	Ta
06/25/1985	11:47:29	Li	11/04/1985	19:03:35	Le	03/16/1986	08:22:46	Ge
06/27/1985	14:37:05	Sc	11/07/1985	02:18:16	Vi	03/18/1986	21:04:21	Cn
06/29/1985	16:30:10	Sg	11/09/1985	05:51:38	Li	03/21/1986	07:38:24	Le
07/01/1985	18:22:00	Cp	11/11/1985	06:30:47	Sc	03/23/1986	14:39:22	Vi
07/03/1985	21:35:47	Aq	11/13/1985	05:52:14	Sg	03/25/1986	18:22:24	Li
07/06/1985	03:40:07	Pi	11/15/1985	05:53:11	Cp	03/27/1986	20:05:14	Sc
07/08/1985	13:20:32	Ar	11/17/1985	08:25:26	Aq	03/29/1986	21:20:14	Sg
07/11/1985	01:43:59	Ta	11/19/1985	14:42:15	Pi	03/31/1986	23:25:08	Cp
07/13/1985	14:23:12	Ge	11/22/1985	00:42:26	Ar	04/03/1986	03:11:02	Aq
07/16/1985	00:54:12	Cn	11/24/1985	13:06:47	Ta	04/05/1986	09:03:25	Pi
07/18/1985	08:24:57	Le	11/27/1985	02:07:54	Ge	04/07/1986	17:12:02	Ar
07/20/1985	13:29:12	Vi	11/29/1985	14:23:01	Cn	04/10/1986	03:36:05	Ta
07/22/1985	17:09:55	Li	12/02/1985	00:59:18	Le	04/12/1986	15:50:40	Ge
07/24/1985	20:15:59	Sc	12/04/1985	09:13:59	Vi	04/15/1986	04:41:58	Cn
07/26/1985	23:12:26	Sg	12/06/1985	14:33:16	Li	04/17/1986	16:09:37	Le
07/29/1985	02:20:53	Cp	12/08/1985	16:56:18	Sc	04/20/1986	00:23:56	Vi
07/31/1985	06:25:18	Aq	12/10/1985	17:13:10	Sg	04/22/1986	04:49:58	Li
08/02/1985	12:33:24	Pi	12/12/1985	16:59:30	Cp	04/24/1986	06:15:27	Sc
08/04/1985	21:42:36	Ar	12/14/1985	18:14:51	Aq	04/26/1986	06:16:09	Sg
08/07/1985	09:41:15	Ta	12/16/1985	22:49:55	Pi	04/28/1986	06:40:52	Cp
08/09/1985	22:31:18	Ge	12/19/1985	07:36:30	Ar	04/30/1986	09:05:40	Aq
08/12/1985	09:28:09	Cn	12/21/1985	19:40:34	Ta	05/02/1986	14:30:04	Pi

05/04/1986	23:00:48	Ar
05/07/1986	09:58:47	Ta
05/09/1986	22:25:50	Ge
05/12/1986	11:17:48	Cn
05/14/1986	23:15:03	Le
05/17/1986	08:45:06	Vi
05/19/1986	14:40:58	Li
05/21/1986	17:02:08	Sc
05/23/1986	16:56:36	Sg
05/25/1986	16:14:56	Cp
05/27/1986	16:59:50	Aq
05/29/1986	20:54:19	Pi
06/01/1986	04:42:35	Ar
06/03/1986	15:45:05	Ta
06/06/1986	04:26:28	Ge
06/08/1986	17:15:58	Cn
06/11/1986	05:11:10	Le
06/13/1986	15:17:49	Vi
06/15/1986	22:37:50	Li
06/18/1986	02:36:13	Sc
06/20/1986	03:35:35	Sg
06/22/1986	02:59:43	Cp
06/24/1986	02:50:01	Aq
06/26/1986	05:12:34	Pi
06/28/1986	11:34:32	Ar
06/30/1986	21:54:10	Ta
07/03/1986	10:31:50	Ge
07/05/1986	23:19:20	Cn
07/08/1986	10:55:34	Le
07/10/1986	20:49:35	Vi
07/13/1986	04:40:00	Li
07/15/1986	09:58:10	Sc
07/17/1986	12:34:20	Sg
07/19/1986	13:09:36	Cp
07/21/1986	13:17:28	Aq
07/23/1986	14:58:45	Pi
07/25/1986	20:02:16	Ar
07/28/1986	05:11:02	Ta
07/30/1986	17:19:01	Ge
08/02/1986	06:03:54	Cn
08/04/1986	17:26:20	Le
08/07/1986	02:44:21	Vi
08/09/1986	10:04:31	Li
08/11/1986	15:35:39	Sc
08/13/1986	19:17:02	Sg
08/15/1986	21:22:18	Cp
08/17/1986	22:43:59	Aq
08/20/1986	00:51:58	Pi
08/22/1986	05:27:10	Ar
08/24/1986	13:36:21	Ta
08/27/1986	01:00:09	Ge
08/29/1986	13:39:37	Cn
09/01/1986	01:08:20	Le
09/03/1986	10:05:38	Vi
09/05/1986	16:33:18	Li
09/07/1986	21:11:41	Sc
09/10/1986	00:40:15	Sg
09/12/1986	03:27:57	Cp
09/14/1986	06:06:52	Aq
09/16/1986	09:26:43	Pi
09/18/1986	14:33:21	Ar
09/20/1986	22:25:22	Ta
09/23/1986	09:13:31	Ge
09/25/1986	21:44:27	Cn
09/28/1986	09:39:16	Le
09/30/1986	18:57:28	Vi
10/03/1986	01:02:47	Li
10/05/1986	04:35:10	Sc
10/07/1986	06:47:36	Sg
10/09/1986	08:52:17	Cp
10/11/1986	11:44:59	Aq
10/13/1986	16:03:11	Pi
10/15/1986	22:13:00	Ar
10/18/1986	06:35:05	Ta
10/20/1986	17:15:14	Ge
10/23/1986	05:37:14	Cn
10/25/1986	18:02:15	Le
10/28/1986	04:19:55	Vi
10/30/1986	11:04:25	Li
11/01/1986	14:19:19	Sc
11/03/1986	15:19:06	Sg
11/05/1986	15:48:30	Cp
11/07/1986	17:28:30	Aq
11/09/1986	21:29:31	Pi
11/12/1986	04:14:15	Ar
11/14/1986	13:24:15	Ta
11/17/1986	00:26:27	Ge
11/19/1986	12:45:44	Cn
11/22/1986	01:25:05	Le
11/24/1986	12:45:55	Vi
11/26/1986	20:58:56	Li
11/29/1986	01:13:15	Sc
12/01/1986	02:08:03	Sg
12/03/1986	01:28:11	Cp
12/05/1986	01:22:52	Aq
12/07/1986	03:48:22	Pi
12/09/1986	09:48:51	Ar
12/11/1986	19:10:19	Ta
12/14/1986	06:41:22	Ge
12/16/1986	19:09:13	Cn
12/19/1986	07:43:52	Le
12/21/1986	19:30:24	Vi
12/24/1986	05:04:44	Li
12/26/1986	11:06:12	Sc
12/28/1986	13:19:30	Sg
12/30/1986	12:53:57	Cp
01/01/1987	11:53:34	Aq
01/03/1987	12:35:52	Pi
01/05/1987	16:50:50	Ar
01/08/1987	01:12:51	Ta
01/10/1987	12:39:16	Ge
01/13/1987	01:18:22	Cn
01/15/1987	13:44:43	Le
01/18/1987	01:14:49	Vi
01/20/1987	11:09:08	Li
01/22/1987	18:30:16	Sc
01/24/1987	22:35:21	Sg
01/26/1987	23:42:13	Cp
01/28/1987	23:16:52	Aq
01/30/1987	23:24:10	Pi
02/02/1987	02:09:24	Ar
02/04/1987	08:52:57	Ta
02/06/1987	19:23:17	Ge
02/09/1987	07:55:01	Cn
02/11/1987	20:21:11	Le
02/14/1987	07:25:51	Vi
02/16/1987	16:44:19	Li
02/19/1987	00:04:21	Sc
02/21/1987	05:09:02	Sg
02/23/1987	07:56:57	Cp
02/25/1987	09:08:23	Aq
02/27/1987	10:06:41	Pi
03/01/1987	12:36:47	Ar
03/03/1987	18:11:23	Ta
03/06/1987	03:26:25	Ge
03/08/1987	15:24:14	Cn
03/11/1987	03:54:13	Le
03/13/1987	14:55:02	Vi
03/15/1987	23:34:00	Li
03/18/1987	05:56:54	Sc
03/20/1987	10:31:54	Sg
03/22/1987	13:48:20	Cp
03/24/1987	16:18:02	Aq
03/26/1987	18:45:34	Pi
03/28/1987	22:12:06	Ar
03/31/1987	03:45:59	Ta
04/02/1987	12:16:22	Ge
04/04/1987	23:33:25	Cn
04/07/1987	12:03:42	Le
04/09/1987	23:27:53	Vi
04/12/1987	08:05:30	Li
04/14/1987	13:40:36	Sc
04/16/1987	17:01:29	Sg
04/18/1987	19:20:42	Cp
04/20/1987	21:45:04	Aq
04/23/1987	01:01:47	Pi
04/25/1987	05:40:35	Ar
04/27/1987	12:05:57	Ta
04/29/1987	20:42:55	Ge
05/02/1987	07:39:04	Cn
05/04/1987	20:06:26	Le
05/07/1987	08:07:08	Vi
05/09/1987	17:28:48	Li
05/11/1987	23:09:13	Sc
05/14/1987	01:40:59	Sg
05/16/1987	02:36:33	Cp
05/18/1987	03:42:26	Aq
05/20/1987	06:23:57	Pi
05/22/1987	11:22:58	Ar
05/24/1987	18:38:55	Ta
05/27/1987	03:55:07	Ge
05/29/1987	14:59:08	Cn
06/01/1987	03:25:20	Le
06/03/1987	15:56:11	Vi

06/06/1987	02:24:17	Li
06/08/1987	09:06:16	Sc
06/10/1987	11:52:51	Sg
06/12/1987	12:04:36	Cp
06/14/1987	11:44:42	Aq
06/16/1987	12:54:17	Pi
06/18/1987	16:56:09	Ar
06/21/1987	00:08:47	Ta
06/23/1987	09:54:32	Ge
06/25/1987	21:22:04	Cn
06/28/1987	09:52:03	Le
06/30/1987	22:33:58	Vi
07/03/1987	09:54:38	Li
07/05/1987	18:02:52	Sc
07/07/1987	22:05:02	Sg
07/09/1987	22:43:24	Aq
07/11/1987	21:49:11	Aq
07/13/1987	21:35:59	Pi
07/16/1987	00:00:15	Ar
07/18/1987	06:04:16	Ta
07/20/1987	15:32:33	Ge
07/23/1987	03:13:01	Cn
07/25/1987	15:49:39	Le
07/28/1987	04:25:31	Vi
07/30/1987	15:59:25	Li
08/02/1987	01:09:18	Sc
08/04/1987	06:47:03	Sg
08/06/1987	08:51:24	Cp
08/08/1987	08:36:39	Aq
08/10/1987	08:01:00	Pi
08/12/1987	09:09:21	Ar
08/14/1987	13:38:08	Ta
08/16/1987	21:58:33	Ge
08/19/1987	09:18:59	Cn
08/21/1987	21:57:50	Le
08/24/1987	10:23:11	Vi
08/26/1987	21:35:22	Li
08/29/1987	06:49:12	Sc
08/31/1987	13:23:57	Sg
09/02/1987	17:03:49	Cp
09/04/1987	18:21:30	Aq
09/06/1987	18:36:33	Pi
09/08/1987	19:33:59	Ar
09/10/1987	22:57:07	Ta
09/13/1987	05:54:32	Ge
09/15/1987	16:21:56	Cn
09/18/1987	04:50:08	Le
09/20/1987	17:13:03	Vi
09/23/1987	03:58:11	Li
09/25/1987	12:30:02	Sc
09/27/1987	18:48:50	Sg
09/29/1987	23:08:07	Cp
10/02/1987	01:51:16	Aq
10/04/1987	03:39:07	Pi
10/06/1987	05:34:41	Ar
10/08/1987	08:57:21	Ta
10/10/1987	15:03:33	Ge
10/13/1987	00:30:39	Cn

10/15/1987	12:34:03	Le
10/18/1987	01:05:54	Vi
10/20/1987	11:49:52	Li
10/22/1987	19:41:30	Sc
10/25/1987	00:56:57	Sg
10/27/1987	04:32:48	Cp
10/29/1987	07:26:44	Aq
10/31/1987	10:19:27	Pi
11/02/1987	13:39:43	Ar
11/04/1987	18:01:56	Ta
11/07/1987	00:15:57	Ge
11/09/1987	09:10:07	Cn
11/11/1987	20:44:54	Le
11/14/1987	09:29:19	Vi
11/16/1987	20:48:16	Li
11/19/1987	04:46:40	Sc
11/21/1987	09:16:18	Sg
11/23/1987	11:31:37	Cp
11/25/1987	13:12:36	Aq
11/27/1987	15:40:29	Pi
11/29/1987	19:35:47	Ar
12/02/1987	01:05:30	Ta
12/04/1987	08:13:26	Ge
12/06/1987	17:19:59	Cn
12/09/1987	04:40:09	Le
12/11/1987	17:30:03	Vi
12/14/1987	05:39:55	Li
12/16/1987	14:41:05	Sc
12/18/1987	19:32:49	Sg
12/20/1987	21:07:30	Cp
12/22/1987	21:19:45	Aq
12/24/1987	22:10:02	Pi
12/27/1987	01:05:13	Ar
12/29/1987	06:36:30	Ta
12/31/1987	14:28:38	Ge
01/03/1988	00:16:32	Cn
01/05/1988	11:47:13	Le
01/08/1988	00:35:02	Vi
01/10/1988	13:17:13	Li
01/12/1988	23:39:09	Sc
01/15/1988	05:58:08	Sg
01/17/1988	08:15:10	Cp
01/19/1988	08:01:50	Aq
01/21/1988	07:26:36	Pi
01/23/1988	08:30:53	Ar
01/25/1988	12:36:18	Ta
01/27/1988	20:02:09	Ge
01/30/1988	06:11:14	Cn
02/01/1988	18:05:58	Le
02/04/1988	06:54:18	Vi
02/06/1988	19:35:59	Li
02/09/1988	06:41:39	Sc
02/11/1988	14:35:35	Sg
02/13/1988	18:36:12	Cp
02/15/1988	19:25:03	Aq
02/17/1988	18:43:45	Pi
02/19/1988	18:34:53	Ar
02/21/1988	20:50:28	Ta

02/24/1988	02:42:00	Ge
02/26/1988	12:11:45	Cn
02/29/1988	00:12:02	Le
03/02/1988	13:06:16	Vi
03/05/1988	01:31:57	Li
03/07/1988	12:27:00	Sc
03/09/1988	20:58:41	Sg
03/12/1988	02:31:02	Cp
03/14/1988	05:07:39	Aq
03/16/1988	05:41:56	Pi
03/18/1988	05:45:05	Ar
03/20/1988	07:04:59	Ta
03/22/1988	11:21:00	Ge
03/24/1988	19:27:17	Cn
03/27/1988	06:53:41	Le
03/29/1988	19:48:34	Vi
04/01/1988	08:05:00	Li
04/03/1988	18:25:41	Sc
04/06/1988	02:28:43	Sg
04/08/1988	08:19:21	Cp
04/10/1988	12:10:14	Aq
04/12/1988	14:24:10	Pi
04/14/1988	15:46:34	Ar
04/16/1988	17:31:05	Ta
04/18/1988	21:09:56	Ge
04/21/1988	04:04:24	Cn
04/23/1988	14:34:08	Le
04/26/1988	03:15:49	Vi
04/28/1988	15:37:21	Li
05/01/1988	01:39:07	Sc
05/03/1988	08:52:12	Sg
05/05/1988	13:53:48	Cp
05/07/1988	17:36:44	Aq
05/09/1988	20:38:44	Pi
05/11/1988	23:23:19	Ar
05/14/1988	02:21:51	Ta
05/16/1988	06:31:23	Ge
05/18/1988	13:05:21	Cn
05/20/1988	22:51:30	Le
05/23/1988	11:12:25	Vi
05/25/1988	23:49:10	Li
05/28/1988	10:06:09	Sc
05/30/1988	16:57:10	Sg
06/01/1988	20:58:29	Cp
06/03/1988	23:33:37	Aq
06/06/1988	02:00:19	Pi
06/08/1988	05:03:46	Ar
06/10/1988	09:02:13	Ta
06/12/1988	14:14:23	Ge
06/14/1988	21:18:48	Cn
06/17/1988	06:57:14	Le
06/19/1988	19:03:25	Vi
06/22/1988	07:57:04	Li
06/24/1988	18:58:16	Sc
06/27/1988	02:17:42	Sg
06/29/1988	05:59:42	Cp
07/01/1988	07:29:32	Aq
07/03/1988	08:33:22	Pi

07/05/1988	10:36:55	Ar	11/15/1988	02:36:19	Aq	03/27/1989	06:53:55	Sg
07/07/1988	14:26:46	Ta	11/17/1988	06:33:43	Pi	03/29/1989	16:25:29	Cp
07/09/1988	20:16:05	Ge	11/19/1988	09:12:19	Ar	03/31/1989	22:44:48	Aq
07/12/1988	04:08:15	Cn	11/21/1988	11:01:46	Ta	04/03/1989	01:36:51	Pi
07/14/1988	14:11:09	Le	11/23/1988	13:11:33	Ge	04/05/1989	01:50:47	Ar
07/17/1988	02:17:15	Vi	11/25/1988	17:19:32	Cn	04/07/1989	01:07:15	Ta
07/19/1988	15:21:43	Li	11/28/1988	00:51:42	Le	04/09/1989	01:30:57	Ge
07/22/1988	03:12:59	Sc	11/30/1988	11:59:30	Vi	04/11/1989	04:57:54	Cn
07/24/1988	11:41:48	Sg	12/03/1988	00:55:54	Li	04/13/1989	12:30:59	Le
07/26/1988	16:06:51	Cp	12/05/1988	12:51:11	Sc	04/15/1989	23:39:08	Vi
07/28/1988	17:24:43	Aq	12/07/1988	21:55:24	Sg	04/18/1989	12:31:23	Li
07/30/1988	17:22:44	Pi	12/10/1988	04:06:45	Cp	04/21/1989	01:13:08	Sc
08/01/1988	17:53:03	Ar	12/12/1988	08:25:23	Aq	04/23/1989	12:38:14	Sg
08/03/1988	20:23:59	Ta	12/14/1988	11:52:55	Pi	04/25/1989	22:15:01	Cp
08/06/1988	01:42:42	Ge	12/16/1988	15:03:02	Ar	04/28/1989	05:32:56	Aq
08/08/1988	09:52:12	Cn	12/18/1988	18:10:47	Ta	04/30/1989	10:03:08	Pi
08/10/1988	20:26:17	Le	12/20/1988	21:42:38	Ge	05/02/1989	11:50:26	Ar
08/13/1988	08:45:32	Vi	12/23/1988	02:34:41	Cn	05/04/1989	11:54:53	Ta
08/15/1988	21:51:39	Li	12/25/1988	09:57:24	Le	05/06/1989	12:03:09	Ge
08/18/1988	10:11:46	Sc	12/27/1988	20:27:21	Vi	05/08/1989	14:19:28	Cn
08/20/1988	19:54:36	Sg	12/30/1988	09:09:26	Li	05/10/1989	20:22:45	Le
08/23/1988	01:48:54	Cp	01/01/1989	21:33:46	Sc	05/13/1989	06:30:03	Vi
08/25/1988	04:04:38	Aq	01/04/1989	07:11:30	Sg	05/15/1989	19:07:05	Li
08/27/1988	04:00:58	Pi	01/06/1989	13:13:52	Cp	05/18/1989	07:47:34	Sc
08/29/1988	03:29:07	Ar	01/08/1989	16:30:31	Aq	05/20/1989	18:51:43	Sg
08/31/1988	04:22:20	Ta	01/10/1989	18:30:50	Pi	05/23/1989	03:53:53	Cp
09/02/1988	08:11:12	Ge	01/12/1989	20:35:34	Ar	05/25/1989	11:00:59	Aq
09/04/1988	15:36:51	Cn	01/14/1989	23:35:42	Ta	05/27/1989	16:13:02	Pi
09/07/1988	02:14:09	Le	01/17/1989	03:56:33	Ge	05/29/1989	19:25:20	Ar
09/09/1988	14:47:40	Vi	01/19/1989	09:56:52	Cn	05/31/1989	20:59:18	Ta
09/12/1988	03:50:57	Li	01/21/1989	18:02:20	Le	06/02/1989	22:02:12	Ge
09/14/1988	16:07:08	Sc	01/24/1989	04:32:21	Vi	06/05/1989	00:16:54	Cn
09/17/1988	02:25:11	Sg	01/26/1989	17:01:29	Li	06/07/1989	05:28:07	Le
09/19/1988	09:44:59	Cp	01/29/1989	05:48:41	Sc	06/09/1989	14:29:23	Vi
09/21/1988	13:42:49	Aq	01/31/1989	16:30:04	Sg	06/12/1989	02:30:59	Li
09/23/1988	14:50:34	Pi	02/02/1989	23:29:36	Cp	06/14/1989	15:11:00	Sc
09/25/1988	14:29:23	Ar	02/05/1989	02:50:48	Aq	06/17/1989	02:12:18	Sg
09/27/1988	14:28:45	Ta	02/07/1989	03:52:00	Pi	06/19/1989	10:41:23	Cp
09/29/1988	16:42:54	Ge	02/09/1989	04:17:42	Ar	06/21/1989	16:56:38	Aq
10/01/1988	22:38:31	Cn	02/11/1989	05:44:47	Ta	06/23/1989	21:36:05	Pi
10/04/1988	08:30:43	Le	02/13/1989	09:22:12	Ge	06/26/1989	01:05:57	Ar
10/06/1988	21:01:13	Vi	02/15/1989	15:39:58	Cn	06/28/1989	03:45:03	Ta
10/09/1988	10:03:20	Li	02/18/1989	00:32:41	Le	06/30/1989	06:08:05	Ge
10/11/1988	21:57:47	Sc	02/20/1989	11:34:18	Vi	07/02/1989	09:18:41	Cn
10/14/1988	07:57:44	Sg	02/23/1989	00:04:41	Li	07/04/1989	14:37:15	Le
10/16/1988	15:44:26	Cp	02/25/1989	12:56:54	Sc	07/06/1989	23:04:19	Vi
10/18/1988	21:04:48	Aq	02/28/1989	00:29:06	Sg	07/09/1989	10:30:18	Li
10/20/1988	23:58:27	Pi	03/02/1989	08:57:45	Cp	07/11/1989	23:08:58	Sc
10/23/1988	00:58:52	Ar	03/04/1989	13:36:17	Aq	07/14/1989	10:31:00	Sg
10/25/1988	01:22:09	Ta	03/06/1989	14:58:35	Pi	07/16/1989	19:01:03	Cp
10/27/1988	02:55:25	Ge	03/08/1989	14:36:18	Ar	07/19/1989	00:35:13	Aq
10/29/1988	07:28:13	Cn	03/10/1989	14:25:02	Ta	07/21/1989	04:06:41	Pi
10/31/1988	16:03:22	Le	03/12/1989	16:16:07	Ge	07/23/1989	06:40:31	Ar
11/03/1988	04:01:36	Vi	03/14/1989	21:27:15	Cn	07/25/1989	09:09:53	Ta
11/05/1988	17:03:50	Li	03/17/1989	06:12:43	Le	07/27/1989	12:14:44	Ge
11/08/1988	04:46:12	Sc	03/19/1989	17:39:25	Vi	07/29/1989	16:31:36	Cn
11/10/1988	14:05:34	Sg	03/22/1989	06:23:46	Li	07/31/1989	22:40:59	Le
11/12/1988	21:12:12	Cp	03/24/1989	19:10:21	Sc	08/03/1989	07:18:48	Vi

08/05/1989	18:28:00	Li	12/15/1989	10:41:26	Le	04/26/1990	20:11:55	Ge
08/08/1989	07:04:54	Sc	12/17/1989	17:19:22	Vi	04/28/1990	20:39:06	Cn
08/10/1989	19:02:11	Sg	12/20/1989	03:45:16	Li	05/01/1990	00:08:20	Le
08/13/1989	04:16:12	Cp	12/22/1989	16:18:18	Sc	05/03/1990	07:17:51	Vi
08/15/1989	09:58:45	Aq	12/25/1989	04:37:03	Sg	05/05/1990	17:28:16	Li
08/17/1989	12:45:32	Pi	12/27/1989	15:10:17	Cp	05/08/1990	05:22:18	Sc
08/19/1989	13:58:45	Ar	12/29/1989	23:37:37	Aq	05/10/1990	17:56:01	Sg
08/21/1989	15:10:23	Ta	01/01/1990	06:10:04	Pi	05/13/1990	06:20:54	Cp
08/23/1989	17:38:35	Ge	01/03/1990	10:56:17	Ar	05/15/1990	17:30:06	Aq
08/25/1989	22:13:02	Cn	01/05/1990	14:03:52	Ta	05/18/1990	01:53:45	Pi
08/28/1989	05:11:34	Le	01/07/1990	16:01:32	Ge	05/20/1990	06:31:19	Ar
08/30/1989	14:29:15	Vi	01/09/1990	17:51:52	Cn	05/22/1990	07:42:03	Ta
09/02/1989	01:47:16	Li	01/11/1990	21:02:13	Le	05/24/1990	06:59:45	Ge
09/04/1989	14:23:05	Sc	01/14/1990	02:57:23	Vi	05/26/1990	06:33:42	Cn
09/07/1989	02:50:39	Sg	01/16/1990	12:17:32	Li	05/28/1990	08:29:09	Le
09/09/1989	13:13:00	Cp	01/19/1990	00:15:56	Sc	05/30/1990	14:07:38	Vi
09/11/1989	20:01:36	Aq	01/21/1990	12:43:42	Sg	06/01/1990	23:30:45	Li
09/13/1989	23:07:32	Pi	01/23/1990	23:27:17	Cp	06/04/1990	11:21:29	Sc
09/15/1989	23:38:11	Ar	01/26/1990	07:24:54	Aq	06/06/1990	23:59:27	Sg
09/17/1989	23:22:18	Ta	01/28/1990	12:50:37	Pi	06/09/1990	12:11:38	Cp
09/20/1989	00:15:40	Ge	01/30/1990	16:33:58	Ar	06/11/1990	23:08:58	Aq
09/22/1989	03:50:13	Cn	02/01/1990	19:27:01	Ta	06/14/1990	07:59:56	Pi
09/24/1989	10:44:03	Le	02/03/1990	22:12:15	Ge	06/16/1990	13:54:44	Ar
09/26/1989	20:32:15	Vi	02/06/1990	01:26:44	Cn	06/18/1990	16:42:37	Ta
09/29/1989	08:14:39	Li	02/08/1990	05:51:23	Le	06/20/1990	17:14:26	Ge
10/01/1989	20:52:43	Sc	02/10/1990	12:13:01	Vi	06/22/1990	17:09:29	Cn
10/04/1989	09:29:15	Sg	02/12/1990	21:09:13	Li	06/24/1990	18:24:54	Le
10/06/1989	20:45:07	Cp	02/15/1990	08:34:18	Sc	06/26/1990	22:41:53	Vi
10/09/1989	05:06:28	Aq	02/17/1990	21:06:55	Sg	06/29/1990	06:46:56	Li
10/11/1989	09:37:21	Pi	02/20/1990	08:30:02	Cp	07/01/1990	18:00:48	Sc
10/13/1989	10:41:20	Ar	02/22/1990	16:52:08	Aq	07/04/1990	06:35:25	Sg
10/15/1989	09:52:22	Ta	02/24/1990	21:49:26	Pi	07/06/1990	18:39:30	Cp
10/17/1989	09:19:12	Ge	02/27/1990	00:16:16	Ar	07/09/1990	05:06:30	Aq
10/19/1989	11:09:17	Cn	03/01/1990	01:42:46	Ta	07/11/1990	13:29:09	Pi
10/21/1989	16:47:25	Le	03/03/1990	03:37:26	Ge	07/13/1990	19:36:17	Ar
10/24/1989	02:14:49	Vi	03/05/1990	07:02:19	Cn	07/15/1990	23:28:38	Ta
10/26/1989	14:10:59	Li	03/07/1990	12:24:27	Le	07/18/1990	01:31:37	Ge
10/29/1989	02:55:50	Sc	03/09/1990	19:46:57	Vi	07/20/1990	02:43:35	Cn
10/31/1989	15:22:36	Sg	03/12/1990	05:08:47	Li	07/22/1990	04:28:35	Le
11/03/1989	02:46:28	Cp	03/14/1990	16:24:53	Sc	07/24/1990	08:17:27	Vi
11/05/1989	12:09:13	Aq	03/17/1990	04:56:03	Sg	07/26/1990	15:18:34	Li
11/07/1989	18:24:32	Pi	03/19/1990	17:01:30	Cp	07/29/1990	01:39:05	Sc
11/09/1989	21:07:55	Ar	03/22/1990	02:31:01	Aq	07/31/1990	13:59:42	Sg
11/11/1989	21:09:10	Ta	03/24/1990	08:08:25	Pi	08/03/1990	02:08:30	Cp
11/13/1989	20:18:38	Ge	03/26/1990	10:15:19	Ar	08/05/1990	12:18:54	Aq
11/15/1989	20:51:06	Cn	03/28/1990	10:26:17	Ta	08/07/1990	19:54:11	Pi
11/18/1989	00:45:30	Le	03/30/1990	10:42:01	Ge	08/10/1990	01:12:38	Ar
11/20/1989	08:54:15	Vi	04/01/1990	12:49:35	Cn	08/12/1990	04:54:34	Ta
11/22/1989	20:25:03	Li	04/03/1990	17:49:44	Le	08/14/1990	07:41:23	Ge
11/25/1989	09:13:05	Sc	04/06/1990	01:41:34	Vi	08/16/1990	10:12:11	Cn
11/27/1989	21:29:47	Sg	04/08/1990	11:44:21	Li	08/18/1990	13:11:03	Le
11/30/1989	08:26:07	Cp	04/10/1990	23:17:33	Sc	08/20/1990	17:32:57	Vi
12/02/1989	17:41:54	Aq	04/13/1990	11:47:37	Sg	08/23/1990	00:16:34	Li
12/05/1989	00:47:38	Pi	04/16/1990	00:14:39	Cp	08/25/1990	09:56:07	Sc
12/07/1989	05:11:20	Ar	04/18/1990	10:52:35	Aq	08/27/1990	21:57:26	Sg
12/09/1989	06:58:43	Ta	04/20/1990	17:56:38	Pi	08/30/1990	10:22:48	Cp
12/11/1989	07:14:50	Ge	04/22/1990	20:58:12	Ar	09/01/1990	20:50:52	Aq
12/13/1989	07:48:59	Cn	04/24/1990	21:02:35	Ta	09/04/1990	04:05:34	Pi

09/06/1990	08:23:00	Ar	01/16/1991	09:04:18	Aq	05/27/1991	22:21:01	Sg
09/08/1990	10:55:16	Ta	01/18/1991	19:23:10	Pi	05/30/1991	10:40:25	Cp
09/10/1990	13:04:32	Ge	01/21/1991	03:27:29	Ar	06/01/1991	23:41:32	Aq
09/12/1990	15:52:39	Cn	01/23/1991	09:00:34	Ta	06/04/1991	11:36:17	Pi
09/14/1990	19:51:56	Le	01/25/1991	12:06:21	Ge	06/06/1991	20:25:05	Ar
09/17/1990	01:18:32	Vi	01/27/1991	13:22:54	Cn	06/09/1991	01:12:32	Ta
09/19/1990	08:33:56	Li	01/29/1991	14:03:24	Le	06/11/1991	02:36:26	Ge
09/21/1990	18:05:37	Sc	01/31/1991	15:43:58	Vi	06/13/1991	02:16:30	Cn
09/24/1990	05:52:06	Sg	02/02/1991	20:02:09	Li	06/15/1991	02:10:27	Le
09/26/1990	18:36:23	Cp	02/05/1991	04:01:10	Sc	06/17/1991	04:02:52	Vi
09/29/1990	05:53:43	Aq	02/07/1991	15:23:06	Sg	06/19/1991	09:01:11	Li
10/01/1990	13:42:10	Pi	02/10/1991	04:15:38	Cp	06/21/1991	17:18:22	Sc
10/03/1990	17:41:47	Ar	02/12/1991	16:16:23	Aq	06/24/1991	04:15:59	Sg
10/05/1990	19:05:53	Ta	02/15/1991	01:58:42	Pi	06/26/1991	16:49:20	Cp
10/07/1990	19:47:00	Ge	02/17/1991	09:11:26	Ar	06/29/1991	05:47:21	Aq
10/09/1990	21:29:19	Cn	02/19/1991	14:24:05	Ta	07/01/1991	17:50:51	Pi
10/12/1990	01:16:17	Le	02/21/1991	18:10:17	Ge	07/04/1991	03:33:29	Ar
10/14/1990	07:20:33	Vi	02/23/1991	20:56:19	Cn	07/06/1991	09:51:46	Ta
10/16/1990	15:26:26	Li	02/25/1991	23:12:34	Le	07/08/1991	12:41:36	Ge
10/19/1990	01:23:53	Sc	02/28/1991	01:49:58	Vi	07/10/1991	13:02:42	Cn
10/21/1990	13:09:13	Sg	03/02/1991	06:03:07	Li	07/12/1991	12:35:02	Le
10/24/1990	02:02:55	Cp	03/04/1991	13:08:17	Sc	07/14/1991	13:11:40	Vi
10/26/1990	14:13:59	Aq	03/06/1991	23:34:52	Sg	07/16/1991	16:34:01	Li
10/28/1990	23:21:42	Pi	03/09/1991	12:13:40	Cp	07/18/1991	23:40:39	Sc
10/31/1990	04:14:15	Ar	03/12/1991	00:30:47	Aq	07/21/1991	10:16:27	Sg
11/02/1990	05:31:27	Ta	03/14/1991	10:10:40	Pi	07/23/1991	22:55:15	Cp
11/04/1990	05:05:43	Ge	03/16/1991	16:37:30	Ar	07/26/1991	11:48:57	Aq
11/06/1990	05:07:26	Cn	03/18/1991	20:40:22	Ta	07/28/1991	23:34:36	Pi
11/08/1990	07:24:01	Le	03/20/1991	23:36:34	Ge	07/31/1991	09:20:08	Ar
11/10/1990	12:48:03	Vi	03/23/1991	02:27:20	Cn	08/02/1991	16:31:34	Ta
11/12/1990	21:08:23	Li	03/25/1991	05:43:19	Le	08/04/1991	20:54:15	Ge
11/15/1990	07:39:06	Sc	03/27/1991	09:40:44	Vi	08/06/1991	22:46:55	Cn
11/17/1990	19:39:04	Sg	03/29/1991	14:49:26	Li	08/08/1991	23:09:20	Le
11/20/1990	08:31:31	Cp	03/31/1991	22:01:00	Sc	08/10/1991	23:34:48	Vi
11/22/1990	21:06:58	Aq	04/03/1991	07:58:48	Sg	08/13/1991	01:51:50	Li
11/25/1990	07:31:42	Pi	04/05/1991	20:19:34	Cp	08/15/1991	07:33:36	Sc
11/27/1990	14:06:08	Ar	04/08/1991	08:59:34	Aq	08/17/1991	17:10:41	Sg
11/29/1990	16:37:06	Ta	04/10/1991	19:17:29	Pi	08/20/1991	05:34:13	Cp
12/01/1990	16:22:32	Ge	04/13/1991	01:49:27	Ar	08/22/1991	18:26:44	Aq
12/03/1990	15:27:20	Cn	04/15/1991	05:05:33	Ta	08/25/1991	05:51:05	Pi
12/05/1990	16:00:01	Le	04/17/1991	06:41:05	Ge	08/27/1991	15:00:50	Ar
12/07/1990	19:38:45	Vi	04/19/1991	08:17:20	Cn	08/29/1991	21:59:36	Ta
12/10/1990	02:59:58	Li	04/21/1991	11:04:11	Le	09/01/1991	03:02:08	Ge
12/12/1990	13:27:34	Sc	04/23/1991	15:29:14	Vi	09/03/1991	06:19:25	Cn
12/15/1990	01:43:48	Sg	04/25/1991	21:36:02	Li	09/05/1991	08:12:59	Le
12/17/1990	14:34:43	Cp	04/28/1991	05:33:46	Sc	09/07/1991	09:34:59	Vi
12/20/1990	02:59:01	Aq	04/30/1991	15:42:01	Sg	09/09/1991	11:51:32	Li
12/22/1990	13:47:41	Pi	05/03/1991	03:54:32	Cp	09/11/1991	16:42:09	Sc
12/24/1990	21:44:56	Ar	05/05/1991	16:50:52	Aq	09/14/1991	01:14:18	Sg
12/27/1990	02:08:53	Ta	05/08/1991	04:04:15	Pi	09/16/1991	13:03:36	Cp
12/29/1990	03:25:45	Ge	05/10/1991	11:34:24	Ar	09/19/1991	01:57:35	Aq
12/31/1990	03:02:13	Cn	05/12/1991	15:07:12	Ta	09/21/1991	13:20:15	Pi
01/02/1991	02:54:10	Le	05/14/1991	16:01:46	Ge	09/23/1991	21:55:34	Ar
01/04/1991	04:56:44	Vi	05/16/1991	16:13:48	Cn	09/26/1991	03:59:14	Ta
01/06/1991	10:33:12	Li	05/18/1991	17:29:57	Le	09/28/1991	08:25:24	Ge
01/08/1991	19:59:04	Sc	05/20/1991	21:00:10	Vi	09/30/1991	11:58:10	Cn
01/11/1991	08:06:08	Sg	05/23/1991	03:07:34	Li	10/02/1991	14:58:27	Le
01/13/1991	21:00:12	Cp	05/25/1991	11:41:20	Sc	10/04/1991	17:44:34	Vi

Date	Time	Sign	Date	Time	Sign	Date	Time	Sign
10/06/1991	21:00:17	Li	02/16/1992	10:15:05	Le	06/27/1992	19:13:46	Ge
10/09/1991	01:59:49	Sc	02/18/1992	09:46:37	Vi	06/29/1992	21:41:58	Cn
10/11/1991	09:57:45	Sg	02/20/1992	10:04:34	Li	07/01/1992	22:15:00	Le
10/13/1991	21:10:15	Cp	02/22/1992	13:11:12	Sc	07/03/1992	22:37:18	Vi
10/16/1991	10:04:21	Aq	02/24/1992	20:26:13	Sg	07/06/1992	00:27:13	Li
10/18/1991	21:52:47	Pi	02/27/1992	07:33:07	Cp	07/08/1992	04:53:23	Sc
10/21/1991	06:33:00	Ar	02/29/1992	20:34:00	Aq	07/10/1992	12:17:12	Sg
10/23/1991	11:55:25	Ta	03/03/1992	09:10:45	Pi	07/12/1992	22:15:34	Cp
10/25/1991	15:08:38	Ge	03/05/1992	20:06:37	Ar	07/15/1992	10:02:41	Aq
10/27/1991	17:36:54	Cn	03/08/1992	05:04:57	Ta	07/17/1992	22:44:12	Pi
10/29/1991	20:20:12	Le	03/10/1992	12:03:21	Ge	07/20/1992	11:07:17	Ar
10/31/1991	23:46:35	Vi	03/12/1992	16:49:33	Cn	07/22/1992	21:35:48	Ta
11/03/1991	04:12:31	Li	03/14/1992	19:20:22	Le	07/25/1992	04:44:12	Ge
11/05/1991	10:08:38	Sc	03/16/1992	20:13:12	Vi	07/27/1992	08:08:06	Cn
11/07/1991	18:21:06	Sg	03/18/1992	20:54:33	Li	07/29/1992	08:39:08	Le
11/10/1991	05:16:13	Cp	03/20/1992	23:19:44	Sc	07/31/1992	08:01:08	Vi
11/12/1991	18:06:10	Aq	03/23/1992	05:13:01	Sg	08/02/1992	08:16:57	Li
11/15/1991	06:33:14	Pi	03/25/1992	15:08:30	Cp	08/04/1992	11:16:03	Sc
11/17/1991	16:07:32	Ar	03/28/1992	03:44:21	Aq	08/06/1992	17:56:59	Sg
11/19/1991	21:49:00	Ta	03/30/1992	16:23:06	Pi	08/09/1992	04:00:18	Cp
11/22/1991	00:22:25	Ge	04/02/1992	03:03:51	Ar	08/11/1992	16:06:29	Aq
11/24/1991	01:25:20	Cn	04/04/1992	11:17:51	Ta	08/14/1992	04:50:55	Pi
11/26/1991	02:37:24	Le	04/06/1992	17:32:43	Ge	08/16/1992	17:11:20	Ar
11/28/1991	05:11:56	Vi	04/08/1992	22:18:09	Cn	08/19/1992	04:09:40	Ta
11/30/1991	09:46:48	Li	04/11/1992	01:45:54	Le	08/21/1992	12:36:10	Ge
12/02/1991	16:33:02	Sc	04/13/1992	04:08:54	Vi	08/23/1992	17:36:22	Cn
12/05/1991	01:32:19	Sg	04/15/1992	06:10:14	Li	08/25/1992	19:14:58	Le
12/07/1991	12:40:57	Cp	04/17/1992	09:09:39	Sc	08/27/1992	18:46:23	Vi
12/10/1991	01:26:33	Aq	04/19/1992	14:40:10	Sg	08/29/1992	18:10:37	Li
12/12/1991	14:19:06	Pi	04/21/1992	23:40:33	Cp	08/31/1992	19:38:23	Sc
12/15/1991	01:06:29	Ar	04/24/1992	11:38:24	Aq	09/03/1992	00:49:59	Sg
12/17/1991	08:09:37	Ta	04/27/1992	00:19:44	Pi	09/05/1992	10:05:54	Cp
12/19/1991	11:21:19	Ge	04/29/1992	11:13:18	Ar	09/07/1992	22:08:18	Aq
12/21/1991	11:54:32	Cn	05/01/1992	19:09:15	Ta	09/10/1992	10:55:59	Pi
12/23/1991	11:38:27	Le	05/04/1992	00:28:09	Ge	09/12/1992	23:02:08	Ar
12/25/1991	12:23:35	Vi	05/06/1992	04:09:27	Cn	09/15/1992	09:46:53	Ta
12/27/1991	15:37:27	Li	05/08/1992	07:07:04	Le	09/17/1992	18:39:41	Ge
12/29/1991	22:03:11	Sc	05/10/1992	09:55:59	Vi	09/20/1992	00:58:54	Cn
01/01/1992	07:30:02	Sg	05/12/1992	13:04:58	Li	09/22/1992	04:18:44	Le
01/03/1992	19:09:01	Cp	05/14/1992	17:14:57	Sc	09/24/1992	05:07:57	Vi
01/06/1992	07:59:03	Aq	05/16/1992	23:21:39	Sg	09/26/1992	04:55:20	Li
01/08/1992	20:51:59	Pi	05/19/1992	08:12:35	Cp	09/28/1992	05:44:02	Sc
01/11/1992	08:22:25	Ar	05/21/1992	19:43:32	Aq	09/30/1992	09:33:33	Sg
01/13/1992	17:00:09	Ta	05/24/1992	08:25:06	Pi	10/02/1992	17:28:56	Cp
01/15/1992	21:54:33	Ge	05/26/1992	19:52:28	Ar	10/05/1992	04:52:46	Aq
01/17/1992	23:25:59	Cn	05/29/1992	04:16:01	Ta	10/07/1992	17:37:40	Pi
01/19/1992	22:56:40	Le	05/31/1992	09:18:55	Ge	10/10/1992	05:35:56	Ar
01/21/1992	22:21:55	Vi	06/02/1992	11:57:34	Cn	10/12/1992	15:48:17	Ta
01/23/1992	23:42:11	Li	06/04/1992	13:34:49	Le	10/15/1992	00:08:09	Ge
01/26/1992	04:31:58	Sc	06/06/1992	15:27:41	Vi	10/17/1992	06:35:40	Cn
01/28/1992	13:19:34	Sg	06/08/1992	18:33:07	Li	10/19/1992	11:00:59	Le
01/31/1992	01:07:22	Cp	06/10/1992	23:26:36	Sc	10/21/1992	13:27:23	Vi
02/02/1992	14:08:33	Aq	06/13/1992	06:28:48	Sg	10/23/1992	14:39:21	Li
02/05/1992	02:50:35	Pi	06/15/1992	15:49:49	Cp	10/25/1992	16:04:18	Sc
02/07/1992	14:14:56	Ar	06/18/1992	03:18:45	Aq	10/27/1992	19:28:47	Sg
02/09/1992	23:35:38	Ta	06/20/1992	15:59:44	Pi	10/30/1992	02:17:52	Cp
02/12/1992	06:07:50	Ge	06/23/1992	04:03:03	Ar	11/01/1992	12:43:07	Aq
02/14/1992	09:30:38	Cn	06/25/1992	13:28:24	Ta	11/04/1992	01:12:33	Pi

11/06/1992	13:19:14	Ar	03/18/1993	00:52:13	Aq	07/28/1993	02:12:45	Sg
11/08/1992	23:18:52	Ta	03/20/1993	13:10:32	Pi	07/30/1993	08:26:36	Cp
11/11/1992	06:49:26	Ge	03/23/1993	01:51:16	Ar	08/01/1993	16:36:28	Aq
11/13/1992	12:19:00	Cn	03/25/1993	13:59:05	Ta	08/04/1993	02:43:30	Pi
11/15/1992	16:22:55	Le	03/28/1993	00:47:50	Ge	08/06/1993	14:39:14	Ar
11/17/1992	19:28:02	Vi	03/30/1993	09:13:58	Cn	08/09/1993	03:22:29	Ta
11/19/1992	22:02:34	Li	04/01/1993	14:21:09	Le	08/11/1993	14:46:39	Ge
11/22/1992	00:51:45	Sc	04/03/1993	16:10:17	Vi	08/13/1993	22:46:16	Cn
11/24/1992	05:00:50	Sg	04/05/1993	15:54:19	Li	08/16/1993	02:43:23	Le
11/26/1992	11:38:08	Cp	04/07/1993	15:31:51	Sc	08/18/1993	03:40:47	Vi
11/28/1992	21:18:58	Aq	04/09/1993	17:09:45	Sg	08/20/1993	03:35:09	Li
12/01/1992	09:23:21	Pi	04/11/1993	22:23:59	Cp	08/22/1993	04:27:28	Sc
12/03/1992	21:48:35	Ar	04/14/1993	07:35:43	Aq	08/24/1993	07:45:19	Sg
12/06/1992	08:16:16	Ta	04/16/1993	19:32:26	Pi	08/26/1993	13:57:46	Cp
12/08/1992	15:36:33	Ge	04/19/1993	08:14:20	Ar	08/28/1993	22:41:35	Aq
12/10/1992	20:05:16	Cn	04/21/1993	20:07:44	Ta	08/31/1993	09:18:31	Pi
12/12/1992	22:46:59	Le	04/24/1993	06:26:37	Ge	09/02/1993	21:20:46	Ar
12/15/1992	00:55:51	Vi	04/26/1993	14:45:22	Cn	09/05/1993	10:09:22	Ta
12/17/1992	03:33:01	Li	04/28/1993	20:39:16	Le	09/07/1993	22:15:55	Ge
12/19/1992	07:19:37	Sc	04/30/1993	23:59:51	Vi	09/10/1993	07:36:36	Cn
12/21/1992	12:42:28	Sg	05/03/1993	01:19:58	Li	09/12/1993	12:51:16	Le
12/23/1992	20:04:17	Cp	05/05/1993	01:57:12	Sc	09/14/1993	14:20:00	Vi
12/26/1992	05:43:02	Aq	05/07/1993	03:34:29	Sg	09/16/1993	13:43:48	Li
12/28/1992	17:27:58	Pi	05/09/1993	07:50:53	Cp	09/18/1993	13:14:36	Sc
12/31/1992	06:06:41	Ar	05/11/1993	15:43:57	Aq	09/20/1993	14:53:17	Sg
01/02/1993	17:29:56	Ta	05/14/1993	02:50:29	Pi	09/22/1993	19:53:44	Cp
01/05/1993	01:41:52	Ge	05/16/1993	15:24:04	Ar	09/25/1993	04:18:42	Aq
01/07/1993	06:10:09	Cn	05/19/1993	03:16:18	Ta	09/27/1993	15:12:48	Pi
01/09/1993	07:49:18	Le	05/21/1993	13:07:07	Ge	09/30/1993	03:28:40	Ar
01/11/1993	08:20:15	Vi	05/23/1993	20:37:55	Cn	10/02/1993	16:13:07	Ta
01/13/1993	09:30:14	Li	05/26/1993	02:02:59	Le	10/05/1993	04:26:47	Ge
01/15/1993	12:41:44	Sc	05/28/1993	05:46:15	Vi	10/07/1993	14:42:20	Cn
01/17/1993	18:30:27	Sg	05/30/1993	08:18:01	Li	10/09/1993	21:33:33	Le
01/20/1993	02:46:15	Cp	06/01/1993	10:22:25	Sc	10/12/1993	00:35:47	Vi
01/22/1993	13:00:25	Aq	06/03/1993	13:01:03	Sg	10/14/1993	00:47:20	Li
01/25/1993	00:47:08	Pi	06/05/1993	17:26:04	Cp	10/16/1993	00:00:47	Sc
01/27/1993	13:27:35	Ar	06/08/1993	00:39:20	Aq	10/18/1993	00:23:15	Sg
01/30/1993	01:36:51	Ta	06/10/1993	10:56:49	Pi	10/20/1993	03:41:59	Cp
02/01/1993	11:14:29	Ge	06/12/1993	23:13:45	Ar	10/22/1993	10:48:56	Aq
02/03/1993	16:56:21	Cn	06/15/1993	11:19:14	Ta	10/24/1993	21:17:17	Pi
02/05/1993	18:51:03	Le	06/17/1993	21:11:48	Ge	10/27/1993	09:39:04	Ar
02/07/1993	18:29:00	Vi	06/20/1993	04:05:00	Cn	10/29/1993	22:20:06	Ta
02/09/1993	17:58:18	Li	06/22/1993	08:26:11	Le	11/01/1993	10:12:35	Ge
02/11/1993	19:23:29	Sc	06/24/1993	11:18:09	Vi	11/03/1993	20:24:33	Cn
02/14/1993	00:07:31	Sg	06/26/1993	13:45:28	Li	11/06/1993	04:06:24	Le
02/16/1993	08:20:09	Cp	06/28/1993	16:37:19	Sc	11/08/1993	08:47:07	Vi
02/18/1993	19:05:05	Aq	06/30/1993	20:27:59	Sg	11/10/1993	10:42:16	Li
02/21/1993	07:11:42	Pi	07/03/1993	01:48:29	Cp	11/12/1993	10:59:34	Sc
02/23/1993	19:50:15	Ar	07/05/1993	09:14:05	Aq	11/14/1993	11:20:27	Sg
02/26/1993	08:11:20	Ta	07/07/1993	19:09:33	Pi	11/16/1993	13:34:10	Cp
02/28/1993	18:52:10	Ge	07/10/1993	07:11:05	Ar	11/18/1993	19:07:47	Aq
03/03/1993	02:16:06	Cn	07/12/1993	19:37:14	Ta	11/21/1993	04:27:23	Pi
03/05/1993	05:40:17	Le	07/15/1993	06:06:31	Ge	11/23/1993	16:30:31	Ar
03/07/1993	05:52:13	Vi	07/17/1993	13:07:35	Cn	11/26/1993	05:14:01	Ta
03/09/1993	04:46:11	Li	07/19/1993	16:47:09	Le	11/28/1993	16:47:33	Ge
03/11/1993	04:39:42	Sc	07/21/1993	18:23:50	Vi	12/01/1993	02:17:00	Cn
03/13/1993	07:33:29	Sg	07/23/1993	19:39:27	Li	12/03/1993	09:32:45	Le
03/15/1993	14:27:52	Cp	07/25/1993	22:00:00	Sc	12/05/1993	14:43:01	Vi

Date	Time	Sign	Date	Time	Sign	Date	Time	Sign
12/07/1993	18:03:27	Li	04/19/1994	04:44:49	Le	08/28/1994	19:07:25	Ge
12/09/1993	20:04:12	Sc	04/21/1994	09:57:53	Vi	08/31/1994	06:59:53	Cn
12/11/1993	21:39:13	Sg	04/23/1994	11:40:03	Li	09/02/1994	15:36:59	Le
12/14/1993	00:06:00	Cp	04/25/1994	11:18:06	Sc	09/04/1994	20:33:27	Vi
12/16/1993	04:51:27	Aq	04/27/1994	10:48:13	Sg	09/06/1994	22:56:35	Li
12/18/1993	12:58:47	Pi	04/29/1994	12:04:52	Cp	09/09/1994	00:25:35	Sc
12/21/1993	00:18:52	Ar	05/01/1994	16:34:24	Aq	09/11/1994	02:25:06	Sg
12/23/1993	13:04:33	Ta	05/04/1994	00:46:43	Pi	09/13/1994	05:44:17	Cp
12/26/1993	00:45:39	Ge	05/06/1994	12:01:08	Ar	09/15/1994	10:42:21	Aq
12/28/1993	09:45:57	Cn	05/09/1994	00:50:15	Ta	09/17/1994	17:31:04	Pi
12/30/1993	15:59:12	Le	05/11/1994	13:43:27	Ge	09/20/1994	02:29:34	Ar
01/01/1994	20:14:41	Vi	05/14/1994	01:26:55	Cn	09/22/1994	13:47:25	Ta
01/03/1994	23:30:47	Li	05/16/1994	10:58:19	Le	09/25/1994	02:41:17	Ge
01/06/1994	02:28:44	Sc	05/18/1994	17:30:43	Vi	09/27/1994	15:11:40	Cn
01/08/1994	05:33:53	Sg	05/20/1994	20:54:29	Li	09/30/1994	00:55:08	Le
01/10/1994	09:15:49	Cp	05/22/1994	21:50:42	Sc	10/02/1994	06:39:18	Vi
01/12/1994	14:25:05	Aq	05/24/1994	21:42:48	Sg	10/04/1994	08:56:08	Li
01/14/1994	22:03:37	Pi	05/26/1994	22:16:49	Cp	10/06/1994	09:21:49	Sc
01/17/1994	08:41:52	Ar	05/29/1994	01:18:53	Aq	10/08/1994	09:46:52	Sg
01/19/1994	21:21:51	Ta	05/31/1994	08:03:20	Pi	10/10/1994	11:43:54	Cp
01/22/1994	09:34:30	Ge	06/02/1994	18:31:02	Ar	10/12/1994	16:09:17	Aq
01/24/1994	18:54:50	Cn	06/05/1994	07:13:58	Ta	10/14/1994	23:18:13	Pi
01/27/1994	00:38:06	Le	06/07/1994	20:03:09	Ge	10/17/1994	08:56:05	Ar
01/29/1994	03:38:51	Vi	06/10/1994	07:21:42	Cn	10/19/1994	20:34:16	Ta
01/31/1994	05:33:44	Li	06/12/1994	16:28:35	Le	10/22/1994	09:27:35	Ge
02/02/1994	07:49:21	Sc	06/14/1994	23:16:08	Vi	10/24/1994	22:15:20	Cn
02/04/1994	11:14:24	Sg	06/17/1994	03:48:00	Li	10/27/1994	09:04:33	Le
02/06/1994	16:01:37	Cp	06/19/1994	06:19:49	Sc	10/29/1994	16:21:10	Vi
02/08/1994	22:16:27	Aq	06/21/1994	07:32:03	Sg	10/31/1994	19:46:06	Li
02/11/1994	06:22:34	Pi	06/23/1994	08:36:45	Cp	11/02/1994	20:19:19	Sc
02/13/1994	16:49:15	Ar	06/25/1994	11:09:37	Aq	11/04/1994	19:45:51	Sg
02/16/1994	05:19:36	Ta	06/27/1994	16:44:26	Pi	11/06/1994	20:01:40	Cp
02/18/1994	18:05:22	Ge	06/30/1994	02:06:33	Ar	11/08/1994	22:48:01	Aq
02/21/1994	04:27:10	Cn	07/02/1994	14:23:00	Ta	11/11/1994	05:03:59	Pi
02/23/1994	10:47:31	Le	07/05/1994	03:12:20	Ge	11/13/1994	14:43:43	Ar
02/25/1994	13:27:06	Vi	07/07/1994	14:17:25	Cn	11/16/1994	02:43:51	Ta
02/27/1994	14:05:59	Li	07/09/1994	22:43:16	Le	11/18/1994	15:41:15	Ge
03/01/1994	14:43:08	Sc	07/12/1994	04:48:09	Vi	11/21/1994	04:20:56	Cn
03/03/1994	16:53:34	Sg	07/14/1994	09:14:36	Li	11/23/1994	15:33:00	Le
03/05/1994	21:24:03	Cp	07/16/1994	12:34:40	Sc	11/26/1994	00:08:38	Vi
03/08/1994	04:14:54	Aq	07/18/1994	15:09:16	Sg	11/28/1994	05:22:10	Li
03/10/1994	13:09:19	Pi	07/20/1994	17:30:13	Cp	11/30/1994	07:21:23	Sc
03/12/1994	23:58:39	Ar	07/22/1994	20:38:16	Aq	12/02/1994	07:12:45	Sg
03/15/1994	12:27:23	Ta	07/25/1994	01:56:06	Pi	12/04/1994	06:42:29	Cp
03/18/1994	01:28:51	Ge	07/27/1994	10:30:37	Ar	12/06/1994	07:51:32	Aq
03/20/1994	12:53:43	Cn	07/29/1994	22:12:53	Ta	12/08/1994	12:24:14	Pi
03/22/1994	20:39:03	Le	08/01/1994	11:04:42	Ge	12/10/1994	21:03:24	Ar
03/25/1994	00:13:48	Vi	08/03/1994	22:22:14	Cn	12/13/1994	08:55:48	Ta
03/27/1994	00:46:14	Li	08/06/1994	06:30:43	Le	12/15/1994	21:59:47	Ge
03/29/1994	00:14:51	Sc	08/08/1994	11:42:04	Vi	12/18/1994	10:24:35	Cn
03/31/1994	00:41:05	Sg	08/10/1994	15:06:33	Li	12/20/1994	21:12:52	Le
04/02/1994	03:37:31	Cp	08/12/1994	17:55:47	Sc	12/23/1994	06:00:44	Vi
04/04/1994	09:45:21	Aq	08/14/1994	20:53:01	Sg	12/25/1994	12:27:25	Li
04/06/1994	18:50:55	Pi	08/17/1994	00:17:53	Cp	12/27/1994	16:17:03	Sc
04/09/1994	06:08:40	Ar	08/19/1994	04:33:40	Aq	12/29/1994	17:45:29	Sg
04/11/1994	18:47:33	Ta	08/21/1994	10:27:11	Pi	12/31/1994	17:57:28	Cp
04/14/1994	07:47:38	Ge	08/23/1994	18:54:38	Ar	01/02/1995	18:38:48	Aq
04/16/1994	19:40:59	Cn	08/26/1994	06:13:20	Ta	01/04/1995	21:49:00	Pi

01/07/1995	04:56:31	Ar	05/19/1995	07:39:25	Aq	09/28/1995	22:30:13	Sg
01/09/1995	15:58:12	Ta	05/21/1995	11:39:56	Pi	10/01/1995	01:10:15	Cp
01/12/1995	04:57:27	Ge	05/23/1995	19:13:00	Ar	10/03/1995	03:59:26	Aq
01/14/1995	17:19:56	Cn	05/26/1995	05:46:33	Ta	10/05/1995	07:35:06	Pi
01/17/1995	03:36:25	Le	05/28/1995	18:06:51	Ge	10/07/1995	12:41:31	Ar
01/19/1995	11:39:27	Vi	05/31/1995	06:59:16	Cn	10/09/1995	20:05:01	Ta
01/21/1995	17:53:35	Li	06/02/1995	19:16:56	Le	10/12/1995	06:09:35	Ge
01/23/1995	22:32:11	Sc	06/05/1995	05:46:08	Vi	10/14/1995	18:20:02	Cn
01/26/1995	01:36:32	Sg	06/07/1995	13:13:04	Li	10/17/1995	06:46:13	Le
01/28/1995	03:26:09	Cp	06/09/1995	17:03:16	Sc	10/19/1995	17:11:24	Vi
01/30/1995	05:02:54	Aq	06/11/1995	17:49:49	Sg	10/22/1995	00:15:08	Li
02/01/1995	08:05:03	Pi	06/13/1995	17:04:58	Cp	10/24/1995	04:06:31	Sc
02/03/1995	14:12:30	Ar	06/15/1995	16:52:01	Aq	10/26/1995	05:56:09	Sg
02/06/1995	00:08:34	Ta	06/17/1995	19:13:07	Pi	10/28/1995	07:14:37	Cp
02/08/1995	12:43:36	Ge	06/20/1995	01:28:57	Ar	10/30/1995	09:23:24	Aq
02/11/1995	01:16:50	Cn	06/22/1995	11:35:24	Ta	11/01/1995	13:17:30	Pi
02/13/1995	11:31:05	Le	06/25/1995	00:02:09	Ge	11/03/1995	19:20:38	Ar
02/15/1995	18:51:38	Vi	06/27/1995	12:56:10	Cn	11/06/1995	03:35:10	Ta
02/18/1995	00:00:18	Li	06/30/1995	01:01:33	Le	11/08/1995	13:54:33	Ge
02/20/1995	03:55:02	Sc	07/02/1995	11:35:16	Vi	11/11/1995	01:56:34	Cn
02/22/1995	07:12:37	Sg	07/04/1995	19:55:13	Li	11/13/1995	14:37:06	Le
02/24/1995	10:10:34	Cp	07/07/1995	01:18:45	Sc	11/16/1995	02:02:07	Vi
02/26/1995	13:13:51	Aq	07/09/1995	03:37:28	Sg	11/18/1995	10:17:36	Li
02/28/1995	17:15:46	Pi	07/11/1995	03:43:24	Cp	11/20/1995	14:40:19	Sc
03/02/1995	23:29:47	Ar	07/13/1995	03:20:50	Aq	11/22/1995	15:56:15	Sg
03/05/1995	08:50:18	Ta	07/15/1995	04:37:03	Pi	11/24/1995	15:48:10	Cp
03/07/1995	20:54:59	Ge	07/17/1995	09:22:59	Ar	11/26/1995	16:15:17	Aq
03/10/1995	09:40:08	Cn	07/19/1995	18:20:16	Ta	11/28/1995	18:58:54	Pi
03/12/1995	20:28:02	Le	07/22/1995	06:23:10	Ge	12/01/1995	00:50:58	Ar
03/15/1995	03:54:25	Vi	07/24/1995	19:15:50	Cn	12/03/1995	09:39:54	Ta
03/17/1995	08:17:42	Li	07/27/1995	07:06:41	Le	12/05/1995	20:34:35	Ge
03/19/1995	10:52:14	Sc	07/29/1995	17:11:53	Vi	12/08/1995	08:44:17	Cn
03/21/1995	12:57:21	Sg	08/01/1995	01:23:25	Li	12/10/1995	21:24:18	Le
03/23/1995	15:31:23	Cp	08/03/1995	07:29:14	Sc	12/13/1995	09:26:27	Vi
03/25/1995	19:09:40	Aq	08/05/1995	11:13:57	Sg	12/15/1995	19:09:02	Li
03/28/1995	00:18:01	Pi	08/07/1995	12:51:47	Cp	12/18/1995	01:06:57	Sc
03/30/1995	07:25:38	Ar	08/09/1995	13:27:36	Aq	12/20/1995	03:13:13	Sg
04/01/1995	16:58:36	Ta	08/11/1995	14:46:14	Pi	12/22/1995	02:46:00	Cp
04/04/1995	04:49:00	Ge	08/13/1995	18:40:47	Ar	12/24/1995	01:51:50	Aq
04/06/1995	17:39:51	Cn	08/16/1995	02:25:09	Ta	12/26/1995	02:44:47	Pi
04/09/1995	05:15:32	Le	08/18/1995	13:39:53	Ge	12/28/1995	07:05:58	Ar
04/11/1995	13:38:49	Vi	08/21/1995	02:23:39	Cn	12/30/1995	15:20:52	Ta
04/13/1995	18:20:02	Li	08/23/1995	14:12:36	Le	01/02/1996	02:29:13	Ge
04/15/1995	20:12:56	Sc	08/25/1995	23:50:26	Vi	01/04/1996	14:55:43	Cn
04/17/1995	20:51:31	Sg	08/28/1995	07:14:55	Li	01/07/1996	03:30:31	Le
04/19/1995	21:53:31	Cp	08/30/1995	12:51:10	Sc	01/09/1996	15:29:21	Vi
04/22/1995	00:37:52	Aq	09/01/1995	16:56:50	Sg	01/12/1996	01:55:01	Li
04/24/1995	05:50:33	Pi	09/03/1995	19:44:52	Cp	01/14/1996	09:29:55	Sc
04/26/1995	13:41:08	Ar	09/05/1995	21:47:03	Aq	01/16/1996	13:24:54	Sg
04/28/1995	23:52:59	Ta	09/08/1995	00:07:51	Pi	01/18/1996	14:06:52	Cp
05/01/1995	11:53:05	Ge	09/10/1995	04:13:58	Ar	01/20/1996	13:14:38	Aq
05/04/1995	00:44:45	Cn	09/12/1995	11:21:30	Ta	01/22/1996	13:01:49	Pi
05/06/1995	12:54:53	Le	09/14/1995	21:48:04	Ge	01/24/1996	15:36:43	Ar
05/08/1995	22:33:22	Vi	09/17/1995	10:15:41	Cn	01/26/1996	22:16:20	Ta
05/11/1995	04:30:00	Li	09/19/1995	22:19:28	Le	01/29/1996	08:42:29	Ge
05/13/1995	06:53:08	Sc	09/22/1995	08:01:17	Vi	01/31/1996	21:10:34	Cn
05/15/1995	06:58:24	Sg	09/24/1995	14:49:35	Li	02/03/1996	09:45:41	Le
05/17/1995	06:35:42	Cp	09/26/1995	19:20:08	Sc	02/05/1996	21:22:09	Vi

02/08/1996	07:29:48	Li	06/18/1996	23:21:42	Le	10/28/1996	13:34:35	Ge
02/10/1996	15:35:01	Sc	06/21/1996	12:06:39	Vi	10/30/1996	21:56:30	Cn
02/12/1996	20:57:59	Sg	06/23/1996	23:37:31	Li	11/02/1996	09:15:53	Le
02/14/1996	23:29:31	Cp	06/26/1996	07:53:25	Sc	11/04/1996	21:57:14	Vi
02/16/1996	23:59:38	Aq	06/28/1996	12:00:53	Sg	11/07/1996	09:28:36	Li
02/19/1996	00:09:05	Pi	06/30/1996	12:46:55	Cp	11/09/1996	18:01:47	Sc
02/21/1996	01:58:17	Ar	07/02/1996	12:05:05	Aq	11/11/1996	23:26:30	Sg
02/23/1996	07:08:21	Ta	07/04/1996	12:06:47	Pi	11/14/1996	02:43:44	Cp
02/25/1996	16:13:51	Ge	07/06/1996	14:41:50	Ar	11/16/1996	05:14:01	Aq
02/28/1996	04:10:18	Cn	07/08/1996	20:43:17	Ta	11/18/1996	07:59:51	Pi
03/01/1996	16:47:06	Le	07/11/1996	05:52:28	Ge	11/20/1996	11:33:42	Ar
03/04/1996	04:12:50	Vi	07/13/1996	17:07:45	Cn	11/22/1996	16:11:52	Ta
03/06/1996	13:40:19	Li	07/16/1996	05:31:26	Le	11/24/1996	22:19:36	Ge
03/08/1996	21:05:20	Sc	07/18/1996	18:16:23	Vi	11/27/1996	06:37:27	Cn
03/11/1996	02:32:26	Sg	07/21/1996	06:13:42	Li	11/29/1996	17:29:56	Le
03/13/1996	06:07:42	Cp	07/23/1996	15:42:47	Sc	12/02/1996	06:10:43	Vi
03/15/1996	08:15:10	Aq	07/25/1996	21:23:38	Sg	12/04/1996	18:23:25	Li
03/17/1996	09:50:16	Pi	07/27/1996	23:17:16	Cp	12/07/1996	03:38:33	Sc
03/19/1996	12:15:23	Ar	07/29/1996	22:47:26	Aq	12/09/1996	08:58:25	Sg
03/21/1996	16:58:40	Ta	07/31/1996	22:00:36	Pi	12/11/1996	11:14:32	Cp
03/24/1996	00:59:30	Ge	08/02/1996	23:04:49	Ar	12/13/1996	12:13:54	Aq
03/26/1996	12:05:51	Cn	08/05/1996	03:33:09	Ta	12/15/1996	13:43:50	Pi
03/29/1996	00:36:54	Le	08/07/1996	11:48:43	Ge	12/17/1996	16:55:18	Ar
03/31/1996	12:14:31	Vi	08/09/1996	22:57:26	Cn	12/19/1996	22:09:31	Ta
04/02/1996	21:26:21	Li	08/12/1996	11:28:53	Le	12/22/1996	05:17:14	Ge
04/05/1996	03:56:55	Sc	08/15/1996	00:07:08	Vi	12/24/1996	14:14:07	Cn
04/07/1996	08:21:23	Sg	08/17/1996	11:54:59	Li	12/27/1996	01:08:45	Le
04/09/1996	11:30:08	Cp	08/19/1996	21:50:16	Sc	12/29/1996	13:44:47	Vi
04/11/1996	14:09:32	Aq	08/22/1996	04:48:15	Sg	01/01/1997	02:31:47	Li
04/13/1996	16:59:53	Pi	08/24/1996	08:21:45	Cp	01/03/1997	13:01:40	Sc
04/15/1996	20:42:34	Ar	08/26/1996	09:10:19	Aq	01/05/1997	19:27:22	Sg
04/18/1996	02:05:20	Ta	08/28/1996	08:48:40	Pi	01/07/1997	21:54:38	Cp
04/20/1996	09:54:11	Ge	08/30/1996	09:15:08	Ar	01/09/1997	21:59:45	Aq
04/22/1996	20:24:45	Cn	09/01/1996	12:19:36	Ta	01/11/1997	21:50:46	Pi
04/25/1996	08:44:24	Le	09/03/1996	19:08:09	Ge	01/13/1997	23:21:36	Ar
04/27/1996	20:48:39	Vi	09/06/1996	05:29:22	Cn	01/16/1997	03:39:54	Ta
04/30/1996	06:27:06	Li	09/08/1996	17:53:56	Le	01/18/1997	10:53:12	Ge
05/02/1996	12:42:29	Sc	09/11/1996	06:28:19	Vi	01/20/1997	20:28:36	Cn
05/04/1996	16:04:42	Sg	09/13/1996	17:51:01	Li	01/23/1997	07:49:52	Le
05/06/1996	17:53:48	Cp	09/16/1996	03:19:42	Sc	01/25/1997	20:26:22	Vi
05/08/1996	19:38:49	Aq	09/18/1996	10:30:36	Sg	01/28/1997	09:21:17	Li
05/10/1996	22:28:51	Pi	09/20/1996	15:12:19	Cp	01/30/1997	20:47:55	Sc
05/13/1996	03:00:20	Ar	09/22/1996	17:39:22	Aq	02/02/1997	04:50:41	Sg
05/15/1996	09:24:36	Ta	09/24/1996	18:42:57	Pi	02/04/1997	08:44:25	Cp
05/17/1996	17:47:49	Ge	09/26/1996	19:45:34	Ar	02/06/1997	09:21:09	Aq
05/20/1996	04:16:00	Cn	09/28/1996	22:23:36	Ta	02/08/1997	08:33:41	Pi
05/22/1996	16:27:53	Le	10/01/1996	04:01:33	Ge	02/10/1997	08:29:23	Ar
05/25/1996	04:58:30	Vi	10/03/1996	13:14:24	Cn	02/12/1997	10:56:14	Ta
05/27/1996	15:33:28	Li	10/06/1996	01:11:41	Le	02/14/1997	16:53:21	Ge
05/29/1996	22:30:25	Sc	10/08/1996	13:48:35	Vi	02/17/1997	02:12:35	Cn
06/01/1996	01:42:48	Sg	10/11/1996	01:00:15	Li	02/19/1997	13:52:28	Le
06/03/1996	02:29:02	Cp	10/13/1996	09:45:33	Sc	02/22/1997	02:38:16	Vi
06/05/1996	02:44:35	Aq	10/15/1996	16:07:11	Sg	02/24/1997	15:23:01	Li
06/07/1996	04:19:02	Pi	10/17/1996	20:37:11	Cp	02/27/1997	02:56:41	Sc
06/09/1996	08:22:57	Ar	10/19/1996	23:51:02	Aq	03/01/1997	12:00:40	Sg
06/11/1996	15:10:42	Ta	10/22/1996	02:22:01	Pi	03/03/1997	17:38:33	Cp
06/14/1996	00:15:56	Ge	10/24/1996	04:50:08	Ar	03/05/1997	19:54:30	Aq
06/16/1996	11:07:51	Cn	10/26/1996	08:11:23	Ta	03/07/1997	19:56:55	Pi

03/09/1997	19:32:39	Ar	07/20/1997	07:28:45	Aq	11/29/1997	11:28:19	Sg
03/11/1997	20:37:24	Ta	07/22/1997	07:59:38	Pi	12/01/1997	18:38:21	Cp
03/14/1997	00:48:28	Ge	07/24/1997	09:02:56	Ar	12/03/1997	23:57:44	Aq
03/16/1997	08:50:43	Cn	07/26/1997	11:53:14	Ta	12/06/1997	04:07:17	Pi
03/18/1997	20:08:15	Le	07/28/1997	17:04:13	Ge	12/08/1997	07:23:48	Ar
03/21/1997	08:59:27	Vi	07/31/1997	00:38:16	Cn	12/10/1997	09:59:53	Ta
03/23/1997	21:35:15	Li	08/02/1997	10:26:51	Le	12/12/1997	12:34:59	Ge
03/26/1997	08:41:59	Sc	08/04/1997	22:15:04	Vi	12/14/1997	16:24:56	Cn
03/28/1997	17:39:52	Sg	08/07/1997	11:16:55	Li	12/16/1997	22:57:38	Le
03/31/1997	00:06:49	Cp	08/09/1997	23:50:12	Sc	12/19/1997	08:59:41	Vi
04/02/1997	03:58:48	Aq	08/12/1997	09:44:57	Sg	12/21/1997	21:34:51	Li
04/04/1997	05:42:06	Pi	08/14/1997	15:42:07	Cp	12/24/1997	10:07:17	Sc
04/06/1997	06:19:02	Ar	08/16/1997	17:58:04	Aq	12/26/1997	20:07:15	Sg
04/08/1997	07:20:25	Ta	08/18/1997	18:00:49	Pi	12/29/1997	02:48:28	Cp
04/10/1997	10:27:57	Ge	08/20/1997	17:44:43	Ar	12/31/1997	06:58:28	Aq
04/12/1997	17:03:22	Cn	08/22/1997	18:57:18	Ta	01/02/1998	09:55:55	Pi
04/15/1997	03:21:49	Le	08/24/1997	22:56:06	Ge	01/04/1998	12:43:08	Ar
04/17/1997	16:00:14	Vi	08/27/1997	06:10:31	Cn	01/06/1998	15:52:17	Ta
04/20/1997	04:36:26	Li	08/29/1997	16:18:43	Le	01/08/1998	19:42:00	Ge
04/22/1997	15:18:55	Sc	09/01/1997	04:26:52	Vi	01/11/1998	00:42:59	Cn
04/24/1997	23:31:58	Sg	09/03/1997	17:29:34	Li	01/13/1998	07:45:16	Le
04/27/1997	05:32:24	Cp	09/06/1997	06:09:34	Sc	01/15/1998	17:31:10	Vi
04/29/1997	09:50:17	Aq	09/08/1997	16:54:28	Sg	01/18/1998	05:44:07	Li
05/01/1997	12:50:10	Pi	09/11/1997	00:23:14	Cp	01/20/1998	18:34:18	Sc
05/03/1997	14:59:06	Ar	09/13/1997	04:09:59	Aq	01/23/1998	05:25:08	Sg
05/05/1997	17:04:25	Ta	09/15/1997	04:59:12	Pi	01/25/1998	12:39:19	Cp
05/07/1997	20:20:34	Ge	09/17/1997	04:24:49	Ar	01/27/1998	16:26:57	Aq
05/10/1997	02:12:41	Cn	09/19/1997	04:21:15	Ta	01/29/1998	18:08:26	Pi
05/12/1997	11:32:57	Le	09/21/1997	06:38:34	Ge	01/31/1998	19:20:54	Ar
05/14/1997	23:43:30	Vi	09/23/1997	12:32:57	Cn	02/02/1998	21:24:36	Ta
05/17/1997	12:26:49	Li	09/25/1997	22:12:24	Le	02/05/1998	01:09:25	Ge
05/19/1997	23:11:33	Sc	09/28/1997	10:27:27	Vi	02/07/1998	06:57:29	Cn
05/22/1997	06:50:43	Sg	09/30/1997	23:32:11	Li	02/09/1998	14:56:53	Le
05/24/1997	11:51:06	Cp	10/03/1997	11:57:17	Sc	02/12/1998	01:09:32	Vi
05/26/1997	15:20:12	Aq	10/05/1997	22:42:49	Sg	02/14/1998	13:17:17	Li
05/28/1997	18:17:58	Pi	10/08/1997	07:03:43	Cp	02/17/1998	02:12:48	Sc
05/30/1997	21:17:42	Ar	10/10/1997	12:38:41	Aq	02/19/1998	13:56:01	Sg
06/02/1997	00:38:55	Ta	10/12/1997	14:59:23	Pi	02/21/1998	22:29:34	Cp
06/04/1997	04:54:34	Ge	10/14/1997	15:24:48	Ar	02/24/1998	03:10:06	Aq
06/06/1997	11:02:01	Cn	10/16/1997	15:15:49	Ta	02/26/1998	04:42:06	Pi
06/08/1997	19:58:00	Le	10/18/1997	16:26:27	Ge	02/28/1998	04:42:05	Ar
06/11/1997	07:43:06	Vi	10/20/1997	20:45:14	Cn	03/02/1998	05:00:26	Ta
06/13/1997	20:35:19	Li	10/23/1997	05:09:50	Le	03/04/1998	07:14:43	Ge
06/16/1997	07:50:50	Sc	10/25/1997	16:59:24	Vi	03/06/1998	12:26:36	Cn
06/18/1997	15:38:59	Sg	10/28/1997	06:04:54	Li	03/08/1998	20:45:37	Le
06/20/1997	20:02:27	Cp	10/30/1997	18:15:25	Sc	03/11/1998	07:35:09	Vi
06/22/1997	22:20:32	Aq	11/02/1997	04:26:40	Sg	03/13/1998	19:57:54	Li
06/25/1997	00:08:50	Pi	11/04/1997	12:30:44	Cp	03/16/1998	08:50:39	Sc
06/27/1997	02:38:29	Ar	11/06/1997	18:33:27	Aq	03/18/1998	20:56:18	Sg
06/29/1997	06:23:16	Ta	11/08/1997	22:34:35	Pi	03/21/1998	06:43:30	Cp
07/01/1997	11:35:21	Ge	11/11/1997	00:43:35	Ar	03/23/1998	13:01:30	Aq
07/03/1997	18:32:36	Cn	11/13/1997	01:44:56	Ta	03/25/1998	15:42:38	Pi
07/06/1997	03:44:52	Le	11/15/1997	03:04:45	Ge	03/27/1998	15:48:37	Ar
07/08/1997	15:21:41	Vi	11/17/1997	06:32:12	Cn	03/29/1998	15:06:14	Ta
07/11/1997	04:20:41	Li	11/19/1997	13:37:56	Le	03/31/1998	15:37:36	Ge
07/13/1997	16:20:20	Sc	11/22/1997	00:32:44	Vi	04/02/1998	19:09:39	Cn
07/16/1997	01:02:26	Sg	11/24/1997	13:29:23	Li	04/05/1998	02:35:41	Le
07/18/1997	05:45:16	Cp	11/27/1997	01:43:07	Sc	04/07/1998	13:25:26	Vi

04/10/1998	02:04:30	Li	08/19/1998	20:00:34	Le	12/30/1998	07:21:51	Ge
04/12/1998	14:55:33	Sc	08/22/1998	04:21:22	Vi	01/01/1999	08:14:54	Cn
04/15/1998	02:52:23	Sg	08/24/1998	15:01:49	Li	01/03/1999	10:31:01	Le
04/17/1998	13:04:59	Cp	08/27/1998	03:25:24	Sc	01/05/1999	15:49:05	Vi
04/19/1998	20:41:28	Aq	08/29/1998	15:55:16	Sg	01/08/1999	00:52:45	Li
04/22/1998	01:05:40	Pi	09/01/1998	02:22:54	Cp	01/10/1999	12:48:42	Sc
04/24/1998	02:30:30	Ar	09/03/1998	09:20:50	Aq	01/13/1999	01:23:05	Sg
04/26/1998	02:08:46	Ta	09/05/1998	12:47:40	Pi	01/15/1999	12:28:33	Cp
04/28/1998	01:55:24	Ge	09/07/1998	13:52:30	Ar	01/17/1999	21:11:14	Aq
04/30/1998	03:56:48	Cn	09/09/1998	14:16:21	Ta	01/20/1999	03:39:59	Pi
05/02/1998	09:49:20	Le	09/11/1998	15:40:14	Ge	01/22/1999	08:24:43	Ar
05/04/1998	19:46:45	Vi	09/13/1998	19:20:04	Cn	01/24/1999	11:52:16	Ta
05/07/1998	08:18:41	Li	09/16/1998	01:47:56	Le	01/26/1999	14:29:24	Ge
05/09/1998	21:10:11	Sc	09/18/1998	10:51:52	Vi	01/28/1999	16:56:50	Cn
05/12/1998	08:47:57	Sg	09/20/1998	21:57:02	Li	01/30/1999	20:15:40	Le
05/14/1998	18:38:46	Cp	09/23/1998	10:21:42	Sc	02/02/1999	01:37:15	Vi
05/17/1998	02:30:22	Aq	09/25/1998	23:04:45	Sg	02/04/1999	09:55:38	Li
05/19/1998	08:03:19	Pi	09/28/1998	10:30:08	Cp	02/06/1999	21:06:08	Sc
05/21/1998	11:05:39	Ar	09/30/1998	18:53:24	Aq	02/09/1999	09:38:05	Sg
05/23/1998	12:06:01	Ta	10/02/1998	23:23:10	Pi	02/11/1999	21:09:57	Cp
05/25/1998	12:25:17	Ge	10/05/1998	00:32:02	Ar	02/14/1999	05:56:46	Aq
05/27/1998	13:58:25	Cn	10/06/1998	23:57:17	Ta	02/16/1999	11:39:44	Pi
05/29/1998	18:37:56	Le	10/08/1998	23:43:33	Ge	02/18/1999	15:06:22	Ar
06/01/1998	03:20:49	Vi	10/11/1998	01:48:25	Cn	02/20/1999	17:28:48	Ta
06/03/1998	15:16:53	Li	10/13/1998	07:25:09	Le	02/22/1999	19:53:40	Ge
06/06/1998	04:05:35	Sc	10/15/1998	16:31:58	Vi	02/24/1999	23:08:39	Cn
06/08/1998	15:34:21	Sg	10/18/1998	04:02:11	Li	02/27/1999	03:44:09	Le
06/11/1998	00:50:30	Cp	10/20/1998	16:36:25	Sc	03/01/1999	10:04:35	Vi
06/13/1998	08:02:55	Aq	10/23/1998	05:16:04	Sg	03/03/1999	18:34:18	Li
06/15/1998	13:31:23	Pi	10/25/1998	17:04:51	Cp	03/06/1999	05:22:07	Sc
06/17/1998	17:22:53	Ar	10/28/1998	02:44:29	Aq	03/08/1999	17:45:51	Sg
06/19/1998	19:47:28	Ta	10/30/1998	08:58:13	Pi	03/11/1999	05:53:38	Cp
06/21/1998	21:26:15	Ge	11/01/1998	11:26:59	Ar	03/13/1999	15:31:55	Aq
06/23/1998	23:39:00	Cn	11/03/1998	11:11:59	Ta	03/15/1999	21:30:12	Pi
06/26/1998	04:03:50	Le	11/05/1998	10:10:46	Ge	03/18/1999	00:12:54	Ar
06/28/1998	11:54:24	Vi	11/07/1998	10:39:23	Cn	03/20/1999	01:08:37	Ta
06/30/1998	23:04:53	Li	11/09/1998	14:32:57	Le	03/22/1999	02:05:11	Ge
07/03/1998	11:45:17	Sc	11/11/1998	22:36:55	Vi	03/24/1999	04:33:24	Cn
07/05/1998	23:23:48	Sg	11/14/1998	09:57:33	Li	03/26/1999	09:22:16	Le
07/08/1998	08:27:21	Cp	11/16/1998	22:40:54	Sc	03/28/1999	16:34:27	Vi
07/10/1998	14:52:08	Aq	11/19/1998	11:12:39	Sg	03/31/1999	01:49:22	Li
07/12/1998	19:22:15	Pi	11/21/1998	22:45:23	Cp	04/02/1999	12:48:35	Sc
07/14/1998	22:44:47	Ar	11/24/1998	08:43:25	Aq	04/05/1999	01:07:28	Sg
07/17/1998	01:33:21	Ta	11/26/1998	16:14:23	Pi	04/07/1999	13:39:02	Cp
07/19/1998	04:18:05	Ge	11/28/1998	20:33:52	Ar	04/10/1999	00:24:23	Aq
07/21/1998	07:42:49	Cn	11/30/1998	21:52:32	Ta	04/12/1999	07:34:41	Pi
07/23/1998	12:48:31	Le	12/02/1998	21:29:36	Ge	04/14/1999	10:45:54	Ar
07/25/1998	20:33:36	Vi	12/04/1998	21:27:43	Cn	04/16/1999	11:07:14	Ta
07/28/1998	07:14:14	Li	12/06/1998	23:55:23	Le	04/18/1999	10:39:01	Ge
07/30/1998	19:44:31	Sc	12/09/1998	06:21:26	Vi	04/20/1999	11:27:18	Cn
08/02/1998	07:47:45	Sg	12/11/1998	16:43:03	Li	04/22/1999	15:05:45	Le
08/04/1998	17:17:49	Cp	12/14/1998	05:16:26	Sc	04/24/1999	22:04:00	Vi
08/06/1998	23:31:09	Aq	12/16/1998	17:47:29	Sg	04/27/1999	07:46:17	Li
08/09/1998	03:04:09	Pi	12/19/1998	04:55:04	Cp	04/29/1999	19:12:32	Sc
08/11/1998	05:10:20	Ar	12/21/1998	14:16:40	Aq	05/02/1999	07:36:08	Sg
08/13/1998	07:04:27	Ta	12/23/1998	21:45:00	Pi	05/04/1999	20:11:51	Cp
08/15/1998	09:45:53	Ge	12/26/1998	03:03:32	Ar	05/07/1999	07:40:29	Aq
08/17/1998	13:55:22	Cn	12/28/1998	06:04:48	Ta	05/09/1999	16:16:03	Pi

05/11/1999	20:53:02	Ar	09/20/1999	18:38:09	Aq	01/30/2000	04:17:33	Sg
05/13/1999	21:56:18	Ta	09/23/1999	02:51:18	Pi	02/01/2000	17:09:50	Cp
05/15/1999	21:07:18	Ge	09/25/1999	07:33:37	Ar	02/04/2000	05:31:06	Aq
05/17/1999	20:39:31	Cn	09/27/1999	09:50:43	Ta	02/06/2000	16:01:47	Pi
05/19/1999	22:37:01	Le	09/29/1999	11:20:54	Ge	02/09/2000	00:17:23	Ar
05/22/1999	04:15:12	Vi	10/01/1999	13:31:31	Cn	02/11/2000	06:20:45	Ta
05/24/1999	13:29:00	Li	10/03/1999	17:13:20	Le	02/13/2000	10:22:46	Ge
05/27/1999	01:04:56	Sc	10/05/1999	22:39:49	Vi	02/15/2000	12:44:58	Cn
05/29/1999	13:37:20	Sg	10/08/1999	05:51:54	Li	02/17/2000	14:11:22	Le
06/01/1999	02:05:33	Cp	10/10/1999	15:01:28	Sc	02/19/2000	15:53:27	Vi
06/03/1999	13:36:51	Aq	10/13/1999	02:18:32	Sg	02/21/2000	19:21:28	Li
06/05/1999	23:00:33	Pi	10/15/1999	15:03:40	Cp	02/24/2000	01:57:54	Sc
06/08/1999	05:07:44	Ar	10/18/1999	03:17:01	Aq	02/26/2000	12:10:01	Sg
06/10/1999	07:43:31	Ta	10/20/1999	12:32:46	Pi	02/29/2000	00:45:12	Cp
06/12/1999	07:48:15	Ge	10/22/1999	17:41:29	Ar	03/02/2000	13:14:20	Aq
06/14/1999	07:14:01	Cn	10/24/1999	19:25:06	Ta	03/04/2000	23:30:05	Pi
06/16/1999	08:07:15	Le	10/26/1999	19:33:27	Ge	03/07/2000	06:54:14	Ar
06/18/1999	12:12:03	Vi	10/28/1999	20:09:13	Cn	03/09/2000	12:00:52	Ta
06/20/1999	20:10:28	Li	10/30/1999	22:47:05	Le	03/11/2000	15:45:40	Ge
06/23/1999	07:18:01	Sc	11/02/1999	04:07:07	Vi	03/13/2000	18:51:18	Cn
06/25/1999	19:51:10	Sg	11/04/1999	11:56:45	Li	03/15/2000	21:43:10	Le
06/28/1999	08:11:50	Cp	11/06/1999	21:45:39	Sc	03/18/2000	00:48:33	Vi
06/30/1999	19:19:22	Aq	11/09/1999	09:15:00	Sg	03/20/2000	04:56:58	Li
07/03/1999	04:34:27	Pi	11/11/1999	22:00:11	Cp	03/22/2000	11:17:35	Sc
07/05/1999	11:21:26	Ar	11/14/1999	10:45:37	Aq	03/24/2000	20:42:59	Sg
07/07/1999	15:21:49	Ta	11/16/1999	21:20:49	Pi	03/27/2000	08:50:50	Cp
07/09/1999	16:59:49	Ge	11/19/1999	03:57:16	Ar	03/29/2000	21:34:24	Aq
07/11/1999	17:27:16	Cn	11/21/1999	06:26:05	Ta	04/01/2000	08:12:18	Pi
07/13/1999	18:25:39	Le	11/23/1999	06:13:37	Ge	04/03/2000	15:21:52	Ar
07/15/1999	21:38:46	Vi	11/25/1999	05:29:01	Cn	04/05/2000	19:29:02	Ta
07/18/1999	04:19:20	Li	11/27/1999	06:18:43	Le	04/07/2000	21:58:20	Ge
07/20/1999	14:30:06	Sc	11/29/1999	10:11:02	Vi	04/10/2000	00:15:52	Cn
07/23/1999	02:48:10	Sg	12/01/1999	17:29:23	Li	04/12/2000	03:15:57	Le
07/25/1999	15:08:23	Cp	12/04/1999	03:35:23	Sc	04/14/2000	07:18:46	Vi
07/28/1999	01:54:21	Aq	12/06/1999	15:27:28	Sg	04/16/2000	12:35:42	Li
07/30/1999	10:27:12	Pi	12/09/1999	04:13:39	Cp	04/18/2000	19:35:28	Sc
08/01/1999	16:46:53	Ar	12/11/1999	16:58:55	Aq	04/21/2000	04:57:38	Sg
08/03/1999	21:08:38	Ta	12/14/1999	04:17:43	Pi	04/23/2000	16:47:15	Cp
08/05/1999	23:57:07	Ge	12/16/1999	12:30:08	Ar	04/26/2000	05:41:56	Aq
08/08/1999	01:52:34	Cn	12/18/1999	16:45:16	Ta	04/28/2000	17:06:03	Pi
08/10/1999	03:55:30	Le	12/20/1999	17:38:48	Ge	05/01/2000	00:54:35	Ar
08/12/1999	07:21:36	Vi	12/22/1999	16:52:19	Cn	05/03/2000	04:53:56	Ta
08/14/1999	13:23:58	Li	12/24/1999	16:31:54	Le	05/05/2000	06:23:22	Ge
08/16/1999	22:40:04	Sc	12/26/1999	18:34:14	Vi	05/07/2000	07:13:51	Cn
08/19/1999	10:31:33	Sg	12/29/1999	00:14:28	Li	05/09/2000	09:01:17	Le
08/21/1999	22:59:21	Cp	12/31/1999	09:36:28	Sc	05/11/2000	12:41:03	Vi
08/24/1999	09:49:07	Aq	01/02/2000	21:31:49	Sg	05/13/2000	18:27:22	Li
08/26/1999	17:49:43	Pi	01/05/2000	10:23:52	Cp	05/16/2000	02:16:31	Sc
08/28/1999	23:09:12	Ar	01/07/2000	22:52:50	Aq	05/18/2000	12:09:23	Sg
08/31/1999	02:40:40	Ta	01/10/2000	09:59:12	Pi	05/21/2000	00:01:04	Cp
09/02/1999	05:24:54	Ge	01/12/2000	18:48:26	Ar	05/23/2000	13:00:24	Aq
09/04/1999	08:09:36	Cn	01/15/2000	00:37:55	Ta	05/26/2000	01:07:33	Pi
09/06/1999	11:28:58	Le	01/17/2000	03:24:59	Ge	05/28/2000	10:07:44	Ar
09/08/1999	15:56:37	Vi	01/19/2000	04:01:00	Cn	05/30/2000	15:02:03	Ta
09/10/1999	22:15:51	Li	01/21/2000	03:58:28	Le	06/01/2000	16:34:24	Ge
09/13/1999	07:08:23	Sc	01/23/2000	05:07:27	Vi	06/03/2000	16:29:55	Cn
09/15/1999	18:34:54	Sg	01/25/2000	09:09:19	Li	06/05/2000	16:45:36	Le
09/18/1999	07:13:30	Cp	01/27/2000	17:01:15	Sc	06/07/2000	18:57:15	Vi

06/09/2000	23:58:35	Li
06/12/2000	07:54:58	Sc
06/14/2000	18:18:01	Sg
06/17/2000	06:26:33	Cp
06/19/2000	19:26:04	Aq
06/22/2000	07:51:45	Pi
06/24/2000	17:55:33	Ar
06/27/2000	00:18:41	Ta
06/29/2000	02:59:25	Ge
07/01/2000	03:09:25	Cn
07/03/2000	02:37:53	Le
07/05/2000	03:19:04	Vi
07/07/2000	06:46:50	Li
07/09/2000	13:48:22	Sc
07/12/2000	00:05:45	Sg
07/14/2000	12:27:39	Cp
07/17/2000	01:26:42	Aq
07/19/2000	13:44:06	Pi
07/22/2000	00:09:25	Ar
07/24/2000	07:43:42	Ta
07/26/2000	12:01:29	Ge
07/28/2000	13:29:42	Cn
07/30/2000	13:23:34	Le
08/01/2000	13:27:13	Vi
08/03/2000	15:31:27	Li
08/05/2000	21:04:19	Sc
08/08/2000	06:30:14	Sg
08/10/2000	18:43:46	Cp
08/13/2000	07:42:51	Aq
08/15/2000	19:41:13	Pi
08/18/2000	05:43:50	Ar
08/20/2000	13:30:54	Ta
08/22/2000	18:54:49	Ge
08/24/2000	21:59:37	Cn
08/26/2000	23:16:54	Le
08/28/2000	23:55:10	Vi
08/31/2000	01:33:02	Li
09/02/2000	05:55:11	Sc
09/04/2000	14:08:22	Sg
09/07/2000	01:47:03	Cp
09/09/2000	14:44:30	Aq
09/12/2000	02:34:10	Pi
09/14/2000	12:00:16	Ar
09/16/2000	19:05:17	Ta
09/19/2000	00:22:06	Ge
09/21/2000	04:15:43	Cn
09/23/2000	07:00:00	Le
09/25/2000	09:01:50	Vi
09/27/2000	11:21:47	Li
09/29/2000	15:29:41	Sc
10/01/2000	22:49:57	Sg
10/04/2000	09:42:29	Cp
10/06/2000	22:33:19	Aq
10/09/2000	10:36:12	Pi
10/11/2000	19:51:16	Ar
10/14/2000	02:06:08	Ta
10/16/2000	06:18:53	Ge
10/18/2000	09:37:00	Cn
10/20/2000	12:42:12	Le
10/22/2000	15:52:28	Vi
10/24/2000	19:29:52	Li
10/27/2000	00:23:24	Sc
10/29/2000	07:40:28	Sg
10/31/2000	18:01:36	Cp
11/03/2000	06:40:48	Aq
11/05/2000	19:12:38	Pi
11/08/2000	05:02:19	Ar
11/10/2000	11:11:48	Ta
11/12/2000	14:27:22	Ge
11/14/2000	16:21:04	Cn
11/16/2000	18:18:52	Le
11/18/2000	21:15:18	Vi
11/21/2000	01:34:56	Li
11/23/2000	07:32:56	Sc
11/25/2000	15:32:56	Sg
11/28/2000	01:57:15	Cp
11/30/2000	14:26:33	Aq
12/03/2000	03:22:44	Pi
12/05/2000	14:17:24	Ar
12/07/2000	21:26:38	Ta
12/10/2000	00:50:27	Ge
12/12/2000	01:48:34	Cn
12/14/2000	02:08:40	Le
12/16/2000	03:29:44	Vi
12/18/2000	07:00:59	Li
12/20/2000	13:11:48	Sc
12/22/2000	21:57:10	Sg
12/25/2000	08:53:44	Cp
12/27/2000	21:25:24	Aq
12/30/2000	10:27:08	Pi
01/01/2001	22:14:06	Ar

Index